STOCHASTIC CONTROL
FOR ECONOMIC MODELS

Economics Handbook Series

Anderson: *National Income Theory and Its Price Theoretic Foundations*
Atkison and Stiglitz: *Lectures on Public Economics*
Carlson: *Economic Security in the United States*
Chacholiades: *International Monetary Theory and Policy*
Chacholiades: *International Trade Theory and Policy*
Hansen: *A Survey of General Equilibrium Systems*
Hansen: *The American Economy*
Harris: *The Economics of Harvard*
Harris: *Monetary Theory*
Harrod: *The British Economy*
Henderson and Quandt: *Microeconomic Theory: A Mathematical Approach*
Hirsch: *The Economics of State and Local Government*
Hirsch: *Urban Economic Analysis*
Jones: *An Introduction to Modern Theories of Economic Growth*
Kendrick: *Stochastic Control for Economic Models*
Kindleberger and Herrick: *Economic Development*
Maddala: *Econometrics*
Nourse: *Regional Economics*
Ott, Ott, and Yoo: *Macroeconomic Theory*
Quirk and Saposnik: *Introduction to General Equilibrium Theory and Welfare Economics*
Taylor: *A History of Economic Thought*
Taylor: *Macro Models for Developing Countries*
Theil, Boot, and Kloek: *Operations Research and Quantitative Economics*
Walton and McKersie: *A Behavioral Theory of Labor Negotiations*

STOCHASTIC CONTROL FOR ECONOMIC MODELS

David Kendrick

The University of Texas

McGraw-Hill Book Company

New York   St. Louis   San Francisco   Auckland   Bogotá   Hamburg
Johannesburg   London   Madrid   Mexico   Montreal   New Delhi
Panama   Paris   São Paulo   Singapore   Sydney   Tokyo   Toronto

This book was set in Times Roman by Science Typographers, Inc.
The editors were Diane D. Heiberg and Madelaine Eichberg;
the production supervisor was Leroy A. Young.
The drawings were done by VIP Graphics.
Kingsport Press, Inc., was printer and binder.

STOCHASTIC CONTROL FOR ECONOMIC MODELS

Copyright © 1981 by McGraw-Hill, Inc. All rights reserved.
Printed in the United States of America. No part of this publication
may be reproduced, stored in a retrieval system, or transmitted, in any
form or by any means, electronic, mechanical, photocopying, recording,
or otherwise, without the prior written permission of the publisher.

1 2 3 4 5 6 7 8 9 0 K P K P 8 9 8 7 6 5 4 3 2 1

Library of Congress Cataloging in Publication Data

Kendrick, David A
    Stochastic control for economic models.

    (Economics handbook series)
    Bibliography: p.
    Includes index.
    1. Economics—Mathematical models. 2. Econometrics.
3. Stochastic analysis. 4. Control theory.
I. Title. II. Series: Economics handbook series
(New York)
HB141.K44   330′.0724   80-20397
ISBN 0-07-033962-7

To Gail

CONTENTS

		Preface	xi
	1	Introduction	1
Part 1		**Deterministic Control**	
	2	**Quadratic Linear Problems**	**5**
	2-1	Problem Statement	6
	2-2	Solution Method	10
	3	**General Nonlinear Models**	**17**
	3-1	Problem Statement	18
	3-2	Quadratic Linear Approximation Method	19
	3-3	Gradient Methods	22
	3-4	Special Problems	24
	4	**Example of Deterministic Control**	**26**
	4-1	System Equations	26
	4-2	The Criterion Function	31
Part 2		**Passive-Learning Stochastic Control**	
	5	**Additive Uncertainty**	**35**
	5-1	Uncertainty in Economic Problems	35
	5-2	Methods of Modeling Uncertainty	36
	5-3	Learning: Passive and Active	37
	5-4	Additive Error Terms	39

6 Multiplicative Uncertainty — 41
- 6-1 Statement of the Problem — 41
- 6-2 Period N — 43
- 6-3 Period $N-1$ — 45
- 6-4 Period k — 48
- 6-5 Expected Values of Matrix Products — 49
- 6-6 Methods of Passive-Learning Stochastic Control — 50

7 Example of Passive-Learning Stochastic Control — 51
- 7-1 The Problem — 51
- 7-2 The Optimal Control for Period 0 — 52
- 7-3 Projections of Means and Covariances to Period 1 — 56

Part 3 Active-Learning Stochastic Control

8 Overview — 63
- 8-1 Problem Statement — 64
- 8-2 The Monte Carlo Procedure — 67
- 8-3 The Adaptive-Control Problem: Initiation — 68
- 8-4 Search for the Optimal Control in Period k — 68
- 8-5 The Update — 72
- 8-6 Other Algorithms — 72

9 Nonlinear Active-Learning Stochastic Control (with Bo Hyun Kang) — 74
- 9-1 Introduction — 74
- 9-2 Problem Statement — 74
- 9-3 Dynamic-Programming Problem and Search Method — 76
- 9-4 Computing the Approximate Cost-to-Go — 76
- 9-5 Obtaining a Deterministic Approximation for the Cost-to-Go — 84
- 9-6 Projection of Covariance Matrices — 85
- 9-7 Summary of the Search for the Optimal Control in Period k — 89
- 9-8 Updating the Covariance Matrix — 90
- 9-9 Summary of the Algorithm — 90

10 Quadratic Linear Active-Learning Stochastic Control (with Bo Hyun Kang) — 91
- 10-1 Introduction — 91
- 10-2 Problem Statement — 91
- 10-3 The Approximate Optimal Cost-to-Go — 94
- 10-4 Dual-Control Algorithm — 98
- 10-5 Updating State and Parameter Estimates — 104

11 Example: The MacRae Problem — 105
- 11-1 Introduction — 105
- 11-2 Problem Statement: MacRae Problem — 105
- 11-3 Calculation of the Cost-to-Go — 107
- 11-4 The Search — 113

12 Example: A Macroeconomic Model with Measurement Error — 116
- 12-1 Introduction — 116
- 12-2 The Model and Data — 117
- 12-3 Adaptive versus Certainty-Equivalence Policies — 120
- 12-4 Results from a Single Monte Carlo Run — 122
- 12-5 Summary — 139

Appendices — 142
- A Second-Order Expansion of the System Equations — 143
- B Expected Value of Vector and Matrix Products — 146
- C Equivalence of Some Matrix Riccati Recursions — 149
- D Second Order Kalman Filter — 152
- E Alternate Forms of the Cost-to-Go Expression — 159
- F Expected Value of the Product of Two Quadratic Forms (by Jorge Rizo-Patron) — 162
- G Certainty-Equivalence Optimal Cost-to-Go Problem — 177
- H Matrix Recursions for the Augmented System — 179
- I Vector Recursions for the Augmented System — 188
- J Proof That a Constant Term in the Cost-to-Go Is Zero — 193
- K Updating the Augmented State Covariance — 195
- L Derivative of the System Equations with Respect to the Parameters — 198
- M Projection of the Augmented State Vector — 202
- N Updating the Augmented State Vector — 206
- O The Sequential Certainty-Equivalence Method — 208
- P The Reestimation Method — 210
- Q Deterministic, Cautionary, and Probing Components of the Cost-to-Go — 211
- R The Measurement-Error Covariance — 214
- S Data for Deterministic Problem — 217
- T Solution to the Macroeconomic Model with Measurement Error — 220

References — 228

Index — 238

PREFACE

This book is about mathematical methods for optimization of dynamic stochastic systems and about the application of these methods to economic problems.

Most economic problems are dynamic. The economists who analyze these problems study the current state of an economic system and ask how various policies can be used to move the system from its present status to a future more desirable state. The problem may be a macroeconomic one in which the state of the economic systems is described with levels of unemployment and inflation and the instruments are fiscal and monetary policy. It may be a microeconomic problem in which the system is characterized by inventory, sales, and profit levels and the policy variables are investment, production, and prices. It may be an international commodity-stabilization problem in which the state variables are levels of export revenues and inventories and the control variables are buffer-stock sales or purchases.

Most economic problems are stochastic. There is uncertainty about the present state of the system, uncertainty about the response of the system to policy measures, and uncertainty about future events. For example, in macroeconomics some time series are known to contain more noise than others. Also, policy makers are uncertain about the magnitude and timing of responses to changes in tax rates, government spending, and interest rates. In international commodity stabilization there is uncertainty about the effects of price changes on consumption.

The methods presented in this book are tools to give the analyst a better understanding of dynamic systems under uncertainty. The book begins with deterministic dynamic systems and then adds various types of uncertainty until it encompasses dynamic systems with uncertainty about (1) the present state of the system, (2) the response of the system to policy measures, (3) the effects of unseen future events which can be modeled as additive errors, and (4) errors in measurement. In the beginning chapters, the book is more like a textbook, but in the closing chapters it is more like a monograph because there is a relatively widespread agreement about methods of deterministic-model solution while there is still considerable doubt about which of a number of competing methods of stochastic control will prove to be superior.

As a textbook, this book provides a detailed derivation of the main results in deterministic and stochastic control theory. It does this along with numerical examples of each kind of analysis so that one can see exactly how the solutions to such models are obtained on computers. Moreover, it provides the economist or management scientist with an introduction to the kind of notation and mathematics which is used in the copious engineering literature on the subject of control theory, making access to that literature easier. Finally, it rederives some of the results in the engineering literature with the explicit inclusion of the kinds of terms typical of economic models.

As a monograph, this book reports on a project explicitly designed to transfer some of the methodology of control theory from engineers to economists and to apply that methodology to economic problems to see whether it sheds additional light on those problems. The project has been funded by the National Science Foundation and has involved two engineers, Edison Tse and Yaakov Bar-Shalom, and two economists, Fred Norman and the author. Fred and I decided at an early stage in the project that we could best learn from Edison and Yaakov if we programmed their algorithm ourselves. This involved rederiving all the results and then making two separate codings of the algorithm (one by each of us). This procedure enabled us to understand and check both the algorithm and the computer codes.

The principal application is to a macroeconomic stabilization problem which included all the kinds of uncertainty described above. The procedures are enabling us to determine the effects of various kinds of uncertainty on policy levels.

Some readers of this book may find themselves disturbed by the fact that the derivations are given in such detail. This is in contrast with many books in econometrics and mathematical economics, where a theorem is stated and the proof is developed in a terse fashion. However, in contrast to econometrics and mathematical economics, control theory is still a relatively new area of concentration in economics. As a result the notation is not familiar, and the mathematical operations are different from those commonly used by economists. Therefore the derivations included in this book are spelled out in detail either in the text or in appendixes. Readers who are already familiar with the usual control-theory notation and mathematical operations may find parts of the text moving much too slowly for their taste, but the liberal relegation of derivations to appendixes should make the book read more smoothly for these researchers.

The economist who is willing to learn the notation and style of control theory will find the investment well repaid. The effort will make it easier to understand the wealth of results contained in such journals as *IEEE Transactions on Automatic Control*, *Automatica*, and the *Journal of Economic Dynamics and Control* and in conference proceedings like those from the annual IEEE Conference on Decision and Control.

It seems likely that the adaptive-control algorithm developed in Chapters 9 and 10 may eventually be superseded by more efficient algorithms. Thus although one can question the value of learning the notation and operations which are particularly associated with it, many of the operations contained in it are common to a variety of adaptive-control algorithms and much of the notation is common to the larger field of control theory.

Not only the derivations but also the numerical examples given in the book are spelled out in considerable detail. The reason for this is that numerical methods are basic to the development of the work in this field and the existence of some thoroughly documented numerical examples will enhance the development and debugging of new algorithms and codes and the improvement in the efficiency of existing algorithms and codes.

The reader who is interested in a shorter and less detailed discussion of some of the subjects covered in this book is referred to Kendrick (1980).

In addition to Edison Tse, Yaakov Bar-Shalom, and Fred Norman, I am grateful to Bo Hyun Kang and Jorge Rizo-Patron, for their help in preparing some of the materials which constitute this book. I am also indebted to Peggy Mills, for her excellent work as administrative assistant and secretary, and to the National Science Foundation for support of this work under grants SOC 72-05254 and SOC 76-11187. Michael Intriligator, Stephen Turnovsky, Homa Motamen, Mohamad Rismanchian, and Ed Hewett read an earlier draft and provided many helpful comments. Michael Athans provided hospitality in the Laboratory for Information and Decision Sciences and access to the Air Force Geophysical Laboratory Computational Facilities during a year on leave at M.I.T. Connie Kirkland helped with the final typing and reproduction of the manuscript and Susan Lane assisted in the typing. I am grateful to both of them for their help in a tedious task.

Most of all I should like to thank my wife, Gail, for her warm support, even while the demands of her own career were great, and to thank my children, Ann and Colin, for adding so much to the joy and spontaneity in my life.

David Kendrick

CHAPTER ONE

INTRODUCTION

Many problems in economics are naturally formulated as dynamic models, in which control or policy variables are used to move a system over time from a less desirable to a more desirable position. One example is short-run macroeconomic problems. The controls are monetary and fiscal policy, the dynamic system is a macroeconometric model, and the desired position is low levels of inflation and unemployment. Another example is the problem of the firm. Here the controls are pricing and production levels, the dynamic system is a model of production and sales, and the desired position is high levels of profits.

Economists and engineers have been applying control theory to economic problems since the early works of Tustin[1] (1953), Phillips (1954, 1957), Simon (1956), and Theil (1957). These pioneers were followed by a sprinkling of studies in the 1960s by Holt (1962), Fisher (1962), Zellner (1966), and Dobell and Ho (1967) and by many studies in the early 1970s by Chow (1970), Kendrick and Taylor (1970), Prescott (1971, 1972), Livesey (1971), Pindyck (1972, 1973*a*, *b*), Shupp (1972), MacRae (1972), Athans (1972), Aoki (1973), Norman and Norman (1973), and many others. This work has been characterized by the solution of increasingly larger deterministic models and by movements into stochastic control theory.

Surveys of this literature have been published by Arrow (1968), Dobell (1969), Athans and Kendrick (1974), Intriligator (1975), and Kendrick (1976). There are also a number of books on control theory and economics, including

---

[1] A list of references appears after the appendixes.

Chow (1975), Aoki (1976), and Pitchford and Turnovsky (1977). Some of the books on control theory are Athans and Falb (1966), Aoki (1967), and Bryson and Ho (1969).

This book covers deterministic control, passive-learning stochastic control, and active-learning stochastic control. The methods differ in their treatment of uncertainty. All uncertainty is ignored in deterministic control theory. In passive-learning stochastic control the effects of uncertainty on the system are considered, but there is no effort to choose the control so that learning about the uncertainty is enhanced. In active-learning stochastic control, also called adaptive control or dual control, the control is chosen with a view toward both (1) reaching the desired states at present and (2) reducing uncertainty through learning, permitting easier attainment of desired states in the future. Part One is devoted to deterministic control, Part Two to passive-learning stochastic control, and Part Three to active-learning stochastic control.

PART ONE

DETERMINISTIC CONTROL

CHAPTER
TWO

QUADRATIC LINEAR PROBLEMS

Deterministic problems are control problems in which there is no uncertainty. Most economic control problems which have been posed and solved to date are of this variety. Deterministic problems fall into two major groups: (1) quadratic linear problems and (2) general nonlinear problems. This chapter is devoted to quadratic linear problems, and the next chapter discusses general nonlinear problems.

Quadratic linear problems (QLP) are problems in which the criterion function is quadratic and the system equations are linear. In continuous-time problems the criterion is an integral over time, and the system equations are linear differential equations. In discrete-time problems the criterion is a summation over time, and the system equations are difference equations. Discussion in this book is confined to discrete-time models since they lend themselves naturally to the computational approach used here. For a discussion of continuous- and discrete-time models together the reader is referred to Bryson and Ho (1969).

As one progresses from deterministic, to passive-learning stochastic, to active-learning stochastic control methods, the size of the numerical models rapidly declines. For example, deterministic control models now commonly include hundreds of equations, passive-learning stochastic control models usually have tens of equations, and active-learning stochastic control models have fewer than ten equations. This pattern results from the increasing computational complexity inherent in the treatment of uncertainty.

This chapter begins with the statement of the quadratic linear problem as the minimization of a quadratic form subject to a set of first-order linear difference equations. Then two types of common quadratic linear problems which are not exactly in this form are introduced, and the method of converting them into this form is given. The first of these problems is the quadratic linear tracking problem, in which the goal is to cause the state and control variables to follow desired paths as closely as possible. The second problem is a quadratic linear problem with nth-order rather than first-order difference equations.

Following the problem statement in Sec. 2-1, the solution method is described in Sec. 2-2. The solution method used here is the dynamic-programming approach rather than the maximum-principle method since dynamic programming lends itself well to generalization to stochastic control methods. Finally the chapter closes with a short discussion of the feedback rules used to represent the solutions to quadratic linear problems.

2-1 PROBLEM STATEMENT

In control-theory problems the variables are separated into two groups: state variables $\mathbf{x}$ and control variables $\mathbf{u}$. State variables describe the state of the economic system at any point in time, and control variables represent the policy variables, which can be chosen. For example, in macroeconomic control models the state variables are typically levels of inflation and unemployment, as well as levels of consumption, investment, and gross national product. The control variables in these problems are levels of government taxation, government expenditure, and open-market purchases of bonds.

Also since control models are dynamic models, initial conditions are normally specified, and at times terminal conditions are also given. These are conditions on the state variables.

With this nomenclature in mind one can write the quadratic linear control problem as (the prime on a vector indicates transposition)

$$\text{Find} \quad (\mathbf{u}_k)_{k=0}^{N-1}$$

to minimize the criterion

$$J = \tfrac{1}{2}\mathbf{x}_N' \mathbf{W}_N \mathbf{x}_N + \mathbf{w}_N' \mathbf{x}_N + \sum_{k=0}^{N-1} \left(\tfrac{1}{2}\mathbf{x}_k' \mathbf{W}_k \mathbf{x}_k + \mathbf{w}_k' \mathbf{x}_k + \mathbf{x}_k' \mathbf{F}_k \mathbf{u}_k + \tfrac{1}{2}\mathbf{u}_k' \mathbf{\Lambda}_k \mathbf{u}_k + \mathbf{\lambda}_k' \mathbf{u}_k \right) \quad (2\text{-}1)$$

subject to the system equations

$$\mathbf{x}_{k+1} = \mathbf{A}_k \mathbf{x}_k + \mathbf{B}_k \mathbf{u}_k + \mathbf{c}_k \quad \text{for } k = 0, 1, \ldots, N-1 \quad (2\text{-}2)$$

and the initial conditions

$$\mathbf{x}_0 \quad \text{given} \quad (2\text{-}3)$$

where $\mathbf{x}_k$ = state vector for period k with n elements
$\mathbf{u}_k$ = control vector for period k with m elements
$\mathbf{W}_k = n \times n$ matrix
$\mathbf{w}_k = n$-element vector
$\mathbf{F}_k = n \times m$ matrix
$\Lambda_k = m \times m$ matrix
$\lambda_k = m$-element vector
$\mathbf{A}_k = n \times n$ matrix
$\mathbf{B}_k = n \times m$ matrix
$\mathbf{c}_k = n$-element vector

Also the notation

$$(\mathbf{u}_k)_{k=0}^{N-1}$$

means the set of control vectors from period zero through period $N - 1$, that is, $(\mathbf{u}_0, \mathbf{u}_1, \mathbf{u}_2, \ldots, \mathbf{u}_{N-1})$. Period N is the terminal period of the model.

Thus the problem is to find the time paths for the m control variables for the time periods from 0 to $N - 1$ to minimize the quadratic form (2-1) while starting at the initial conditions (2-3) and following the difference equation (2-2).

Most quadratic linear control models in economics are not exactly in the form of (2-1) to (2-3), but they can be easily transformed into that form. For example, the quadratic linear tracking model used by Pindyck (1973a) and Chow (1975) uses a form of the criterion differing from (2-1). Also the model in Pindyck (1973a) has nth-order difference equations rather than first-order equations of the form (2-2). Since (2-1) to (2-3) constitute a general form, we shall use them as the basis for computation algorithms and show what transformations are required on each class of quadratic linear problems to bring them into this form.

Quadratic Linear Tracking Problems

The criterion function in these problems is of the form

$$J = \tfrac{1}{2}[\mathbf{x}_N - \mathbf{x}_N^\#]'\mathbf{W}_N^\#[\mathbf{x}_N - \mathbf{x}_N^\#]$$
$$+ \tfrac{1}{2} \sum_{k=0}^{N-1} \left([\mathbf{x}_k - \mathbf{x}_k^\#]'\mathbf{W}_k^\#[\mathbf{x}_k - \mathbf{x}_k^\#] + [\mathbf{u}_k - \mathbf{u}_k^\#]'\Lambda_k^\#[\mathbf{u}_k - \mathbf{u}_k^\#] \right) \quad (2\text{-}4)$$

where $\mathbf{x}_k^\#$ = desired vector for state vector in period k
$\mathbf{u}_k^\#$ = desired vector for control vector in period k
$\mathbf{W}_k^\#$ = penalty matrix on deviations of state variables from desired paths
$\Lambda_k^\#$ = penalty matrix on control variables for deviations from desired paths

Normally the matrices $\mathbf{W}^\#$ and $\Lambda^\#$ are diagonal.

Table 2-1 Notational equivalence for quadratic linear problems

Equation (2-1)	Equation (2-4)	Equation (2-1)	Equation (2-4)
W_N	$W_N^\#$	F_k	0
w_N	$-W_N^\# x_N^\#$	Λ_K	$\Lambda_K^\#$
W_k	$W_k^\#$	λ_k	$-\Lambda_k^\# u_k^\#$
w_k	$-W_k^\# x_k^\#$		

The equivalence of (2-4) to the criterion in the original problem (2-1) can be seen by expanding (2-4). The results are given in Table 2-1, which shows the notational equivalence between (2-1) and (2-4). The constant term which results from the expansion of (2-4) is not shown in the table since it does not affect the solution and can be dropped from the optimization problem.

One example of the application of quadratic linear tracking problems to economics is Pindyck (1972, 1973a). The state variable x includes consumption, nonresidential investment, residential investment, the price level, unemployment, and short- and long-term interest rates. The control variable includes government expenditures, taxes, and the money supply. Desired paths for both the state variable and the control variables are included as $x_k^\#$ and $u_k^\#$, respectively. The diagonal elements of the matrices $W_k^\#$ and $\Lambda_k^\#$ are used not only to represent different levels of desirability of tracking the targets but also to equivalence relative magnitudes of the different variables.[1]

Lagged State and Control Variables

For many economic problems the difference equations which represent the econometric model cannot be written as a set of first-order difference equations but must be written as second- and higher-order difference equations. The procedure for converting second-order difference equations in states and controls is given here. The procedure for higher-order equations is analogous.

Consider an econometric model with second-order lags in control and state variables

$$x_{k+1} = A_0 x_k + A_1 x_{k-1} + B_0 u_k + B_1 u_{k-1} \quad (2\text{-}5)$$

Then define two new vectors

$$y_k \equiv x_{k-1} \quad (2\text{-}6)$$

and

$$v_k \equiv u_{k-1} \quad (2\text{-}7)$$

---

[1] For other examples of quadratic linear control (but not necessarily tracking problems) the reader is referred to Tustin (1953), Bogaard and Theil (1959), van Eijk and Sandee (1959), Holt (1962), Theil (1964, 1965), Erickson, Leondes, and Norton (1970), Sandblom (1970), Thalberg (1971a, b), Paryani (1972), Friedman (1972), Erickson and Norton (1973), Tinsley, Craine, and Havenner (1974), Shupp (1976a), You (1975), Kaul and Rao (1975), Fischer and Uebe (1975), and Oudet (1976).

and rewrite (2-5) as
$$x_{k+1} = A_0 x_k + A_1 y_k + B_0 u_k + B_1 v_k \qquad (2\text{-}8)$$
Next define the augmented state vector z_k as
$$z_k = \begin{bmatrix} x \\ y \\ v \end{bmatrix}_k \qquad (2\text{-}9)$$
and rewrite (2-6) and (2-7) as
$$y_{k+1} = x_k \qquad (2\text{-}10)$$
and
$$v_{k+1} = u_k \qquad (2\text{-}11)$$
Then Eqs. (2-8), (2-10), and (2-11) can be written as
$$\begin{bmatrix} x \\ y \\ v \end{bmatrix}_{k+1} = \begin{bmatrix} A_0 & A_1 & B_1 \\ I & 0 & 0 \\ 0 & 0 & 0 \end{bmatrix} \begin{bmatrix} x \\ y \\ v \end{bmatrix}_k + \begin{bmatrix} B_0 \\ 0 \\ I \end{bmatrix} u_k \qquad (2\text{-}12)$$
or as
$$z_{k+1} = A z_k + B u_k \qquad (2\text{-}13)$$
with
$$A = \begin{bmatrix} A_0 & A_1 & B_1 \\ I & 0 & 0 \\ 0 & 0 & 0 \end{bmatrix} \quad \text{and} \quad B = \begin{bmatrix} B_0 \\ 0 \\ I \end{bmatrix} \qquad (2\text{-}14)$$

Equation (2-13) is then a first-order linear difference equation in the augmented state vector z.

An example of this can be found in Pindyck (1973a). The original state vector includes 10 elements, and the augmented state vector includes 28 elements [see Pindyck (1973a, p. 97)]. For example, the augmented state vector includes not only prices but also lagged prices and not only unemployment rates but also lagged unemployment rates and unemployment rates lagged two periods.

It can be argued that for computational reasons it is unwise to convert nth-order difference equations of the form (2-5) into augmented systems of first-order equations of the form (2-13). Norman and Jung (1977) have compared the computational efficiency of the two approaches and have concluded that in certain cases it is better not to transform the equations into augmented systems of first-order difference equations.

A slightly different kind of problem occurs in many economic models. The difference equations are written as
$$x_{k+1} = A x_k + B u_{k+1} \qquad (2\text{-}15)$$
i.e., the control vector is not u_k, as in Eq. (2-2), but u_{k+1}. While it may be true that there are some economic problems in which there is an important and immediate effect of the control variable on the state variables, usually the choice of control is actually made at least one time period before it has an affect. For

example, the simple multiplier-acceleration model

$$Y_k = C_k + I_k + G_k$$
$$C_k = a + bY_k \qquad (2\text{-}16)$$
$$I_k = e(Y_k - Y_{k-1})$$

where Y = gross national product
C = consumption
I = investment

reduces to

$$Y_k = \beta Y_{k-1} + \gamma G_k + \delta \qquad (2\text{-}17)$$

with $\quad \beta = -\dfrac{e}{1-b-e} \quad \gamma = \dfrac{1}{1-b-e} \quad \delta = \dfrac{a}{1-b-e}$

However, government expenditures is not actually the decision or control variable since in fact the decision variable is appropriations made by the Congress or obligations made by the administration. Both these variables lead expenditure by at least one quarter. Therefore it is common to add to a model like Eq. (2-17) another relationship like

$$G_{k+1} = O_k \qquad (2\text{-}18)$$

where O_k stands for government obligations. Then substitution of Eq. (2-18) into Eq. (2-17) yields

$$Y_k = \beta Y_{k-1} + \gamma O_{k-1} + \delta \qquad (2\text{-}19)$$

and this model is in the same form as the system equation (2-2).

For models which truly have the simultaneous form of Eq. (2-15) the reader is referred to Chow (1975). The derivations in that book are made for system equations of the form (2-15). Although the difference between Eqs. (2-15) and (2-2) may be viewed as simply a matter of labels, in the stochastic control context when one is dealing with the real timing of events and the arrival of information, the matter may be more than just one of labels.

This concludes the demonstration of how a variety of types of quadratic linear economic control models can be reduced to the form (2-1) to (2-3). Next the problem (2-1) to (2-3) will be solved by the method of dynamic programming to obtain the feedback-control solution.

2-2 SOLUTION METHOD

The crucial notion from dynamic programming[1] is that of the optimal cost-to-go. Since the idea is more simply thought of in space than in time, a spatial example is used here; later the method will be applied in time.

---

[1] See Intriligator (1971, chap. 13) for a discussion of dynamic-programming methods.

Consider an aircraft flying from New York to London. Different routes are flown each time the Atlantic is crossed because of the constantly shifting wind and weather patterns. Next consider flights on two different days when the weather is exactly the same in the eastern half of the crossing but different in the western half. Now suppose that on these two days the plane flies different routes over the western half of the Atlantic but ends up at the same point just as it begins to cross the eastern half. One can ask: Will the plane fly the same route the rest of the way into London on the two different days? Since the weather is the same in the eastern half on the two days, there is no reason not to use the same route for the rest of the way into London.

This is the basic idea of dynamic programming, i.e., that from a given point the route the rest of the way home to the finish will be the same no matter how one happened to get to that point. Also since the route is the same from that point the rest of the way home, the cost-to-go from that point to London is the same no matter how one arrived at the point. It is called the *optimal cost-to-go* since it is the minimum-cost route for the rest of the trip. It is written in symbols as $J^*(\mathbf{x}_k)$, where $\mathbf{x}_k$ is a vector giving the coordinates of a point in space and $J^*(\mathbf{x}_k)$ is the cost of going from the point $\mathbf{x}_k$ to London. The elements of the vector $\mathbf{x}_k$ in this example could be the longitude and latitude of the point in the middle of the ocean.

The next idea is that one can associate with *every* point in the Atlantic a minimum-cost path to London and an associated optimal cost-to-go. If one had this information available on a chart, one could simply look on the chart and say that at a given latitude and longitude one should set the rudder of the aircraft in a certain position in order to arrive at London with minimum cost. This idea gives rise to the notion of a feedback rule of the form

$$\mathbf{u}_k = \mathbf{G}_k \mathbf{x}_k + \mathbf{g}_k \qquad (2\text{-}20)$$

where $\mathbf{x}_k$ = state vector giving location of aircraft at place k
$\mathbf{u}_k$ = control vector consisting of settings for ailerons and rudder
$\mathbf{G}_k$ = matrix of coefficients
$\mathbf{g}_k$ = vector of coefficients

so the feedback rule (2-20) says that when the plane is in a position $\mathbf{x}_k$, the various controls should be set in the positions $\mathbf{u}_k$. Of course the problem is finding the elements of $\mathbf{G}_k$ and $\mathbf{g}_k$—but that is what dynamic programming is all about.[1]

For the problems in this book the primary dimension is not space but time. So the feedback rule index k changes from place k to time k. Then the feedback rule (2-20) is interpreted as "given that the economy is in state $\mathbf{x}_k$ at time k, the best policy to take is the set of policies in the vector $\mathbf{u}_k$." For example, in a commodity-stabilization problem the state vector $\mathbf{x}$ would include elements for price and buffer-stock level, and the control would include an element for

---

[1] For a full discussion of dynamic programming see Bellman (1957) or Bellman and Dreyfus (1962).

12 DETERMINISTIC CONTROL

buffer-stock sales (or purchases). Then the feedback rule (2-20) would be interpreted as "given that the price and stocks are $\mathbf{x}_k$, the amount $\mathbf{u}_k$ should be sold (or bought) by the stabilization scheme managers."[1]

The feedback rule (2-20) is generally nonlinear, rather than linear as in Eq. (2-20), but for an important class of problems, namely the quadratic linear problems that are the subject of this chapter, the feedback rule is linear. Also, the cost-to-go for this class of problems is a quadratic function of the state of the system at time k

$$J^*(\mathbf{x}_k) = J^*(k) = \tfrac{1}{2}\mathbf{x}_k'\mathbf{K}_k\mathbf{x}_k + \mathbf{p}_k'\mathbf{x}_k \tag{2-21}$$

where $\mathbf{K}_k$ is an $n \times n$ matrix which is called the Riccati matrix and $\mathbf{p}_k$ is an n-element vector. In words this equation says that when the system is in the state $\mathbf{x}_k$ at time k, the optimal cost-to-go is a quadratic function of that state. To return momentarily to the New York–to–London flight example, Eq. (2-21) can be interpreted as saying that the cost to go from point $\mathbf{x}_k$ in the middle of the Atlantic is a quadratic function of the latitude and longitude at that point. It seems more reasonable to say that the cost-to-go would be some function of the entire path from $\mathbf{x}_k$ to London, but that is *not* what Eq. (2-21) implies. Instead it states that the optimal cost-to-go from point $\mathbf{x}_k$ to London can be written as a quadratic function of the coordinates of that single point.

To derive the optimal feedback rule for the problem (2-1) to (2-3) one begins at the terminal time and works backward toward the initial time. So if the optimal cost-to-go at time k is defined by Eq. (2-21), the optimal cost-to-go at time N can be written as

$$J^*(\mathbf{x}_N) = J^*(N) = \tfrac{1}{2}\mathbf{x}_N'\mathbf{K}_N\mathbf{x}_N + \mathbf{p}_N'\mathbf{x}_N \tag{2-22}$$

From Eq. (2-1) the costs which are incurred in the terminal period N are

$$\tfrac{1}{2}\mathbf{x}_N'\mathbf{W}_N\mathbf{x}_N + \mathbf{w}_N'\mathbf{x}_N \tag{2-23}$$

so by comparison of Eqs. (2-22) and (2-23) one obtains

$$\mathbf{K}_N = \mathbf{W}_N \tag{2-24}$$

$$\mathbf{p}_N = \mathbf{w}_N \tag{2-25}$$

Equations (2-24) and (2-25) provide the terminal values for a set of difference equations which are used to determine $\mathbf{K}_k$ and $\mathbf{p}_k$ for all time periods. In fact the information in $\mathbf{K}_k$ and $\mathbf{p}_k$ is like price information in that $\mathbf{W}_N$ and $\mathbf{w}_N$ provide information about the value of having the economic systems in state $\mathbf{x}_N$ at time N. Later it will become apparent how the difference equations in $\mathbf{K}$ and $\mathbf{p}$ (which are called the *Riccati equations*) are used to transmit this price information from the last period backward in time to the initial period. The $\mathbf{K}_k$'s and $\mathbf{p}_k$'s will in turn be used to compute the $\mathbf{G}_k$ and $\mathbf{g}_k$ components of the feedback rule (2-20).

---

[1] For an application of control methods to commodity stabilization see Kim, Goreux, and Kendrick (1975).

The optimal cost-to-go for period N is given in Eq. (2-22). Now one can begin working backward in time to get the optimal cost-to-go in period $N - 1$, that is,

$$J^*(N - 1) = \min_{\mathbf{u}_{N-1}} \{J^*(N) + L_{N-1}(\mathbf{x}_{N-1}, \mathbf{u}_{N-1})\} \quad (2\text{-}26)$$

where L_{N-1} is the cost-function term in Eq. (2-1) for period $N - 1$, that is, from Eq. (2-1),

$$L_{N-1}(\mathbf{x}_{N-1}, \mathbf{u}_{N-1}) = \tfrac{1}{2}\mathbf{x}'_{N-1}\mathbf{W}_{N-1}\mathbf{x}_{N-1} + \mathbf{w}'_{N-1}\mathbf{x}_{N-1} + \mathbf{x}'_{N-1}\mathbf{F}_{N-1}\mathbf{u}_{N-1}$$
$$+ \tfrac{1}{2}\mathbf{u}'_{N-1}\mathbf{\Lambda}_{N-1}\mathbf{u}_{N-1} + \boldsymbol{\lambda}'_{N-1}\mathbf{u}_{N-1} \quad (2\text{-}27)$$

Equation (2-26) embodies an important notion from dynamic programming. It says that the optimal cost-to-go at time $N - 1$ will be the minimum over the control at time $N - 1$ of the optimal cost-to-go at state $\mathbf{x}_N$ in time N and the cost incurred in time period $N - 1$, that is, L_{N-1}.

So in the airplane example the optimal cost-to-go from position $N - 1$ in the Atlantic will be the minimum over the available controls at time $N - 1$ of the cost incurred in period $N - 1$ plus the optimal cost-to-go in period N.

Substitution of Eqs. (2-22) and (2-27) into Eq. (2-26) then yields

$$J^*(N - 1) = \min_{\mathbf{u}_{N-1}} \left(\tfrac{1}{2}\mathbf{x}'_N\mathbf{K}_N\mathbf{x}_N + \mathbf{p}'_N\mathbf{x}_N + \tfrac{1}{2}\mathbf{x}'_{N-1}\mathbf{W}_{N-1}\mathbf{x}_{N-1} \right.$$
$$+ \mathbf{w}'_{N-1}\mathbf{x}_{N-1} + \mathbf{x}'_{N-1}\mathbf{F}_{N-1}\mathbf{u}_{N-1}$$
$$\left. + \tfrac{1}{2}\mathbf{u}'_{N-1}\mathbf{\Lambda}_{N-1}\mathbf{u}_{N-1} + \boldsymbol{\lambda}'_{N-1}\mathbf{u}_{N-1} \right) \quad (2\text{-}28)$$

Furthermore, the $\mathbf{x}_N$ in Eq. (2-28) can be written in terms of $\mathbf{x}_{N-1}$ and $\mathbf{u}_{N-1}$ by using the system equations (2-2), i.e.,

$$\mathbf{x}_N = \mathbf{A}_{N-1}\mathbf{x}_{N-1} + \mathbf{B}_{N-1}\mathbf{u}_{N-1} + \mathbf{c}_{N-1} \quad (2\text{-}29)$$

Then substitution of Eq. (2-29) into Eq. (2-28) and collection of like terms yields

$$J^*(N - 1) = \min_{\mathbf{u}_{N-1}} \left(\tfrac{1}{2}\mathbf{x}'_{N-1}\boldsymbol{\Phi}_{N-1}\mathbf{x}_{N-1} + \tfrac{1}{2}\mathbf{u}'_{N-1}\boldsymbol{\Theta}_{N-1}\mathbf{u}_{N-1} \right.$$
$$\left. + \mathbf{x}'_{N-1}\boldsymbol{\Psi}_{N-1}\mathbf{u}_{N-1} + \boldsymbol{\phi}'_{N-1}\mathbf{x}_{N-1} + \boldsymbol{\theta}'_{N-1}\mathbf{u}_{N-1} + \eta_{N-1} \right)$$
$$(2\text{-}30)$$

$$\begin{aligned}
\boldsymbol{\Phi}_{N-1} &= \mathbf{A}'_{N-1}\mathbf{K}_N\mathbf{A}_{N-1} + \mathbf{W}_{N-1} \\
\boldsymbol{\Theta}_{N-1} &= \mathbf{B}'_{N-1}\mathbf{K}_N\mathbf{B}_{N-1} + \mathbf{\Lambda}_{N-1} \\
\boldsymbol{\Psi}_{N-1} &= \mathbf{A}'_{N-1}\mathbf{K}_N\mathbf{B}_{N-1} + \mathbf{F}_{N-1} \\
\boldsymbol{\phi}_{N-1} &= \mathbf{A}'_{N-1}(\mathbf{K}'_N\mathbf{c}_{N-1} + \mathbf{p}_N) + \mathbf{w}_{N-1} \\
\boldsymbol{\theta}_{N-1} &= \mathbf{B}'_{N-1}(\mathbf{K}'_N\mathbf{c}_{N-1} + \mathbf{p}_N) + \boldsymbol{\lambda}_{N-1} \\
\eta_{N-1} &= \mathbf{c}'_{N-1}\mathbf{K}_N\mathbf{c}_{N-1} + \mathbf{p}'_N\mathbf{c}_{N-1}
\end{aligned} \quad (2\text{-}31)$$

Next the minimization for $\mathbf{u}_{N-1}$ in Eq. (2-30) is performed to yield the first-order condition

$$\mathbf{u}'_{N-1}\boldsymbol{\Theta}_{N-1} + \mathbf{x}'_{N-1}\boldsymbol{\Psi}_{N-1} + \boldsymbol{\theta}'_{N-1} = \mathbf{0} \qquad (2\text{-}32)$$

This first-order condition can then be solved for $\mathbf{u}_{N-1}$ in terms of $\mathbf{x}_{N-1}$ to obtain the feedback rule for period $N-1$, that is,

$$\mathbf{u}_{N-1} = \mathbf{G}_{N-1}\mathbf{x}_{N-1} + \mathbf{g}_{N-1} \qquad (2\text{-}33)$$

where $\mathbf{G}_{N-1} = -(\boldsymbol{\Theta}'_{N-1})^{-1}\boldsymbol{\Psi}_{N-1}$ and $\mathbf{g}_{N-1} = -(\boldsymbol{\Theta}'_{N-1})^{-1}\boldsymbol{\theta}_{N-1}$ (2-34)

This is the feedback rule for period $N-1$; however, one needs the feedback rule for a general period k, not just for the next-to-last period $N-1$. To accomplish this look back at Eq. (2-26), which gives the optimal cost-to-go for period $N-1$. One can use the optimal cost-to-go for period $N-2$ to obtain the feedback rule for period $N-2$ and then see whether the results can be generalized to period k. The optimal cost-to-go for period $N-2$ can then be written, by analogy to Eq. (2-26), as

$$J^*(N-2) = \min_{\mathbf{u}_{N-2}} \{J^*(N-1) + L_{N-2}(\mathbf{x}_{N-2}, \mathbf{u}_{N-2})\} \qquad (2\text{-}35)$$

The second part of Eq. (2-35) is obtained simply by inspecting Eq. (2-1) for the cost terms which are appropriate to period $N-2$

$$L_{N-2}(\mathbf{x}_{N-2}, \mathbf{u}_{N-2}) = \tfrac{1}{2}\mathbf{x}'_{N-2}\mathbf{W}_{N-2}\mathbf{x}_{N-2} + \mathbf{w}'_{N-2}\mathbf{x}_{N-2} + \mathbf{x}'_{N-2}\mathbf{F}_{N-2}\mathbf{u}_{N-2}$$
$$+ \tfrac{1}{2}\mathbf{u}'_{N-2}\boldsymbol{\Lambda}_{N-2}\mathbf{u}_{N-2} + \boldsymbol{\lambda}'_{N-2}\mathbf{u}_{N-2} \qquad (2\text{-}36)$$

but the first term in Eq. (2-35) is slightly more difficult to obtain.

Equation (2-30) gives an expression for J^*_{N-1}, but it includes terms in both $\mathbf{x}_{N-1}$ and $\mathbf{u}_{N-1}$. If one is to state the optimal cost-to-go strictly as a function of the state $\mathbf{x}_{N-1}$, then $\mathbf{u}_{N-1}$ must be substituted out. Since this can be done by using the feedback rule (2-33), substitution of Eq. (2-33) into Eq. (2-30) and collection of like terms yields

$$J^*(N-1) = \tfrac{1}{2}\mathbf{x}'_{N-1}\mathbf{K}_{N-1}\mathbf{x}_{N-1} + \mathbf{p}'_{N-1}\mathbf{x}_{N-1} \qquad (2\text{-}37)$$

where $\mathbf{K}_{N-1} = \boldsymbol{\Phi}_{N-1} + \mathbf{G}'_{N-1}\boldsymbol{\Theta}_{N-1}\mathbf{G}_{N-1} + 2\boldsymbol{\Psi}_{N-1}\mathbf{G}_{N-1}$ (2-38)

$$\mathbf{p}_{N-1} = (\boldsymbol{\Psi}_{N-1} + \mathbf{G}'_{N-1}\boldsymbol{\Theta}'_{N-1})\mathbf{g}_{N-1} + \mathbf{G}'_{N-1}\boldsymbol{\theta}_{N-1} + \boldsymbol{\phi}_{N-1} \qquad (2\text{-}39)$$

The matrix $\mathbf{K}$ and the vector $\mathbf{p}$ have been used in Eq. (2-37) just as they were in the optimal cost-to-go term for $J^*(N)$ in Eq. (2-22).

Next Eqs. (2-36) and (2-37) can be substituted into Eq. (2-35) to obtain an expression for the optimal cost-to-go at time $N-2$ in terms of $\mathbf{x}_{N-1}$, $\mathbf{x}_{N-2}$, and $\mathbf{u}_{N-2}$. Then $\mathbf{x}_{N-1}$ can be substituted out of this expression by using the system equations (2-2). This leaves the optimal cost-to-go as a function of $\mathbf{x}_{N-2}$ and $\mathbf{u}_{N-2}$ only. Then the first-order condition is obtained by taking the derivative with respect to $\mathbf{u}_{N-2}$, and the resulting set of equations is solved for $\mathbf{u}_{N-2}$ in terms of x_{N-2}. This provides the feedback rule for period $N-2$

$$u_{N-2} = G_{N-2} x_{N-2} + g_{N-2} \qquad (2\text{-}40)$$

where $\quad G_{N-2} = -(\Theta'_{N-2})^{-1} \Psi'_{N-2} \quad$ and $\quad g_{N-2} = -(\Theta'_{N-2})^{-1} \theta_{N-2}$
$$\qquad (2\text{-}41)$$

with
$$\begin{aligned}
\Phi_{N-2} &= A'_{N-2} K_{N-1} A_{N-2} + W_{N-2} \\
\Theta_{N-2} &= B'_{N-2} K_{N-1} B_{N-2} + \Lambda_{N-2} \\
\Psi_{N-2} &= A'_{N-2} K_{N-1} B_{N-2} + F_{N-2} \\
\phi_{N-2} &= A'_{N-2} K_{N-1} c_{N-2} + A'_{N-2} p_{N-1} + w_{N-2} \\
\theta_{N-2} &= B'_{N-2} K_{N-1} c_{N-2} + B'_{N-2} p_{N-1} + \lambda_{N-2} \\
\eta_{N-2} &= c'_{N-2} K_{N-1} c_{N-2} + p_{N-1} c_{N-2}
\end{aligned} \qquad (2\text{-}42)$$

Then exactly as was done for period $N-1$ the optimal cost-to-go for period $N-2$ as a function of the state x_{N-2} alone can be obtained by substituting the feedback rule (2-40) back into the expression for the cost-to-go in terms of x_{N-2} and u_{N-2}. This procedure yields

$$J^*(N-2) = \tfrac{1}{2} x'_{N-2} K_{N-2} x_{N-2} + p'_{N-2} x_{N-2} \qquad (2\text{-}43)$$

where
$$K_{N-2} = \Phi_{N-2} + G'_{N-2} \Theta_{N-2} G_{N-2} + 2\Psi_{N-2} G_{N-2} \qquad (2\text{-}44)$$

$$p_{N-2} = (\Psi_{N-2} + G'_{N-2} \Theta'_{N-2}) g_{N-2} + G'_{N-2} \theta_{N-2} + \phi_{N-2} \qquad (2\text{-}45)$$

The feedback rule for periods $N-1$ and $N-2$ have now been obtained; comparing Eqs. (2-33) and (2-40) shows them both to be of the form

$$u_k = G_k x_k + g_k \qquad (2\text{-}46)$$

with $\quad G_k = -(\Theta'_k)^{-1} \Psi'_k \quad$ and $\quad g_k = -(\Theta'_k)^{-1} \theta_k \qquad (2\text{-}47)$

So Eq. (2-46) is the optimal feedback rule for the problem (2-1) to (2-3). Also by comparing Eqs. (2-44) and (2-45) with Eqs. (2-38) and (2-39) one can write the Riccati equations for the problem as

$$K_k = \Phi_k + G'_k \Theta_k G_k + 2\Psi_k G_k \qquad (2\text{-}48)$$

$$p_k = (\Psi_k + G'_k \Theta'_k) g_k + G'_k \theta_k + \phi_k \qquad (2\text{-}49)$$

with
$$\begin{aligned}
\Phi_k &= A'_k K_{k+1} A_k + W_k & \Theta_k &= B'_k K_{k+1} B_k + \Lambda_k \\
\Psi_k &= A'_k K_{k+1} B_k + F_k & \phi_k &= A'_k (K_{k+1} c_k + p_{k+1}) + w_k \\
\theta_k &= B'_k (K_{k+1} c_k + p_{k+1}) + \lambda_k & \eta_k &= c'_k K_{k+1} c_k + p'_{k+1} c_k
\end{aligned} \qquad (2\text{-}50)$$

In summary, then, the optimal control problem (2-1) to (2-3) is solved by beginning with the terminal conditions (2-24) and (2-25) on K_N and p_N and then integrating the Riccati equations (2-48) and (2-49) backward in time. With the K_k and p_k computed for all time periods, the G_k and g_k for each time period can be calculated with Eq. (2-47). These in turn are used in the feedback rule (2-46). First the initial condition x_0 in Eq. (2-3) is used in the feedback rule (2-46) to compute $\mathbf{u}_0$. Then $\mathbf{u}_0$ and $\mathbf{x}_0$ are used in the system equations (2-2) to calculate $\mathbf{x}_1$. Then $\mathbf{x}_1$ is used in the feedback rule to calculate $\mathbf{u}_1$. The calculations proceed in this fashion until all the $\mathbf{x}_k$'s and $\mathbf{u}_k$'s have been obtained.

For comparability to other texts and to increase the intuitive nature of the solution slightly it is worthwhile to define the feedback matrices and the Riccati equations in terms of the original matrices of the problem (2-1) to (2-3), i.e., in terms of $\mathbf{A}$, $\mathbf{B}$, $\mathbf{c}$, $\mathbf{W}$, and Λ instead of in terms of the intermediate matrix and vector elements Φ, Θ, Ψ, ϕ, θ, and η. This can be accomplished by substituting the intermediate results in Eqs. (2-50) into the feedback matrices defined in Eq. (2-47) and the Riccati equations (2-48) and (2-49), yielding the feedback rule

$$\mathbf{u}_k = \mathbf{G}_k \mathbf{x}_k + \mathbf{g}_k \qquad (2\text{-}51)$$

where
$$\mathbf{G}_k = -[\mathbf{B}'_k \mathbf{K}_{k+1} \mathbf{B}_k + \Lambda'_k]^{-1}[\mathbf{F}'_k + \mathbf{B}'_k \mathbf{K}_{k+1} \mathbf{A}_k]$$

$$\mathbf{g}_k = -[\mathbf{B}'_k \mathbf{K}_{k+1} \mathbf{B}_k + \Lambda'_k]^{-1}[\mathbf{B}'_k[\mathbf{K}_{k+1} \mathbf{c}_k + \mathbf{p}_{k+1}] + \boldsymbol{\lambda}_k] \qquad (2\text{-}52)$$

with the Riccati equations

$$\mathbf{K}_k = \mathbf{A}'_k \mathbf{K}_{k+1} \mathbf{A}_k + \mathbf{W}_k$$
$$- [\mathbf{A}'_k \mathbf{K}_{k+1} \mathbf{B}_k + \mathbf{F}_k][\mathbf{B}'_k \mathbf{K}_{k+1} \mathbf{B}_k + \Lambda_k]^{-1}[\mathbf{F}'_k + \mathbf{B}'_k \mathbf{K}_{k+1} \mathbf{A}_k] \qquad (2\text{-}53)$$

$$\mathbf{p}_k = -[\mathbf{A}'_k \mathbf{K}_{k+1} \mathbf{B}_k + \mathbf{F}_k][\mathbf{B}'_k \mathbf{K}_{k+1} \mathbf{B}_k + \Lambda'_k]^{-1}[\mathbf{B}_k[\mathbf{K}_{k+1} \mathbf{c}_k + \mathbf{p}_{k+1}] + \boldsymbol{\lambda}_k]$$
$$+ \mathbf{A}'_k[\mathbf{K}_{k+1} \mathbf{c}_k + \mathbf{p}_{k+1}] + \mathbf{w}_k \qquad (2\text{-}54)$$

and with terminal conditions

$$\mathbf{K}_N = \mathbf{W}_N \qquad (2\text{-}55)$$

and
$$\mathbf{p}_N = \mathbf{w}_N \qquad (2\text{-}56)$$

The difference-equation nature of the Riccati equations is much clearer in Eqs. (2-53) and (2-54) than it was in Eqs. (2-48) and (2-49). It is also apparent how the equations can be integrated backward in time from the terminal conditions (2-55) and (2-56). Furthermore these equations indicate how the pricelike information in the $\mathbf{W}$, $\mathbf{w}$, Λ, and $\boldsymbol{\lambda}$ elements in the criterion function is integrated backward in time in the Riccati equations and then used in the $\mathbf{G}$ and $\mathbf{g}$ elements of the feedback rule as the solution is brought forward in time using the feedback rule and the system equations.

Comparability to results for the quadratic linear problem published in other texts and articles can be obtained by using the fact that the cross term in the criterion $\mathbf{x}'\mathbf{F}\mathbf{u}$ is frequently not used and that the constant term in the system equations $\mathbf{c}_k$ is usually omitted. When both $\mathbf{F}$ and $\mathbf{c}$ are set to zero, the results stated above can be considerably simplified. Also, for comparability of the results above to those derived for quadratic linear tracking problems it is necessary to use the notational equivalence given in Table 2-1.

CHAPTER
THREE

GENERAL NONLINEAR MODELS

The previous chapter dealt with the restricted case of deterministic models with quadratic criterion functions and linear system equations. In this chapter the deterministic assumption is maintained, but the quadratic linear assumptions are dropped. Thus both the criterion function and the system equations can take general nonlinear forms. If the model is written in continuous time, the criterion will be an integral over time and the system equations will be differential equations. If the model is written in discrete time, the criterion will be a summation over time periods and the system equations will be difference equations. Since the basic approach used throughout this book is one of numerical solution of the models, and since continuous-time problems are transformed into discrete-time problems when they are solved on digital computers, only discrete-time problems are discussed here.[1]

This chapter begins with a statement of the general nonlinear problems in Sec. 3-1.[2] This is followed by a discussion of approximation methods for solving the problem. The approximation methods use a second-order approximation of the criterion function and a first-order approximation of the system equations. The approximation problem is then in the form of the quadratic linear problems

---

[1] For a discussion of continuous-time problems see Miller (1979), Intriligator (1971), or Pitchford and Turnovsky (1977).

[2] Examples of the application of nonlinear control theory to economic problems include Livesey (1971, 1978), Cheng and Wan (1972), Shupp (1972), Norman and Norman (1973), Fitzgerald, Johnston, and Bayes (1973), Holbrook (1973, 1974, 1975), Woodside (1973), Friedman and Howrey (1973), Healy and Summers (1974), Sandblom (1975), Fair (1974, 1976, 1978a, b), Rouzier (1974), Healey and Medina (1975), Gupta et al. (1975), Craine, Havenner, and Tinsley (1976), Ando, Norman, and Palash (1978), Athans et al. (1975), Palash (1977), and Klein (1979).

discussed in the previous chapter. The approximation QLP is then solved iteratively until the results converge.

While this approximation method may be adequate for solving some nonlinear optimization problems, convergence may be too slow. Therefore it is common to solve this class of problems with one of a variety of gradient methods. These methods commonly employ the maximum principle and then use iterative means to satisfy the optimality conditions. Basically, they integrate costate equations backward in time and state equations forward in time to satisfy these conditions and then check to see whether the derivative of the hamiltonian with respect to the control variable has gone to zero. If it has not, the controls are moved in the direction of the gradient and the costate and state equations are integrated again. This procedure is repeated until the derivative is close enough to zero. These gradient methods are discussed in Sec. 3-3.

Even these gradient methods are inadequate to solve many economic optimization problems. Many economic models are very large, containing hundreds of nonlinear equations. To solve these problems on computers where the high-speed memory is limited, the sparsity of the model is exploited. Since not every variable enters every equation, it is not necessary to store large matrices fully; only the nonzero elements need be stored and manipulated. An introduction to this topic will be provided in Sec. 3-4.

3-1 PROBLEM STATEMENT

The problem is to find the vector of control variables $\mathbf{u}_k$ in each time period k

$$(\mathbf{u}_k)_{k=0}^{N-1} = (\mathbf{u}_0, \mathbf{u}_1, \mathbf{u}_2, \ldots, \mathbf{u}_{N-1})$$

which will minimize the criterion function

$$J = L_N(\mathbf{x}_N) + \sum_{k=0}^{N-1} L_k(\mathbf{x}_k, \mathbf{u}_k) \qquad (3\text{-}1)$$

where $\mathbf{x}_k$ = vector of state variables
$\mathbf{u}_k$ = vector of control variables
L_k = scalar function

The last period, period N, is separated from the other time periods to simplify the specification of terminal conditions. Also the criterion function is assumed to be additive over time. This assumption is not essential, but its use greatly simplifies the analysis. In Chap. 2 the functions L_k were assumed to be quadratic forms; here they will remain general nonlinear forms.

The criterion function (3-1) is minimized subject to the system equations

$$\mathbf{x}_{k+1} = \mathbf{f}_k(\mathbf{x}_k, \mathbf{u}_k) \qquad k = 0, 1, \ldots, N-1 \qquad (3\text{-}2)$$

and the initial conditions

$$\mathbf{x}_0 = \text{given} \tag{3-3}$$

where $\mathbf{f}$ is a vector-valued function. The system equations are written in explicit form; i.e., the variable $\mathbf{x}_{k+1}$ is an explicit function of $\mathbf{x}_k$ and $\mathbf{u}_k$. Some econometric models are developed in implicit form; i.e., the system equations are written in the form

$$\mathbf{g}_k(\mathbf{x}_{k+1}, \mathbf{x}_k, \mathbf{u}_k) = \mathbf{0} \tag{3-4}$$

For a discussion of computational methods which are specific to such problems see Drud (1976).

The problem (3-1) to (3-3) can be solved by a variety of methods. A discussion of a quadratic linear approximation method is given next, followed by an elaboration of gradient methods.

3-2 QUADRATIC LINEAR APPROXIMATION METHOD

The problem (3-1) to (3-3) can be approximated by a second-order expansion of the criterion function and a first-order expansion of the system equations.[1] The resulting approximation problem can be solved using the quadratic linear problem methods discussed in the previous chapter. This procedure can be iterated, the equations being expanded each time around the solution obtained on the previous iteration. The iterations are continued until satisfactory convergence is obtained.

First consider a second-order expansion of the criterion function. This expansion is done about a path[2]

$$(\mathbf{x}_{o,k+1}, \mathbf{u}_{ok})_{k=0}^{N-1}$$

which is chosen as close to the expected optimal path as possible. This second-order expansion of the criterion function is written as[3]

$$\begin{aligned} J = & \mathbf{L}'_{\mathbf{x}N}[\mathbf{x}_N - \mathbf{x}_{oN}] + \tfrac{1}{2}[\mathbf{x}_N - \mathbf{x}_{oN}]' \mathbf{L}_{\mathbf{xx},N}[\mathbf{x}_N - \mathbf{x}_{oN}] \\ & + \sum_{k=0}^{N-1} [\mathbf{L}'_{\mathbf{x}k} \quad \mathbf{L}'_{\mathbf{u}k}] \begin{bmatrix} \mathbf{x}_k - \mathbf{x}_{ok} \\ \mathbf{u}_k - \mathbf{u}_{ok} \end{bmatrix} \\ & + \tfrac{1}{2}[[\mathbf{x}_k - \mathbf{x}_{ok}]'[\mathbf{u}_k - \mathbf{u}_{ok}]'] \begin{bmatrix} \mathbf{L}_{\mathbf{xx}} & \mathbf{L}_{\mathbf{xu}} \\ \mathbf{L}_{\mathbf{ux}} & \mathbf{L}_{\mathbf{uu}} \end{bmatrix}_k \begin{bmatrix} \mathbf{x}_k - \mathbf{x}_{ok} \\ \mathbf{u}_k - \mathbf{u}_{ok} \end{bmatrix} \end{aligned} \tag{3-5}$$

---

[1] The method described here is like Garbade (1975a, chap. 2; 1975b).
[2] A lowercase o is used to denote the nominal path, and 0 is used to denote the period zero.
[3] This notation differs from the convention of treating gradient vectors as row vectors. Thus the usual notation would treat, for example, $\mathbf{L}_{\mathbf{x}N}$ as a row vector and the transpose shown in Eq. (3-5) would not be necessary. Departure from that convention was adopted here so that *all* vectors can be treated as column vectors unless an explicit transpose is given, in which case they are row vectors.

where $\mathbf{L}_{\mathbf{x}k}$ is the vector of the derivatives of the function L with respect to each element in the vector $\mathbf{x}$ at time k, that is,

$$\mathbf{L}_{\mathbf{x}k} = \begin{bmatrix} \dfrac{\partial L_k}{\partial x_{1k}} \\ \vdots \\ \dfrac{\partial L_k}{\partial x_{nk}} \end{bmatrix} \tag{3-5a}$$

with x_{ik} the ith element in n vector $\mathbf{x}_k$. $\mathbf{L}_{\mathbf{u}k}$ is the vector of the derivatives of the function L with respect to each element in the vector $\mathbf{u}$ at time k, that is,

$$\mathbf{L}_{\mathbf{u}k} = \begin{bmatrix} \dfrac{\partial L_k}{\partial u_{1k}} \\ \vdots \\ \dfrac{\partial L_k}{\partial u_{mk}} \end{bmatrix} \tag{3-5b}$$

with u_{ik} the ith element in the m vector $\mathbf{u}_k$. Also $\mathbf{L}_{\mathbf{xx},k}$ is the matrix of second derivatives of the function L_k with respect to the elements in the vector $\mathbf{x}_k$

$$\mathbf{L}_{\mathbf{xx},k} = \begin{bmatrix} \dfrac{\partial^2 L_k}{\partial x_{1k} \partial x_{1k}} & \cdots & \dfrac{\partial^2 L_k}{\partial x_{1k} \partial x_{nk}} \\ \vdots & & \vdots \\ \dfrac{\partial^2 L_k}{\partial x_{nk} \partial x_{1k}} & \cdots & \dfrac{\partial^2 L_k}{\partial x_{nk} \partial x_{nk}} \end{bmatrix} \tag{3-5c}$$

$\mathbf{L}_{\mathbf{xu},k}$ is the matrix of cross partial derivatives of the function L_k with respect to the elements of the vectors $\mathbf{x}_k$ and $\mathbf{u}_k$

$$\mathbf{L}_{\mathbf{xu},k} = \begin{bmatrix} \dfrac{\partial^2 L_k}{\partial x_{1k} \partial u_{1k}} & \cdots & \dfrac{\partial^2 L_k}{\partial x_{1k} \partial u_{mk}} \\ \vdots & & \vdots \\ \dfrac{\partial^2 L_k}{\partial x_{nk} \partial u_{1k}} & \cdots & \dfrac{\partial^2 L_k}{\partial x_{nk} \partial u_{mk}} \end{bmatrix} = \mathbf{L}'_{\mathbf{ux},k} \tag{3-5d}$$

and $\mathbf{L}_{\mathbf{uu},k}$ is the matrix of second derivatives of the function L_k with respect to the elements in the vector $\mathbf{u}_k$

$$\mathbf{L}_{\mathbf{uu},k} = \begin{bmatrix} \dfrac{\partial^2 L_k}{\partial u_{1k} \partial u_{1k}} & \cdots & \dfrac{\partial^2 L_k}{\partial u_{1k} \partial u_{mk}} \\ \vdots & & \vdots \\ \dfrac{\partial^2 L_k}{\partial u_{mk} \partial u_{1k}} & \cdots & \dfrac{\partial^2 L_k}{\partial u_{mk} \partial u_{mk}} \end{bmatrix} \tag{3-5e}$$

The approximate criterion (3-5) is minimized subject to first-order expansion of the system equations around the path

$$(\mathbf{x}_{o,k+1}, \mathbf{u}_{ok})_{k=0}^{N-1}$$

that is

$$\mathbf{x}_{k+1} = \mathbf{f}_k + \mathbf{f}_{\mathbf{x}k}[\mathbf{x}_k - \mathbf{x}_{ok}] + \mathbf{f}_{\mathbf{u}k}[\mathbf{u}_k - \mathbf{u}_{ok}] \qquad k = 0, 1, \ldots, N-1 \quad (3\text{-}6)$$

where $\mathbf{f}_k$ is the vector-valued system equations evaluated on the path

$$(\mathbf{x}_{o,k+1}, \mathbf{u}_{ok})_{k=1}^{N-1}$$

$\mathbf{f}_{\mathbf{x}k}$ is the matrix of first-order derivatives of each of the functions f_k^j in $\mathbf{f}_k$ with respect to each of the variables x_{ik} in $\mathbf{x}_k$

$$\mathbf{f}_{\mathbf{x}k} = \begin{bmatrix} (\mathbf{f}_{\mathbf{x}k}^1)' \\ \vdots \\ (\mathbf{f}_{\mathbf{x}k}^n)' \end{bmatrix} = \begin{bmatrix} \dfrac{\partial f_k^1}{\partial x_{1k}} & \cdots & \dfrac{\partial f_k^1}{\partial x_{nk}} \\ \vdots & & \vdots \\ \dfrac{\partial f_k^n}{\partial x_{1k}} & \cdots & \dfrac{\partial f_k^n}{\partial x_{nk}} \end{bmatrix} \qquad (3\text{-}6a)$$

and $\mathbf{f}_{\mathbf{u}k}$ is the matrix of first-order derivatives of each of the functions f_k^j in $\mathbf{f}_k$ with respect to each of the variables u_{ik} in $\mathbf{u}_k$

$$\mathbf{f}_{\mathbf{u}k} = \begin{bmatrix} (\mathbf{f}_{\mathbf{u}k}^1)' \\ \vdots \\ (\mathbf{f}_{\mathbf{u}k}^n)' \end{bmatrix} = \begin{bmatrix} \dfrac{\partial f_k^1}{\partial u_{1k}} & \cdots & \dfrac{\partial f_k^1}{\partial u_{mk}} \\ \vdots & & \vdots \\ \dfrac{\partial f_k^n}{\partial u_{1k}} & \cdots & \dfrac{\partial f_k^n}{\partial u_{mk}} \end{bmatrix} \qquad (3\text{-}6b)$$

Thus the notation

$$\mathbf{f}_{\mathbf{x}k}[\mathbf{x}_k - \mathbf{x}_{ok}]$$

in Eq. (3-6) does not represent a matrix of derivatives evaluated at the point $\mathbf{x}_k - \mathbf{x}_{ok}$ but the matrix of derivatives $\mathbf{f}_{\mathbf{x}k}$ evaluated at $\mathbf{x}_{ok}$ multiplied by the vector $\mathbf{x}_k - \mathbf{x}_{ok}$.

The approximation problem (3-5) and (3-6) is the same form as the quadratic linear problem (2-1) and (2-2) discussed in the previous chapter. The equivalence between the matrices of these two problems is given in Table 3-1.

Table 3-1 Equivalence of the matrices and vectors in QLP and the approximation QLP

QLP (2-1) and (2-2)	Approximation QLP (3-5) and (3-6)	QLP (2-1) and (2-2)	Approximation QLP (3-5) and (3-6)
$\mathbf{W}_N$	$\mathbf{L}_{\mathbf{xx},N}$	$\mathbf{\Lambda}_k$	$\mathbf{L}_{\mathbf{uu},k}$
$\mathbf{w}_N$	$\mathbf{L}_{\mathbf{x}N} - \mathbf{L}'_{\mathbf{xx},N}\mathbf{x}_{oN}$	$\boldsymbol{\lambda}_k$	$\mathbf{L}_{\mathbf{u}k} - \mathbf{L}'_{\mathbf{uu},k}\mathbf{u}_{ok} - \mathbf{L}'_{\mathbf{xu}}\mathbf{x}_{ok}$
$\mathbf{W}_k$	$\mathbf{L}_{\mathbf{xx},k}$	$\mathbf{A}_k$	$\mathbf{f}_{\mathbf{x}k}$
$\mathbf{w}_k$	$\mathbf{L}_{\mathbf{x}k} - \mathbf{L}'_{\mathbf{xx},k}\mathbf{x}_{ok} - \mathbf{L}_{\mathbf{xu},k}\mathbf{u}_{ok}$	$\mathbf{B}_k$	$\mathbf{f}_{\mathbf{u}k}$
$\mathbf{F}_k$	$\mathbf{L}_{\mathbf{xu},k}$	$\mathbf{c}_k$	$-(\mathbf{f}_{\mathbf{x}k}\mathbf{x}_{ok} + \mathbf{f}_{\mathbf{u}k}\mathbf{u}_{ok})$

Thus the problem (3-5) and (3-6) with the initial condition (3-3) is solved to obtain the optimal path

$$(\mathbf{x}^*_{k+1}, \mathbf{u}^*_k)_{k=0}^{N-1}$$

using the algorithm of the previous chapter. Then the iteration procedure is used to obtain a new nominal path

$$(\mathbf{x}_{o,k+1}, \mathbf{u}_{ok})_{k=0}^{N-1}$$

in the following manner. Let

$$(\mathbf{x}^\rho_{o,k+1}, \mathbf{u}^\rho_k)_{k=0}^{N-1}$$

be the nominal path about which the expansion is done on the ρth iteration. Then

$$\mathbf{u}^{\rho+1}_{o,k} = \alpha[\mathbf{u}^*_k - \mathbf{u}^\rho_{ok}] + \mathbf{u}^\rho_{ok} \tag{3-7}$$

where α is the step size. So the new nominal control path on iteration $\rho + 1$ will be the same as the path on the previous iteration plus some fraction α of the difference between the nominal path and the optimal path. The choice of α can of course be critical. If it is chosen too small, the iteration proceeds too slowly, and if it is chosen too large, the iterations may jump back and forth across the optimal path. In the next section on gradient methods several other methods of choosing both the direction in which to change the control between iterations and the distance to move it will be discussed. Once $\mathbf{u}^{\rho+1}_{ok}$ has been computed from Eq. (3-7), it can be used in the original nonlinear system equations (3-2) to compute the implied $\mathbf{x}^{\rho+1}_{ok}$. The iteration is then repeated using this new nominal path.

3-3 GRADIENT METHODS

Gradient methods are iterative optimization methods in which the control variables are moved in the gradient (downhill) direction at each iteration. The control is changed at each iteration until the gradient is sufficiently close to zero and the optimal solution is obtained at that point. This type of algorithm is most easily understood by writing the first-order conditions for the optimization problem and showing how they are satisfied.

The problem is to minimize

$$J = L_N(\mathbf{x}_N) + \sum_{k=0}^{N-1} L_k(\mathbf{x}_k, \mathbf{u}_k) \tag{3-1}$$

subject to

$$\mathbf{x}_{k+1} = \mathbf{f}_k(\mathbf{x}_k, \mathbf{u}_k) \tag{3-2}$$

$$\mathbf{x}_0 \text{ given} \tag{3-3}$$

GENERAL NONLINEAR MODELS

For this problem we construct the hamiltonian H_k by appending the system equations to the criterion function with a lagrangian (or costate) variable λ for each time period as

$$H_k = L_k(x_k, u_k) + \lambda'_{k+1} f_k(\mathbf{x}_k, \mathbf{u}_k) \tag{3-8}$$

Then the first-order conditions can be stated as[1]

Systems (or state) equations: $\quad \mathbf{x}_{k+1} = \mathbf{f}_k(\mathbf{x}_k, \mathbf{u}_k) \quad k = 0, 1, \ldots, N-1 \quad (3\text{-}9)$

Costate equations: $\quad \boldsymbol{\lambda}_k = \mathbf{L}_{\mathbf{x}k} + \boldsymbol{\lambda}'_{k+1} \mathbf{f}_{\mathbf{x}k} \quad k = 1, 2, \ldots, N-1 \quad (3\text{-}10)$

Optimality conditions: $\quad \mathbf{H}_{\mathbf{u}k} = \mathbf{L}_{\mathbf{u}k} + \boldsymbol{\lambda}'_{k+1} \mathbf{f}_{\mathbf{u}k} = 0 \quad k = 0, 1, \ldots, N-1$

$$\tag{3-11}$$

Terminal conditions: $\quad\quad\quad\quad\quad \boldsymbol{\lambda}'_N = \mathbf{L}_{\mathbf{x}N} \quad\quad\quad\quad\quad (3\text{-}12)$

Initial conditions: $\quad\quad\quad\quad\quad\quad \mathbf{x}_0 = \text{given} \quad\quad\quad\quad\quad (3\text{-}13)$

where $\mathbf{L}_{\mathbf{x}k}$, $\mathbf{L}_{\mathbf{u}k}$, $\mathbf{f}_{\mathbf{x}k}$, and $\mathbf{f}_{\mathbf{u}k}$ are defined in Eqs. (3-5a), (3-5b), (3-6a), and (3-6b), respectively. Also $\boldsymbol{\lambda}_k$ is a vector with n elements and $\mathbf{H}_{\mathbf{u}k}$ is a vector with m elements which is defined by Eq. (3-11).

The first-order conditions (3-9) to (3-12) are then met in an iterative fashion. First a nominal set of control variables for iteration $\rho = 0$ is chosen

$$(\mathbf{u}_k^\rho)_{k=0}^{N-1}$$

Then the control variables and the initial conditions (3-13) are used to integrate the system Eq. (3-9) forward in time. That is, $\mathbf{u}_0$ and $\mathbf{x}_0$ are used in Eq. (3-9) to calculate $\mathbf{x}_1$. Then $\mathbf{x}_1$ and $\mathbf{u}_1$ are used to calculate $\mathbf{x}_2$, etc. Finally at terminal time N, $\mathbf{x}_N$ is obtained and is used in turn in the terminal condition (3-12) to determine $\boldsymbol{\lambda}_N$.

Next the costate equations are integrated backward in time from period N to period 1 to obtain $\boldsymbol{\lambda}_N$ through $\boldsymbol{\lambda}_1$. At this point all the first-order conditions are satisfied except the optimality conditions (3-11), and even these may be satisfied. To check this, $\mathbf{H}_{\mathbf{u}k}$ is calculated for all time periods using the nominal control

$$(\mathbf{u}_k^\rho)_{k=0}^{N-1}$$

and the states and costates calculated from them in the manner described above. If all the elements in the vector $\mathbf{H}_{\mathbf{u}k}$ are sufficiently close to zero for all time periods, the problem is solved, but this will ordinarily not be the case.

Thus the problem is to move the controls in such a direction that the optimality conditions are more likely to be met on the next iteration. This is where the gradient procedure is employed. First a decision is made to move the control in the direction of the gradient $\mathbf{H}_{\mathbf{u}k}$ from the control values of iteration ρ

---

[1] See Kendrick and Taylor (1971) and Bryson and Ho (1969, chap. 7, secs. 7 and 8).

to obtain the control values at iteration $\rho + 1$

$$\mathbf{u}_k^{\rho+1} = \mathbf{u}_k^{\rho} - \alpha \mathbf{H}_{\mathbf{u}k} \qquad k = 0, 1, \ldots, N-1 \qquad (3\text{-}14)$$

where α is the distance to move in the gradient direction. (In practice the control is usually moved not in the gradient direction but in the *conjugate* gradient direction.)[1] So the *direction* of movement is known but the *distance* is not known. However, α is usually chosen by doing a one-dimensional search in the gradient (or conjugate-gradient) direction until the hamiltonian H_k is minimized. A variety of line-search methods are in use, including those due to Shanno (1977) and to Gill et al. (1976).

Once the new nominal control has been determined from (3-14), the process is repeated again beginning with the system Eq. (3-9). The iterations are continued until the optimality conditions are satisfied to the desired accuracy.

3-4 SPECIAL PROBLEMS

The algorithm described in Sec. 3-3 is sufficient to solve many economic models, but it does not address a number of difficulties arising from efforts to solve certain classes of dynamic economic optimization problems, e.g., accuracy and roundoff errors, large model size, and presence of inequality constraints on state variables. This section provides a brief discussion of each of these issues and gives references to more extensive discussions.

Accuracy and Roundoff Errors

Many large econometric models are not defined in the explicit form of the system equations

$$\mathbf{x}_{k+1} = \mathbf{f}_k(\mathbf{x}_k, \mathbf{u}_k) \qquad (3\text{-}2)$$

but in an implicit form

$$\mathbf{g}_k(\mathbf{x}_{k+1}, \mathbf{x}_k, \mathbf{u}_k) = 0 \qquad (3\text{-}4)$$

Therefore it is necessary to solve the set of simultaneous equations (3-4) at each step in the solution of the optimization problem. Since Eq. (3-4) may contain several hundred equations, this is no simple task. Furthermore, if the numerical methods employed are not sufficiently accurate, the derivatives $\mathbf{H}_{\mathbf{u}k}$ which are used in the algorithm will be off and the search for the optimum will be made in the wrong direction.[2]

---

[1] This is the procedure which was used by Kendrick and Taylor (1970). For a description see Lasdon, Mitter and Warren, (1967), and Fletcher and Reeves (1964). For other gradient methods see Polack and Ribière (1969), Perry (1976), Davidon (1959), Fletcher and Powell (1963), and computer codes which embody several of these methods, namely MINOS, by Murtagh and Saunders (1977), and LSGRG, by Mantell and Lasdon (1977).

[2] For a discussion of this problem see Ando, Norman, and Palash (1978).

Large Model Size

A large econometric model may have 300 to 500 state equations. Thus the matrix $\mathbf{f}_{xk}$ may have as many as 250,000 elements. If a problem has 10 time periods, 2.5 million words of memory will be required to store the $\mathbf{f}_{xk}$ matrices alone. Of course it is also necessary to store $\mathbf{f}_{uk}$, $\mathbf{H}_{uk}$, $\mathbf{L}_{uk}$, and $\mathbf{L}_{xk}$. Thus the storage requirements will easily surpass several million words of core storage. Even the largest of today's computers will be strained to the limit by such large high-speed-memory requirements. Therefore, it is necessary to exploit the fact that the matrix $\mathbf{f}_{xk}$ will have only a relatively small number of elements that are not zero; i.e., the matrix will be very sparse. Computer codes have been constructed to store and manipulate only the nonzero elements of the matrices. Examples of this class of codes are MINOS, by Murtagh and Saunders (1977), LSGRG, by Mantell and Lasdon (1977), and CONOPT, by Drud and Meeraus.[2] It is beyond the scope of this book to discuss sparsity techniques, but a clear discussion is available in Drud (1976).

Inequality Constraints on State Variables

The method described in the previous section is adequate if there are constraints on control variables but not on state variables since the linear search can be halted when a constraint is reached. However, when there are constraints on state variables or on combinations of state and control variables, that method is not adequate. Instead the generalized reduced gradient (GRG) methods are employed.[2] Fortunately they are embodied in a number of computer codes, including the three mentioned above.

---

[1] The Drud and Meeraus code is not yet fully documented, but a call for problems and the addresses of the authors are given in A. Drud and A. Meeraus, *J. Econ. Dynam. Control*, 2(1): 133–4 (1980).

[2] For a discussion see Drud (1976, sec. 6.3).

CHAPTER
FOUR

EXAMPLE OF DETERMINISTIC CONTROL

This chapter employs a small macroeconomic model to demonstrate how an economic-stabilization problem can be cast into the deterministic control framework and how that framework may alter one's thinking about the problem. A small quarterly macroeconomic model of the United States economy is developed, estimated, and converted into the format used by control theorists. A criterion function is then specified for this model.

4-1 SYSTEM EQUATIONS

The body of a control-theory macroeconometric model, called the system equations, constitutes the set of difference equations which describe the evolution of the economy over time. In this section the simplest multiplier-accelerator model is presented, estimated, and converted into control-theory format.

The simple multiplier-accelerator model is written as

$$C_k = a + bY_k \tag{4-1}$$

$$I_k = e + f(Y_k - Y_{k-1}) \tag{4-2}$$

$$Y_k = C_k + I_k + G_k \tag{4-3}$$

where C_k = consumption
I_k = investment
Y_k = gross national product
G_k = government spending

In order to fit this model to the data, it is necessary to be somewhat more precise in the definition of each variable; let

C_k = total personal consumption expenditures, 1958 dollars (GC58)
I_k = gross private domestic investment, 1958 dollars (GPI58)
Y_k = gross national product, 1958 dollars, less net exports of goods and services, 1958 dollars (YN = GNP58 − GNET58)
G_k = total government purchases of goods and services, 1958 dollars (GGE58)

In particular, data from the National Bureau of Economic Research time-series data bank for the period 1947-II to 1973-II were used. Fitting Eqs. (4-1) and (4-2) by ordinary least squares then yields

$$C_k = -14.5 + .67 Y_k \qquad \begin{matrix} R^2 = .99 \\ DW = .15 \end{matrix} \qquad (4\text{-}4)$$
$$ (2.84) \quad (.005)$$

and

$$I_k = 73.7 + 1.53(Y_k - Y_{k-1}) \qquad \begin{matrix} R^2 = .17 \\ DW = .17 \end{matrix} \qquad (4\text{-}5)$$
$$ (2.58) \quad (.34)$$

The fit is adequate for the consumption function, but the Durbin-Watson statistic is too low. Also, the explanatory power of the investment equation and the Durbin-Watson statistic are too low.

One can obtain a model which retains most of the simplicity of Eqs. (4-1) to (4-3) while mitigating the problems above by using a partial-adjustment model. Also the accelerator (4-2) is rewritten to make investment a function of changes in consumption instead of changes in GNP. The latter change is made in order to reduce the length of lags in the control model and thereby reduce the size of the model, which is used later in the book for adaptive-control experiments. The resulting model can be written

$$C_k^* = a + bY_k \qquad (4\text{-}6)$$
$$C_k = C_{k-1} + \gamma(C_k^* - C_{k-1}) \qquad (4\text{-}7)$$
$$I_k^* = e + f(C_k - C_{k-1}) \qquad (4\text{-}8)$$
$$I_k = I_{k-1} + \theta(I_k^* - I_{k-1}) \qquad (4\text{-}9)$$
$$Y_k = C_k + I_k + G_k \qquad (4\text{-}10)$$

where C_k^* = desired consumption
I_k^* = desired investment
γ = partial adjustment coefficient for investment
θ = partial adjustment coefficient for consumption

The model (4-6) to (4-10) can be rewritten to eliminate the unobservable variables by substituting Eq. (4-6) into Eq. (4-7) and Eq. (4-8) into Eq. (4-9), to obtain

$$C_k = (1 - \gamma)C_{k-1} + \gamma b Y_k + \gamma a \qquad (4\text{-}11)$$

and
$$I_k = (1 - \theta)I_{k-1} + \theta fC_k - \theta fC_{k-1} + \theta e \quad (4\text{-}12)$$

Then the national-income identity (4-10) can be substituted into Eq. (4-11) and the resulting model written as

$$C_k = \alpha_0 + \alpha_1 I_k + \alpha_2 C_{k-1} + \alpha_3 G_k \quad (4\text{-}13)$$

$$I_k = \beta_0 + \beta_1 C_k + \beta_2 C_{k-1} + \beta_3 I_{k-1} \quad (4\text{-}14)$$

where
$$\alpha_0 = \frac{\gamma a}{1 - \gamma b} \qquad \alpha_1 = \alpha_3 = \frac{\gamma b}{1 - \gamma b} \qquad \alpha_2 = \frac{1 - \gamma}{1 - \gamma b}$$

$$\beta_0 = \theta e \qquad \beta_1 = -\beta_2 = \theta f \qquad \beta_3 = 1 - \theta$$

The structural form of Eqs. (4-13) and (4-14) can be written as

$$\begin{aligned}
C_k - \alpha_1 I_k - \alpha_2 C_{k-1} \quad\quad\quad\quad - \alpha_3 G_k - \alpha_0 &= \varepsilon_1 \\
-\beta_1 C_k + \quad I_k - \beta_2 C_{k-1} - \beta_3 I_{k-1} \quad\quad\quad\quad - \beta_0 &= \varepsilon_2
\end{aligned} \quad (4\text{-}15)$$

with the spacing used to emphasize that G_k enters the first equation but not the second and I_{k-1} enters the second equation but not the first. Then Eq. (4-15) can be written in the usual econometric notation as

$$\hat{\mathbf{B}}\hat{\mathbf{y}}_k + \hat{\boldsymbol{\Gamma}}\hat{\mathbf{x}}_k = \hat{\mathbf{u}}_k \quad (4\text{-}16)$$

$$\hat{\mathbf{y}}_k = \begin{bmatrix} C_k \\ I_k \end{bmatrix} \qquad \hat{\mathbf{x}}_k = \begin{bmatrix} C_{k-1} \\ I_{k-1} \\ G_k \\ v_k \end{bmatrix} \text{ where } v_k = 1 \text{ for all } k \qquad \hat{\mathbf{u}}_k = \begin{bmatrix} \varepsilon_{1k} \\ \varepsilon_{2k} \end{bmatrix} \quad (4\text{-}17)$$

$$\hat{\mathbf{B}} = \begin{bmatrix} \hat{\beta}_{11} & \hat{\beta}_{12} \\ \hat{\beta}_{21} & \hat{\beta}_{22} \end{bmatrix} = \begin{bmatrix} 1 & -\alpha_1 \\ -\beta_1 & 1 \end{bmatrix}$$

$$\hat{\boldsymbol{\Gamma}} = \begin{bmatrix} \hat{\gamma}_{11} & \hat{\gamma}_{12} & \hat{\gamma}_{13} & \hat{\gamma}_{14} \\ \hat{\gamma}_{21} & \hat{\gamma}_{22} & \hat{\gamma}_{23} & \hat{\gamma}_{24} \end{bmatrix} = \begin{bmatrix} -\alpha_2 & 0 & -\alpha_3 & -\alpha_0 \\ -\beta_2 & -\beta_3 & 0 & -\beta_0 \end{bmatrix} \quad (4\text{-}18)$$

In Eq. (4-16) the hat over the variables has been used to distinguish the notation commonly used in econometrics textbooks from the notation used in control-theory textbooks. Table 4-1 provides a comparison of some of the common notation used in these two fields.

The reduced form of Eq. (4-16) can then be written

$$\hat{\mathbf{y}}_k = \hat{\boldsymbol{\Pi}}\hat{\mathbf{x}}_k + \hat{\mathbf{v}}_k \quad (4\text{-}19)$$

where $\quad \hat{\boldsymbol{\Pi}} = \hat{\mathbf{B}}^{-1}\hat{\boldsymbol{\Gamma}} \qquad \hat{\mathbf{v}}_k = \hat{\mathbf{B}}^{-1}\hat{\mathbf{u}}_k \qquad \hat{\boldsymbol{\Pi}} = \begin{bmatrix} \pi_{11} & \pi_{12} & \pi_{13} & \pi_{14} \\ \pi_{21} & \pi_{22} & \pi_{23} & \pi_{24} \end{bmatrix}$

Table 4-1 Common notation in econometrics and in control-theory textbooks

Symbol	Use in econometrics	Use in control theory
	Vectors	
y	Endogenous variables	Observation variables
x	Predetermined variables	State variables
u	Error terms	Control variables
v	Error terms	Not used
	Matrices	
B	Endogenous-variable coefficients in structural form	Control-variable coefficients
Γ	Predetermined-variable coefficients in structural form	Not used
Π	Predetermined-variable coefficients in structural form	Not used

The identification of the model (4-15) can be checked with the help of the following variables:[1]

G = number of endogenous variables in model
G^Δ = number of endogenous variables appearing in gth equation
$G^{\Delta\Delta} = G - G^\Delta$
K = number of predetermined variables in model
K^* = number of predetermined variables appearing in gth equation
$K^{**} = K - K^*$

With these definitions, an equation is said to satisfy the order condition for identifiability if

$$K^{**} \geq G^\Delta - 1 \tag{4-20}$$

For the model (4-15), $G = 2$ and $K = 4$. Also for the first equation $G^\Delta = 2$, since both endogenous variables appear in that equation. On the other hand, $K^* = 3$, since, from Eq. (4-18), I_{k-1} does not appear in the first equation. Thus the inequality (4-20) becomes

$$K - K^* = K^{**} \geq G^\Delta - 1$$
$$4 - 3 = 1 \geq 2 - 1$$
$$1 = 1 \tag{4-21}$$

---

[1] See Kmenta (1971, pp. 539–546).

30 DETERMINISTIC CONTROL

When, as in this case, the inequality holds as an equality, the equation is said to be *exactly identified*.

Similarly for the second equation in (4-15), $G^\Delta = 2$ and $K^* = 3$, since, from Eq. (4-18), G_k does not enter the equation. Thus the inequality (4-20) holds as an equality for the second equation, and it is also exactly identified.

When all the equations of the model are exactly identified, the ordinary (unrestricted) least-squares estimates are consistent estimates of the π's. These estimates will also be equivalent to maximum-likelihood estimates and will possess the properties of asymptotic efficiency and asymptotic normality.[1]

The reduced-form equations (4-19) were estimated by ordinary least squares on the TROLL system at M.I.T. for the period 1947-II through 1969-I, to obtain[2]

$$C_k = 1.014 C_{k-1} + .002 I_{k-1} - .004 G_k - 1.312 \qquad \begin{array}{l} R^2 = .998 \\ DW = 2.19 \end{array} \qquad (4\text{-}22)$$
$$(.016) \phantom{C_{k-1} +} (.047) \phantom{I_{k-1} -} (.031) (1.52)$$

$$I_k = .093 C_{k-1} + .753 I_{k-1} - .100 G_k + .448 \qquad \begin{array}{l} R^2 = .938 \\ DW = 1.62 \end{array} \qquad (4\text{-}23)$$
$$(.023) \phantom{C_{k-1} +} (.068) \phantom{I_{k-1} -} (.044) (2.164)$$

As can be seen from quick examination, this model has some characteristics which make it something less than the perfect model for conducting stabilization experiments. First, the coefficient in the first equation on C_{k-1} of 1.014 gives the model an explosive character. Second, the small coefficient on G_k of $-.004$ in the same equation renders government policy very weak in affecting consumption. Also the predominant effect of government spending on private consumption (as on investment in the second equation) is a "crowding out" effect. Thus increases in government spending result in decreases in both consumption and investment. This effect is of course not of significant magnitude in the consumption equation but is significant in the investment equation.

While these characteristics make it somewhat undesirable for stabilization experiments, the model in Eqs. (4-22) and (4-23) has the virtue of being derived and estimated in a straightforward manner from the Keynesian textbook model which is widely taught in freshman economics textbooks. Also, as will become apparent in Chap. 12, in the experiments with active-learning stochastic control the model is rich enough to begin to provide some insights into the relative magnitudes involved. The consumption path proves to be uninteresting, but the investment path shows considerable realism in the stochastic control experiments.[3]

Before the model (4-22) and (4-23) is written in control-theory notation, it is convenient to define government spending as equal to government obligations the previous quarter

$$G_{k+1} = O_k = \text{government obligations} \qquad (4\text{-}24)$$

---

[1] See Kmenta (1971, p. 551).
[2] These data are listed in Appendix S.
[3] For a more interesting example of deterministic control see Pindyck (1973a). A smaller model is used here so that it can also be used for stochastic control in later chapters.

Then by using Eqs. (4-22) and (4-23) the model can be written as the systems equations of a control model

$$x_{k+1} = Ax_k + Bu_k + c \qquad (4\text{-}25)$$

where

$$x_k = \begin{bmatrix} C_k \\ I_k \end{bmatrix} \qquad u_k = [O_k]$$

$$A = \begin{bmatrix} 1.014 & .002 \\ .093 & .753 \end{bmatrix} \qquad B = \begin{bmatrix} -.004 \\ -.100 \end{bmatrix} \qquad c = \begin{bmatrix} -1.312 \\ .448 \end{bmatrix}$$

Also the initial state variable for the model is

$$x_0 = \begin{bmatrix} 460.1 \\ 113.1 \end{bmatrix}$$

where the first element corresponds to private-consumption expenditures and the second element to gross private domestic investment in billions of 1958 dollars for 1969-I.

4-2 THE CRITERION FUNCTION

The criterion function is written to minimize the deviation of control- and state-variable paths from desired paths

$$J = \tfrac{1}{2}[x_N - \tilde{x}_N]'W_N[x_N - \tilde{x}_N]$$
$$+ \frac{1}{2}\sum_{k=0}^{N-1}\{[x_k - \tilde{x}_k]'W_k[x_k - \tilde{x}_k] + [u_k - \tilde{u}_k]'\Lambda_k[u_k - \tilde{u}_k]\}$$

(4-26)

where $\tilde{x}$ = desired state vector
$\tilde{u}$ = desired control vector
W = matrix of weights on state-variable deviations from desired paths
Λ = matrix of weights on control-variable deviations from desired paths

There has been considerable debate about the desirability of using quadratic rather than more general nonlinear functional forms for the criterion in macroeconomic problems.[1] The arguments for using quadratic functions are:

Computational simplicity. Since the first-order conditions for quadratic linear problems are linear, solution methods for solving such problems can be highly efficient.

Ease of explanation. It is likely that it will be easier to discuss desired paths and relative weights in quadratic penalty functions with politicians than to discuss general nonlinear utility functions.

---

[1] See for example Palash (1977) and related comments by Shupp (1977) and Livesey (1977).

Table 4-2 Solution to a macro control problem

	States						
	1	2	3	4	5	6	7
C	464.8	469.6	474.5	479.4	484.4	489.5	494.6
I	112.8	112.9	113.4	114.2	115.3	116.7	118.3
				Controls			
	0	1	2	3	4	5	6
O	156.4	156.8	157.2	157.4	157.2	156.7	155.6

The arguments against using the quadratic are:

Accuracy. The quadratic does not capture the true nature of political preferences.

Symmetric nature. Symmetric penalties about a given point are not desirable.[1]

For the problem at hand, the quadratic formulation has been adopted. The paths $\tilde{x}$ and $\tilde{u}$ were chosen by assuming desired growth rates of .75 percent per quarter. The initial conditions for these desired paths are the actual data for the economy for 1969-I, that is,

$$\tilde{x}_k = [1.0075]^k \begin{bmatrix} 460.1 \\ 113.1 \end{bmatrix} \quad k = 0, 1, \ldots, N$$

$$\tilde{u}_k = [1.0075]^k [153.644] \quad k = 0, 1, \ldots, N-1$$

The weighting matrices are chosen to represent the decision makers' preferences over the desired paths. For example, when unemployment levels and inflation rates are among the state variables, relatively higher penalties may be assigned to one or the other to represent political preferences.[2] Also the weights can be used to represent the fact that politicians may care much more about deviations of the economy from desired paths in some quarters than in others [see Fair (1978a, b)]. For example, the penalty matrices may be

$$W_N = \begin{bmatrix} 100 & 0 \\ 0 & 100 \end{bmatrix} \quad W_k = \begin{bmatrix} 1 & 0 \\ 0 & 1 \end{bmatrix} \text{ where } k = 1, 2, \ldots, N-1$$

$$\Lambda_k = [1]$$

In this scheme the politician cares 100 times as much about deviations of the economy from its desired path in the last quarter (say the quarter before an election) than in other quarters.

The solution to this problem is given in Table 4-2.

---

[1] See Friedman (1972), however, for an asymmetric quadratic penalty function.
[2] For a discussion and application of this procedure to a larger model see Pindyck (1973a).

PART TWO

PASSIVE-LEARNING STOCHASTIC CONTROL

CHAPTER
FIVE

ADDITIVE UNCERTAINTY

5-1 UNCERTAINTY IN ECONOMIC PROBLEMS

Uncertainty is pervasive in dynamic economic problems, but it is frequently ignored for three reasons:

1. It is assumed that the effect of the uncertainty in the economic system under study is small enough to have no noticeable affect on the outcome.
2. It is conjectured that even if the uncertainty were considered, the resulting optimal policy would not be different.
3. It is thought that the incorporation of uncertainty into the analysis will make the problem intractable.

Now consider in turn each of these reasons for ignoring uncertainty. First comes the argument that its effects are small and thus can be ignored. This may be true. However, one does not know about this until uncertainty is systematically incorporated into the analysis and the system is analyzed both with and without the uncertainty. In some cases this analysis can be done by comparing terms in mathematical expressions. In other cases it is necessary to compare numerical results since analytical mathematics is insufficient. It emerges from those numerical results that in some cases the *degree* of uncertainty matters. For example if variances are sufficiently small, there is no significant effect on the solution.

Second, the case is put forward that even when the uncertainty is considered in posing the problem, its effects do not appear in optimality conditions. This is the classic case of certainty equivalence, in which a deterministic problem is equivalent to the stochastic problem. This occurs in special cases of economic problems under uncertainty, particularly when the uncertainty can be modeled in an additive fashion. The latter part of this chapter is devoted to a discussion of the circumstances under which certainty equivalence holds. However, there are many economic problems where certainty equivalence does not hold.

Finally, it is thought that the incorporation of uncertainty into the analysis will make it intractable. This is unfortunately sometimes true, but even in these cases it is frequently possible to obtain *approximate* numerical solutions. These methods are relatively new to economics, and it is not yet known whether the quality of the approximation is sufficiently good. However, this knowledge will come in due course as experimentation with the methods increases. Approximation methods are used in the last part of this book on active-learning control problems. Whether or not approximation is necessary depends on how the uncertainty is modeled.

5-2 METHODS OF MODELING UNCERTAINTY

Uncertainty in economic problems can be separated into two broad classes: uncertainty in the economic system and uncertainty in the measurement of the system. Although most work with economics of uncertainty has been with the first type, econometricians are returning increasingly to work on measurement error.[1]

Uncertainty in the system is commonly modeled in one of two ways: additive error terms and parameter uncertainty. Additive error (or noise) terms is the most common treatment of uncertainty. Cases of this type can usually be treated with the certainty-equivalence procedures discussed later in this chapter. Parameter uncertainty is more difficult to treat since certainty-equivalence methods do not apply. However, procedures are available for analyzing this problem. Furthermore, they are sufficiently simple in computational terms to be applicable to large models involving hundreds of equations. This is the subject of Chap. 6.

When the uncertainty is in the parameters, it can be modeled with two kinds of assumptions. The simplest assumption is that the parameters are in fact constant but that the *estimates* of the parameters are unknown and stochastic. This case is analyzed later in this book. The alternative is that the parameters are themselves stochastic, a more difficult problem. Methods for analyzing this problem are discussed in this book, but no numerical examples of this type are given.[2] This completes the discussion of uncertainty in the system equations and leaves only the uncertainty in the measurement relations.

In engineering applications of control-theory measurement errors on various physical devices such as radar are used in the analysis. Since these devices are

---

[1] See for example Geraci (1976).
[2] For a discussion of this problem see also Sarris and Athans (1973).

used to measure state variables, the existence of measurement error means that the states are not known exactly but are estimated. Thus the engineering models include estimates of the mean and covariance of the state vector. These notions are also being adopted in economics. Certainty measurements of economic systems are also noisy, so it is reasonable to assume that although the state variables are not known exactly, estimates of their means and covariances can be made. The models used in the last chapters of this book will include measurement errors.

The various kinds of uncertainty require different methods of analysis. One of the most important differences in the treatment of uncertainty is the distinction between passive and active learning.

5-3 LEARNING: PASSIVE AND ACTIVE

Passive learning is a familiar concept in economics, though the term has not been widely used.[1] It refers to the fact that new data are collected in each time period and are periodically used to reestimate the parameters in economic models. When measurement errors are present, this concept can be extended to include reestimation of the state of the system at each period after data have been collected.

In contrast, active learning not only includes the idea of reestimation but also the notion that the existence of future measurements should be considered when choosing the control variables. That is, one should take account of the fact that changes in a control variable at time k will affect the yield of information in future time periods. Stated another way, perturbations to the system today will provide more accurate estimation of state variables and parameters in future time periods. Furthermore, the more accurate estimates will permit better control of the system in subsequent periods.

An example from guidance systems will serve to illustrate this point. The control theorist Karl Astrom and his colleagues have used stochastic control methods for developing a control system for large oil tankers. Whenever a tanker takes on or discharges crude oil, the response of the ship to changes in the wheel setting is different. With a passive-learning scheme the ship pulls away from the dock and the system reestimates the response parameters every few minutes as the ship is maneuvered out of the harbor. With an active-learning scheme the control system perturbates the controls on purpose to learn faster about the response of the ship to different control settings.

In order to make these concepts somewhat precise it is useful to set out the scheme proposed by Bar-Shalom and Tse (1976b) and to distinguish between various types of control schemes. In order to do this some additional notation

---

[1] See Rausser (1977) for a more complete discussion of active- and passive-learning stochastic control.

must be developed. Recall the notation

$$\mathbf{x}_k = \text{state vector in period } k$$
$$\mathbf{u}_k = \text{control vector in period } k$$

and consider a model with system equations

$$\mathbf{x}_{k+1} = \mathbf{f}_k(\mathbf{x}_k, \mathbf{u}_k, \boldsymbol{\xi}_k) \qquad k = 0, 1, \ldots, N-1 \qquad (5\text{-}1)$$

where $\boldsymbol{\xi}_k$ is the vector of process noise terms at time k. Further, as discussed above, assume that measurements are taken on the state of the system and that there is error in these measurements; i.e.,

$$\mathbf{y}_k = \mathbf{h}_k(\mathbf{x}_k, \boldsymbol{\zeta}_k) \qquad k = 0, 1, \ldots, N \qquad (5\text{-}2)$$

where $\mathbf{y}_k$ is the measurement vector and $\boldsymbol{\zeta}_k$ is the measurement error (noise). Next define variables which represent the collection of state and control variables, respectively, for all the time periods in the model

$$\mathbf{X}_0^N = (\mathbf{x}_j)_{j=0}^N \qquad \mathbf{U}_0^{N-1} = (\mathbf{u}_j)_{j=0}^{N-1}$$

Also define the set of all observations between period 1 and period k as

$$\mathbf{Y}^k = (\mathbf{y}_j)_{j=1}^k$$

Next the notation

$$\mathbf{M}^k = \left(\mathbf{h}_j(\mathbf{x}_j, \boldsymbol{\zeta}_j)\right)_{j=1}^k$$

is used to represent the knowledge that a measurement is made. Note the distinction between $\mathbf{Y}$ and $\mathbf{M}$. $\mathbf{Y}$ represents the actual measurement, but $\mathbf{M}$ represents the knowledge that a measurement will be made without specifying what the actual measurement will be.

Finally the notation

$$\mathbf{S}^k = P\!\left(\mathbf{x}_0, (\boldsymbol{\xi}_j)_{j=0}^k, (\boldsymbol{\zeta}_j)_{j=1}^k\right)$$

is used to represent the probability distribution of the initial state vector, the system error terms, and the measurement error term. A subset of these data

$$\mathbf{S}^* = P\!\left(\mathbf{x}_0, (\boldsymbol{\xi}_j)_{j=0}^{N-1}\right)$$

is defined for use in the definition of one kind of control policy.

With this notation in mind the following breakdown of control policies made by Bar-Shalom and Tse (1976b) can be stated. First comes the open-loop policy, which ignores all measurement relationships, i.e.,

$$\mathbf{u}_k^{\text{OL}} = \mathbf{g}_k(\mathbf{S}^*) \qquad k = 0, 1, \ldots, N-1$$

Next comes feedback (or passive-learning) policy, which uses the measurement relations through period k, that is,

$$\mathbf{u}_k^F = \mathbf{g}_k(\mathbf{Y}^k, \mathbf{U}^{k-1}, \mathbf{M}^k, \mathbf{S}^k) \qquad k = 0, 1, \ldots, N-1$$

This policy makes use of both the actual measurement $\mathbf{y}^k$ and the knowledge that measurements are made through period k. Finally there is the closed-loop (or active-learning) policy

$$\mathbf{u}_k^{CL} = \mathbf{g}_k(\mathbf{Y}^k, \mathbf{U}^{k-1}, \mathbf{M}^{N-1}, \mathbf{S}^{N-1}) \qquad k = 0, 1, \ldots, N-1$$

which not only uses the state observation through period k but also takes account of the fact that the system will be measured in future time periods, i.e., for $\mathbf{M}^{N-1}$ and $\mathbf{S}^{N-1}$.

In practice this means that in choosing the control under a passive-learning scheme one ignores the future covariances of the states and parameters while under an active-learning scheme one considers the impact of the present choice of control on the future covariances of states and controls. The idea is not that one can use actual future measurements (since they are not available) but can anticipate that present perturbations of the controls will improve the accuracy of future estimates as represented by the covariance matrices for future states and controls.

This completes the introductory material for the remainder of the book on stochastic control as well as the introductory material for Part Two, which is on passive-learning stochastic control. Now a discussion of the first kind of passive-learning stochastic control, namely additive uncertainty, will be given. This will be followed in Chap. 6 by a discussion of an algorithm for the treatment of multiplicative uncertainty.

5-4 ADDITIVE ERROR TERMS

The most common form of uncertainty in economic models is an additive error term, i.e., a random error term is added to the system equations so that they become

$$\mathbf{x}_{k+1} = \mathbf{f}_k(\mathbf{x}_k, \mathbf{u}_k) + \boldsymbol{\xi}_k \tag{5-3}$$

where $\boldsymbol{\xi}_k$ is a vector of additive error terms. Furthermore it is assumed that the error terms (1) have zero mean, (2) have the covariance $\mathbf{Q}_k$, and (3) are serially uncorrelated; i.e.,

$$E\{\boldsymbol{\xi}_k\} = 0 \qquad E\{\boldsymbol{\xi}_k \boldsymbol{\xi}_k'\} = \mathbf{Q}_k \qquad E\{\boldsymbol{\xi}_k \boldsymbol{\xi}_\theta'\}_{\theta \neq k} = \mathbf{0} \tag{5-4}$$

The mean-zero assumption is not crucial since the nonzero mean can be added into the $\mathbf{f}_k$ function. Also the serial-correlation assumption is not crucial since it can be treated by augmenting the state equations.[1]

The criterion function is no longer deterministic but is an expectation taken over the random quantities. Thus the problem is to find $(\mathbf{u}_k)_{k=0}^{N-1}$ to minimize

$$J = E\{C\} = E\left\{ L_N(\mathbf{x}_N) + \sum_{k=0}^{N-1} L_k(\mathbf{x}_k, \mathbf{u}_k) \right\} \tag{5-5}$$

---

[1] Correlated error terms in control problems are discussed in Pagan (1975).

subject to Eqs. (5-3) and (5-4) and given initial conditions x_0 for the state variables.

If L is quadratic and f is linear, the certainty-equivalence conditions hold and the results of Simon (1956) and Theil (1957) can be applied. This means that the expected value of the random components can be taken and the problem solved as a deterministic model. Alternatively, when L is not quadratic, the postponed-linear-approximation method of Ashley (1976) can be applied.[1]

Also for the general case when L is not quadratic and f is not linear, approximation methods are available. For example, see Athans (1972). An application of this approach to macroeconomic stabilization problems is given in Garbade (1975a) and to a commodity-stabilization problem is given in Kim, Goreux, and Kendrick (1975). The latter is the cocoa-market stabilization study.[2]

As with most approximation methods a Taylor expansion is made around a nominal path. It is customary to choose the nominal path by taking expectations of all random variables and solving the resulting deterministic problem. In the cocoa-market stabilization problem the resulting deterministic nonlinear control problem was solved using the differential dynamic-programming method of Jacobson and Mayne (1970). In contrast, Garbade used the quadratic linear approximation method discussed in Chap. 3. These procedures yield a nominal path

$$(x_{o,k+1}, u_{o,k})_{k=0}^{N-1}$$

Next a second-order Taylor expansion of the criterion function (5-5) and a first-order expansion of the system equations (5-3) are made along the nominal path, as described in Sec. 3-2. Finally, the resulting quadratic linear control problem is solved. This yields a feedback rule of the form

$$u_k = u_{ok} + G_k[x_k - x_{ok}] + g_k \tag{5-6}$$

One merit of this procedure is that the quadratic approximation in the criterion functions works like a tracking problem in the sense that the problem is solved to minimize some weighted sum of terms in $[x_k - x_{ok}]$ and $[u_k - u_{ok}]$ for all k. Thus the quality of the approximation is enhanced by the fact that the criterion works to keep the optimal path for both the controls and states close to the nominal paths about which the approximation is made. When this method is used for stabilization problems, the effect of this is to stabilize about the certainty-equivalence path. In some cases this may not be desirable.[3]

---

[1] For a generalization of this result to adaptive-control problems see Ashley (1979).

[2] For other applications of control theory to models with additive error terms see, for microeconomics, Kendrick, Rao, and Wells (1970), a water-pollution control problem; for macroeconomics (1) United States Economy, Pindyck and Roberts (1974), Chow (1972), Brito and Hester (1974), and Gordon (1974); (2) United Kingdom Economy, Bray (1974, 1975) and Wall and Westcott (1974, 1975); (3) theoretical models, Kareken, Muench, and Wallace (1973), Phelps and Taylor (1977), and Sargent and Wallace (1975).

[3] See Denham (1964) for an alternative procedure for choosing the nominal path with consideration of the uncertainty.

CHAPTER SIX

MULTIPLICATIVE UNCERTAINTY

If all uncertainty in economic problems could be treated as additive uncertainty, the method of the previous chapter could be applied; however, many economic problems of interest include multiplicative uncertainty. Consider, for example, agricultural problems. The total output is represented as the yield of the crop per acre times the number of acres planted. But since the yield is a random variable, multiplicative uncertainty occurs because the acreage is a state or control variable and the yield multiplies the acreage. Or consider policy choice in macroeconomic models. Since the coefficients in these models are estimated, they should be treated as random variables and once again multiplicative uncertainty is introduced.

The optimal control problem with multiplicative uncertainty is stated in the next section. Then dynamic-programming methods are used to derive the optimal control just as was done in Chap. 2 for deterministic problems. As in Chap. 2, the analysis is restricted to problems with quadratic criterion functions and linear system equations. Unlike Chap. 2, however, an expectations operator is introduced into the criterion function. Therefore special attention is paid in this chapter to methods of taking expectations of products of matrices. The chapter closes with a brief discussion of methods of updating the estimates of the unknown parameters.

6-1 STATEMENT OF THE PROBLEM

The system equations for the problem are written exactly as they were in Chap. 5 with an additive error term except that the parameters are considered to be stochastic rather than fixed. Thus the system equations are written

$$\mathbf{x}_{k+1} = \mathbf{A}_k \mathbf{x}_k + \mathbf{B}_k \mathbf{u}_k + \mathbf{c}_k + \boldsymbol{\xi}_k \qquad k = 0, 1, \ldots, N-1 \qquad (6\text{-}1)$$

with
$$\mathbf{x}_0 = \text{given}$$

Means and covariance for the parameters are assumed to be known:

Means:
$$\begin{aligned} &E\{a_{ij}\} && \text{for all } i,j \\ &E\{b_{ij}\} && \text{for all } i,j \\ &E\{c_j\} && \text{for all } j \end{aligned} \qquad (6\text{-}2)$$

Covariances:
$$\begin{aligned} &\text{cov}(a_{ij} a_{kl}) && \text{for all } i,j,k,l \\ &\text{cov}(b_{ij} b_{kl}) && \text{for all } i,j,k,l \\ &\text{cov}(c_i c_j) && \text{for all } i,j \\ &\text{cov}(a_{ij} b_{kl}) && \text{for all } i,j,k,l \\ &\text{cov}(a_{ij} c_k) && \text{for all } i,j,k \\ &\text{cov}(b_{ij} c_k) && \text{for all } i,j,k \end{aligned} \qquad (6\text{-}3)$$

The elements in Eq. (6-3) are the familiar covariance matrices obtained when estimating equations with econometrics packages. For example, consider the coefficients in the first row of the matrix $\mathbf{A}$ as the coefficients of a single equation. Then the first element in Eq. (6-3) becomes

$$\text{cov}(a_{1j} a_{1k}) \qquad \text{for all } j,k$$

which is the familiar Σ matrix for the coefficients of a single equation, in this case Σ_{11} since it is for the first equation. Of course in the first element of Eq. (6-3) there is a matrix like this for each equation, namely Σ_{11}, Σ_{22}, etc., and then there are also off-diagonal matrices which provide the covariance between the coefficients of each equation with every other equation. These matrices are obtained when one is performing simultaneous-equation estimation.

Next consider the criterion function for the problem. It is the expected value of a quadratic function; i.e., the problem is to find the controls $(\mathbf{u}_k)_{k=0}^{N-1}$ to minimize

$$J = E\left\{ L_N(\mathbf{x}_N) + \sum_{k=0}^{N-1} L_k(\mathbf{x}_k, \mathbf{u}_k) \right\} \qquad (6\text{-}4)$$

where E is the expectations operator. The functions L_N and L_k are the same quadratic functions as in Chap. 2

$$L_N(\mathbf{x}_N) = \tfrac{1}{2}\mathbf{x}_N' \mathbf{W}_N \mathbf{x}_N + \mathbf{w}_N' \mathbf{x}_N \qquad (6\text{-}5)$$

and
$$L_k(\mathbf{x}_k, \mathbf{u}_k) = \tfrac{1}{2}\mathbf{x}_k' \mathbf{W}_k \mathbf{x}_k + \mathbf{w}_k' \mathbf{x}_k + \mathbf{x}_k' \mathbf{F}_k \mathbf{u}_k + \tfrac{1}{2}\mathbf{u}_k' \Lambda_k \mathbf{u}_k + \boldsymbol{\lambda}_k' \mathbf{u}_k$$
$$k = 0, 1, \ldots, N-1 \qquad (6\text{-}6)$$

where N = last time period
k = all other time periods
$\mathbf{x}$ = state vector
$\mathbf{u}$ = control vector
$\mathbf{W}, \Lambda, \mathbf{F}$ = matrices
$\mathbf{w}, \boldsymbol{\lambda}$ = vectors

So in summary, the problem is to minimize the criterion function (6-4) subject to the system equations (6-1).

The problem is solved by using dynamic-programming methods and working backward in time.[1] First the problem is solved for period N and then for period $N - 1$. This leads to the solution for the general period k.

6-2 PERIOD N

It is useful to introduce notation for the cost-to-go, keeping in mind that it is usually written as the cost-to-go when one is $N - j$ periods from the end. Thus the deterministic cost-to-go $N - j$ periods from the terminal period is written as

$$C_{N-j} = L_N(\mathbf{x}_N) + \sum_{k=j}^{N-1} L_k(\mathbf{x}_k, \mathbf{u}_k) \qquad (6\text{-}7)$$

Thus C_{N-j} is the cost-to-go with $N - j$ periods to go. With this notation C_0 is the cost-to-go with zero periods remaining, and C_N is the cost-to-go with all N periods remaining, i.e.,

$$C_0 = L_N(\mathbf{x}_N) \qquad (6\text{-}8)$$

and
$$C_N = L_N(\mathbf{x}_N) + \sum_{k=0}^{N-1} L_k(\mathbf{x}_k, \mathbf{u}_k) \qquad (6\text{-}9)$$

The expected cost-to-go J is defined in the same manner as the random cost-to-go C

$J_N = E\{C_N\}$ = expected cost-to-go for full N periods
$J_{N-j} = E\{C_{N-j}\}$ = expected cost-to-go at period j with $N-j$ periods remaining
$J_0 = E\{C_0\}$ = expected cost-to-go for terminal period

---

[1] The derivation here follows the procedure of Farison, Graham, and Shelton (1967) and Aoki (1967, pp. 44–47). Related algorithms have been developed by Bar-Shalom and Sivan (1969), Curry (1969), Tse and Athans (1972), and Ku and Athans (1973). Yaakov Bar-Shalom provided private communications that helped in developing the derivations used here. Also a few elements from Tse, Bar-Shalom, and Meier (1973) and Bar-Shalom, Tse, and Larson (1974) have been used. For a similar derivation see Chow (1975, chap. 10). For an alternative treatment of multiplicative uncertainty see Turnovsky (1975, 1977).

Finally, J^* is defined as the *optimal* expected cost-to-go. It is written in an elaborate manner for the general period $N - j$ as

$$J^*_{N-j} = \min_{\mathbf{u}_j} E\left\{ \cdots \min_{\mathbf{u}_{N-2}} E\left\{ \min_{\mathbf{u}_{N-1}} E\{C_{N-j}|\mathcal{P}^{N-1}\}|\mathcal{P}^{N-2}\right\} \cdots |\mathcal{P}^j \right\} \quad (6\text{-}10)$$

where $\mathcal{P}^j = (\mathbf{x}_j, \Sigma_j)$ is the mean and covariance of the unknown elements. The expectations are nested in Eq. (6-10). That is, the inside expectation in the nested expressions is

$$\min_{\mathbf{u}_{N-1}} E\{C_{N-j}|\mathcal{P}^{N-1}\} \quad (6\text{-}11)$$

This expression means the minimum over the control variables in the next to last period of the expectation of the term in the braces. Recall that since no control is chosen in the last period, the control in the next-to-last period is the final set of control variables chosen for the problem. The terms in the braces are the cost-to-go $N - j$ periods from the end conditional on the information $\mathcal{P}^{N-1}$ being available. The information $\mathcal{P}^j$ is defined as the means and covariances of the parameters at time j. The symbols J^* and C have indices which indicate the number of periods remaining; all other symbols like u and $\mathcal{P}$ have subscripts and superscripts indicating the period in which the action occurs. Thus in a problem with eight time periods C_2 means the cost-to-go with two periods remaining, i.e., the cost-to-go at period 6 ($C_{N-6} = C_{8-6} = C_2$).

Returning to the entire nested expression (6-10), one sees that each control $\mathbf{u}_j$ must be chosen with the information available only through time j. For example, $\mathbf{u}_3$ is chosen with the means and covariances available in period 3, while $\mathbf{u}_6$ has the advantage of being chosen three periods later when better estimates of the means and covariances will be available.

If the general expression (6-10) is specialized to zero periods to go, i.e., to the last period, it becomes

$$J^*_0 = E\{C_0|\mathcal{P}^{N-1}\} \quad (6\text{-}12)$$

Substitution of Eq. (6-8) into Eq. (6-12) yields

$$J^*_0 = E\{L_N(\mathbf{x}_N)|\mathcal{P}^{N-1}\} \quad (6\text{-}13)$$

When Eq. (6-5) is used, this becomes

$$J^*_0 = E\{\tfrac{1}{2}\mathbf{x}'_N \mathbf{W}_N \mathbf{x}_N + \mathbf{w}'_N \mathbf{x}_N\} \quad (6\text{-}14)$$

The information variable $\mathcal{P}^{N-1}$ is dropped here in order to simplify the notation. Then the expectation in Eq. (6-14) can be taken to yield

$$J^*_0 = \tfrac{1}{2}\mathbf{x}'_N E\{\mathbf{W}_N\}\mathbf{x}_N + E\{\mathbf{w}_N\}'\mathbf{x}_N \quad (6\text{-}15)$$

This expression gives the optimal cost-to-go with no periods remaining.

Next recall from Chap. 2 that it was assumed for the deterministic problem that the optimal cost-to-go is a quadratic function of the state of the system. That assumption is used here, and the expected cost-to-go with zero periods to go is written as

$$J_0^* = \nu_N + \mathbf{p}_N' \mathbf{x}_N + \tfrac{1}{2}\mathbf{x}_N' \mathbf{K}_N \mathbf{x}_N \qquad (6\text{-}16)$$

where the scalar ν, the vector $\mathbf{p}$, and the matrix $\mathbf{K}$ are the parameters of the quadratic function. These parameters are determined recursively in the optimization procedure described in the remainder of this chapter.

Then comparing Eqs. (6-15) and (6-16), one obtains the terminal conditions for the Riccati equations, namely

$$\mathbf{K}_N = E\{\mathbf{W}_N\} = \mathbf{W}_N \qquad \mathbf{p}_N = E\{\mathbf{w}_N\} = \mathbf{w}_N \qquad \nu_N = 0 \qquad (6\text{-}17)$$

This completes the discussion for period N. Consider next the period before the last one, namely period $N - 1$.

6-3 PERIOD $N - 1$

Recall from Chap. 2 the discussion of the dynamic-programming principle of optimality, which states that the optimal cost-to-go with $N - j$ periods remaining will equal the minimum over the choice of the control at time j of the cost incurred during period j plus the optimal cost-to-go with $N - j - 1$ periods remaining, i.e.,

$$J_{N-j}^* = \min_{\mathbf{u}_j} E\{L_j(\mathbf{x}_j, \mathbf{u}_j) + J_{N-j-1}^* | \mathcal{P}^j\} \qquad (6\text{-}18)$$

Equation (6-18) can be used to obtain the optimal cost-to-go in period $N - 1$. For this case it is written with $j = N - 1$ as

$$J_{N-(N-1)}^* = \min_{\mathbf{u}_{N-1}} E\{L_{N-1}(\mathbf{x}_{N-1}, \mathbf{u}_{N-1}) + J_{N-(N-1)-1}^* | \mathcal{P}^{N-1}\}$$

or as

$$J_1^* = \min_{\mathbf{u}_{N-1}} E\{L_{N-1}(\mathbf{x}_{N-1}, \mathbf{u}_{N-1}) + J_0^* | \mathcal{P}^{N-1}\} \qquad (6\text{-}19)$$

Thus the optimal cost-to-go with one period remaining is the minimum over the control at time $N - 1$ of the expected value of the sum of the cost incurred in period $N - 1$ and the optimal cost-to-go with zero periods remaining. Both these terms have already been developed. The cost in each period is in Eq. (6-6), and the optimal cost-to-go with zero periods remaining is in Eq. (6-14). Substituting these two expressions into Eq. (6-19) yields

$$J_1^* = \min_{\mathbf{u}_{N-1}} E\{\tfrac{1}{2}\mathbf{x}_N' \mathbf{W}_N \mathbf{x}_N + \mathbf{w}_N' \mathbf{x}_N + \tfrac{1}{2}\mathbf{x}_{N-1}' \mathbf{W}_{N-1} \mathbf{x}_{N-1} + \mathbf{w}_{N-1}' \mathbf{x}_{N-1}$$
$$+ \mathbf{x}_{N-1}' \mathbf{F}_{N-1} \mathbf{u}_{N-1} + \tfrac{1}{2}\mathbf{u}_{N-1}' \Lambda_{N-1} \mathbf{u}_{N-1} + \lambda_{N-1}' \mathbf{u}_{N-1}\} \qquad (6\text{-}20)$$

The logical steps to follow, as shown in Eq. (6-20), are to take the expected value and then to find the minimum over $\mathbf{u}_{N-1}$. However, it is helpful to write the entire expression in terms of $\mathbf{x}_{N-1}$ and $\mathbf{u}_{N-1}$ by using the systems equations (6-1) to substitute out the $\mathbf{x}_N$ terms. Before doing so, however, we shall review

46 PASSIVE-LEARNING STOCHASTIC CONTROL

the steps that remain:

1. Substituting the system equations into the optimal cost-to-go expression
2. Applying the expectations operator
3. Applying the minimization operator
4. Obtaining the feedback rule from the first-order conditions
5. Substituting the feedback rule back into the optimal cost-to-go in order to obtain the Riccati recursions

These are the same steps used in Chap. 2 except for the application of the expectations operator in step 2.

The substitution of the system equations (6-1) into Eq. (6-20) and the use of the Nth-period Riccati equations (6-17) yields the optimal cost-to-go entirely in terms of $\mathbf{x}_{N-1}$ and $\mathbf{u}_{N-1}$.

$$J_1^* = \min_{\mathbf{u}_{N-1}} E\{\tfrac{1}{2}\mathbf{x}'_{N-1}\boldsymbol{\Phi}_{N-1}\mathbf{x}_{N-1} + \boldsymbol{\phi}'_{N-1}\mathbf{x}_{N-1} + \mathbf{x}'_{N-1}\boldsymbol{\Psi}_{N-1}\mathbf{u}_{N-1}$$
$$+ \tfrac{1}{2}\mathbf{u}'_{N-1}\boldsymbol{\Theta}_{N-1}\mathbf{u}_{N-1} + \boldsymbol{\theta}'_{N-1}\mathbf{u}_{N-1} + \tfrac{1}{2}\boldsymbol{\xi}'_{N-1}\boldsymbol{\Omega}_{N-1}\boldsymbol{\xi}_{N-1}$$
$$+ \omega'_{N-1}\boldsymbol{\xi}_{N-1} + \mathbf{x}'_{N-1}\boldsymbol{\Upsilon}_{N-1}\boldsymbol{\xi}_{N-1} + \mathbf{u}'_{N-1}\boldsymbol{\Gamma}_{N-1}\boldsymbol{\xi}_{N-1} + \eta_{N-1}|\mathcal{P}^{N-1}\}$$
(6-21)

where

$$\boldsymbol{\Phi}_{N-1} = \mathbf{W}_{N-1} + \mathbf{A}'_{N-1}\mathbf{K}_N\mathbf{A}_{N-1} \quad \boldsymbol{\phi}_{N-1} = \mathbf{A}'_{N-1}(\mathbf{K}_N\mathbf{c}_{N-1} + \mathbf{p}_N) + \mathbf{w}_{N-1}$$
$$\boldsymbol{\Psi}_{N-1} = \mathbf{F}_{N-1} + \mathbf{A}'_{N-1}\mathbf{K}_N\mathbf{B}_{N-1} \quad \boldsymbol{\Theta}_{N-1} = \boldsymbol{\Lambda}_{N-1} + \mathbf{B}'_{N-1}\mathbf{K}_N\mathbf{B}_{N-1}$$
$$\boldsymbol{\theta}_{N-1} = \mathbf{B}'_{N-1}(\mathbf{K}_N\mathbf{c}_{N-1} + \mathbf{p}_N) + \boldsymbol{\lambda}_{N-1} \quad \boldsymbol{\Omega}_{N-1} = \mathbf{K}_N \quad (6\text{-}22)$$
$$\omega_{N-1} = \mathbf{K}_N\mathbf{c}_{N-1} + \mathbf{p}_N \quad \boldsymbol{\Upsilon}_{N-1} = \mathbf{A}'_{N-1}\mathbf{K}_N$$
$$\boldsymbol{\Gamma}_{N-1} = \mathbf{B}'_{N-1}\mathbf{K}_N \quad \eta_{N-1} = \mathbf{c}'_{N-1}\mathbf{K}_N\mathbf{c}_{N-1} + \mathbf{p}'_N\mathbf{c}_{N-1}$$

Next we perform the expectations and minimization operations in Eq. (6-20). Taking the expectation in Eq. (6-21) yields

$$J_1^* = \min_{\mathbf{u}_{N-1}} \left[\tfrac{1}{2}\mathbf{x}'_{N-1}E\{\boldsymbol{\Phi}_{N-1}\}\mathbf{x}_{N-1} + E\{\boldsymbol{\phi}_{N-1}\}'\mathbf{x}_{N-1} + \mathbf{x}'_{N-1}E\{\boldsymbol{\Psi}_{N-1}\}\mathbf{u}_{N-1} \right.$$
$$+ \tfrac{1}{2}\mathbf{u}'_{N-1}E\{\boldsymbol{\Theta}_{N-1}\}\mathbf{u}_{N-1} + E\{\boldsymbol{\theta}_{N-1}\}'\mathbf{u}_{N-1} + \tfrac{1}{2}E\{\boldsymbol{\xi}'_{N-1}\boldsymbol{\Omega}_{N-1}\boldsymbol{\xi}_{N-1}\}$$
$$+ E\{\eta_{N-1}\} \Big]$$
(6-23)

The expected value of the additive error term $\boldsymbol{\xi}$ is assumed to be zero, so all terms involving *only* the expected value are dropped. In contrast, the covariance of the noise term is not zero, and so the term involving it remains. Since the state variables $\mathbf{x}_k$ are assumed to be observed without error, they are a deterministic quantity. Also the control variables $\mathbf{u}_k$ are deterministic. This leaves expectations of matrices and vectors in Eq. (6-23). From Eq. (6-22) some of these expectations are of products of matrices. They are rather complicated, and a full explanation of this process will be given in Sec. 6-5.

Now the minimization operation in Eq. (6-23) can be performed. This yields the first-order condition

$$\mathbf{x}'_{N-1}E\{\mathbf{\Psi}_{N-1}\} + \mathbf{u}'_{N-1}E\{\mathbf{\Theta}_{N-1}\} + (E\{\boldsymbol{\theta}_{N-1}\})' = \mathbf{0} \tag{6-24}$$

The feedback rule can then be obtained from Eq. (6-24) as

$$\mathbf{u}_{N-1} = \mathbf{G}^\dagger_{N-1}\mathbf{x}_{N-1} + \mathbf{g}^\dagger_{N-1} \tag{6-25}$$

where

$$\mathbf{G}^\dagger_{N-1} = -(E\{\mathbf{\Theta}'_{N-1}\})^{-1}(E\{\mathbf{\Psi}_{N-1}\})' \qquad \mathbf{g}^\dagger_{N-1} = -(E\{\mathbf{\Theta}'_{N-1}\})^{-1}(E\{\boldsymbol{\theta}_{N-1}\}) \tag{6-26}$$

The feedback rule (6-25) and (6-26) provides the optimality condition sought for period $N-1$. It is instructive to compare it with the feedback rule for period $N-1$ in the deterministic problem, Eqs. (2-33) and (2-34). The rules are identical except that the $\mathbf{G}^\dagger$ and $\mathbf{g}^\dagger$ feedback gain matrix and vector are now products of expectations of matrices.

In order to be able to evaluate $\mathbf{G}^\dagger$ and $\mathbf{g}^\dagger$ one must calculate the Riccati matrix and vector $\mathbf{K}$ and $\mathbf{p}$, and to do that one needs a recursion in these elements. This recursion is obtained by substituting the feedback rule (6-25) back into the optimal cost-to-go expression (6-23) in order to eliminate $\mathbf{u}_{N-1}$ and to be able to write the optimal cost-to-go entirely in terms of $\mathbf{x}_{N-1}$. This substitution yields the optimal cost-to-go

$$J_1^* = \tfrac{1}{2}\mathbf{x}'_{N-1}\mathbf{K}_{N-1}\mathbf{x}_{N-1} + \mathbf{p}'_{N-1}\mathbf{x}_{N-1} + \nu_{N-1} \tag{6-27}$$

where

$$\begin{aligned}
\mathbf{K}_{N-1} &= E\{\mathbf{\Phi}_{N-1}\} - E\{\mathbf{\Psi}_{N-1}\}(E\{\mathbf{\Theta}_{N-1}\})^{-1}(E\{\mathbf{\Psi}_{N-1}\})' \\
\mathbf{p}_{N-1} &= E\{\boldsymbol{\phi}_{N-1}\} - E\{\mathbf{\Psi}_{N-1}\}(E\{\mathbf{\Theta}_{N-1}\})^{-1}E\{\boldsymbol{\theta}_{N-1}\} \\
\nu_{N-1} &= -\tfrac{1}{2}(E\{\boldsymbol{\theta}_{N-1}\})'E\{\mathbf{\Theta}_{N-1}\}E\{\boldsymbol{\theta}_{N-1}\} + \tfrac{1}{2}E\{\boldsymbol{\xi}'_{N-1}\mathbf{\Omega}_{N-1}\boldsymbol{\xi}_{N-1}\} + E\{\eta_{N-1}\}
\end{aligned} \tag{6-28}$$

In order to see the recursive nature of these Riccati equations it is necessary to rewrite them in terms of the original parameters of the problem. This can be done by substituting Eq. (6-22) into Eq. (6-28) to obtain

$$\mathbf{K}_{N-1} = \mathbf{W}_{N-1} + E\{\mathbf{A}'_{N-1}\mathbf{K}_N\mathbf{A}_{N-1}\} - (\mathbf{F}_{N-1} + E\{\mathbf{A}'_{N-1}\mathbf{K}_N\mathbf{B}_{N-1}\})$$
$$\times (\mathbf{\Lambda}_{N-1} + E\{\mathbf{B}'_{N-1}\mathbf{K}_N\mathbf{B}_{N-1}\})^{-1}(E\{\mathbf{B}'_{N-1}\mathbf{K}_N\mathbf{A}_{N-1}\} + \mathbf{F}'_{N-1}) \tag{6-29}$$

$$\mathbf{p}_{N-1} = E\{\mathbf{A}'_{N-1}\mathbf{K}_N\mathbf{c}_{N-1}\} + E\{\mathbf{A}_{N-1}\}'\mathbf{p}_N + \mathbf{w}_{N-1}$$
$$- [\mathbf{F}_{N-1} + E\{\mathbf{A}'_{N-1}\mathbf{K}_N\mathbf{B}_{N-1}\}][\mathbf{\Lambda}_{N-1} + E\{\mathbf{B}'_{N-1}\mathbf{K}_N\mathbf{B}_{N-1}\}]^{-1}$$
$$\times [E\{\mathbf{B}'_{N-1}\mathbf{K}_N\mathbf{c}_{N-1}\} + E\{\mathbf{B}_{N-1}\}'\mathbf{p}_N + \boldsymbol{\lambda}_{N-1}]$$

The Riccati equation for $\mathbf{K}$ is seen to be a difference equation with values of $\mathbf{K}_N$ on the right-hand side and $\mathbf{K}_{N-1}$ on the left-hand side. Since the terminal

condition for this equation
$$\mathbf{K}_N = \mathbf{W}_N$$
was obtained in Eq. (6-17), one can evaluate $\mathbf{K}_{N-1}$ by using Eq. (6-29). This is sometimes called *backward integration* since the integration occurs backward in time. In fact, the reader may recall from Chap. 2 that this is how quadratic linear control problems are solved. First the Riccati equations are integrated backward in time, and the feedback-gain matrices $\mathbf{G}^\dagger$ and $\mathbf{g}^\dagger$ can be computed so that the system equations and the feedback rule can be used in tandom as they are integrated forward in time to find the optimal paths for the states and controls. Also the $\mathbf{p}$ equation in Eq. (6-29) can be integrated backward by using the terminal conditions for both $\mathbf{K}$ and $\mathbf{p}$ in Eq. (6-17)
$$\mathbf{K}_N = \mathbf{W}_N \qquad \mathbf{p}_N = \mathbf{w}_N$$
The v equation in Eq. (6-28) is not evaluated here since it does not affect the optimal control path but only the optimal cost-to-go.

The optimal control problem has now been solved by dynamic programming for periods N and $N - 1$. The process can now be repeated for periods $N - 2, N - 3$, etc. It is not necessary to show this here since the basic structure of the solution is already present. The derivations will not be given, and the feedback and Riccati equations for the typical period k will simply be stated.

6-4 PERIOD k

The optimal feedback rule for period k is, from Eq. (6-25),
$$\mathbf{u}_k = \mathbf{G}_k^\dagger \mathbf{x}_k + \mathbf{g}_k^\dagger \qquad (6\text{-}30)$$
where, from Eq. (6-26),
$$\mathbf{G}_k^\dagger = -(E\{\mathbf{\Theta}_k'\})^{-1}(E\{\mathbf{\Psi}_k\})' \qquad \mathbf{g}_k^\dagger = -(E\{\mathbf{\Theta}_k\})^{-1} E\{\boldsymbol{\theta}_k\} \qquad (6\text{-}31)$$
Then, from Eq. (6-22),
$$\begin{aligned}
E\{\mathbf{\Phi}_k\} &= \mathbf{W}_k + E\{\mathbf{A}_k' \mathbf{K}_{k+1} \mathbf{A}_k\} \\
E\{\boldsymbol{\phi}_k\} &= E\{\mathbf{A}_k' \mathbf{K}_{k+1} \mathbf{c}_k\} + E\{\mathbf{A}_k\}' \mathbf{p}_{k+1} + \mathbf{w}_k \\
E\{\mathbf{\Psi}_k\} &= \mathbf{F}_k + E\{\mathbf{A}_k' \mathbf{K}_{k+1} \mathbf{B}_k\} \qquad (6\text{-}32) \\
E\{\mathbf{\Theta}_k\} &= \mathbf{\Lambda}_k + E\{\mathbf{B}_k' \mathbf{K}_{k+1} \mathbf{B}_k\} \\
E\{\boldsymbol{\theta}_k\} &= E\{\mathbf{B}_k' \mathbf{K}_{k+1} \mathbf{c}_k\} + E\{\mathbf{B}_k\}' \mathbf{p}_{k+1} + \boldsymbol{\lambda}_k
\end{aligned}$$
Also the Riccati equations can be written using Eq. (6-28) as
$$\begin{aligned}
\mathbf{K}_k &= E\{\mathbf{\Phi}_k\} - E\{\mathbf{\Psi}_k\}(E\{\mathbf{\Theta}_k\})^{-1}(E\{\mathbf{\Psi}_k\})' \\
\mathbf{p}_k &= E\{\boldsymbol{\phi}_k\} - E\{\mathbf{\Psi}_k\}(E\{\mathbf{\Theta}_k\})^{-1} E\{\boldsymbol{\theta}_k\}
\end{aligned} \qquad (6\text{-}33)$$

or, in terms of the original matrices of the problem, by using Eq. (6-29), as

$$\mathbf{K}_k = \mathbf{W}_k + E\{\mathbf{A}'_k \mathbf{K}_{k+1} \mathbf{A}_k\} - [\mathbf{F}_k + E\{\mathbf{A}'_k \mathbf{K}_{k+1} \mathbf{B}_k\}]$$
$$\times [\mathbf{\Lambda}_k + E\{\mathbf{B}'_k \mathbf{K}_{k+1} \mathbf{B}_k\}]^{-1} [E\{\mathbf{B}'_k \mathbf{K}_{k-1} \mathbf{A}_k\} + \mathbf{F}'_k]$$
$$\mathbf{p}_k = E\{\mathbf{A}'_k \mathbf{K}_{k+1} \mathbf{c}_k\} + E\{\mathbf{A}_k\}' \mathbf{p}_{k+1} + \mathbf{w}_k - [\mathbf{F}_k + E\{\mathbf{A}'_k \mathbf{K}_{k+1} \mathbf{B}_k\}]$$
$$\times [\mathbf{\Lambda}_k + E\{\mathbf{B}'_k \mathbf{K}_{k+1} \mathbf{B}_k\}]^{-1} [E\{\mathbf{B}'_k \mathbf{K}_{k+1} \mathbf{c}_k\} + E\{\mathbf{B}_k\}' \mathbf{p}_{k+1} + \mathbf{\lambda}_k]$$

(6-34)

In summary the problem is solved by using the terminal conditions (6-17) in Eq. (6-34) to integrate the Riccati equations backward in time. Then the $\mathbf{G}^\dagger$ and $\mathbf{g}^\dagger$ elements can be computed for all time periods. Next the initial condition on the states, $\mathbf{x}_0$, is used in the feedback rule (6-30) to compute $\mathbf{u}_0$. Then $\mathbf{u}_0$ and $\mathbf{x}_0$ are used in the system equations (6-1) to compute $\mathbf{x}_1$. Then $\mathbf{x}_1$ is used in the feedback rule to get $\mathbf{u}_1$. In this manner the system equations are integrated forward in time and the optimal controls and states are calculated for all time periods.

6-5 EXPECTED VALUES OF MATRIX PRODUCTS

One loose end remains to be cleared up. This is the method for calculating the expected value of matrix vector products.
Consider the general case

$$E\{\mathbf{A}'\mathbf{KB}\} \quad (6\text{-}35)$$

where $\mathbf{A}$, $\mathbf{K}$, and $\mathbf{B}$ are all matrices. The $\mathbf{A}$ and $\mathbf{B}$ matrices are assumed to be random, and the $\mathbf{K}$ matrix is assumed to be deterministic. If $\mathbf{A}$ and/or $\mathbf{B}$ is a vector, the method suggested here is somewhat simplified. Define the matrix

$$\mathbf{D} \equiv \mathbf{A}'\mathbf{KB}$$

so that

$$E\{\mathbf{D}\} = E\{\mathbf{A}'\mathbf{KB}\}$$

and consider a single element in $\mathbf{D}$, namely d_{ij}. Then

$$E\{d_{ij}\} = E\{\mathbf{a}'_i \mathbf{K} \mathbf{b}_j\} \quad (6\text{-}36)$$

where $\mathbf{a}_i$ is the ith column of $\mathbf{A}$ and $\mathbf{b}_j$ is the jth column of $\mathbf{B}$. From the result in Appendix B the expectation in Eq. (6-36) can be written as

$$E\{d_{ij}\} = (E\{\mathbf{a}_i\})' \mathbf{K} E\{\mathbf{b}_j\} + \text{tr}[\mathbf{K} \mathbf{\Sigma}_{\mathbf{b}_j \mathbf{a}_i}] \quad (6\text{-}37)$$

where
$$\mathbf{\Sigma}_{\mathbf{b}_j \mathbf{a}_i} = E\{[\mathbf{b}_j - E\{\mathbf{b}_j\}][\mathbf{a}_i - E\{\mathbf{a}_i\}]'\}$$

is the covariance matrix for the jth column of $\mathbf{B}$ and the ith column of $\mathbf{A}$ and $\text{tr}[\cdot]$ is the trace operator, i.e., the sum of the diagonal elements of the matrix in the brackets. While Eq. (6-37) is the form of this expectations operator which is commonly used in displaying mathematical results, it is not the most efficient form to use in computers.[1] Observe that Eq. (6-36) can be written and rewritten as

$$E\{d_{ij}\} = E\{\mathbf{a}'_i \mathbf{K} \mathbf{b}_j\} = E\left\{\sum_s a_{si}\left(\sum_r k_{sr} b_{rj}\right)\right\} \quad (6\text{-}38)$$

Where Σ is an ordinary summation sign (not a covariance matrix) and k_{sr} is the element in the sth row and rth column of the matrix $\mathbf{K}$. Continuing from Eq. (6-38), one obtains

$$E\{d_{ij}\} = E\left\{\sum_s \sum_r a_{si} k_{sr} b_{rj}\right\} = \sum_s \sum_r E\{a_{si} k_{sr} b_{rj}\} = \sum_s \sum_r k_{sr} E\{a_{si} b_{rj}\}$$

Thus

$$E\{d_{ij}\} = \sum_s \sum_r k_{sr}[(Ea_{si})(Eb_{rj}) + \text{cov}(a_{si} b_{rj})] \quad (6\text{-}39)$$

gives the form desired. The advantage of using Eq. (6-39) instead of Eq. (6-37) is that it is not necessary to store the matrix $\Sigma_{\mathbf{b}_j \mathbf{a}_i}$ and to compute the $\mathbf{K}\Sigma$ product and take its trace. Only the scalar elements $\text{cov}(a_{si} b_{rj})$ are necessary.

This completes the discussion of the methods for obtaining the control of each time period, since the expectations evaluations discussed here can be coupled with the Riccati equations, feedback law, and system equations discussed in Sec. 6-4. Before ending the chapter, however, it is useful to describe briefly two methods of passive-learning stochastic control.

6-6 METHODS OF PASSIVE-LEARNING STOCHASTIC CONTROL

Methods of stochastic control include a procedure for choosing the control at each time period and a procedure for updating parameter estimates at each time period. The differences in the names for the procedures depend on the method for choosing the control at each time period. For example, if the control at each time period is chosen while ignoring the uncertainty in the parameters, the method is called *sequential certainty equivalence*, *update certainty equivalence* [Rausser (1977)], or *heuristic certainty equivalence* [Norman, (1976)]. In contrast, if the control is chosen at each time period using the multiplicative uncertainty, the method is called *open-loop feedback*.[2]

---

[1] This procedure was suggested to the author by Fred Norman.

[2] Rausser (1977) distinguishes between open-loop feedback and sequential stochastic control. In sequential stochastic control in his nomenclature the derivation of the control rule is based on the assumption that future observations will be made but they will not be used to adapt the probability distribution of the parameters. He classifies as open-loop feedback studies those of Aoki (1967), Bar-Shalom and Sivan (1969), Curry (1969), Ku and Athans (1973), and Tse and Athans (1972). He classifies as sequential stochastic control the studies of Rausser and Freebairn (1974), Zellner (1971), Chow (1975, chap. 10), and Prescott (1971).

CHAPTER SEVEN
EXAMPLE OF PASSIVE-LEARNING STOCHASTIC CONTROL

7-1 THE PROBLEM

This chapter contains the solution of a two-period, one-unknown-parameter problem used by MacRae (1972),[1] i.e., find (u_0, u_1) to minimize

$$J = E\left\{ \sum_{k=1}^{N} \left(\tfrac{1}{2}qx_k^2 + \tfrac{1}{2}ru_{k-1}^2\right) \right\}$$

subject to

$$x_{k+1} = ax_k + bu_k + c + \xi_k \qquad k = 0, 1$$

with x_0 given.

Also[2]
$$\xi_k \sim N(0, Q) \qquad b_0 \sim N(\mu_b, \Sigma_{0|0}^{bb})$$

i.e., both ξ_k and b_0 are assumed to be normally distributed with means and variances as indicated.

---

[1] This chapter has been written with an eye toward its use in debugging computer programs. For this reason, the calculations are presented in considerable detail with all intermediate results explicitly shown.
[2] This notation means that ξ_k is a normally distributed random variable with mean zero and covariance Q.

52 PASSIVE-LEARNING STOCHASTIC CONTROL

Consider the case with[1]

$$N = 2 \quad q = 1 \quad r = 1 \quad a = .7$$
$$\mu_b = -.5 \quad \Sigma_{0|0}^{bb} = .5 \quad c = 3.5 \quad Q = .2 \quad x_0 = 0$$

This corresponds to the $(q:r) = (5:5)$ case in Table 2 of MacRae (1972) with $N = 2$. She solves only for the first-period control. In contrast, sample calculations will be presented here for a single Monte Carlo run in which the optimal policy for both period 0 and period 1 are calculated.[2]

Begin by solving the open-loop-feedback problem from period k to period N.[3]

7-2 THE OPTIMAL CONTROL FOR PERIOD 0

The solution to the open-loop-feedback problem is given in Eq. (6-30), i.e.,

$$\mathbf{u}_k = \mathbf{G}_k^{\dagger} \mathbf{x}_k + \mathbf{g}_k^{\dagger} \tag{7-1}$$

where, from Eq. (6-31),

$$\mathbf{G}_k^{\dagger} = -(E\{\mathbf{\Theta}_k'\})^{-1}(E\{\mathbf{\Psi}_k\})'$$
$$\mathbf{g}_k^{\dagger} = -(E\{\mathbf{\Theta}_k'\})^{-1}(E\{\boldsymbol{\theta}_k\}) \tag{7-2}$$

with, from Eq. (6-32),

$$E\{\mathbf{\Theta}_k\} = \mathbf{\Lambda}_k + E\{\mathbf{B}_k' \mathbf{K}_{k+1} \mathbf{B}_k\}$$
$$E\{\mathbf{\Psi}_k\} = \mathbf{F}_k + E\{\mathbf{A}_k' \mathbf{K}_{k+1} \mathbf{B}_k\} \tag{7-3}$$
$$E\{\boldsymbol{\theta}_k\} = E\{\mathbf{B}_k' \mathbf{K}_{k+1} \mathbf{c}_k\} + E\{\mathbf{B}_k\}' \mathbf{p}_{k+1} + \boldsymbol{\lambda}_k$$

Also, the $\mathbf{K}$ and $\mathbf{p}$ recursions are defined in Eq. (6-33) as

$$\mathbf{K}_k = E\{\mathbf{\Phi}_k\} - E\{\mathbf{\Psi}_k\}(E\{\mathbf{\Theta}_k\})^{-1}(E\{\mathbf{\Psi}_k\})' \quad \mathbf{K}_N = \mathbf{W}_N$$
$$\mathbf{p}_k = E\{\boldsymbol{\phi}_k\} - E\{\mathbf{\Psi}_k\}(E\{\mathbf{\Theta}_k\})^{-1} E\{\boldsymbol{\theta}_k\} \quad \mathbf{p}_N = \mathbf{w}_N \tag{7-4}$$

with, from Eq. (6-32),

$$E\{\mathbf{\Phi}_k\} = \mathbf{W}_k + E\{\mathbf{A}_k' \mathbf{K}_{k+1} \mathbf{A}_k\}$$
$$E\{\boldsymbol{\phi}_k\} = E\{\mathbf{A}_k' \mathbf{K}_{k+1} \mathbf{c}_k\} + E\{\mathbf{A}_k\}' \mathbf{p}_{k+1} + \mathbf{w}_k \tag{7-5}$$

---

[1] $\Sigma_{0|0}^{bb}$ is the variance of b. The reason for this elaborate notation is given in subsequent chapters.

[2] For other examples of the application of passive-learning stochastic control methods to economic problems with multiplicative random variables see Fisher (1962), Zellner and Geisel (1968), Burger, Kalish, and Babb (1971), Henderson and Turnovsky (1972), Bowman and Laporte (1972), Chow (1973), Turnovsky (1973, 1974, 1975, 1977), Kendrick (1973), Aoki (1974a,b), Cooper and Fischer (1975), Shupp (1976b, c), and Walsh and Cruz (1975).

[3] The results are of course a function of the particular random quantities generated. However, the calculations are done here for a single set of random quantities to show how the calculations are performed.

EXAMPLE OF PASSIVE-LEARNING STOCHASTIC CONTROL 53

Also compare the criterion function for this problem with the criteria for the quadratic linear problem (2-1) to obtain

$$w_k = 0 \qquad \lambda_k = 0 \qquad (7\text{-}6)$$

For the problem at hand

$$A_k = a = .7 \qquad B_k = \mu_b = -.5 \qquad c_k = c = 3.5$$
$$W_N = W_k = q = 1 \qquad \Lambda_k = r = 1 \qquad F_k = 0 \qquad (7\text{-}7)$$

and

$$\Sigma^{bb}_{0|0} = .5 \qquad \hat{\theta}_{0|0} = \mu_b = -.5 \qquad (7\text{-}8)$$

In order to obtain the solution u_k, one can work backward through the relationships above, obtaining Eq. (7-5), then Eq. (7-4), then Eq. (7-3), then Eq. (7-2), and finally Eq. (7-1). Begin with Eq. (7-5)

$$E\Phi_1 = W_1 + E\{A'K_2 A\} \qquad (7\text{-}9)$$

Then from Eqs. (7-4) and (7-7) we have $K_2 = W_2 = 1$, and from Eq. (6-39)

$$E\{A'K_2 A\} = K_2[(Ea)(Ea) + \text{cov}(aa)]$$
$$= K_2[a^2 + \text{cov}(a)] = K_2 a^2$$
$$= (1)(.7)^2 = .49$$

So Eq. (7-9) becomes

$$E\{\Phi_1\} = 1 + .49 = 1.49 \qquad (7\text{-}10)$$

Also, from Eq. (7-5),

$$E\{\phi_1\} = E\{A'K_2 c\} + E\{A\}' p_2 + w_1 \qquad (7\text{-}11)$$

and from Eq. (6-39)

$$E\{A'K_2 c\} = K_2[E\{a\}E\{c\} + \text{cov}(ac)]$$
$$= K_2(ac + 0) = K_2 ac$$
$$= (1)(.7)(3.5) = 2.45 \qquad (7\text{-}12)$$

Also,

$$E\{A\}' p_2 = a p_2$$

but

$$p_2 = w_2 \quad \text{from Eq. (7-4)}$$
$$0 \quad \text{from Eq. (7-6)}$$

and so

$$E\{A\}' p_2 = (.7)(0) = 0 \qquad (7\text{-}13)$$

Finally, from Eq. (7-6),

$$w_1 = 0 \qquad (7\text{-}14)$$

Then from Eqs. (7-11) to (7-14)

$$E\{\phi_1\} = 2.45 + 0 + 0 = 2.45 \qquad (7\text{-}15)$$

This completes the evaluation of Eq. (7-5).

In order to evaluate Eq. (7-4) it is necessary first to evaluate the elements in Eq. (7-3). Begin with $E\{\Theta_k\}$

$$E\{\Theta_1\} = \Lambda_1 + E\{\mathbf{B'K_2B}\} \tag{7-16}$$

From Eq. (6-39)

$$E\{\mathbf{B'K_2B}\} = K_2[\mu_b\mu_b + \text{cov}(bb)]$$
$$= (1)[(-.5)(-.5) + .5] = .75 \tag{7-17}$$

Then using Eqs. (7-17) and (7-7) in Eq. (7-16) yields

$$E\{\Theta_1\} = 1 + .75 = 1.75$$

Therefore,

$$(E\{\Theta_1\})^{-1} = .5714 \tag{7-18}$$

The next element in Eq. (7-3) is

$$E\{\Psi_1\} = \mathbf{F}_1 + E\{\mathbf{A'K_2B}\} \tag{7-19}$$

Then, from Eq. (6-39),

$$E\{\mathbf{A'K_2B}\} = K_2[(Ea)(Eb) + \text{cov}(ab)]$$
$$= (1)[(.7)(-.5) + 0] = -.35 \tag{7-20}$$

Using Eqs. (7-20) and (7-7) in (7-19) yields

$$E\{\Psi_1\} = 0 - .35 = -.35 \tag{7-21}$$

The last element in Eq. (7-3) is

$$E\{\theta_1\} = E\{\mathbf{B'K_2c}\} + E\{\mathbf{B}\}'\mathbf{p}_2 + \lambda_1 \tag{7-22}$$

From Eq. (6-39)

$$E\{\mathbf{B'K_2c}\} = K_2[\mu_b c + \text{cov}(bc)] = (1)[(-.5)(3.5) + 0] = -1.75 \tag{7-23}$$

From Eqs. (7-4) and (7-6)

$$E\{\mathbf{B}\}'\mathbf{p}_2 = \mu_b w_2 = (-.5)(0) = 0 \tag{7-24}$$

From Eq. (7-6)

$$\lambda_1 = 0 \tag{7-25}$$

Therefore, substitution of Eqs. (7-23) to (7-25) in Eq. (7-22) yields

$$E\{\theta_1\} = -1.75 + 0 + 0 = -1.75 \tag{7-26}$$

This completes the evaluation of Eq. (7-3). Now Eq. (7-4) can be evaluated

$$K_1 = E\{\Phi_1\} - E\{\Psi_1\}(E\{\Theta_1\})^{-1}(E\{\Psi_1\})' \tag{7-27}$$

Substitution of Eqs. (7-10), (7-21), and (7-18) into Eq. (7-27) yields

$$K_1 = 1.49 - (-.35)(.5714)(-.35) = 1.42$$

EXAMPLE OF PASSIVE-LEARNING STOCHASTIC CONTROL 55

Also from Eq. (7-4)
$$\mathbf{p}_1 = E\{\boldsymbol{\phi}_1\} - E\{\boldsymbol{\Psi}_1\}(E\{\boldsymbol{\Theta}_1\})^{-1}E\{\boldsymbol{\theta}_1\} \tag{7-28}$$
Substitution of Eqs. (7-15), (7-21), (7-18), and (7-26) into Eq. (7-28) yields
$$\mathbf{p}_1 = 2.45 - (-.35)(.5714)(-1.75) = 2.1$$
This completes the evaluation of Eqs. (7-4) and (7-3) and leaves only Eqs. (7-2) and (7-1).

The $\mathbf{G}^\dagger$ and $\mathbf{g}^\dagger$ elements of the feedback rule (7-1) can now be evaluated with Eq. (7-2). Begin with $\mathbf{G}^\dagger$. Calculation of $\mathbf{u}_1$ is not necessary, but calculation of $\mathbf{u}_0$ is. Therefore, from Eq. (7-1) $\mathbf{G}_0^\dagger$ rather than $\mathbf{G}_1^\dagger$ needs to be calculated. From Eq. (7-2)
$$\mathbf{G}_0^\dagger = -(E\{\boldsymbol{\Theta}_0\})^{-1}(E\{\boldsymbol{\Psi}_0\})' \tag{7-29}$$
From Eq. (7-3)
$$E\{\boldsymbol{\Theta}_0\} = \Lambda_0 + E\{\mathbf{B}'\mathbf{K}_1\mathbf{B}\} \tag{7-30}$$
From Eq. (6-39)
$$E\{\mathbf{B}'\mathbf{K}_1\mathbf{B}\} = K_1[\mu_b\mu_b + \text{cov}(bb)]$$
$$= 1.42[(-.5)(-.5) + .5] = 1.065 \tag{7-31}$$
Then substitution of Eq. (7-31) into Eq. (7-30) and using Eq. (7-7) yields
$$E\{\boldsymbol{\Theta}_0\} = 1 + 1.065 = 2.065$$
Therefore,
$$(E\{\boldsymbol{\Theta}_0\})^{-1} = \frac{1}{2.065} = .484 \tag{7-32}$$
From Eq. (7-3)
$$E\{\boldsymbol{\Psi}_0\} = F_0 + E\{\mathbf{A}'\mathbf{K}_1\mathbf{B}\}$$
$$= 0 + K_1[a\mu_b + \text{cov}(ab)]$$
$$= 1.42[(.7)(-.5) + 0] = -.497 \tag{7-33}$$
Finally, substitution of Eqs. (7-32) and (7-33) into (7-29) yields
$$\mathbf{G}_0^\dagger = -(.484)(-.497) = .2405 \tag{7-34}$$
Next evaluate $\mathbf{g}_0^\dagger$ with Eq. (7-2):
$$\mathbf{g}_0^\dagger = -(E\{\boldsymbol{\Theta}_0\})^{-1}E\{\boldsymbol{\theta}_0\} \tag{7-35}$$
The inverse $(E\{\boldsymbol{\Theta}_0\})^{-1}$ was calculated in Eq. (7-32), and so only $E\boldsymbol{\theta}_0$ remains. To obtain it use Eq. (7-3)
$$E\{\boldsymbol{\theta}_0\} = E\{\mathbf{B}'\mathbf{K}_1\mathbf{c}\} + E\{\mathbf{B}\}'\mathbf{p}_1 + \lambda_0$$
$$= K_1[\mu_b c + \text{cov}(bc)] + \mu_b \mathbf{p}_1 + \lambda_0$$
$$= 1.42[(-.5)(3.5) + 0] + (-.5)(2.1) + 0 = -3.535 \tag{7-36}$$

Then substitution of Eqs. (7-32) and (7-36) into Eq. (7-35) yields

$$g_0^\dagger = -(.484)(-3.535) = 1.712 \qquad (7\text{-}37)$$

This completes the evaluation of Eq. (7-2).

Finally, u_0 can be evaluated with Eq. (7-1) using Eqs. (7-34) and (7-37) as

$$u_0 = G_0^\dagger x_0 + g_0^\dagger = (.2405)(0) + 1.712 = 1.712$$

This result checks with the $(q:r) = (5:5)$ case with $N = 2$ in MacRae (1972, table 2, p. 446).

In summary the calculations for the optimal period 0 control yield the following results:

Period	2	1	0
K	1.0	1.42	
p	0	2.10	
$G^\dagger$			2.40
$g^\dagger$			1.712
u^{OLF}			1.712

Finally, set

$$u_0^\dagger = u_0^{OLF} = 1.712$$

7-3 PROJECTIONS OF MEANS AND COVARIANCES TO PERIOD 1

In order to perform the calculations for the projections and the optimal control for period 1, it is necessary to use some results from appendixes which are developed along with Chap. 10. It is therefore recommended that the reader proceed to Chaps. 8 to 10 and then return to these calculations.

The method employed in the remainder of this chapter is the same as that outlined in Appendix O for the sequential certainty-equivalence method, except for step 2, which is replaced by the computation of the open-loop feedback policy, as has been done above.

The steps in the method of Appendix O follow.

Step 1 Generate the random vectors for the system noise ξ_k and the measurement noise ζ_k. Since there is no measurement noise in this problem, only the system noise ξ_k must be generated. In doing this the covariance $Q = .2$ is used to generate

$$\xi_0 = .3 \quad \text{and} \quad \xi_1 = .43$$

The solution will of course differ for each set of random-noise terms. These values are used only as an example.

Step 2 Solve for the open-loop feedback control for period 0 as in Sec. 7-2.

Step 3 Obtain the actual value of the state vector with
$$x_1 = Ax_0 + Bu_0^\dagger + c + \xi_0$$
$$= (.7)(0) + (-.5)(1.712) + 3.5 + .3 = 2.944$$
and of the measurement vector with
$$y_1 = Hx_1 + \zeta_1 = (1)(2.944) + 0 = 2.944$$

Step 4 Get $\hat{x}_{1|0}$ and $\hat{\theta}_{1|0}$ by using (M-8) and (M-9) of Appendix M
$$\hat{x}_{1|0} = A_0(\hat{\theta}_{0|0})\hat{x}_{0|0} + B_0(\hat{\theta}_{0|0})u_0^\dagger + c_k(\hat{\theta}_{0|0}) + \sum_{i \in X} e^i \operatorname{tr}(a_\theta^i \Sigma_{0|0}^{\theta x}) \quad (7\text{-}38)$$
and
$$\hat{\theta}_{1|0} = D\hat{\theta}_{0|0} \quad (7\text{-}39)$$

Since $\Sigma_{0|0}^{\theta x} = 0$ and $D = 1$, Eqs. (7-38) and (7-39) become
$$\hat{x}_{1|0} = (.7)(0) + (-.5)(1.712) + 3.5 + 0 = 2.644$$
$$\hat{\theta}_{1|0} = \hat{\theta}_{0|0} = -.5$$

Step 5 Get $\Sigma_{k+1|k}$ by using Eqs. (M-16) to (M-19) and the fact that $\Sigma_{0|0}^{xx} = \Sigma_{0|0}^{\theta x} = 0$, that is,
$$\Sigma_{1|0}^{xx} = f_{\theta 0}^x \Sigma_{0|0}^{\theta \theta}(f_{\theta 0}^x)' + Q$$
where
$$f_{\theta 0}^x = \sum_i e_i \hat{x}_{0|0}' a_\theta^i + \sum_i e_i u_0^\dagger b_\theta^i + \sum_i e_i c_\theta^i$$
$$= \hat{x}_{0|0}' a_\theta + u_0^\dagger b_\theta + c_\theta$$
$$= (0)(0) + (1.712)(1) + 0 = 1.712$$

Therefore,
$$\Sigma_{1|0}^{xx} = (1.712)(.5)(1.712) + .2 = 1.465 + .2 = 1.665 \quad (7\text{-}40)$$

From Eq. (M-18)
$$\Sigma_{1|0}^{\theta x} = D\Sigma_{0|0}^{\theta \theta}(f_{\theta 0}^x)' = (1)(.5)(1.712) = .856 \quad (7\text{-}41)$$

From Eq. (M-19)
$$\Sigma_{1|0}^{\theta \theta} = D\Sigma_{0|0}^{\theta \theta} D + G_0 = (1)(.5)(1) + 0 = .5 \quad (7\text{-}42)$$

Step 6 Use Eqs. (K-17) to (K-19) along with the results in Eqs. (7-40) to (7-42) to get $\Sigma_{1|1}$, that is,
$$\Sigma_{1|1}^{xx} = \Sigma_{1|0}^{xx} - \Sigma_{1|0}^{xx} H_1' S_1^{-1} H_1 \Sigma_{1|0}^{xx}$$
where, from Eq. (K-15),
$$S_1 = H_1 \Sigma_{1|0}^{xx} H_1' + R = (1)(1.665)(1) + 0 = 1.665$$

so that [1]

$$\Sigma^{xx}_{1|1} = 1.665 - (1.665)(1)(1.665)^{-1}(1)(1.665) = 0$$

Then, from Eq. (K-18),

$$\Sigma^{\theta x}_{1|1} = \Sigma^{\theta x}_{1|0} - \Sigma^{\theta x}_{1|0} H'_1 S_1^{-1} H_1 \Sigma^{xx}_{1|0}$$
$$= .856 - (.856)(1)(1.665)^{-1}(1)(1.665) = 0$$

And from Eq. (K-19)

$$\Sigma^{\theta\theta}_{1|1} = \Sigma^{\theta\theta}_{1|0} - \Sigma^{\theta x}_{1|0} H'_1 S_1^{-1} H_1 \Sigma^{x\theta}_{1|0}$$
$$= .5 - (.86)(1)(1.665)^{-1}(1)(.856) = .06$$

Step 7 Update the mean $\hat{x}_{1|1}$ and $\hat{\theta}_{1|1}$ by using Eqs. (N-7) and (N-8)

$$\hat{x}_{1|1} = \hat{x}_{1|0} + \Sigma^{xx}_{1|0} H'_1 S_1^{-1} (y_1 - H_1 \hat{x}_{1|0})$$
$$= 2.644 + (1.665)(1)(1.665)^{-1}(2.944 - (1)2.644) = 2.944$$

and

$$\hat{\theta}_{1|1} = \hat{\theta}_{1|0} + \Sigma^{\theta x}_{1|0} H'_1 S_1^{-1} (y_1 - H_1 \hat{x}_{1|0})$$
$$= -.5 + (.856)(1)(1.665)^{-1}(2.944 - 2.644) = -.346$$

In summary the results for time periods 0 and 1 are as follows:

Period	0|0	1|0	1|1
x	0	2.644	2.944
θ	-.5	-.5	-.346
Σ^{xx}	0	1.665	0
$\Sigma^{\theta x}$	0	.856	0
$\Sigma^{\theta\theta}$	.5	.5	.06

and

Period	0	1
x^{OLF}	0	2.944
u^{OLF}	1.712	

[1] With no measurement error in the problem that state covariance returns to zero after each measurement.

Similarly the summary results for periods 1 and 2 are:

Period	1|1	2|1	2|2
x	2.944	4.997	5.179
θ	$-$.346	$-$.346	$-$.296
Σ^{xx}	0	.359	0
$\Sigma^{\theta x}$	0	.098	0
$\Sigma^{\theta\theta}$	.06	.060	.033

and

Period	1	2
x^{OLF}	2.944	5.179
u^{OLF}	1.630	

So the optimal OLF control values are

$$u_0^{OLF} = 1.712 \qquad u_1^{OLF} = 1.630$$

and the total criterion value is

$$J^{OLF} = 20.54$$

PART THREE

ACTIVE-LEARNING STOCHASTIC CONTROL

If a man will begin with certainties, he shall end with doubts; but if he will be content to being with doubts, he shall end in certainties.

Francis Bacon,
The Advancement of Learning,
bk. I, chap. V, sec. 8,
1605

CHAPTER
EIGHT
OVERVIEW

Active-learning stochastic control has also been called adaptive control or dual control. The name "dual" emphasizes the double role that the choice of control plays in active-learning stochastic control. On the one hand, the control is chosen to guide the system in a desired direction. On the other hand, it is chosen to decrease the uncertainty about the system's response. This would seem to imply that there were two elements in the criterion function, one for performance and one for learning. Not so! There is only one element, the *expected* performance. However, minimization of the expected cost includes a trade-off between performance and learning. If the system's parameters are not well known, a choice of control in period k which detracts from present performance but which yields improved parameter estimates in later periods may result in overall better performance in the time periods covered by the model.

Thus active-learning stochastic control is sometimes characterized by the idea that the controls will be used in the earlier time periods to perturb the system so as to improve parameter estimates and thereby permit better performance in later time periods. Of course one expects to observe the perturbations being done in such a manner that they will improve estimates of the crucial parameters, i.e., of the parameters which most affect the performance. This contrasts with the present procedure used in large econometric models of the United States economy, in which the constant terms in equations are frequently updated and modified. In fact it may not be these terms but terms which are multiplied by the states or by the controls which are most important and which deserve the special updating attention.

A political analog can be drawn to active-learning stochastic control. A slate of officers from a party enters office prepared to improve the performance of the economy. They realize that they do not know exactly how the economy will respond to their policies, so they try small changes in various policies in the early quarters of their term in office. Then with the improved estimates so obtained they do a better job of directing the economy in the waning quarters of the term while they are running for reelection. Of course this is a long way from current political practice. Even the idea that an administration might "perturb" the economy to improve the knowledge of its response to stimulation is worrisome to many people. Of course it is also of concern that policy actions are taken when officials are highly uncertain about the response of the economy. One example of this is the uncertainty associated with the lag in response of the economy to changes in monetary policy. Some economists feel that the response comes within one or two quarters, and others argue that the response may take six or eight quarters. If policies are chosen with the belief that the short response time holds when in fact the long response time holds, the effects on the economy may be most unfortunate.

This chapter includes a discussion of one of the algorithms that has been proposed for adaptive control, the algorithm of Tse, Bar-Shalom, and Meier (1973). The description occupies most of this chapter and is followed by detailed descriptions of the linear and nonlinear versions of the algorithm in Chaps. 9 and 10. The applications of the algorithm are given in Chaps. 11 and 12.

Since this chapter is an overview, some notation and concepts are not explained in great detail, the purpose being to survey the forest before plunging in among the trees.

This is not the only adaptive-control algorithm which has been applied to economic problems. Some of the other studies are those by Prescott (1967, 1971), MacRae (1972, 1975), Rausser and Freebairn (1974), Abel (1975) using the Chow (1975) algorithm, Upadhyay (1975) using the Deshpande, Upadhyay, and Lainoitis (1973) algorithm, Sarris and Athans (1973), and Taylor (1973, 1974). Also earlier results from the use of the Tse, Bar-Shalom, and Meier algorithm are reported in Kendrick (1979). As yet there is no clear ranking of these various algorithms; their relative performance appears to be problem-specific [see Norman (1976) and Bar-Shalom and Tse (1976a)].

The chapter begins with a statement of the problem, followed by a discussion of the Monte Carlo procedure used with the algorithm. The algorithm is then described in three sections. The closing section of the chapter provides a brief description of the relationship of this algorithm to some of the others which have been proposed.

8-1 PROBLEM STATEMENT

Recall from previous discussion that the notation J_N represents the expected cost-to-go with N periods remaining and that C_N is the random cost-to-go with N periods remaining. The subscripts on these two elements represent the number of periods to go. In contrast, the time subscripts on all other variables represent the period in which the variable occurs. For example L_N is the cost in the Nth period and x_N is the state variable in the Nth period. With this notation in mind the problem can be stated as one of finding $(\mathbf{u}_k)_{k=0}^{N-1}$ to minimize the cost functional

$$J_N = E\{C_N\} \tag{8-1}$$

where
$$C_N = L_N(\mathbf{x}_N) + \sum_{k=0}^{N-1} L_k(\mathbf{x}_k, \mathbf{u}_k) \tag{8-2}$$

It is useful to further divide L_k into three components

$$L_k(\mathbf{x}_k, \mathbf{u}_k) = \nu_k(\mathbf{x}_k) + \omega_k(\mathbf{x}_k, \mathbf{u}_k) + \phi_k(\mathbf{u}_k)$$

since at a later stage it will be desirable to drop all terms in the criterion which do not include the control variables.

The system equations are written with an additive-noise term as

$$\mathbf{x}_{k+1} = \mathbf{f}_k(\mathbf{x}_k, \mathbf{u}_k) + \boldsymbol{\xi}_k \tag{8-3}$$

where $\boldsymbol{\xi}_k$ is the additive-noise term. Next a new element is introduced, namely the measurement relationship

$$\mathbf{y}_k = \mathbf{h}_k(\mathbf{x}_k) + \boldsymbol{\zeta}_k \tag{8-4}$$

where $\mathbf{y}_k$ = measurement vector
$\mathbf{h}$ = measurement functions
$\boldsymbol{\zeta}$ = measurement-noise terms

Equation (8-4) represents the fact that the state variables may be measured not exactly but with error. Almost all economic statistics are acknowledged to include measurement error although this fact is rarely introduced into the analysis. Here it will be included. Equation (8-4) can also be used to represent the fact that although the state variables cannot be observed directly, other variables which are a function of the state variables can be observed. For example, it may be that we cannot observe the money stock directly but we can observe some components of it which can be used to estimate what the money stock is. Equation (8-4) even raises the possibility of multiple measurements on each state variable, i.e., there may be several variables which are observable and which are functions of a state variable while the state variable itself cannot be measured directly.

Next consider the statistical properties of the random elements in the problem

$$\begin{aligned} E\{\mathbf{x}_0\} &= \hat{\mathbf{x}}_{0|0} & \mathrm{cov}(\mathbf{x}_0) &= \Sigma_{0|0} \\ E\{\boldsymbol{\xi}_k\} &= \mathbf{0} & \mathrm{cov}(\boldsymbol{\xi}_k) &= \mathbf{Q}_k \\ E\{\boldsymbol{\zeta}_k\} &= \mathbf{0} & \mathrm{cov}(\boldsymbol{\zeta}_k) &= \mathbf{R}_k \end{aligned} \tag{8-5}$$

It is assumed that $\mathbf{x}_0$ and the system- and measurement-noise terms are independent gaussian vectors with the statistics shown in Eq. (8-5). One bit of new notation is introduced in Eq. (8-5), namely $\Sigma_{0|0}$. This means the covariance of the state vector at time zero as estimated with data through time zero. Later, notation of the form $\Sigma_{k+1|k}$ will be used to represent a covariance matrix at time $k + 1$ as projected with data available at time k.

As a result of assuming that the state vector is measured with error, it is no longer true that x is known perfectly; instead estimates of the mean of the state variables $\hat{x}$ and of the covariance of the state vector Σ can be made.

In summary the problem is to select the controls to minimize the criteria (8-1) and (8-2) subject to the system equations (8-3), the measurement equations (8-4), and the statistics (8-5).

A flowchart outlining the main procedures for solving this problem is given in Fig. 8-1. The algorithm may be thought of as consisting of three nested do loops. Alternatively, one can think of the problem as consisting of three parts: a Monte Carlo procedure containing a dynamic optimization problem, which in turn contains a static optimization problem.

The outside do loop with the index ρ is the Monte Carlo do loop. In each Monte Carlo run, as discussed in the next section, all the required random terms for the problem are generated at the outset. Then the problem is solved for these manifestations of the random elements. The Monte Carlo loop is repeated as many times as required to establish the statistical reliability of the comparisons of the adaptive-control method with other methods.

The second do loop is the time-period counter k. The problem is solved for N time periods. This is the middle loop, or the dynamic optimization problem shown in Fig. 8-1. At the beginning of this loop in each time period k the certainty-equivalence (CE) problem for the remaining time periods is solved and the control is set equal to u_k^{CE}. This procedure is described in Sec. 8-3. The control variable is then modified iteratively in the third, or inside, do loop until the optimal control for period k is found.

This third do loop, shown at the bottom of Fig. 8-1, is the static optimization problem. In each pass through this loop the approximate cost-to-go with $N - k$ periods remaining is evaluated. If the optimal control has been found, the search is halted; otherwise a new search value is chosen for the control and the evaluation is repeated. As described in Sec. 8-4, this search may be either a gradient procedure or a grid search.

Once the optimal control for period k has been found in the bottom loop, that control is applied to the system along with the random elements. New states in the period $k + 1$ are obtained, and the estimates of the mean and covariance of the state are updated to period $k + 1$, as described in Sec. 8-5.

8-2 THE MONTE CARLO PROCEDURE

At this stage of the research on stochastic control methods in economics there is substantial interest in comparing various methods and algorithms. For example,

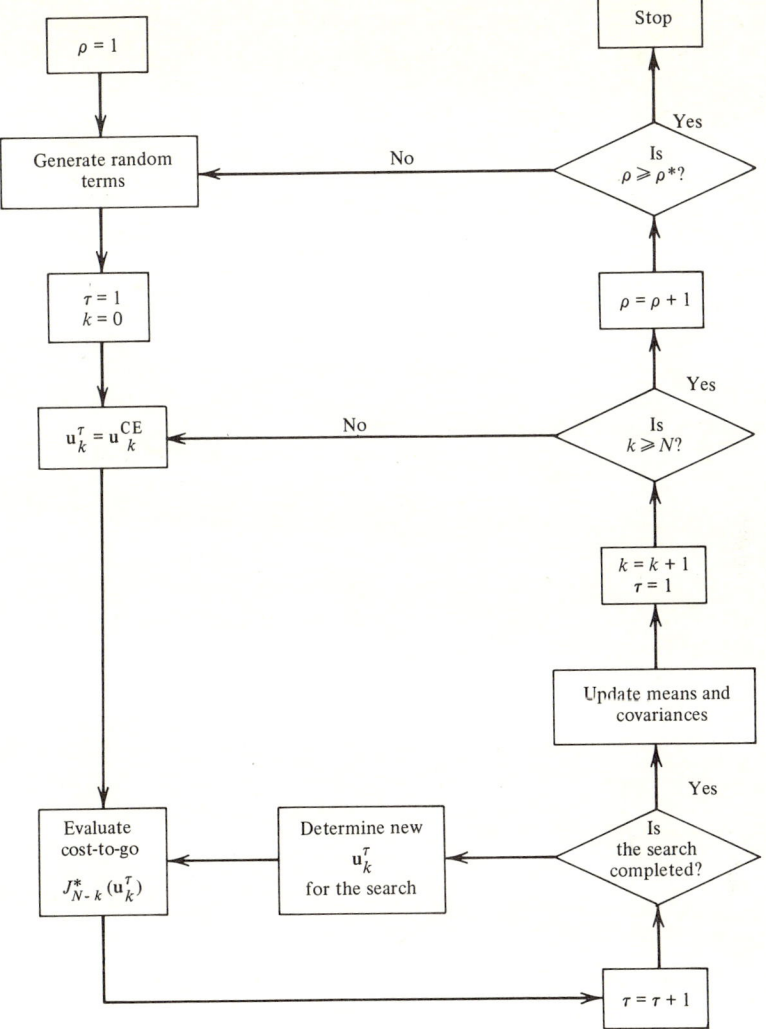

Figure 8-1 Flowchart of an adaptive-control algorithm; ρ = Monte Carlo run counter, k = time-period counter, τ = search-iteration counter.

there is a comparison in Chap. 12 of deterministic, passive-learning stochastic, and active-learning stochastic control applied to a small econometric model of the United States economy.

When comparing stochastic control procedures it is necessary to make repeated trials with different samples of the random variables. For the problem at hand there are three groups of random variables:

1. The initial state variables $\mathbf{x}_0$
2. The system-equation noise terms $\boldsymbol{\xi}_k$
3. The measurement-equation noise terms $\boldsymbol{\zeta}_k$

The n random elements in $\mathbf{x}_0$ are obtained from a Monte Carlo generator which is provided the initial state-variable covariance $\boldsymbol{\Sigma}_{0|0}$. In a similar manner the $n \times N$ system-equation noise terms $\boldsymbol{\xi}_k$ ($k = 0, 1, \ldots, N - 1$) are obtained by using the covariance $\mathbf{Q}_k$, and the $r \times N$ measurement error terms are obtained by using the covariance $\mathbf{R}_k$. Here n is the dimension of the state vector $\mathbf{x}$, and r is the dimension of the measurement vector $\mathbf{y}$.

This completes the first (or outermost) of the three do loops. The second do loop runs over the index of time periods k. Its initiation is discussed next.

8-3 THE ADAPTIVE-CONTROL PROBLEM: INITIATION

The solution method begins with setting the time-period counter k to zero. In economics it is common to label the first time period as period 1, while in parts of control theory period 0 is used. The control convention is followed here. A review of Fig. 8-1 shows that the search-iteration counter is initialized to $\tau = 1$ at this stage.

The initialization of the search is necessary at this stage; i.e., it is necessary to choose a value $\mathbf{u}_k^\tau$ for $k = 0$ and $\tau = 1$, that is $\mathbf{u}_0^1$, with which to begin the search for the optimal control. This is done by solving the certainty-equivalence problem for periods k through N to obtain

$$\left(\mathbf{x}_{j+1}^{CE}, \mathbf{u}_j^{CE}\right)_{j=0}^{N-1}$$

Then the control is set as $\mathbf{u}_0^1 = \mathbf{u}_0^{CE}$.

This completes the initialization and clears the way for the beginning of the search for the optimal control in the third do loop.

8-4 SEARCH FOR THE OPTIMAL CONTROL IN PERIOD k

A final glance at Fig. 8-1 shows that this third do loop consists of an iteration on the counter τ while searching for the optimal control with the approximate cost-to-go evaluated in each iteration. Figure 8-2 provides a more detailed description of this part of the algorithm. It also reveals that there is still a fourth nested do loop, which did not appear in Fig. 8-1 but which is shown in the more detailed breakdown of Fig. 8-2. This fourth do loop is used to project the covariances to period N.

The basic method used here is to calculate the optimal cost-to-go which corresponds to the search value of the control $\mathbf{u}_k^\tau$ for each iteration τ until the

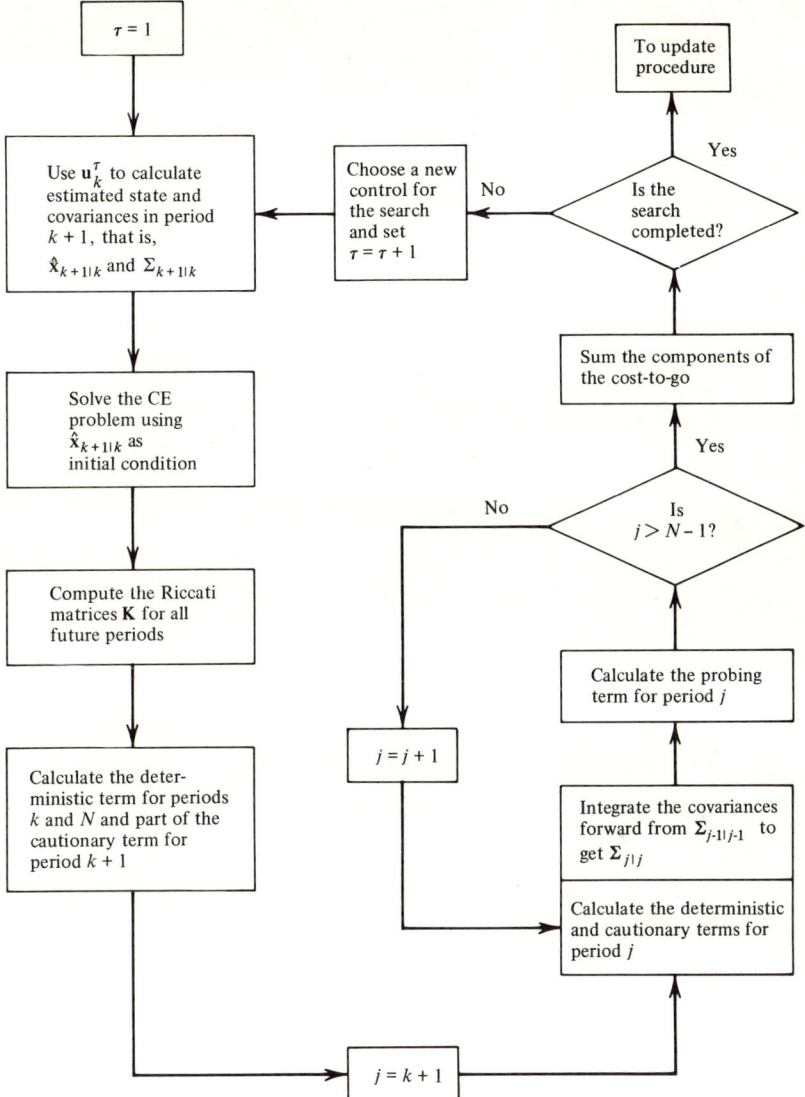

Figure 8-2 Flowchart of the search for $\mathbf{u}_k^*$; τ = search-iteration counter.

optimal control $\mathbf{u}_k^*$ for period k has been found. The search method may be a gradient procedure or a grid search.

At each iteration in the search it is necessary to evaluate the cost-to-go, but since the problem is nonlinear, the cost-to-go is extremely difficult to evaluate [see Aoki (1967)]. Therefore an approximate cost-to-go is obtained by using a second-order expansion of both the criterion and the system equations about a nominal path.

The nominal path is obtained in two steps. First the value for x_{k+1} is obtained by using the current search value of the control u_k^τ and a second-order expansion of the system equations. This step is shown in the second box down on the left-hand side of Fig. 8-2. Then this value of x_{k+1} (really $\hat{x}_{k+1|k}$, since it is a projection of $k + 1$ using data from period k) is used as the initial condition for a certainty-equivalence problem from period $k + 1$ through N. This provides the nominal path

$$(x_{o,j+1}, u_{oj})_{j=k+1}^{N}$$

about which the expansions can then be done. This step is shown in the third box down on the left-hand side of Fig. 8-2.

The approximate optimal cost-to-go can then be written as a function of the following elements:

u_k^τ = search value of control for period k at iteration τ

$(x_{o,j+1}, u_{oj})_{j=k+1}^{N-1}$ = nominal paths for the state and control variables

$\Sigma_{k+1|k}$ = covariance of state variables at time $k+1$ as projected with data available at time k

$(Q_j)_{j=k+1}^{N}$ = covariance of system-equation noise terms

$(\Sigma_{j|j})_{j=k+1}^{N-1}$ = post-observation covariance matrix for all future time periods

Also, all terms in the approximate optimal cost-to-go which do not depend on the search value of the control are dropped; the notation used for this is

$J_{d,N-k}^*$ = approximate optimal cost-to-go once terms which are not dependent on u_k^τ have been dropped

Thus the general form of the function can be written as

$$J_{d,N-k}^* = \min_{u_k} f\left(u_k^\tau, (x_{o,j+1}, u_{oj})_{j=k+1}^{N-1}, \Sigma_{k+1|k}, (Q_j)_{j=k+1}^{N-1}, (\Sigma_{j|j})_{j=k+1}^{N-1}\right) \tag{8-6}$$

For better understanding it is useful to divide Eq. (8-6) into three components [Bar-Shalom and Tse (1976a)], called the *deterministic*, *cautionary*, and *probing* terms. They are written in general functional form as

$$J_{d,N-k}^* = \min_{u_k} (J_{D,N-k} + J_{C,N-k} + J_{P,N-k}) \tag{8-7}$$

where $J_{D,N-k}$ = deterministic component = $f\left(u_k^\tau, (x_{o,j+1}, u_{oj})_{j=k+1}^{N-1}\right)$ (8-8)

$J_{C,N-k}$ = cautionary term = $f\left(\Sigma_{k+1|k}, (Q_j)_{j=k+1}^{N-1}\right)$ (8-9)

$J_{P,N-k}$ = probing term = $f\left((\Sigma_{j|j})_{j=k+1}^{N-1}\right)$ (8-10)

The deterministic component is a function of only the search value of the control and the nominal path. It contains no covariance terms.

The cautionary component is a function of $\Sigma_{k+1|k}$, which is the covariance of the state variable at time $k + 1$ as projected with data available at time k. This represents the uncertainty in the response of the system to a control applied at time k *before* the state of the system can be observed again at time $k + 1$ and a new control applied to bring the system back onto the desired path. The name "cautionary" comes from the fact that such uncertainty normally biases the choice of the control variable in a conservative direction since one is uncertain about the magnitudes of the response to expect. This component is also a function of the covariance of the system equations error terms. This does not necessarily fit well into a component called cautionary. Thus it shows that the separation into these particular three components is somewhat arbitrary. Perhaps it would be better to separate these terms into yet a fourth component.

The probing component is a function of the covariance matrix $\Sigma_{j|j}$ for all future time periods. This is the uncertainty associated with the state vector at each time period after the measurement has been taken at that time period and the covariance matrix has been updated. Since probing or perturbation of the system early in time will tend to reduce the uncertainty and to make the elements of these matrices smaller later, this term is called the probing term.

Now return to Fig. 8-2. The next step, shown in the fourth box down on the left-hand side of the figure, is to compute the Riccati matrices **K**. Analogous to the Riccati matrices in the deterministic and multiplicative-uncertainty problems, there are also Riccati matrices in this problem. They can be computed for all future time periods by integrating backward from terminal conditions.

Next, since the nominal path is known, the deterministic component of the approximate cost-to-go can be computed. Also the part of the cautionary term involving $\Sigma_{k+1|k}$ can be computed at this stage since that matrix is available. It was computed in the step shown in the second box from the top on the left along with the projected mean of the state variable $\hat{x}_{k+1|k}$.

Next the algorithm enters the fourth of the nested do loops, which projects the covariance matrices $\Sigma_{j|j}$ forward all the way to period N and uses these terms to compute the probing component. Also the part of the cautionary component which involves $\mathbf{Q}_j$ is computed in this do loop.

Once the do loop has been completed, the total approximate cost-to-go can be obtained by adding the three components. This is then used to determine whether or not the search is complete.

If the search is a grid search and the vector $\mathbf{u}_k$ consists of a single control, the problem reduces to a line search. This is the method used in the example in Chap. 12. The approximate cost-to-go is evaluated at many points on the interval between the highest and lowest likely values for the controls. The search value of the control which yields the lowest cost-to-go is then chosen as the optimal control.

With a gradient technique the third loop is used as the procedure for evaluating the function at each iteration. The gradient method then proceeds until satisfactory convergence has been obtained.

It is useful to note the computational complexity of the problem at this stage. The iterations in the search for the optimal control require the backward integration of the Riccati equations and the forward integration of the covariance equations at each step. The search must in turn be carried out for each time period of the problem in the second of the nested do loops. Furthermore, the entire problem must be solved for each of the Monte Carlo runs. This means that only a fairly limited number of Monte Carlo runs can be made for even small econometric models.

Return now to the search in Fig. 8-2. If the search is not completed, the iteration counter is increased and the evaluation of the cost-to-go is repeated. If the search is completed, the update procedure is entered in the concluding phase of the solution of the adaptive-control problem.

8-5 THE UPDATE

Once the search is completed and the optimal control $\mathbf{u}_k^*$ for period k has been obtained, this control is used along with the additive-noise terms in Eq. (8-3) to obtain $\mathbf{x}_{k+1}$. The vector $\mathbf{x}_{k+1}$ is used in turn in the measurement relationship Eq. (8-4) along with the measurement error term to get $\mathbf{y}_{k+1}$. The measurement is used to obtain updated estimates of the mean and covariance of the state vector at time $k + 1$ using data obtained through period $k + 1$, that is, $\hat{\mathbf{x}}_{k+1|k+1}$ and $\Sigma_{k+1|k+1}$. This is shown on the right-hand side of Fig. 8-1.

Next the time-period index k is increased by 1 and a test is made to see whether all N periods have been completed. If not, the certainty-equivalence control for the new time period is computed and the search is made again. If all N periods have been completed, the Monte Carlo run counter is increased by 1 and a test is made to see whether the desired number of Monte Carlo runs has been completed.

8-6 OTHER ALGORITHMS

As discussed in the introduction to this chapter, a variety of other algorithms are available for solving active-learning stochastic control problems, but very little work on comparison of algorithms has been down.

It is beyond the scope of this book to provide a detailed comparison of the various algorithms, but a brief comparison to three other algorithms is provided, namely those of Norman (1976), MacRae (1975), and Chow (1975, chap. 10).

Norman's algorithm is like the algorithm described above except that a couple of simplifications are adopted: (1) he assumes that there is no measurement error, and (2) he employs a first-order rather than a second-order expansion of the cost-to-go function (hence the name first-order dual control).

MacRae also uses the assumption of no measurement noise. Thus the Σ matrix used in Chap. 10 of this book consists of one component, $\Sigma^{\theta\theta}$, instead of four components.

With this assumption MacRae derives an updating rule for the inverse of the covariance matrix of the form

$$\Gamma_k^{-1} = f(\Gamma_{k-1}^{-1}) \tag{8-11}$$

This same type of relationship can be derived by assuming (in the notation of Chap. 10) that $\mathbf{D} = \mathbf{I}$, $\mathbf{H} = \mathbf{I}$, $\Sigma^{xx} = \mathbf{0}$, and $\mathbf{R} = \mathbf{0}$, that is, by assuming that the parameters of the problem are constant over time and that the state variables can be measured exactly. Then Eq. (10-60) can be substituted into Eq. (10-69) to obtain a relationship like Eq. (8-11).

In MacRae's algorithm the update relationship (8-11) is appended to the criterion function with lagrangian variables, and the resulting function is minimized.

Chow's algorithm also relies on the assumption of perfect measurement of the state vector, but it is more general than the algorithm used in this book in at least one way. Chow's development includes cross terms from different time periods. Another difference is in the path about which the second-order approximation is made. In the Tse, Bar-Shalom, and Meier algorithm this path is rechosen at each iteration in the search path; in Chow's algorithm it is selected before the search is begun and not altered during the search. Finally in the development of the algorithm Chow takes the expectation first and then performs the second-order expansion while Tse, Bar-Shalom, and Meier reverse these steps.

This completes the brief review of other algorithms and the survey of the adaptive-control algorithm used in this book. The next two chapters include a detailed development of the nonlinear algorithm and the application of this algorithm to a quadratic linear control problem with unknown parameters. The reader who is more interested in the application of stochastic control to economics than in the algorithms may prefer to skip to Chap. 12, which includes an application to a small econometric model of the United States economy.

CHAPTER NINE

NONLINEAR ACTIVE-LEARNING STOCHASTIC CONTROL

with
Bo Hyun Kang

9-1 INTRODUCTION

This chapter provides a detailed description and derivation of the Tse, Bar-Shalom, and Meier (1973) algorithm.[1] It also extends that algorithm to cover cases where (1) a constant term is given explicitly in the systems equations and (2) the criterion function includes a cross term in **x** and **u**.

9-2 PROBLEM STATEMENT

The problem is to select $\mathbf{U}^{N-1} = (\mathbf{u}_k)_{k=0}^{N-1}$ to minimize the cost functional

$$J_N = E\{C_N\} \tag{9-1}$$

where

$$C_N = L_N(\mathbf{x}_N) + \sum_{k=0}^{N-1} L_k(\mathbf{x}_k, \mathbf{u}_k) \tag{9-2}$$

---

[1] See also Bar-Shalom, Tse, and Larson (1974).

where the expectation $E\{\cdot\}$ is taken over all random variables. The subscripts denote the time period. It will be convenient at times to divide the cost function into three component functions, one including only terms in **x**, another including only terms in **u**, and a third including cross terms in **x** and **u**, that is,

$$L_k(\mathbf{x}_k, \mathbf{u}_k) = \nu_k(\mathbf{x})_k + \omega_k(\mathbf{x}_k, \mathbf{u}_k) + \phi_k(\mathbf{u}_k) \tag{9-3}$$

The cost functional is to be minimized subject to the system equations

$$\mathbf{x}_{k+1} = \mathbf{f}_k(\mathbf{x}_k, \mathbf{u}_k) + \boldsymbol{\xi}_k \qquad k = 0, 1, \ldots, N-1 \tag{9-4}$$

and the measurement equations

$$\mathbf{y}_k = \mathbf{h}_k(\mathbf{x}_k) + \boldsymbol{\zeta}_k \qquad k = 1, \ldots, N \tag{9-5}$$

where **x** = n-element state vector
u = m-element control vector
y = r-element observation vector

It is assumed that $\mathbf{x}_0$ and $(\boldsymbol{\xi}_k, \boldsymbol{\zeta}_{k+1})_{k=0}^{N-1}$ are independent gaussian vectors with statistics

$$\begin{aligned} E\{\mathbf{x}_0\} &= \hat{\mathbf{x}}_{0|0} & \text{cov}(\mathbf{x}_0) &= \boldsymbol{\Sigma}_{0|0} \\ E\{\boldsymbol{\xi}_k\} &= 0 & \text{cov}(\boldsymbol{\xi}_k) &= \mathbf{Q}_k \\ E\{\boldsymbol{\zeta}_k\} &= 0 & \text{cov}(\boldsymbol{\zeta}_k) &= \mathbf{R}_k \end{aligned} \tag{9-6}$$

As discussed in Chap. 5, we seek a control which is a *closed-loop* rather than a *feedback* control [see Bar-Shalom and Tse (1976b)], the distinction being that the feedback control depends only on past measurements and random variables while the closed-loop control includes some consideration of future measurements and random variables. In fact the control used here is of the form

$$\mathbf{u}_k = \mathbf{u}_k(\mathbf{Y}^k, \mathbf{U}^{k-1}, C_N, \mathbf{D}, \boldsymbol{\Sigma}^{N-1}, \mathbf{Q}^{N-1}, \mathbf{R}^N) \tag{9-7}$$

where

$$\mathbf{Y}^k = (\mathbf{y}_j)_{j=1}^k \qquad \mathbf{U}^{k-1} = (\mathbf{u}_j)_{j=0}^{k-1} \qquad \mathbf{Q}^{N-1} = (\mathbf{Q}_j)_{j=0}^{N-1} \qquad \mathbf{R}^N = (\mathbf{R}_j)_{j=1}^N$$

and where C_N is the cost functional, **D** is the systems dynamics $\mathbf{f}_k(\cdot)$ for $k = 0, 1, \ldots, N-1$, and $\boldsymbol{\Sigma}^{N-1} = (\boldsymbol{\Sigma}_j)_{j=k}^{N-1}$, where $\boldsymbol{\Sigma}_k$ is an estimate of $\boldsymbol{\Sigma}$ at k based on $\mathbf{Y}^k$ and $\mathbf{U}^{k-1}$ and $(\boldsymbol{\Sigma}_j)_{k+1}^{N-1}$ is a projection of $\boldsymbol{\Sigma}$ for future time periods based on $\mathbf{Y}^k$, $\mathbf{U}^{k-1}$, and the statistical description of the future measurements. So the control depends on the estimated state-variable covariance matrix at time k and on projections of this same matrix which take account of the fact that system noises will be increasing the variance but also that future measurements can be used to decrease the variance of the state vector. Also, it is assumed here that **Q** and **R** are known for all future time periods.

The dual-control method used here is said to be a wide-sense method in that it employs the first and second moments $\hat{\mathbf{x}}$ and $\boldsymbol{\Sigma}$ in computing the optimal control. Higher moments are ignored.

9-3 DYNAMIC-PROGRAMMING PROBLEM AND SEARCH METHOD

As stated in Eq. (6-18), the dynamic-programming problem at time k is to find $\mathbf{u}_k$ to minimize the expected cost-to-go, i.e.,

$$J^*_{N-k} = \min_{\mathbf{u}_k} E\{L_k(\mathbf{x}_k, \mathbf{u}_k) + J^*_{N-k-1} | \mathbf{Y}^k, \mathbf{U}^{k-1}\} \tag{9-8}$$

The first problem then is to describe the search method over the space $\mathbf{u}_k$.

Since the search for the optimal control $\mathbf{u}^*_k$ is initiated from the certainty-equivalence control $\mathbf{u}^{CE}_k$, it is necessary first to solve the certainty-equivalence problem.

Repeated values of $\mathbf{u}_k$ are chosen, and the cost-to-go is evaluated for each set of control values. If $\mathbf{u}_k$ is a scalar quantity, a line search is appropriate; in Tse and Bar-Shalom (1973) a quadratic fit method is used. If $\mathbf{u}_k$ is a vector, more general gradient or grid-search methods can be used. However, the function $J^*_{N-k}(\mathbf{u}_k)$ may have multiple local optima. Therefore, if gradient methods are used, they should be given multiple starting points. Because of the presence of local optima, Kendrick (1979) employed both a quasi-Newton gradient method and a grid-search technique.[1]

9-4 COMPUTING THE APPROXIMATE COST-TO-GO

In order to evaluate Eq. (9-8), an approximate cost-to-go must be computed, and this requires a nominal path on which the second-order Taylor expansion of J^*_{N-k-1} can be evaluated.

Choosing the Nominal Path

The nominal path is $(\mathbf{x}^{CE}_{j+1}, \mathbf{u}^{CE}_j)_{j=k+1}^{N-1}$, that is, the certainty-equivalence path of values which minimize the cost functional from time $k+1$ to N with all random variables set to their mean values. In order to solve the problem one must have the value $\mathbf{x}_{k+1}$ as an initial condition. This value is obtained by using the current search value of $\mathbf{u}_k$ to obtain an estimate $\hat{\mathbf{x}}_{k+1|k}$ of the state at time $k+1$ as projected with data available at time k. In order to do this, consider the system equation (9-4)

$$\mathbf{x}_{k+1} = \mathbf{f}_k(\mathbf{x}_k, \mathbf{u}_k) + \boldsymbol{\xi}_k \tag{9-9}$$

and expand it to second order about $\hat{\mathbf{x}}_{k|k}$, the current estimate of the state, and

---

[1] The gradient technique used was ZXMIN from the IMSL Library (1974).

$\mathbf{u}_k^\tau$, the current search value of $\mathbf{u}_k$. This yields (see Appendix A for derivation)

$$\mathbf{x}_{k+1} \approx \mathbf{f}_k(\hat{\mathbf{x}}_{k|k}, \mathbf{u}_k^\tau) + [\mathbf{f}_\mathbf{x}][\mathbf{x}_k - \hat{\mathbf{x}}_{k|k}]$$
$$+ [\mathbf{f}_\mathbf{u}][\mathbf{u}_k - \mathbf{u}_k^\tau] + \tfrac{1}{2}\sum_i \mathbf{e}^i[\mathbf{x}_k - \hat{\mathbf{x}}_{k|k}]' \mathbf{f}_{\mathbf{xx}}^i[\mathbf{x}_k - \hat{\mathbf{x}}_{k|k}]$$
$$+ \tfrac{1}{2}\sum_i \mathbf{e}^i[\mathbf{u}_k - \mathbf{u}_k^\tau]' \mathbf{f}_{\mathbf{uu}}^i[\mathbf{u}_k - \mathbf{u}_k^\tau]$$
$$+ \sum_i \mathbf{e}^i[\mathbf{u}_k - \mathbf{u}_k^\tau]' \mathbf{f}_{\mathbf{ux}}^i[\mathbf{x}_k - \hat{\mathbf{x}}_{k|k}] + \xi_k \qquad (9\text{-}10)$$

Taking the expected value of Eq. (9-10) with data through period k and setting $\mathbf{u}_k = \mathbf{u}_k^\tau$, since we wish to find $\hat{\mathbf{x}}_{k+1|k}$ conditional on $\mathbf{u}_k = \mathbf{u}_k^\tau$, yields

$$\hat{\mathbf{x}}_{k+1|k} \approx \mathbf{f}_k(\hat{\mathbf{x}}_{k|k}, \mathbf{u}_k^\tau) + \tfrac{1}{2} E\left\{ \sum_i \mathbf{e}^i[\mathbf{x}_k - \hat{\mathbf{x}}_{k|k}]' \mathbf{f}_{\mathbf{xx}}^i[\mathbf{x}_k - \hat{\mathbf{x}}_{k|k}] \right\} \qquad (9\text{-}11)$$

In Appendix B it is shown that the expected value of a quadratic form is

$$E\{\mathbf{x}'\mathbf{A}\mathbf{x}\} = \hat{\mathbf{x}}\mathbf{A}\hat{\mathbf{x}} + \mathrm{tr}\,[\mathbf{A}\Sigma] \qquad (9\text{-}12)$$

where $\hat{\mathbf{x}} = E\{\mathbf{x}\}$ and $\Sigma = \mathrm{cov}(\mathbf{x})$. The application of this result to Eq. (9-11) yields

$$\hat{\mathbf{x}}_{k+1|k} = \mathbf{f}_k(\hat{\mathbf{x}}_{k|k}, \mathbf{u}_k^\tau) + \tfrac{1}{2}\sum_i \mathbf{e}^i \,\mathrm{tr}\!\left[\mathbf{f}_{\mathbf{xx}}^i \Sigma_{k|k}\right] \qquad (9\text{-}13)$$

since $E\{\mathbf{x}_k\} = \hat{\mathbf{x}}_{k|k}$ and $\Sigma_{k|k} = E\{[\mathbf{x}_k - \hat{\mathbf{x}}_{k|k}][\mathbf{x}_k - \hat{\mathbf{x}}_{k|k}]'\}$.

Therefore, given the current statistics on $\mathbf{x}$, namely $(\hat{\mathbf{x}}_{k|k}, \Sigma_{k|k})$, and the current search value of the control $\mathbf{u}_k$, one can use Eq. (9-13) to obtain $\hat{\mathbf{x}}_{k+1|k}$, next period's state as estimated with data available through period k.

As indicated above, $\hat{\mathbf{x}}_{k+1|k}$ then provides the initial condition for the certainty-equivalence problem to find a nominal path from periods $k + 1$ to N. If the resulting certainty-equivalence problem is a quadratic linear problem, the Riccati method can be used. If the problem is a general nonlinear problem, a gradient method like the conjugate gradient used by Kendrick and Taylor (1970) or a variable-metric algorithm used by Norman and Norman (1973) can be used. Now define the nominal path as $(\mathbf{x}_{o,j+1}, \mathbf{u}_{oj})_{j=k+1}^{N-1}$ and set it equal to the certainty-equivalence path $(\mathbf{x}_{j+1}^{CE}, \mathbf{u}_j^{CE})_{j=k+1}^{N-1}$.

Second-Order Expansion of the Optimal Cost-to-Go

The optimal cost-to-go at period $k + 1$ can be written as

$$J_{N-k-1}^* = \min_{\mathbf{u}_{k+1}} E\left\{ \cdots \min_{\mathbf{u}_{N-1}} E\{ C_{N-k-1} | \mathcal{P}^{N-1} \} \cdots \mathcal{P}^{k+1} \right\} \qquad (9\text{-}14)$$

where
$$C_{N-k-1} = L_N(\mathbf{x}_N) + \sum_{j=k+1}^{N-1} L_j(\mathbf{x}_j, \mathbf{u}_j) \qquad (9\text{-}15)$$

$$\mathcal{P}^k = (\hat{\mathbf{x}}_{k|k}, \Sigma_{k|k})$$

A second-order expansion of Eq. (9-15) about the nominal path is then

$$C_{N-k-1} = C_{o,N-k-1} + \Delta C_{N-k-1} \qquad (9\text{-}16)$$

where $C_{o,N-k-1}$ are the zeroth-order terms in the expansion and ΔC_{N-k-1} are the first- and second-order terms. Then

$$C_{o,N-k-1} = L_N(\mathbf{x}_{o,N}) + \sum_{j=k+1}^{N-1} L_j(\mathbf{x}_{oj}, \mathbf{u}_{oj}) \qquad (9\text{-}17)$$

and
$$\Delta C_{N-k-1} = \mathbf{L}_{N\mathbf{x}} \delta \mathbf{x}_N + \tfrac{1}{2} \delta \mathbf{x}'_N \mathbf{L}_{N,\mathbf{xx}} \delta \mathbf{x}_N$$
$$+ \sum_{j=k+1}^{N-1} \left(\mathbf{L}'_{j\mathbf{x}} \delta \mathbf{x}_j + \tfrac{1}{2} \delta \mathbf{x}'_j \mathbf{L}_{j,\mathbf{xx}} \delta \mathbf{x}_j + \delta \mathbf{x}_j \mathbf{L}_{j,\mathbf{xu}} \delta \mathbf{u}_j \right.$$
$$\left. + \mathbf{L}'_{j\mathbf{u}} \delta \mathbf{u}_j + \tfrac{1}{2} \delta \mathbf{u}'_j \mathbf{L}_{j,\mathbf{uu}} \delta \mathbf{u}_j \right) \qquad (9\text{-}18)$$

where $\mathbf{L}_{N\mathbf{x}}$, $\mathbf{L}_{j\mathbf{x}}$, and $\mathbf{L}_{j\mathbf{u}}$ are the gradients and $\mathbf{L}_{N,\mathbf{xx}}$, $\mathbf{L}_{j,\mathbf{xx}}$, $\mathbf{L}_{j,\mathbf{xu}}$, and $\mathbf{L}_{j,\mathbf{uu}}$ are the hessians evaluated at $\mathbf{x}_{oN}$, $\mathbf{x}_{oj}$, and $\mathbf{u}_{oj}$ and

$$\delta \mathbf{x}_j = \mathbf{x}_j - \mathbf{x}_{oj} \qquad \delta \mathbf{u}_j = \mathbf{u}_j - \mathbf{u}_{oj}$$

Substitution of Eqs. (9-16) to (9-18) into Eq. (9-14) then yields an approximate optimal cost-to-go of the form

$$J^*_{N-k-1} = J^*_{o,N-k-1} + \Delta J^*_{N-k-1} \qquad (9\text{-}19)$$

where
$$J^*_{o,N-k-1} = C_{o,N-k-1} \qquad (9\text{-}20)$$

$$\Delta J^*_{N-k-1} = \min_{\delta \mathbf{u}_{k+1}} E \left\{ \cdots \min_{\delta \mathbf{u}_{N-1}} E \{ \Delta C_{N-k-1} | \mathcal{P}^{N-1} \} \cdots \mathcal{P}^{k+1} \right\} \qquad (9\text{-}21)$$

Here the motivation for dividing J^* into zeroth-order terms and first- and second-order terms becomes apparent. The expectation of the zeroth-order term is simply itself since it contains no random variables but only the nominal-path variables. The first- and second-order terms now constitute a separate optimization problem with a quadratic criterion. This criterion is maximized subject to system equations, which are constituted from the expansion of the original system equations. This can be obtained by rewriting Eq. (9-10) in perturbation form as

$$\delta \mathbf{x}_{k+1} = \mathbf{f}_\mathbf{x} \delta \mathbf{x}_k + \mathbf{f}_\mathbf{u} \delta \mathbf{u}_k$$
$$+ \sum_{i=1}^{N} \mathbf{e}^i \left(\tfrac{1}{2} \delta \mathbf{x}'_k \mathbf{f}^i_{\mathbf{xx}} \delta \mathbf{x}_k + \delta \mathbf{x}'_k \mathbf{f}^i_{\mathbf{xu}} \delta \mathbf{u}_k + \tfrac{1}{2} \delta \mathbf{u}'_k \mathbf{f}^i_{\mathbf{uu}} \delta \mathbf{u}_k \right) + \boldsymbol{\xi}_k \qquad (9\text{-}22)$$

where all the derivatives are evaluated on the nominal path and are for period k unless otherwise noted.

Now Eqs. (9-21) and (9-22) constitute a problem with a quadratic criterion and quadratic system equations. It is assumed that the solution to this problem can be represented up to second-order terms by the quadratic form

$$\Delta J^*_{N-k-1} = g_{k+1} + E\{ \mathbf{p}'_{k+1} \delta \mathbf{x}_{k+1} + \tfrac{1}{2} \delta \mathbf{x}'_{k+1} \mathbf{K}_{k+1} \delta \mathbf{x}_{k+1} | \mathcal{P}^{k+1} \} \qquad (9\text{-}23)$$

where **g**, **p**, and **K** are parameters to be determined below. Equation (9-23) embodies the important observation that the approximate optimal cost-to-go is a quadratic function of the current state of the system.

In the following section the recursion equations for the parameters **g**, **p**, and **K** will be derived, and it will be demonstrated that the assumed quadratic form (9-23) is correct.

Solution of the Perturbation Problem for J^*_{N-k-1}

In Eq. (9-8) the optimal cost-to-go was written as

$$J^*_{N-j} = \min_{\mathbf{u}_j} E\{L_j(\mathbf{x}_j, \mathbf{u}_j) + J^*_{N-j-1} | Y^j, U^{j-1}\} \tag{9-24}$$

Expanding Eq. (9-24) to second order around the path $(\mathbf{x}_{oj}, \mathbf{u}_{oj})$ yields

$$J^*_{N-j} = \min_{\delta \mathbf{u}_j} E\{L_j(\mathbf{x}_{oj}, \mathbf{u}_{oj}) + \mathbf{L}'_x \delta \mathbf{x}_j + \tfrac{1}{2}\delta \mathbf{x}'_j \mathbf{L}_{xx} \delta \mathbf{x}_j + \delta \mathbf{x}'_j \mathbf{L}_{xu} \delta \mathbf{u}_j$$
$$+ \mathbf{L}'_u \delta \mathbf{u}_j + \tfrac{1}{2} \delta \mathbf{u}'_j \mathbf{L}_{uu} \delta \mathbf{u}_j + J^*_{o,N-j-1} + \Delta J^*_{N-j-1} | Y^j, U^{j-1}\}$$

Removal of the constant terms provides

$$J^*_{N-j} - L_j(\mathbf{x}_{oj}, \mathbf{u}_{oj}) - J^*_{o,N-j-1} = \min_{\delta \mathbf{u}_j} E\{\mathbf{L}'_x \delta \mathbf{x}_j + \tfrac{1}{2}\delta \mathbf{x}'_j \mathbf{L}_{xx} \delta \mathbf{x}_j + \delta \mathbf{x}'_j \mathbf{L}_{xu} \delta \mathbf{u}_j$$
$$+ \mathbf{L}'_u \delta \mathbf{u}_j + \tfrac{1}{2} \delta \mathbf{u}'_j \mathbf{L}_{uu} \delta \mathbf{u}_j + \Delta J^*_{N-j-1} | Y^j, U^{j-1}\} \tag{9-25}$$

Substitution of the optimal cost-to-go for the perturbation problem ΔJ^*_{N-j-1} from Eq. (9-23) yields

$$\Delta J^*_{N-j} = J^*_{N-j} - J^*_{o,N-j} = \min_{\delta \mathbf{u}_j} E\{\mathbf{L}'_x \delta \mathbf{x}_j + \tfrac{1}{2}\delta \mathbf{x}'_j \mathbf{L}_{xx} \delta \mathbf{x}_j + \delta \mathbf{x}'_j \mathbf{L}_{xu} \delta \mathbf{u}_j$$
$$+ \mathbf{L}'_u \delta \mathbf{u}_j + \tfrac{1}{2} \delta \mathbf{u}'_j \mathbf{L}_{uu} \delta \mathbf{u}_j$$
$$+ E\{g_{j+1} + \mathbf{p}'_{j+1} \delta \mathbf{x}_{j+1} + \tfrac{1}{2}\delta \mathbf{x}'_j \mathbf{K}_{j+1} \delta \mathbf{x}_{j+1} | \mathcal{P}^{j+1}\} | \mathcal{P}^j\} \tag{9-26}$$

The expression above indicates the method that Bar-Shalom, Tse, and Larson (1974) use to demonstrate that the solution to the quadratic quadratic-perturbation control problem can be written as a quadratic form (9-23). No proof as such is stated, but a partial proof is given by the method of induction. It is assumed in Eq. (9-26) that the optimal cost-to-go for the perturbation problem for period $j+1$ is a quadratic form, and it is then shown that the optimal cost-to-go in period j will also be a quadratic form. The demonstration could thus be converted into a proof by showing that the optimal cost-to-go at the final time (period N) is a quadratic form. It then follows through the induction that this holds for all other time periods.

To proceed with the demonstration (and with the derivation of the recursions for **g**, **p**, and **K**) it is necessary to transform Eq. (9-26) so that it is a function of δx_j only and not of δx_{j+1} and δu_j. The method of removing these last two sets of terms is to use the second-order expansion of the system equations (9-22) to eliminate δx_{j+1} and then to find the optimal control rule for δu_j as a function of δx_j in order to eliminate the δu_j's.

Substitution of Eq. (9-22) into Eq. (9-26) yields

$$\Delta J_{N-j}^* = \min_{\delta u_j} E \bigg\{ L_x' \delta x_j + \tfrac{1}{2} \delta x_j' L_{xx} \delta x_j + \delta x_j' L_{xu} \delta u_j$$

$$+ L_u' \delta u_j + \tfrac{1}{2} \delta u_j' L_{uu} \delta u_j + g_{j+1}$$

$$+ E \bigg\{ p_{j+1}' \bigg[f_x \delta x_j + f_u \delta u_j + \sum_{i=1}^{N} e^i \big(\tfrac{1}{2} \delta x_j' f_{xx}^i \delta x_j$$

$$+ \delta x_j' f_{xu}^i \delta u_j + \tfrac{1}{2} \delta u_j' f_{uu}^i \delta u_j \big) + \xi_j \bigg]$$

$$+ \tfrac{1}{2} \bigg[f_x \delta x_j + f_u \delta u_j + \sum_{i=1}^{N} e^i \big(\tfrac{1}{2} \delta x_j' f_{xx}^i \delta x_j + \delta x_j' f_{xu}^i \delta u_j + \tfrac{1}{2} \delta u_j' f_{uu}^i \delta u_j \big) + \xi_j \bigg]'$$

$$K_{j+1} \bigg[f_x \delta x_j + f_u \delta u_j + \sum_{i=1}^{N} e^i \big(\tfrac{1}{2} \delta x_j' f_{xx}^i \delta x_j$$

$$+ \delta x_j' f_{xu}^i \delta u_j + \tfrac{1}{2} \delta u_j' f_{uu}^i \delta u_j \big) + \xi_j \bigg] \bigg| \mathcal{P}^{j+1} \bigg\} \bigg| \mathcal{P}^j \bigg\}$$

(9-27)

All derivatives, namely L_x, L_{xx}, L_{xu}, L_u, L_{uu}, f_x, f_{xx}^i, f_u, f_{uu}^i, and f_{xu}^i, are for time period j.

Now define

$$H_j \equiv L_j(x_j, u_j) + p_{j+1}' f_j \qquad (9\text{-}28)$$

so that

$$H_x = L_x + p_{j+1}' f_x \qquad H_u = L_u + p_{j+1}' f_u$$

$$H_{xx} = L_{xx} + \sum_{i=1}^{n} e^i p_{j+1}' f_{xx}^i \qquad H_{uu} = L_{uu} + \sum_{i=1}^{n} e^i p_{j+1}' f_{uu}^i \qquad (9\text{-}29)$$

$$H_{xu} = L_{xu} + \sum_{i=1}^{n} e^i p_{j+1}' f_{xu}^i$$

Then simplify Eq. (9-27) by substituting Eq. (9-29) into it and by dropping terms which are higher than second order. The result is

$$\Delta J_{N-j}^* = \min_{\delta u_j} E \big\{ H_x' \delta x_j + H_u' \delta u_j + \tfrac{1}{2} \delta x_j' H_{xx} \delta x_j$$

$$+ \delta x_j' H_{xu} \delta u_j + \tfrac{1}{2} \delta u_j' H_{uu} \delta u_j + g_{j+1}$$

$$+ E \big\{ \tfrac{1}{2} \delta x_j' f_x' K_{j+1} f_x \delta x_j + \delta x_j' f_x' K_{j+1} f_u \delta u_j + \tfrac{1}{2} \delta u_j' f_u' K_{j+1} f_u \delta u_j$$

$$+ \tfrac{1}{2} \xi_j' K_{j+1} \xi_j \big| \mathcal{P}^{j+1} \big\} \big| \mathcal{P}^j \big\}$$

(9-30)

In order to simplify Eq. (9-30) further define

$$\mathcal{H}_{xx} = \mathbf{H}_{xx} + \mathbf{f}'_x \mathbf{K}_{j+1} \mathbf{f}_x \qquad \mathcal{H}_{ux} = \mathbf{H}_{ux} + \mathbf{f}'_u \mathbf{K}_{j+1} \mathbf{f}_x \qquad \mathcal{H}_{uu} = \mathbf{H}_{uu} + \mathbf{f}'_u \mathbf{K}_{j+1} \mathbf{f}_u$$
(9-31)

Then taking the expectation over $\mathcal{P}^{j+1}$ and substituting Eq. (9-31) into Eq. (9-30) yields

$$\Delta J^*_{N-j} = \min_{\delta \mathbf{u}_j} E\{\mathbf{H}'_x \delta \mathbf{x}_j + \mathbf{H}'_u \delta \mathbf{u}_j + g_{j+1}$$

$$+ \tfrac{1}{2} \delta \mathbf{x}'_j \mathcal{H}_{xx} \delta \mathbf{x}_j + \delta \mathbf{x}'_j \mathcal{H}_{xu} \delta \mathbf{u}_j + \tfrac{1}{2} \delta \mathbf{u}'_j \mathcal{H}_{uu} \delta \mathbf{u}_j + \tfrac{1}{2} \boldsymbol{\xi}'_j \mathbf{K}_{j+1} \boldsymbol{\xi}_j | \mathcal{P}^j\}$$
(9-32)

Taking expectations over $\mathcal{P}^j$ and again using the trace operator discussed in Appendix B yields

$$\Delta J^*_{N-j} = \min_{\delta \mathbf{u}_j} \{\mathbf{H}'_x \delta \hat{\mathbf{x}}_{j|j} + \mathbf{H}'_u \delta \mathbf{u}_j + g_{j+1}$$

$$+ \tfrac{1}{2} \delta \hat{\mathbf{x}}'_{j|j} \mathcal{H}_{xx} \delta \hat{\mathbf{x}}_{j|j} + \delta \hat{\mathbf{x}}'_{j|j} \mathcal{H}_{xu} \delta \mathbf{u}_j$$

$$+ \tfrac{1}{2} \delta \mathbf{u}'_j \mathcal{H}_{uu} \delta \mathbf{u}_j + \tfrac{1}{2} \operatorname{tr}[\mathcal{H}_{xx} \boldsymbol{\Sigma}_{j|j}] + \tfrac{1}{2} \operatorname{tr}[\mathbf{K}_{j+1} \mathbf{Q}_j]\} \qquad (9\text{-}33)$$

where

$$\delta \hat{\mathbf{x}}_{j|j} = E\{\delta \mathbf{x}_j | \mathcal{P}^j\}$$

$$\boldsymbol{\Sigma}_{j|j} = E\{[\delta \mathbf{x}_j - \delta \hat{\mathbf{x}}_{j|j}][\delta \mathbf{x}_j - \delta \hat{\mathbf{x}}_{j|j}]' | \mathcal{P}^j\}$$

$$\mathbf{Q}_j = E\{\boldsymbol{\xi}_j \boldsymbol{\xi}'_j | \mathcal{P}^j\}$$

since

$$E\{\boldsymbol{\xi}_j\} = 0$$

The minimization operation in Eq. (9-33) transforms it into

$$\mathbf{H}'_u + \delta \hat{\mathbf{x}}'_{j|j} \mathcal{H}_{xu} + \delta \mathbf{u}'_j \mathcal{H}_{uu} = 0 \qquad (9\text{-}34)$$

or

$$\delta \mathbf{u}_j = -\mathcal{H}_{uu}^{-1}[\mathcal{H}'_{xu} \delta \hat{\mathbf{x}}_{j|j} + \mathbf{H}_u] \qquad (9\text{-}35)$$

which is the optimal perturbation control rule.

Substitution of Eq. (9-35) into Eq. (9-32) and dropping the minimization operator results in

$$\Delta J^*_j = E\{\mathbf{H}'_x \delta \mathbf{x}_j - \mathbf{H}'_u \mathcal{H}_{uu}^{-1} \mathcal{H}'_{xu} \delta \hat{\mathbf{x}}_{j|j} - \mathbf{H}'_u \mathcal{H}_{uu}^{-1} \mathbf{H}_u + g_{j+1} + \tfrac{1}{2} \delta \mathbf{x}'_j \mathcal{H}_{xx} \delta \mathbf{x}_j$$

$$- \delta \mathbf{x}'_j \mathcal{H}_{xu} \mathcal{H}_{uu}^{-1} \mathcal{H}'_{xu} \delta \hat{\mathbf{x}}_{j|j} - \delta \mathbf{x}'_j \mathcal{H}_{xu} \mathcal{H}_{uu}^{-1} \mathbf{H}_u$$

$$+ \tfrac{1}{2}[(\mathbf{H}'_u + \delta \hat{\mathbf{x}}'_{j|j} \mathcal{H}_{xu}) \mathcal{H}_{uu}^{-1}] \mathcal{H}_{uu}[\mathcal{H}_{uu}^{-1}(\mathcal{H}'_{ux} \delta \hat{\mathbf{x}}_{j|j} + \mathbf{H}_u)]$$

$$+ \tfrac{1}{2} \boldsymbol{\xi}'_j \mathbf{K}_{j+1} \boldsymbol{\xi}_j | \mathcal{P}^j\} \qquad (9\text{-}36)$$

Next define

$$\mathcal{Q}_{xx} = \mathcal{H}'_{ux} \mathcal{H}_{uu}^{-1} \mathcal{H}_{ux} \qquad (9\text{-}37)$$

Then substitute Eq. (9-37) into Eq. (9-36) and collect terms to obtain

$$\Delta J^*_{N-j} = E\{g_{j+1} - \tfrac{1}{2}\mathbf{H}'_u \mathcal{H}^{-1}_{uu} \mathbf{H}_u + (\mathbf{H}_x - \mathcal{H}'_{xu}\mathcal{H}^{-1}_{uu}\mathbf{H}_u)' \delta\mathbf{x}_j + \tfrac{1}{2}\delta\mathbf{x}'_j \mathcal{H}_{xx} \delta\mathbf{x}_j$$
$$- \delta\mathbf{x}'_j \mathcal{C}_{xx} \delta\hat{\mathbf{x}}_{j|j} + \tfrac{1}{2}\delta\hat{\mathbf{x}}'_{j|j} \mathcal{C}_{xx} \delta\hat{\mathbf{x}}_{j|j} + \tfrac{1}{2}\boldsymbol{\xi}'_j \mathbf{K}_j \boldsymbol{\xi}_j | \mathcal{P}^j\} \qquad (9\text{-}38)$$

Removal of the constant terms from the expectation leaves (also using $\mathcal{H}'_{xu} = \mathcal{H}_{ux}$)

$$\Delta J^*_{N-j} = g_{j+1} - \tfrac{1}{2}\mathbf{H}'_u \mathcal{H}^{-1}_{uu} \mathbf{H}_u + \tfrac{1}{2}\operatorname{tr}\left[\mathbf{K}_{j+1}\mathbf{Q}_j\right]$$
$$+ E\{[\mathbf{H}_x - \mathcal{H}'_{ux}\mathcal{H}^{-1}_{uu}\mathbf{H}_u]'\delta\mathbf{x}_j + \tfrac{1}{2}\delta\mathbf{x}'_j \mathcal{H}_{xx} \delta\mathbf{x}_j | \mathcal{P}^j\} - \tfrac{1}{2}\delta\hat{\mathbf{x}}'_{j|j} \mathcal{C}_{xx} \hat{\mathbf{x}}_{j|j}$$
$$(9\text{-}39)$$

Now recall from the discussion of the trace operator in Appendix B that

$$E\{\delta\mathbf{x}'_j \mathcal{C}_{xx} \delta\mathbf{x}_j | \mathcal{P}^j\} = \delta\hat{\mathbf{x}}'_{j|j} \mathcal{C}_{xx} \delta\hat{\mathbf{x}}_{j|j} + \operatorname{tr}\left[\mathcal{C}_{xx} \boldsymbol{\Sigma}_{j|j}\right] \qquad (9\text{-}40)$$

Solving Eq. (9-40) for the $\delta\hat{\mathbf{x}}' \mathcal{C} \delta\hat{\mathbf{x}}$ term and substituting the result back into Eq. (9-39) yields

$$\Delta J^*_{N-j} = g_{j+1} - \tfrac{1}{2}\mathbf{H}'_u \mathcal{H}^{-1}_{uu} \mathbf{H}_u + \tfrac{1}{2}\operatorname{tr}\left[\mathbf{K}_{j+1}\mathbf{Q}_j + \mathcal{C}_{xx}\boldsymbol{\Sigma}_{j|j}\right]$$
$$+ E\{(\mathbf{H}_x - \mathcal{H}'_{ux}\mathcal{H}^{-1}_{uu}\mathbf{H}_u)'\delta\mathbf{x}_j + \tfrac{1}{2}\delta\mathbf{x}'_j \mathcal{H}_{xx}\delta\mathbf{x}_j | \mathcal{P}^j\}$$
$$- \tfrac{1}{2}E\{\delta\mathbf{x}'_j \mathcal{C}_{xx}\delta\mathbf{x}_j | \mathcal{P}^j\} \qquad (9\text{-}41)$$

or

$$\Delta J^*_{N-j} = g_j + E\{\mathbf{p}'_j \delta\mathbf{x}_j + \tfrac{1}{2}\delta\mathbf{x}'_j \mathbf{K}_j \delta\mathbf{x}_j | \mathcal{P}^j\} \qquad (9\text{-}42)$$

where

$$g_j = g_{j+1} - \tfrac{1}{2}\mathbf{H}'_u \mathcal{H}^{-1}_{uu} \mathbf{H}_u + \tfrac{1}{2}\operatorname{tr}\left[\mathbf{K}_{j+1}\mathbf{Q}_j + \mathcal{C}_{xx}\boldsymbol{\Sigma}_{j|j}\right] \qquad (9\text{-}43)$$

$$\mathbf{p}_j = \mathbf{H}_x - \mathcal{H}'_{ux}\mathcal{H}^{-1}_{uu}\mathbf{H}_u \qquad (9\text{-}44)$$

and

$$\mathbf{K}_j = \mathcal{H}_{xx} - \mathcal{C}_{xx} \qquad (9\text{-}45)$$

Expression (9-42), which gives the approximate optimal cost-to-go at time j for the perturbation problem, is a quadratic function of the state of the system at time j. Thus the induction has shown that if the approximate optimal cost-to-go at time $j + 1$ is quadratic, it will also be quadratic at time j. Also expressions (9-43) to (9-45) provide the recursions on g, p, and K which were sought.

Slightly different expressions of the recursions on g, p, and K are given in Bar-Shalom, Tse, and Larson (1974) and in Tse, Bar-Shalom, and Meier (1973). Since both sets of results will be used in this book, Appendix C shows the equivalence of the two sets of recursions.

Partial Solution of the g Recursion

Expressions (9-42) to (9-45) provide a method of calculating the perturbation approximate cost-to-go, i.e., the approximate cost-to-go for the first- and second-order terms in the Taylor expansion. These terms can be added to the zeroth-order term in the expansion to get the full approximate cost-to-go. However, before doing that it is useful to partially solve the difference equation for g in order to provide a clear separation of the stochastic terms from the nonstochastic terms in it.

In order to solve Eq. (9-43) define

$$A_j \equiv \tfrac{1}{2} \mathbf{H}'_{\mathbf{u}j} \mathcal{K}^{-1}_{\mathbf{uu},j} \mathbf{H}_{\mathbf{u}j} \tag{9-46}$$

and

$$B_j \equiv \tfrac{1}{2} \operatorname{tr}\left[\mathbf{K}_{j+1} \mathbf{Q}_j + \mathcal{Q}_{\mathbf{xx}} \Sigma_{j|j} \right] \tag{9-47}$$

so that Eq. (9-43) can be written as

$$g_j = g_{j+1} - A_j + B_j \tag{9-48}$$

Then solve Eq. (9-48) by working backward from period N

$$g_{N-1} = g_N - A_{N-1} + B_{N-1} \tag{9-49}$$

$$g_{N-2} = g_{N-1} - A_{N-2} + B_{N-2} \tag{9-50}$$

Then substitute Eq. (9-49) into Eq. (9-50) to obtain

$$g_{N-2} = g_N - A_{N-1} + B_{N-1} - A_{N-2} + B_{N-2}$$

$$= g_N - \sum_{j=N-2}^{N-1} A_j + \sum_{j=N-2}^{N-1} B_j \tag{9-51}$$

or in general

$$g_{N-k} = g_N - \sum_{j=N-k}^{N-1} A_j + \sum_{j=N-k}^{N-1} B_j \tag{9-52}$$

so the g difference equation has been solved for both the A and the B; however, it was desired only to solve it partially for the B term. Therefore we define

$$\gamma_j \equiv \gamma_{j+1} - A_j \qquad \gamma_N = 0 \tag{9-53}$$

or

$$\gamma_{N-1} = \gamma_N - A_{N-1} \tag{9-54}$$

$$\gamma_{N-2} = \gamma_{N-1} - A_{N-2} = \gamma_N - A_{N-1} - A_{N-2} \tag{9-55}$$

or in general

$$\gamma_{N-k} = \gamma_N - \sum_{j=N-k}^{N-1} A_j = - \sum_{j=N-k}^{N-1} A_j \tag{9-56}$$

Substitution of Eq. (9-56) into Eq. (9-52) yields

$$g_{N-k} = g_N + \gamma_{N-k} + \sum_{j=N-k}^{N-1} B_j \tag{9-57}$$

Then the use of the fact that $g_N = 0$ and substitution of the definition of B in Eq. (9-47) back into Eq. (9-57) results in

$$g_{N-k} = \gamma_{N-k} + \frac{1}{2} \sum_{j=N-k}^{N-1} \operatorname{tr}\left[\mathbf{K}_{j+1} \mathbf{Q}_j + \mathcal{Q}_{\mathbf{xx}} \Sigma_{j|j} \right] \tag{9-58}$$

or

$$g_{k+1} = \gamma_{k+1} + \frac{1}{2} \sum_{j=k+1}^{N-1} \operatorname{tr}\left[\mathbf{K}_{j+1} \mathbf{Q}_j + \mathcal{Q}_{\mathbf{xx}} \Sigma_{j|j} \right] \tag{9-59}$$

where

$$\gamma_k \equiv \gamma_{k+1} - \tfrac{1}{2} \mathbf{H}'_{\mathbf{u},k} \mathcal{K}^{-1}_{\mathbf{uu},k} \mathbf{H}_{\mathbf{u},k} \tag{9-60}$$

9-5 OBTAINING A DETERMINISTIC APPROXIMATION FOR THE COST-TO-GO

Substitution of Eq. (9-59) into the perturbation cost-to-go expression (9-23) yields

$$\Delta J^*_{N-k-1} = \gamma_{k+1} + \frac{1}{2} \sum_{j=k+1}^{N-1} \text{tr}\left[\mathbf{K}_{j+1}\mathbf{Q}_j + \mathcal{Q}_{xx}\Sigma_{j|j}\right]$$
$$+ E\left\{\mathbf{p}'_{k+1}\delta\mathbf{x}_{k+1} + \tfrac{1}{2}\delta\mathbf{x}'_{k+1}\mathbf{K}_{k+1}\delta\mathbf{x}_{k+1} \,\middle|\, \mathcal{P}^{k+1}\right\} \quad (9\text{-}61)$$

Expression (9-61) then provides the optimal perturbation cost-to-go (the first- and second-order terms in the Taylor expansion). Next this term is added to the zeroth-order term (9-20). So substitution of Eqs. (9-61) and (9-20) into Eq. (9-19) yields

$$J^*_{N-k-1} = C_{o,N-k-1} + \gamma_{k+1} + \frac{1}{2}\sum_{j=k+1}^{N-1}\text{tr}\left[\mathbf{K}_{j+1}\mathbf{Q}_j + \mathcal{Q}_{xx}\Sigma_{j|j}\right]$$
$$+ E\left\{\mathbf{p}'_{k+1}\delta\mathbf{x}_{k+1} + \tfrac{1}{2}\delta\mathbf{x}'_{k+1}\mathbf{K}_{k+1}\delta\mathbf{x}_{k+1} \,\middle|\, \mathcal{P}^{k+1}\right\} \quad (9\text{-}62)$$

which is the approximate optimal cost-to-go at period $k+1$.

Substitution of Eq. (9-62) into Eq. (9-8) provides the optimal cost-to-go at period k,

$$J^*_{N-k} = \min_{\mathbf{u}_k} E\Bigg\{ L_k(\mathbf{x}_k,\mathbf{u}_k) + C_{o,N-k-1} + \gamma_{k+1}$$
$$+ \frac{1}{2}\sum_{j=k+1}^{N-1}\text{tr}\left[\mathbf{K}_{j+1}\mathbf{Q}'_j + \mathcal{Q}_{xx}\Sigma_{j|j}\right]$$
$$+ E\left\{\mathbf{p}'_{k+1}\delta\mathbf{x}_{k+1} + \tfrac{1}{2}\delta\mathbf{x}'_{k+1}\mathbf{K}_{k+1}\delta\mathbf{x}_{k+1} \,\middle|\, \mathcal{P}^{k+1}\right\} \,\bigg|\, \mathcal{P}^k\Bigg\} \quad (9\text{-}63)$$

Next use the result that

$$E\left\{E\left\{\mathbf{p}'_{k+1}\delta\mathbf{x}_{k+1} + \tfrac{1}{2}\delta\mathbf{x}'_{k+1}\mathbf{K}_{k+1}\delta\mathbf{x}_{k+1} \,\middle|\, \mathcal{P}^{k+1}\right\} \,\middle|\, \mathcal{P}^k\right\}$$
$$= E\left\{\mathbf{p}'_{k+1}\delta\mathbf{x}_{k+1} + \tfrac{1}{2}\delta\mathbf{x}'_{k+1}\mathbf{K}_{k+1}\delta\mathbf{x}_{k+1} \,\middle|\, \mathcal{P}^k\right\}$$
$$(9\text{-}64)$$

i.e., since $\mathcal{P}^{k+1} \supset \mathcal{P}^k$, the expression reduces to one taken over the smaller set. Then

$$E\left\{\mathbf{p}'_{k+1}\delta\mathbf{x}_{k+1} \,\middle|\, \mathcal{P}^k\right\} = \mathbf{p}'_{k+1}E\left\{\delta\mathbf{x}_{k+1} \,\middle|\, \mathcal{P}^k\right\} = 0 \quad (9\text{-}65)$$

and $E\left\{\tfrac{1}{2}\delta\mathbf{x}'_{k+1}\mathbf{K}_{k+1}\delta\mathbf{x}_{k+1} \,\middle|\, \mathcal{P}^k\right\} = \tfrac{1}{2}\delta\hat{\mathbf{x}}'_{k+1|k}\mathbf{K}_{k+1}\delta\hat{\mathbf{x}}_{k+1|k} + \tfrac{1}{2}\text{tr}\left[\mathbf{K}_{k+1}\Sigma_{k+1|k}\right]$
$$= \tfrac{1}{2}\text{tr}\left[\mathbf{K}_{k+1}\Sigma_{k+1|k}\right] \quad (9\text{-}66)$$

since $\delta\hat{\mathbf{x}}_{k+1|k} = 0$ from Eq. (9-65). Substituting the results of Eqs. (9-64) to

(9-66) into Eq. (9-63) and taking the expectation over the remaining terms yields

$$J^*_{N-k} = \min_{\mathbf{u}_k} \left\{ L_k(\mathbf{x}_k, \mathbf{u}_k) + C_{o,N-k-1} + \gamma_{k+1} \right.$$

$$\left. + \frac{1}{2} \sum_{j=k+1}^{N-1} \operatorname{tr}\left[\mathbf{K}_{j+1}\mathbf{Q}_j + \mathcal{Q}_{\mathbf{xx}}\Sigma_{j|j}\right] + \frac{1}{2}\operatorname{tr}\left[\mathbf{K}_{k+1}\Sigma_{k+1|k}\right]\right\} \quad (9\text{-}67)$$

The reader may recall that a search is made over values of $\mathbf{u}_k$ in order to find the minimum of the function (9-67). Since $\mathbf{x}_k$ does not depend on $\mathbf{u}_k$, we can drop this term, leaving only the terms which are dependent on $\mathbf{u}_k$ in Eq. (9-3), i.e.,

$$J^*_{d,N-k} = \min_{\mathbf{u}_k} \left\{ \omega_k(\mathbf{x}_k, \mathbf{u}_k) + \phi_k(\mathbf{u}_k) + C_{o,N-k-1} + \gamma_{k+1} \right.$$

$$\left. + \frac{1}{2}\operatorname{tr}\left[\mathbf{K}_{k+1}\Sigma_{k+1|k}\right] + \frac{1}{2}\sum_{j=k+1}^{N-1}\operatorname{tr}\left[\mathbf{K}_{j+1}\mathbf{Q}_j + \mathcal{Q}_{\mathbf{xx}}\Sigma_{j|j}\right]\right\} \quad (9\text{-}68)$$

where $J^*_{d,N-k}$ is the optimal cost-to-go, which is dependent on $\mathbf{u}_k$.

The expression (9-68) can then be used in the search to find the best choice of $\mathbf{u}_k$ at period k. Alternatively,

$$J^*_{d,N-k} = \min_{\mathbf{u}_k} \left\{ \omega_k(\mathbf{x}_k, \mathbf{u}_k) + \phi_k(\mathbf{u}_k) + J_{o,N-k-1} + \gamma_{k+1} \right.$$

$$+ \frac{1}{2}\operatorname{tr}\left\{ (\Sigma_{k+1|k} - \Sigma_{k+1|k+1})\mathbf{K}_{k+1} + \psi_{o,\mathbf{xx}}\Sigma_{N|N} \right.$$

$$\left.\left. + \sum_{j=k+1}^{N-1}\left[\mathbf{H}_{\mathbf{xx},j}\Sigma_{j|j} + (\Sigma_{j+1|j} - \Sigma_{j+1|j+1})\mathbf{K}_{j+1}\right]\right\}\right\} \quad (9\text{-}69)$$

can be used in the search, since Eq. (9-69) is equivalent to Eq. (9-68).[1] The derivation of Eq. (9-69) from Eq. (9-68) is given in Appendix E.

In order to evaluate either (9-68) or (9-69) one needs the values of $(\Sigma_{j|j})_{j=k+1}^{N-1}$. The next section outlines the method used to project these covariance matrices.

9-6 PROJECTION OF COVARIANCE MATRICES

When projections of economic data are made to compute both future means and variances, one ordinarily finds a rapidly growing variance so that the confidence which can be attached to predictions in the distant future is sharply limited. The

---

[1] Expression (9-69) is the same as the cost-to-go in Tse, Bar-Shalom, and Meier (1973). Expression (9-68) is the same as the cost-to-go in Bar-Shalom, Tse, and Larson (1974).

same phenomenon would occur here except for the fact that it is assumed that future measurements will be made. So the dynamics and the system-equation noise cause the variance to increase and the measurements cause the variance to decrease. Also the noise in the measurement equation modifies the ability of the measurements to decrease the variance.

These notions are embodied in the mathematical model in the distinction between

$$\Sigma_{k+1|k} = E\{[\mathbf{x}_{k+1} - \hat{\mathbf{x}}_{k+1|k}][\mathbf{x}_{k+1} - \hat{\mathbf{x}}_{k+1|k}]'|\mathbf{Y}^k\} \quad (9\text{-}70)$$

and
$$\Sigma_{k+1|k+1} = E\{[\mathbf{x}_{k+1} - \hat{\mathbf{x}}_{k+1|k+1}][\mathbf{x}_{k+1} - \hat{\mathbf{x}}_{k+1|k+1}]'|\mathbf{Y}^{k+1}\} \quad (9\text{-}71)$$

where
$$\hat{\mathbf{x}}_{k+1|k} = E\{\mathbf{x}_{k+1}|\mathbf{Y}^k\}$$

and
$$\hat{\mathbf{x}}_{k+1|k+1} = E\{\mathbf{x}_{k+1}|\mathbf{Y}^{k+1}\} \quad \text{for } \mathbf{Y}^k = (\mathbf{y}_j)_{j=1}^k$$

That is, $\Sigma_{k+1|k}$ is the covariance matrix in period $k + 1$ calculated from observations through period k, and $\Sigma_{k+1|k+1}$ is the covariance matrix in period $k + 1$ as calculated with observations through period $k + 1$.

Consider first the method of obtaining $\Sigma_{k+1|k}$. To do so one can use the system equations (9-4), make a second-order expansion of them as in Eq. (9-10), and set $\mathbf{u}_k = \mathbf{u}_k^\dagger$ to obtain

$$\mathbf{x}_{k+1} \approx \mathbf{f}_k(\hat{\mathbf{x}}_{k|k}, \mathbf{u}_k^\tau) + \mathbf{f}_\mathbf{x}[\mathbf{x}_k - \hat{\mathbf{x}}_{k|k}]$$
$$+ \tfrac{1}{2}\sum_i \mathbf{e}^i[\mathbf{x}_k - \hat{\mathbf{x}}_{k|k}]'\mathbf{f}_{\mathbf{xx}}^i[\mathbf{x}_k - \hat{\mathbf{x}}_{k|k}] + \boldsymbol{\xi}_k \quad (9\text{-}72)$$

Also, the mean-value term $\hat{\mathbf{x}}_{k+1|k}$ was obtained earlier in Eq. (9-13) as

$$\hat{\mathbf{x}}_{k+1|k} \approx \mathbf{f}_k[\hat{\mathbf{x}}_{k|k}, \mathbf{u}_k^\tau] + \tfrac{1}{2}\sum_i \mathbf{e}^i \operatorname{tr}[\mathbf{f}_{\mathbf{xx}}^i \Sigma_{k|k}] \quad (9\text{-}73)$$

Then using Eqs. (9-72) and (9-73), we have

$$\mathbf{x}_{k+1} - \hat{\mathbf{x}}_{k+1|k} = \mathbf{f}_\mathbf{x}[\mathbf{x}_k - \hat{\mathbf{x}}_{k|k}] + \tfrac{1}{2}\sum_i \mathbf{e}^i[\mathbf{x}_k - \hat{\mathbf{x}}_{k|k}]'\mathbf{f}_{\mathbf{xx}}^i[\mathbf{x}_k - \hat{\mathbf{x}}_{k|k}]$$
$$+ \boldsymbol{\xi}_k - \tfrac{1}{2}\sum_i \mathbf{e}^i \operatorname{tr}[\mathbf{f}_{\mathbf{xx}}^i \Sigma_{k|k}] \quad (9\text{-}74)$$

The use of Eq. (9-74) in Eq. (9-70) yields

$$\Sigma_{k+1|k} = E\{[\mathbf{x}_{k+1} - \hat{\mathbf{x}}_{k+1|k}][\mathbf{x}_{k+1} - \hat{\mathbf{x}}_{k+1|k}]'\}$$
$$= E\{\mathbf{f}_\mathbf{x}'[\mathbf{x}_k - \hat{\mathbf{x}}_{k|k}][\mathbf{x}_k - \hat{\mathbf{x}}_{k|k}]'\mathbf{f}_\mathbf{x}\}$$
$$+ \tfrac{1}{4}E\left\{\left[\sum_i \mathbf{e}^i[\mathbf{x}_k - \hat{\mathbf{x}}_{k|k}]'\mathbf{f}_{\mathbf{xx}}^i[\mathbf{x}_k - \hat{\mathbf{x}}_{k|k}]\right]\right.$$
$$\left.\times \left[\sum_j \mathbf{e}^j[\mathbf{x}_k - \hat{\mathbf{x}}_{k|k}]'\mathbf{f}_{\mathbf{xx}}^j[\mathbf{x}_k - \hat{\mathbf{x}}_{k|k}]\right]'\right\}$$

$$+ E\{\xi_k \xi_k'\} + \tfrac{1}{4} E\left\{ \left[\sum_i e^i \operatorname{tr}\left[f_{xx}^i \Sigma_{k|k} \right] \right] \left[\sum_j e^j \operatorname{tr}\left[f_{xx}^j \Sigma_{k|k} \right] \right]' \right\}$$

$$- \tfrac{1}{2} E\left\{ \left[\sum_i e^i [x_k - \hat{x}_{k|k}]' f_{xx}^i [x_k - \hat{x}_{k|k}] \right] \left[\sum e^i \operatorname{tr}\left[f_{xx}^i \Sigma_{k|k} \right] \right]' \right\}$$

(9-75)

since the other cross terms are equal to zero after expectations are taken. Next Eq. (9-75) can be rewritten as

$$\Sigma_{k+1|k} = f_x' \Sigma_{k|k} f_x + \tfrac{1}{4} \sum_i \sum_j e^i e^{j\prime} E\left\{ \left[[x_k - \hat{x}_{k|k}]' f_{xx}^i [x_k - x_{k|k}]\right] \right.$$

$$\left. \times \left[[x_k - \hat{x}_{k|k}]' f_{xx}^j [x_k - \hat{x}_{k|k}]\right]'\right\}$$

$$+ Q_k + \tfrac{1}{4} \left[\sum_i e^i \operatorname{tr}\left[f_{xx}^i \Sigma_{k|k} \right] \right] \left[\sum_j e^j \operatorname{tr}\left[f_{xx}^j \Sigma_{k|k} \right] \right]'$$

$$- \tfrac{1}{2} \left[\sum_j e^j \operatorname{tr}\left[f_{xx}^j \Sigma_{k|k} \right] \right] \left[\sum_i e^i \operatorname{tr}\left[f_{xx}^i \Sigma_{k|k} \right] \right]'$$

(9-76)

Using the result derived in Appendix F that

$$E[(x'Ax)(x'Bx)] = 2 \operatorname{tr}[A\Sigma B\Sigma] + \operatorname{tr}[A\Sigma]\operatorname{tr}[B\Sigma]$$

one obtains[1]

$$\tfrac{1}{4} \sum_i \sum_j e^i e^{j\prime} E\left\{ \left[[x_k - \hat{x}_{k|k}]' f_{xx}^i [x_k - \hat{x}_{k|k}]\right]\left[[x_k - \hat{x}_{k|k}]' f_{xx}^j [x_k - \hat{x}_{k|k}]\right]'\right\}$$

$$= \tfrac{1}{2} \sum_i \sum_j e^i e^{j\prime} \operatorname{tr}\left[f_{xx}^i \Sigma_{k|k} f_{xx}^j \Sigma_{k|k} \right] + \tfrac{1}{4} \sum_i \sum_j e^i e^{j\prime} \operatorname{tr}\left[f_{xx}^i \Sigma_{k|k} \right] \operatorname{tr}\left[f_{xx}^j \Sigma_{k|k} \right]$$

(9-77)

Substitution of Eq. (9-77) into Eq. (9-76) yields

$$\Sigma_{k+1|k} = f_x \Sigma_{k|k} f_x' + Q_k + \tfrac{1}{2} \sum_i \sum_j e^i e^{j\prime} \operatorname{tr}\left[f_{xx}^i \Sigma_{k|k} f_{xx}^j \Sigma_{k|k} \right] \qquad (9\text{-}78)$$

This expression propagates the covariance one period forward through the system equations.

The next step is to devise an expression for $\Sigma_{k+1|k+1}$ based on a knowledge of $\Sigma_{k+1|k}$ and on the covariance of the measurement noise R_{k+1}. This is done by applying the method of the Kalman filter to the measurement equation (9-5)

$$y_k = h_k(x_k) + \zeta_k \qquad (9\text{-}79)$$

---

[1] This result is given in Athans, Wishner, and Bertolini [1968 eq. (48)].

A first-order Taylor expansion of this equation is

$$y_k = h(x_{o,k}) + h_{x,k}[x_k - x_{o,k}] + \zeta_k \tag{9-80}$$

or
$$\delta y_k = h_{x,k} \delta x_k + \zeta_k \tag{9-81}$$

and the $(k+1)$th-period version of Eq. (9-81) is

$$\delta y_{k+1} = h_{x,k+1} \delta x_{k+1} + \zeta_{k+1} \tag{9-82}$$

At the time when the measurement relationship (9-82) is used, the covariance matrix for δx_{k+1},

$$\Sigma_{k+1|k} = E\{[x_{k+1} - \hat{x}_{k+1|k}][x_{k+1} - \hat{x}_{k+1|k}]'|Y^k\} \tag{9-83}$$

is known from Eq. (9-78) above, and the covariance matrix for ζ_{k+1} is given as R.

In Appendix D the Kalman filter for a linear observation equation like Eq. (9-82) is derived following the method given in Bryson and Ho (1969). The notational equivalence between the appendix and Eqs. (9-82) and (9-83) is given in Table 9-1. The result obtained in Appendix D as (D-41) is

$$\Sigma = M - [Mh_x]\left[h'_x Mh_x + R + \frac{1}{2}\sum_i \sum_j e^i e^{j\prime} \operatorname{tr}\left[h^i_{xx} M h^j_{xx} M\right]\right]^{-1}[h'_x M]$$

so the equivalent result for Eqs. (9-82) to (9-83) is

$$\Sigma_{k+1|k+1} = [I - V_{k+1} h'_{x,k+1}]\Sigma_{k+1|k} \tag{9-84}$$

where

$$V_{k+1} = \Sigma_{k+1|k} h'_{x,k+1}$$

$$\times \left[h'_{x,k+1}\Sigma_{k+1|k} h_{x,k+1} + R_{k+1} + \frac{1}{2}\sum_i\sum_j e^i e^{j\prime} \operatorname{tr}\left(h^i_{xx}\Sigma_{k+1|k} h^j_{xx}\Sigma_{k+1|k}\right)\right]^{-1}$$

$$\tag{9-85}$$

Table 9-1 Notational equivalence

Equation (D-17)	Eqs. (9-82) and (9-83)
$z = Hx + v$	$\delta y_{k+1} = h_{x,k+1}\delta x_{k+1} + \zeta_{k+1}$
z	δy_{k+1}
H or h_x	$h_{x,k+1}$
x	δx_{k+1}
v	ζ_{k+1}
$M = \operatorname{cov}(x)$	$\Sigma_{k+1|k} = \operatorname{cov}(\delta x_{k+1}|Y^k)$
$\Sigma = \operatorname{cov}(x|z)$	$\Sigma_{k+1|k+1} = \operatorname{cov}(\delta x_{k+1}|Y^{k+1})$
$R = \operatorname{cov}(v)$	$R = \operatorname{cov}(\zeta_{k+1})$

Expressions (9-84) and (9-85) provide a means of determining $\Sigma_{k+1|k+1}$ from $\Sigma_{k+1|k}$, and Eq. (9-78) can be used to determine $\Sigma_{k+1|k}$ from $\Sigma_{k|k}$. These expressions taken together enable one to make a projection of the state covariance matrix which takes into account (1) the process noise, (2) the measurement noise, and (3) the fact of future measurements.

Examination of Eq. (9-78) shows that the greater the premeasurement state and the state covariance $\Sigma_{k|k}$ the greater the premeasurement state covariance $\Sigma_{k+1|k}$ in the next period. Also Eq. (9-84) shows that the postmeasurement covariance matrix in the next period $\Sigma_{k+1|k+1}$ will be the same as the premeasurement covariance $\Sigma_{k+1|k}$ except that it is decreased by the term $\mathbf{Vh_x}$. Of course $\mathbf{h_x}$ is determined by the nature of the measurement function. $\mathbf{V}$ in turn depends inversely on the measurement-noise covariance $\mathbf{R}$, as shown in Eq. (9-85). Thus the larger $\mathbf{R}$ the smaller the decrease in the state-covariance matrix by the measurement process. Also the larger the premeasurement covariance $\Sigma_{k+1|k}$ the less effective the measurement in reducing the state covariance.

So Eqs. (9-78), (9-84), and (9-85) can be used to project $(\Sigma_{j|j})_{j=k+1}^{N-1}$ beginning from $\Sigma_{k|k}$. These covariance matrices can be used in Eqs. (9-68) or (9-69), along with other terms which are already known, in order to compute the approximate cost-to-go associated with each choice of the control variable $\mathbf{u}_k$ in the search to find that $\mathbf{u}_k$ which provides the minimum cost-to-go. This then completes the discussion of what is done in each time period to find the control $\mathbf{u}_k$ to apply at that period.

9-7 SUMMARY OF THE SEARCH FOR THE OPTIMAL CONTROL IN PERIOD k

In brief summary, the method is to do a search on $\mathbf{u}_k$ by evaluating the cost-to-go [Eq. (9-68)] for each choice of $\mathbf{u}_k$ and then selecting that value of $\mathbf{u}_k$ which minimizes the cost-to-go. The evaluation of Eq. (9-68) requires (1) the solution of the certainty-equivalence problem about a path beginning from $\mathbf{x}_{k+1}$ (which is obtained by applying the current search value of $\mathbf{u}_k$ to the process equations), (2) the evaluation of matrices of partial derivatives along that certainty-equivalence path, and (3) the projection of the covariance matrices Σ for all future time periods. Since all three of the steps must be repeated each time a search value of $\mathbf{u}_k$ is chosen, the evaluation of Eq. (9-68) for each $\mathbf{u}_k$ is a computationally expensive process.

After this control has been chosen, it is applied and the new state $\mathbf{x}_{k+1}$ is determined with the passage of time and the effect of the control. Then an estimate is made of the mean and covariance of the new state of the system, and the search for the optimal control for the next period is begun. The next section provides a discussion of the procedure for *updating* the estimates of the mean and covariance of the system. This is to be distinguished from the process of *projecting* the covariance matrix Σ for all future time periods. The first process will be called updating and the second process will be referred to as projecting.

Tse, Bar-Shalom, and Meier (1973) use the same Kalman filter approach for both updating and projecting Σ; however, that need not necessarily be done. Since the projection must be done as many times as there are search steps in each time period while the updating is done only once each time period, more sophisticated and time-consuming methods for each estimation may be used for updating than for projecting.

9-8 UPDATING THE COVARIANCE MATRIX

Here the second-order Kalman filter method is used for both updating and projection. This method is outlined in Appendix D. The results of this appendix provide the mean and covariance of the state conditional on the measurement, i.e., Eqs. (D-39) and (D-41). Writing these expressions in the notation of the present problem provides

$$\hat{x}_{k+1|k+1} = E\{x_{k+1}|y_{k+1}\}'$$

$$= \hat{x}_{k+1|k} + V_{k+1}[y_{k+1} - h_{x,k+1}\hat{x}_{k+1|k}] \quad (9\text{-}86)$$

$$\Sigma_{k+1|k+1} = [I - V_{k+1}h_{x,k+1}]\Sigma_{k+1|k} \quad (9\text{-}87)$$

where V_{k+1} is defined in Eq. (9-85) and, from Eq. (9-13),

$$\hat{x}_{k+1|k} = f_k(\hat{x}_{k|k}, u_k^*) + \tfrac{1}{2}\sum_i e^i \operatorname{tr}\left[f_{xx}^i \Sigma_{k|k}\right] \quad (9\text{-}88)$$

with u_k^* the optimal control from the search in period k.

9-9 SUMMARY OF THE ALGORITHM

The algorithm begins at period k with estimates of the mean $\hat{x}_{k|k}$ and covariance $\Sigma_{k|k}$ given. A search is then begun to find the optimal control u_k^* to be used in period k. For each trial choice of u_k the optimal cost-to-go function (9-68) is evaluated, and this process is continued until satisfactory convergence is obtained.

The evaluation of Eq. (9-68) involves the steps discussed in Sec. 9-7. After the control u_k^* has been chosen, it is applied to the system and the process is moved one step forward in time. Then a new measure y_k is taken, and updated estimates of the mean and covariance of the state are calculated. Then the search process for the best control for that period is begun.

CHAPTER
TEN

QUADRATIC LINEAR ACTIVE-LEARNING STOCHASTIC CONTROL

with
Bo Hyun Kang

10-1 INTRODUCTION

This chapter applies the algorithm of Chap. 9 to the special case of a problem with a quadratic criterion function and linear system equations. It also provides a detailed derivation and explication of the results in Tse and Bar-Shalom (1973) and extends those results to (1) criterion functions which include a term in the product of state and control variables, (2) system equations in which there is an explicit constant term, and (3) controls **u** which are a vector rather than a scalar.

10-2 PROBLEM STATEMENT

Original System

The problem is to find the values of control variables in a set of linear system equations which will minimize the expected value of a quadratic criterion function when the parameters of the system equations are unknown. Also, the state variables are observed not directly but through a noisy measurement process. This problem can be written as follows:

Select $\mathbf{u}^{N-1} = (\mathbf{u}_k)_{k=0}^{N-1}$ to minimize the cost functional

$$J = E\left\{ L_N(\mathbf{x}_N) + \sum_{k=1}^{N-1} L_k(\mathbf{x}_k, \mathbf{u}_k) \right\} \quad (10\text{-}1)$$

where
$$L_N(\mathbf{x}_N) = \tfrac{1}{2}[\mathbf{x}_N - \tilde{\mathbf{x}}_N]'\mathbf{W}_N[\mathbf{x}_N - \tilde{\mathbf{x}}_N] \quad (10\text{-}2)$$

$$L_k(\mathbf{x}_k, \mathbf{u}_k) = \nu_k(\mathbf{x}_k) + \omega_k(\mathbf{x}_k, \mathbf{u}_k) + \phi_k(\mathbf{u}_k) \quad (10\text{-}3)$$

$$\nu_k(\mathbf{x}_k) = \tfrac{1}{2}[\mathbf{x}_k - \tilde{\mathbf{x}}_k]'\mathbf{W}_k[\mathbf{x}_k - \tilde{\mathbf{x}}_k] \quad (10\text{-}4)$$

$$\omega_k(\mathbf{x}_k, \mathbf{u}_k) = [\mathbf{x}_k - \tilde{\mathbf{x}}_k]'\mathbf{F}_k[\mathbf{u}_k - \tilde{\mathbf{u}}_k] \quad (10\text{-}5)$$

$$\phi_k(\mathbf{u}_k) = \tfrac{1}{2}[\mathbf{u}_k - \tilde{\mathbf{u}}_k]'\Lambda_k[\mathbf{u}_k - \tilde{\mathbf{u}}_k] \quad (10\text{-}6)$$

subject to a discrete-time linear system

$$\begin{aligned}\mathbf{x}_{k+1} &= \mathbf{f}_k(\mathbf{x}_k, \mathbf{u}_k) + \mathbf{v}_k \\ &= \mathbf{A}_k(\boldsymbol{\theta}_k)\mathbf{x}_k + \mathbf{B}_k(\boldsymbol{\theta}_k)\mathbf{u}_k + \mathbf{c}_k(\boldsymbol{\theta}_k) + \mathbf{v}_k, \quad k = 0,1,\ldots,N-1\end{aligned} \quad (10\text{-}7)$$

and the measurement equations

$$\mathbf{y}_k = \mathbf{H}_k(\boldsymbol{\theta}_k)\mathbf{x}_k + \mathbf{w}_k \quad k = 1,\ldots,N \quad (10\text{-}8)$$

where
- $\mathbf{x}_k$ = state vector at time k-n vector
- $\mathbf{u}_k$ = control vector-m vector
- $\tilde{\mathbf{x}}_k$ = desired path for state vector-n vector
- $\tilde{\mathbf{u}}_k$ = desired path for control vector
- $\mathbf{W}_k$ = penalty matrix on state variable deviations from desired path $(n \times n)$
- $\mathbf{F}_k$ = penalty on state control variable deviations from desired path $(n \times m)$
- Λ_k = penalty on control-variable deviations from desired path $(m \times m)$
- $\boldsymbol{\theta}_k$ = s vector containing a subset of the coefficients in $\mathbf{A}$, $\mathbf{B}$, and $\mathbf{c}$
- $\mathbf{A}_k(\boldsymbol{\theta}_k)$ = state-vector coefficient matrix $(n \times n)$
- $\mathbf{B}_k(\boldsymbol{\theta}_k)$ = control-vector coefficient matrix $(n \times m)$
- $\mathbf{c}_k(\boldsymbol{\theta}_k)$ = constant-coefficient vector $(n \times 1)$
- $\mathbf{H}_k(\boldsymbol{\theta}_k)$ = measurement-coefficient matrix $(r \times n)$
- $\mathbf{v}_k$ = system noise $(n \times 1)$
- $\mathbf{w}_k$ = measurement noise $(r \times 1)$
- $\mathbf{y}_k$ = measurement vector $(r \times 1)$

The state vector $\mathbf{x}$ is not directly observed but is indirectly measured through $\mathbf{y}$. Also, it is assumed that the random coefficients $\boldsymbol{\theta}$ may follow a first-order Markov process

$$\boldsymbol{\theta}_{k+1} = \mathbf{D}_k \boldsymbol{\theta}_k + \boldsymbol{\eta}_k \tag{10-9}$$

where $\mathbf{D}_k$ is a known matrix and $\boldsymbol{\eta}_k$ is a random vector ($s \times 1$).

The vectors $\mathbf{v}$, $\mathbf{w}$, $\boldsymbol{\eta}$, $\mathbf{x}_0$, and $\boldsymbol{\theta}_0$ are assumed to be mutually independent normally distributed random vectors with known mean and covariance

$$\mathbf{x}_0 \sim N(\hat{\mathbf{x}}_0, \Sigma_0^{xx}) \quad \boldsymbol{\theta}_0 \sim N(\hat{\boldsymbol{\theta}}_0, \Sigma_0^{\theta\theta}) \quad \mathbf{v}_k \sim N(\mathbf{O}, \mathbf{Q}_k)$$
$$\mathbf{w}_k \sim N(\mathbf{O}, \mathbf{R}_k) \quad \boldsymbol{\eta}_k \sim N(\mathbf{O}, \mathbf{G}_k) \tag{10-10}$$

with Σ_0^{xx}, $\Sigma_0^{\theta\theta}$, $\mathbf{Q}_k$, $\mathbf{R}_k$, $\mathbf{G}_k \geq 0$. Also it is assumed that the unknown parameters enter linearly in $\mathbf{A}$, $\mathbf{B}$, $\mathbf{c}$, and $\mathbf{H}$.

Augmented System

One approach to solving this problem is to treat the random parameters as additional state variables.[1] The state vector $\mathbf{x}$ is therefore augmented by the parameter vector $\boldsymbol{\theta}$ to create a new state vector $\mathbf{z}$,

$$\mathbf{z}_k = \begin{bmatrix} \mathbf{x}_k \\ \boldsymbol{\theta}_k \end{bmatrix} \tag{10-11}$$

The control problem can then be stated as

$$\text{Minimize} \quad J = E \left\{ L_N(\mathbf{z}_N) + \sum_{k=0}^{N-1} L_k(\mathbf{z}_k, \mathbf{u}_k) \right\} \tag{10-12}$$

subject to the system equation

$$\mathbf{z}_{k+1} = \mathbf{f}_k(\mathbf{z}_k, \mathbf{u}_k) + \boldsymbol{\xi}_k \tag{10-13}$$

and the measurement equation

$$\mathbf{y}_k^z = \mathbf{h}_k(\mathbf{z}_k) + \boldsymbol{\zeta}_k \tag{10-14}$$

where

$$L_N(\mathbf{z}_N) = \tfrac{1}{2} \big[[\mathbf{x}_N - \tilde{\mathbf{x}}_N]', \mathbf{O} \big] \begin{bmatrix} \mathbf{W}_N & \mathbf{O} \\ \hline \mathbf{O} & \mathbf{O} \end{bmatrix} \begin{bmatrix} \mathbf{x}_N - \tilde{\mathbf{x}}_N \\ \hline \mathbf{O} \end{bmatrix} \tag{10-15}$$

$$L_k(\mathbf{z}_k, \mathbf{u}_k) = \nu_k(\mathbf{z}_k) + \omega_k(\mathbf{z}_k, \mathbf{u}_k) + \phi_k(\mathbf{u}_k) \tag{10-16}$$

$$\nu_k(\mathbf{z}_k) = \tfrac{1}{2} \big[[\mathbf{x}_k - \tilde{\mathbf{x}}_k]', \mathbf{O} \big] \begin{bmatrix} \mathbf{W}_k & \mathbf{O} \\ \hline \mathbf{O} & \mathbf{O} \end{bmatrix} \begin{bmatrix} \mathbf{x}_k - \tilde{\mathbf{x}}_k \\ \hline \mathbf{O} \end{bmatrix} \tag{10-17}$$

$$\omega_k(\mathbf{z}_k, \mathbf{u}_k) = \big[[\mathbf{x}_k - \tilde{\mathbf{x}}_k]', \mathbf{O} \big] \begin{bmatrix} \mathbf{F}_k \\ \hline \mathbf{O} \end{bmatrix} [\mathbf{u}_k - \tilde{\mathbf{u}}_k] \tag{10-18}$$

$$\phi_k(\mathbf{u}_k) = \tfrac{1}{2} [\mathbf{u}_k - \tilde{\mathbf{u}}_k]' \boldsymbol{\Lambda}_k [\mathbf{u}_k - \tilde{\mathbf{u}}_k] \tag{10-19}$$

---

[1] See Norman (1976) for a method of solving this problem without augmenting the state vector for problems in which there is no measurement error.

$$\mathbf{f}_k(\mathbf{z}_k, \mathbf{u}_k) = \begin{bmatrix} \mathbf{f}^x(\mathbf{z}_k, \mathbf{u}_k) \\ \hdashline \mathbf{f}^\theta(\mathbf{z}_k, \mathbf{u}_k) \end{bmatrix} = \begin{bmatrix} \mathbf{A}_k(\boldsymbol{\theta}_k)\mathbf{x}_k + \mathbf{B}_k(\boldsymbol{\theta}_k)\mathbf{u}_k + \mathbf{c}_k(\boldsymbol{\theta}_k) \\ \hdashline \mathbf{D}_k \boldsymbol{\theta}_k \end{bmatrix} \quad (10\text{-}20)$$

$$\boldsymbol{\xi}_k = \begin{bmatrix} \mathbf{v}_k \\ \hdashline \boldsymbol{\eta}_k \end{bmatrix} \quad (10\text{-}21)$$

$$\mathbf{h}_k(\mathbf{z}_k) = \begin{bmatrix} \mathbf{H}_k(\boldsymbol{\theta}_k)\mathbf{x}_k \\ \hdashline \mathbf{0} \end{bmatrix} \quad (10\text{-}22)$$

$$\boldsymbol{\zeta}_k = \begin{bmatrix} \mathbf{w}_k \\ \hdashline \mathbf{0} \end{bmatrix} \quad (10\text{-}23)$$

Problems (10-1) to (10-10) and (10-11) to (10-23) are equivalent; however, the first is described as a linear quadratic problem with random coefficients and the second as a nonlinear stochastic control problem. In fact the second problem is in the same form as the nonlinear problem discussed in Chap. 9 since that problem is nonlinear in $\mathbf{x}$, $\mathbf{u}$, and $\boldsymbol{\theta}$. Therefore, the method of Chap. 9 can now be applied to the problem.

10-3 THE APPROXIMATE OPTIMAL COST-TO-GO

Two approaches to evaluation of the approximate cost-to-go are discussed here. The first is based on Eq. (9-69), and the second is based on Eq. (9-68). Both approaches have been used in numerical exercises by the author. First the approach of Eq. (9-69) was programmed and debugged. Then at a later date the programs were rewritten to use Eq. (9-68) since this approach offers the opportunity of separating the criterion function into deterministic, cautionary, and probing terms. Since in large part the same mathematics is needed to understand the two approaches, both will be discussed here.

Using the first approach, the approximate cost-to-go conditional on $\mathbf{u}_k$ for the augmented system can be written by using Eq. (9-69) as[1]

$$\begin{aligned} J_{d, N-k} = {} & \omega_k(\mathbf{z}_k, \mathbf{u}_k) + \phi_k(\mathbf{u}_k) + J_{o, k+1} + \gamma_{k+1} \\ & + \tfrac{1}{2} \operatorname{tr} \Big\{ \big[\Sigma_{k+1|k} - \Sigma_{k+1|k+1} \big] \mathbf{K}_{k+1} + \mathbf{L}_{N, \mathbf{z}\mathbf{z}} \Sigma_{N|N} \\ & + \sum_{j=k+1}^{N-1} \big[\mathbf{H}_{\mathbf{z}\mathbf{z}, j} \Sigma_{j|j} + (\Sigma_{j+1|j} - \Sigma_{j+1|j+1}) \mathbf{K}_{j+1} \big] \Big\} \quad (10\text{-}24) \end{aligned}$$

---
[1] Since Eq. (10-24) is conditional on the choice of $\mathbf{u}_k$, the minimum over $\mathbf{u}_k$ operation in Eq. (9-69) is dropped.

where $J_{o,N-k-1}$ is the optimal cost-to-go obtained by solving the certainty-equivalence problem for the unaugmented system along a nominal path.[1] Expression (10-24) can be further simplified by decomposing each term on the right-hand side.

First, from Eq. (10-15),

$$L_N = \tfrac{1}{2}[\mathbf{x}_N - \tilde{\mathbf{x}}_N]'\mathbf{W}_N[\mathbf{x}_N - \tilde{\mathbf{x}}_N] \tag{10-25}$$

Therefore,

$$L_{N,zz} = \left[\begin{array}{c|c} L_{N,xx} & L_{N,x\theta} \\ \hline L_{N,\theta x} & L_{N,\theta\theta} \end{array}\right] = \left[\begin{array}{c|c} \mathbf{W}_N & \mathbf{0} \\ \hline \mathbf{0} & \mathbf{0} \end{array}\right]$$

and

$$L_{N,zz}\Sigma_{N|N} = \left[\begin{array}{c|c} \mathbf{W}_N & \mathbf{0} \\ \hline \mathbf{0} & \mathbf{0} \end{array}\right]\left[\begin{array}{c|c} \Sigma^{xx} & \Sigma^{x\theta} \\ \hline \Sigma^{\theta x} & \Sigma^{\theta\theta} \end{array}\right]_{N|N} = \left[\begin{array}{c|c} \mathbf{W}_N\Sigma^{xx}_{N|N} & \mathbf{W}_N\Sigma^{x\theta}_{N|N} \\ \hline \mathbf{0} & \mathbf{0} \end{array}\right]$$

and therefore,

$$\operatorname{tr}\left[L_{N,zz}\Sigma_{N|N}\right] = \operatorname{tr}\left[\mathbf{W}_N\Sigma^{xx}_{N|N}\right] \tag{10-26}$$

Next in order to evaluate $J_{o,N-k-1}$, it is necessary to solve the certainty-equivalence problem for the unaugmented system. This problem is to choose a nominal control sequence $(\mathbf{u}_{oj})_{j=k+1}^{N-1}$ which minimizes

$$J_{o,N-k-1} = \tfrac{1}{2}[\mathbf{x}_{o,N} - \tilde{\mathbf{x}}_N]'\mathbf{W}_N[\mathbf{x}_{o,N} - \tilde{\mathbf{x}}_N]$$

$$+ \frac{1}{2}\sum_{j=k+1}^{N-1}\left([\mathbf{x}_{o,j} - \tilde{\mathbf{x}}_j]'\mathbf{W}_j[\mathbf{x}_{o,j} - \tilde{\mathbf{x}}_j] + [\mathbf{x}_{o,j} - \tilde{\mathbf{x}}_j]'\mathbf{F}_j[\mathbf{u}_{oj} - \tilde{\mathbf{u}}_j]\right.$$

$$\left. + \tfrac{1}{2}[\mathbf{u}_{o,j} - \tilde{\mathbf{u}}_j]'\Lambda_j[\mathbf{u}_{o,j} - \tilde{\mathbf{u}}_j]\right) \tag{10-27}$$

subject to

$$\mathbf{x}_{o,j+1} = \mathbf{A}_j(\boldsymbol{\theta}_{o,j})\mathbf{x}_{o,j} + \mathbf{B}_j(\boldsymbol{\theta}_{o,j})\mathbf{u}_{o,j} + \mathbf{c}_j(\boldsymbol{\theta}_{o,j}) \quad j = k+1,\ldots,N-1$$

$$\mathbf{x}_{o,k+1} = \hat{\mathbf{x}}_{k+1|k} \tag{10-28}$$

where $\boldsymbol{\theta}_{o,j}, j = k+1,\ldots,N-1$, are generated by

$$\boldsymbol{\theta}_{o,j+1} = \mathbf{D}_j\boldsymbol{\theta}_{o,j} \qquad \boldsymbol{\theta}_{o,k+1} = \hat{\boldsymbol{\theta}}_{k+1|k} \tag{10-29}$$

In this problem it is assumed that all parameters of the system equation (10-28) are known from Eq. (10-29), and this is indicated by using the subscript o.

The certainty-equivalence solution for the above is summarized as follows (the derivation is given in Appendix G). The tilde is used to indicate the **K**, **p**, and η parameters for the certainty-equivalence problem for the unaugmented system to distinguish them from those for the augmented system. The feedback rule for the optimal control is

$$\mathbf{u}_{oj} = \mathbf{G}_j\mathbf{x}_{oj} + \mathbf{g}_j \tag{10-30}$$

---

[1] Note in Appendix E that this term is the same as $C_{o,N-k-1}$.

where $\quad G_j = -\mu_j[F'_j + B'_j\tilde{K}_{j+1}A_j]$ (10-31)

and $\quad g_j = -\mu_j[B'_j(\tilde{K}_{j+1}c_j + \tilde{p}_{j+1}) - F'_j\tilde{x}_j - \Lambda_j\tilde{u}_j]$

with $\quad \mu_j = [B'_j\tilde{K}_{j+1}B_j + \Lambda_j]^{-1}$ (10-32)

The recursions for $\tilde{K}$ and $\tilde{p}$ are [from Eqs. (G-9) and (G-10)]

$$\tilde{K}_j = A'_j\tilde{K}_{j+1}A_j - [A'_j\tilde{K}_{j+1}B_j + F_j]\mu_j[F'_j + B'_j\tilde{K}_{j+1}A_j] + W_j$$

with $\quad \tilde{K}_N = W_N$ (10-33)

and $\quad \tilde{p}_j = -[A'_j\tilde{K}_{j+1}B_j + F_j]\mu_j[B'_j(\tilde{K}_{j+1}c_j + \tilde{p}_{j+1}) - (F'_j\tilde{x}_j + \Lambda_j\tilde{u}_j)]$
$$+ A'_j(\tilde{K}_{j+1}c_j + \tilde{p}_{j+1}) - (W_j\tilde{x}_j + F_j\tilde{u}_j)$$

with $\quad \tilde{p}_N = -W_N\tilde{x}_N$ (10-34)

Finally, the cost-to-go can be written as

$$J^*_{o,N-k-1} = \tfrac{1}{2}\hat{x}'_{k+1|k}\tilde{K}_{k+1}\hat{x}_{k+1|k} + \tilde{p}'_{k+1}\hat{x}_{k+1|k} + \tilde{\eta}_{k+1} \quad (10\text{-}35)$$

Substituting Eqs. (10-18), (10-19), (10-26), and (10-35) into Eq. (10-24), dropping $\tilde{\eta}_{k+1}$, which is independent of the choice of $\mathbf{u}_k$, and using $\gamma_{k+1} = 0$ (see Appendix J), we obtain

$$J_{d,N-k} = [\mathbf{x}_k - \tilde{\mathbf{x}}_k]'F[\mathbf{u}_k - \tilde{\mathbf{u}}_k] + \tfrac{1}{2}[\mathbf{u}_k - \tilde{\mathbf{u}}_k]'\Lambda_k[\mathbf{u}_k - \tilde{\mathbf{u}}_k]$$
$$+ \tfrac{1}{2}\hat{x}'_{k+1|k}\tilde{K}_{k+1}\hat{x}_{k+1|k} + \tilde{p}'_{k+1}\hat{x}_{k+1|k} + \tfrac{1}{2}\operatorname{tr}\Big\{[\Sigma_{k+1|k} - \Sigma_{k+1|k+1}]K_{k+1}$$
$$+ W_N\Sigma^{xx}_{N|N} + \sum_{j=k+1}^{N-1}[H_{zz,j}\Sigma_{j|j} + (\Sigma_{j+1|j} - \Sigma_{j+1|j+1})K_{j+1}]\Big\} \quad (10\text{-}36)$$

where (see Appendix H)

$$H_{zz} = \left[\begin{array}{c|c} W_j & \Sigma e'_i p^x_{j+1}a^i_\theta \\ \hline \sum_{i\in X} e'_i p^x_{j+1}(a^i_\theta)' & O \end{array}\right] \quad (10\text{-}37)$$

$$K_j = \left[\begin{array}{c|c} K^{xx}_j & K^{\theta x'}_j \\ \hline K^{\theta x}_j & K^{\theta\theta}_j \end{array}\right] \quad (10\text{-}38)$$

$$K^{xx}_j = \tilde{K}_j \quad (10\text{-}39)$$

$$K^{\theta x}_j = [(f^x_\theta)'K^{xx}_{j+1} + D'K^{\theta x}_{j+1}]A$$
$$- [[(f^x_\theta)'K^{xx}_{j+1} + D'K^{\theta x}_{j+1}]B + [\Sigma e'_i p^x_{j+1}b^i_\theta]']\mu_j[B'K^{xx}_{j+1}A + F']$$
$$+ \Sigma e'_i p^x_{j+1}a^i_\theta \quad \text{with } K^{\theta x}_N = O \quad (10\text{-}40)$$

in which (see Appendix L)[1]

[1] Expression (10-40) is similar to Tse and Bar-Shalom [1973, eq. (3.15)]. Equation (10-40) contains a term in a^i_θ which should be added to the equation in Tse and Bar-Shalom.

$$\mathbf{f}_\theta^x(k) = \sum_{i \in X} \mathbf{e}_i \hat{\mathbf{x}}'_{k|k} \mathbf{a}_\theta^i(k) + \sum_{i \in X} \mathbf{e}_i (\mathbf{u}_k^\tau)' \mathbf{b}_\theta^i(k) + \sum_{i \in X} \mathbf{e}_i \mathbf{c}_\theta^i(k) \qquad (10\text{-}41)$$

$$\mathbf{K}_j^{\theta\theta} = (\mathbf{f}_\theta^x)' \left[\mathbf{K}_{j+1}^{xx} \mathbf{f}_\theta^x + \mathbf{K}_{j+1}^{x\theta} \mathbf{D} \right] + \mathbf{D}' \left[\mathbf{K}_{j+1}^{\theta x} \mathbf{f}_\theta^x + \mathbf{K}_{j+1}^{\theta\theta} \mathbf{D} \right]$$

$$- \left[\left[(\mathbf{f}_\theta^x)' \mathbf{K}_{j+1}^{xx} + \mathbf{D}' \mathbf{K}_{j+1}^{\theta x} \right] \mathbf{B} + \left[\Sigma \mathbf{e}_i' \mathbf{p}_{j+1}^x \mathbf{b}_\theta^i \right]' \right] \mu$$

$$\left[\mathbf{B}' \left[\mathbf{K}_{j+1}^{xx} \mathbf{f}_\theta^x + \mathbf{K}_{j+1}^{x\theta} \mathbf{D} \right] + \Sigma \mathbf{e}_i' \mathbf{p}_{j+1}^x \mathbf{b}_\theta^i \right] \qquad \text{with } \mathbf{K}_N^{\theta\theta} = 0 \qquad (10\text{-}42)$$

where $\mu = [\Lambda + \mathbf{B}' \mathbf{K}^{xx} \mathbf{B}]^{-1}$.

Also see Appendix I for the derivation of

$$\mathbf{p}_j^x = \tilde{\mathbf{K}}_j \mathbf{x}_{oj} + \tilde{\mathbf{p}}_j \qquad (10\text{-}43)$$

Thus Eq. (10-36) provides one way of evaluating the approximate optimal cost-to-go.

Alternatively, one may use a second approach to evaluation of the cost-to-go in order to separate it into deterministic, cautionary, and probing terms, as in Bar-Shalom and Tse (1976a). To do this, begin with Eq. (9-68) instead of Eq. (9-69). Expression (9-68) is

$$J_{d,N-k}^* = \min_{\mathbf{u}_k} \left\{ \omega_k(\mathbf{z}_k, \mathbf{u}_k) + \phi_k(\mathbf{u}_k) + C_{o,N-k-1} + \gamma_{k+1} \right.$$

$$\left. + \tfrac{1}{2} \operatorname{tr} \left[\mathbf{K}_{k+1} \Sigma_{k+1|k} \right] + \frac{1}{2} \sum_{j=k+1}^{N-1} \operatorname{tr} \left[\mathbf{K}_{j+1} \mathbf{Q}_j^z + \mathcal{Q}_{zz} \Sigma_{j|j} \right] \right\} \qquad (10\text{-}44)$$

(The notation $\mathbf{Q}^z$ is used for the covariance of the system-equation noise terms for the augmented system.) This can be separated into three components as

$$J_{d,N-k}^* = \min_{\mathbf{u}_k} (J_{D,N-k} + J_{C,N-k} + J_{P,N-k}) \qquad (10\text{-}45)$$

where the deterministic component is

$$J_{D,N-k} = \omega_k(\mathbf{z}_k, \mathbf{u}_k) + \phi_k(\mathbf{u}_k) + C_{o,k+1} + \gamma_{k+1} \qquad (10\text{-}46)$$

the cautionary component is

$$J_{C,N-k} = \tfrac{1}{2} \operatorname{tr} \left[\mathbf{K}_{k+1} \Sigma_{k+1|k} \right] + \frac{1}{2} \sum_{j=k+1}^{N-1} \operatorname{tr} \left[\mathbf{K}_{j+1} \mathbf{Q}_j^z \right] \qquad (10\text{-}47)$$

and the probing term is

$$J_{P,N-k} = \frac{1}{2} \sum_{j=k+1}^{N-1} \operatorname{tr} \left[\mathcal{Q}_{zz} \Sigma_{j|j} \right] \qquad (10\text{-}48)$$

Expression (10-46) contains all the deterministic terms, and this is the rationale for separating it from the stochastic terms in Eqs. (10-47) and (10-48). Increases in control do not affect $\mathbf{Q}_j^z$ in Eq. (10-47) but may increase $\Sigma_{k+1|k}$. Therefore, minimization of the cautionary component (10-47) usually requires selecting $\mathbf{u}_k$ so as to decrease the $\mathbf{K}$ weighting matrices and the $\Sigma_{k+1|k}$ term. Since the elements of the matrices $\Sigma_{j|j}$ in Eq. (10-48) can in general be decreased through use of more vigorous control levels $\mathbf{u}_k$, this expression is called the *probing term*.

Expressions (10-46) to (10-48) define the cost components for the augmented system. For both computational efficiency and insight into the nature of the results, it is useful to write these components out in terms of the matrices which are the parts of the augmented system. This is done in Appendix Q. The results are shown below for deterministic terms [from Eq. (Q-3)]

$$\begin{aligned}J_{D,N-k} = &\left[\mathbf{x}_k - \tilde{\mathbf{x}}_k\right]'\mathbf{F}_k[\mathbf{u}_k - \tilde{\mathbf{u}}_k] + \tfrac{1}{2}[\mathbf{u}_k - \tilde{\mathbf{u}}_k]'\Lambda_k[\mathbf{u}_k - \tilde{\mathbf{u}}_k] \\ &+ \tfrac{1}{2}[\mathbf{x}_{o,N} - \tilde{\mathbf{x}}_N]'\mathbf{W}_N[\mathbf{x}_{o,N} - \tilde{\mathbf{x}}_N] \\ &+ \tfrac{1}{2}\sum_{j=k+1}^{N-1}\left([\mathbf{x}_{o,j} - \tilde{\mathbf{x}}_j]'\mathbf{W}_j[\mathbf{x}_{o,j} - \tilde{\mathbf{x}}_j]' + [\mathbf{x}_{oj} - \tilde{\mathbf{x}}_{oj}]'\mathbf{F}_j[\mathbf{u}_{oj} - \tilde{\mathbf{u}}_j]\right. \\ &\left. + [\mathbf{u}_{o,j} - \tilde{\mathbf{u}}_j]'\Lambda_j[\mathbf{u}_{o,j} - \tilde{\mathbf{u}}_j]\right) \quad (10\text{-}49)\end{aligned}$$

cautionary terms [from Eq. (Q-8)]

$$\begin{aligned}J_{C,N-k} = &\tfrac{1}{2}\operatorname{tr}(\mathbf{K}^{xx}_{k+1}\Sigma^{xx}_{k+1|k}) + \operatorname{tr}(\mathbf{K}^{\theta x}_{k+1}\Sigma^{\theta x}_{k+1|k}) \\ &+ \tfrac{1}{2}\operatorname{tr}(\mathbf{K}^{\theta\theta}_{k+1}\Sigma^{\theta\theta}_{k+1|k}) \\ &+ \tfrac{1}{2}\sum_{j=k+1}^{N-1}\left[\operatorname{tr}(\mathbf{K}^{xx}_{j+1}\mathbf{Q}_j) + \operatorname{tr}(\mathbf{K}^{\theta\theta}_{j+1}\mathbf{G}_j)\right] \quad (10\text{-}50)\end{aligned}$$

and probing terms [from Eq. (Q-13)]

$$\begin{aligned}J_{P,N-k} = &\tfrac{1}{2}\sum_{j=k+1}^{N-1}\left\{\operatorname{tr}\left(\left[\mathbf{A}'\mathbf{K}^{xx}_{j+1}\mathbf{B} + \mathbf{F}\right]\mu_j\left[\mathbf{B}'\mathbf{K}^{xx}_{j+1}\mathbf{A} + \mathbf{F}'\right]\Sigma^{xx}_{j|j}\right)\right. \\ &+ 2\operatorname{tr}\left(\left[\mathbf{B}'\mathbf{K}^{xx}_{j+1}\mathbf{A} + \mathbf{F}\right]'\mu_j\left[\mathbf{B}'\left[\mathbf{K}^{xx}_{j+1}\mathbf{f}^x_\theta + \mathbf{K}^{x\theta}_{j+1}\mathbf{D}\right] + \Sigma e_i\mathbf{p}^x\mathbf{b}^j_\theta\right]\Sigma^{\theta x}_{j|j}\right) \\ &+ \operatorname{tr}\left(\left[\left[\mathbf{D}'\mathbf{K}^{\theta x}_{j+1} + \mathbf{f}^{x'}_\theta\mathbf{K}^{xx}_{j+1}\right]\mathbf{B} + \left[\Sigma e_i\mathbf{p}^x\mathbf{b}^j_\theta\right]'\right]\mu_j\right. \\ &\left.\left. \times\left[\mathbf{B}'\left[\mathbf{K}^{xx}_{j+1}\mathbf{f}^x_\theta + \mathbf{K}^{x\theta}_{j+1}\mathbf{D}\right] + \Sigma e_i\mathbf{p}^x\mathbf{b}^j_\theta\right]\Sigma^{\theta\theta}_{j|j}\right)\right\} \quad (10\text{-}51)\end{aligned}$$

With these components in hand the algorithm can now be explained in detail.

10-4 DUAL-CONTROL ALGORITHM

A flowchart of the algorithm is provided in Fig. 10-1. There are two major sections: (1) the search on the left in the figure and (2) the update procedure on the right. The purpose of the search is to determine the best control to use in the current time period $\mathbf{u}_k$, and the update procedures project the system forward one time period and update the estimates of the means and covariances of both the original states and the parameters. The means and covariances are

$$\hat{\mathbf{z}}_{k+1|k+1} = \begin{bmatrix}\hat{\mathbf{x}} \\ \hat{\boldsymbol{\theta}}\end{bmatrix}_{k+1|k+1} \quad\text{and}\quad \Sigma_{k+1|k+1} = \begin{bmatrix}\Sigma^{xx} & \Sigma^{x\theta} \\ \Sigma^{\theta x} & \Sigma^{\theta\theta}\end{bmatrix}_{k+1|k+1}$$

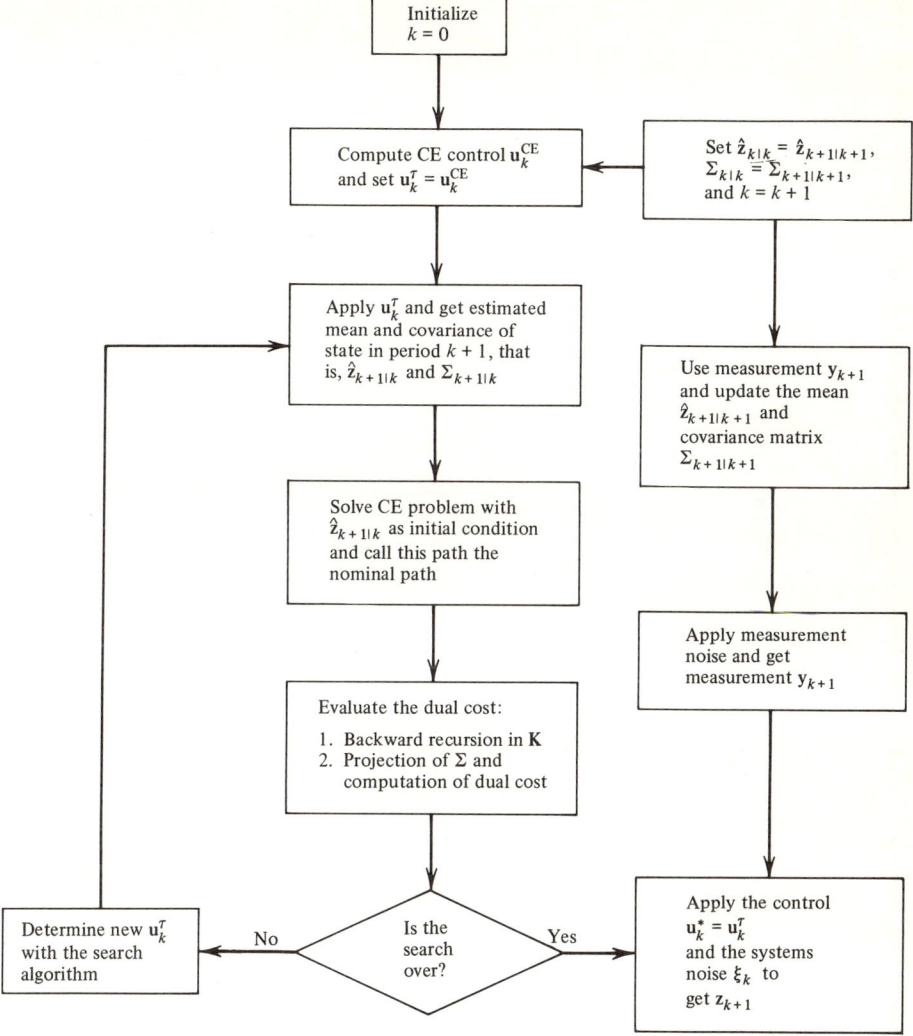

Figure 10-1 Flowchart of the algorithm.

The search procedure is further outlined in Fig. 10-2, which shows three trial values of the control $\mathbf{u}_k^\tau$. In fact more trial values than this are generally used before the search converges.

The trial value $\mathbf{u}_k^\tau$ for the τth trial is used to project the mean and covariance $(\hat{\mathbf{z}}_{k+1|k}, \Sigma_{k+1|k})$ of the state of the system at time $k + 1$ with measurements through time k. These values are then used as the initial condition for the solution of a deterministic optimization (certainty-equivalence) problem from time $k + 1$ to final time N. This problem is a quadratic linear approximation of the nonlinear deterministic problem. The solution to this problem provides the nominal path $(\mathbf{z}_{oj}^\tau, \mathbf{u}_{oj}^\tau)_{j=k+1}^N$ around which the approximate cost-to-go J_d can be determined.

100 ACTIVE-LEARNING STOCHASTIC CONTROL

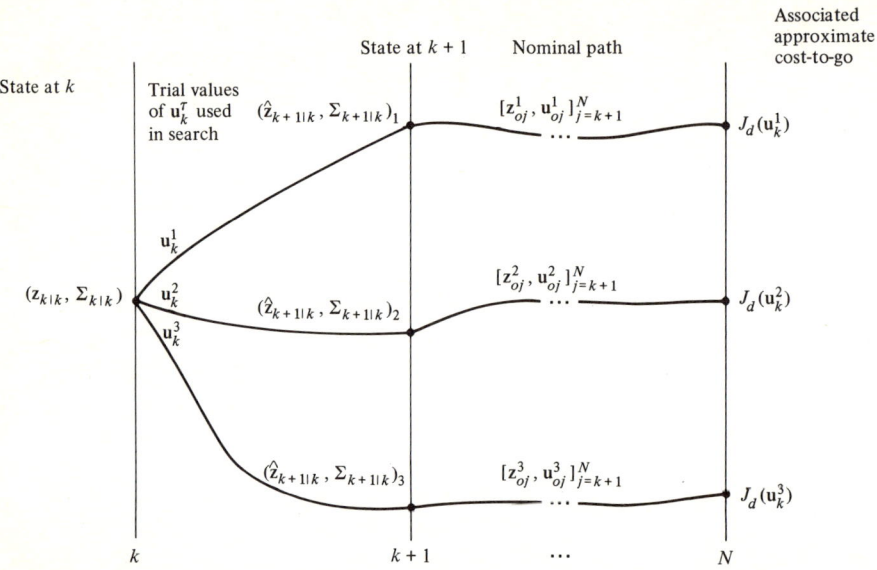

Figure 10-2 Search procedure to determine $\mathbf{u}_k^*$. Set $\mathbf{u}_k^* = \{\mathbf{u}_k^\tau$ for τ that gives $\min_\tau J_d(\mathbf{u}_k^\tau)\}$.

This procedure is repeated for each $\mathbf{u}_k^\tau$ until the search algorithm converges, at which time the optimal control $\mathbf{u}_k^*$ for period k is set equal to that search value $\mathbf{u}_k^\tau$ which minimizes $J_d(\mathbf{u}_k^\tau)$.

Then the update procedure is begun by using $\mathbf{u}_k^*$ and the system noise $\boldsymbol{\xi}_k$, which is obtained from the random-number generator, to determine the state of the system $\mathbf{z}_{k+1}$ at time $k+1$ (see Fig. 10-3). The state cannot be directly observed but is measured through the observed $\mathbf{y}_{k+1}$. The measurement $\mathbf{y}_{k+1}$ is

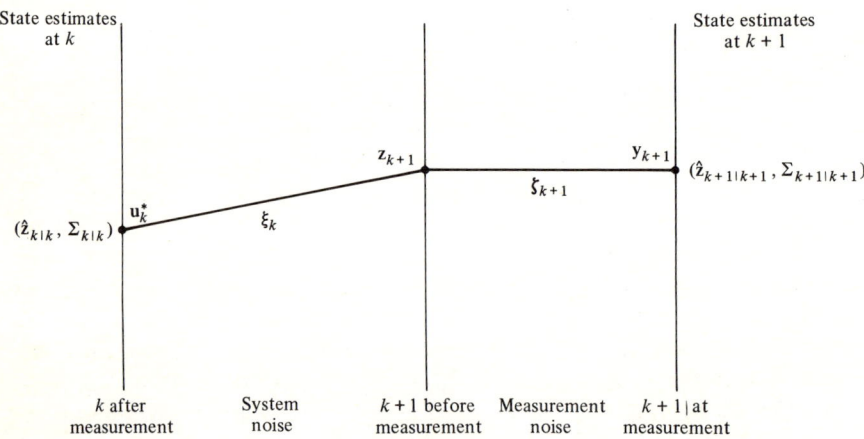

Figure 10-3 Monte Carlo and update procedures.

obtained from the measurement relation, where the measurement noise ζ_{k+1} is included. Then the measurement $\mathbf{y}_{k+1}$ is used with the Kalman filter to update the estimates of the mean and covariance of the augmented state $\hat{\mathbf{z}}_{k+1|k+1}$ and $\Sigma_{k+1|k+1}$.

These two procedures of search and update are then repeated for each time period until the final time period is reached. The cost of the dual-control solution is then calculated for this single Monte Carlo run. A number of Monte Carlo runs are then performed in order to obtain a distribution of the cost associated with the use of the wide-sense dual-control strategy.

The algorithm is now outlined step by step. The algorithm outlined here is based on the evaluation of the cost-to-go and its three components in Eq. (10-45).

At each time period k there are three major steps in the algorithm:

1. Initialization
2. Search for the optimal control $\mathbf{u}_k^*$
3. Updating the estimates of the states and parameters

Initialization

The first step in the initialization is to compute the nominal value of the parameters. If the parameters are constant, this simply means setting $\theta_{o,k}$ to $\theta_{k-1|k-1}$. If they are not constant, it means using Eq. (10-29) to project $\theta_{o,j}$ for $j = k, \ldots, N$ from $\hat{\theta}_{k-1|k-1}$. Once this has been completed, it is necessary to update $\mathbf{A}_j$, $\mathbf{B}_j$, and $\mathbf{c}_j$ for $j = k, \ldots, N$.

Next the Riccati parameters $\tilde{\mathbf{K}}_j$ and $\tilde{\mathbf{p}}_j$ for $j = k+1, \ldots, N$ are calculated by using Eqs. (10-33) and (10-34).

Finally, it is necessary to choose a value of the control $\mathbf{u}_k$ with which to begin the search for the optimal control $\mathbf{u}_k^*$. While this may be done in a variety of ways, it is normally done by solving the certainty-equivalence problem for period k to N and then setting $\mathbf{u}_k^\tau$ for step $\tau = 1$ in the search to the certainty-equivalence solution for period k as given by Eq. (10-30).

Search for the Optimal Control

There are eight steps in this procedure:

1. Use the control $\mathbf{u}_k^\tau$ to get the projected states and covariances in period $k+1$, that is, $\hat{\mathbf{z}}_{k+1|k}$ and $\Sigma_{k+1|k}$.
2. Get the nominal path for period $k+1$ to N by solving the certainty-equivalence problem using the x component of $\hat{\mathbf{z}}_{k+1|k}$ as the initial condition.
3. Compute the Riccati matrices $\mathbf{K}^{\theta x}$ and $\mathbf{K}^{\theta\theta}$ for all periods.
4. Calculate the deterministic component of the cost-to-go for period k and period N.

5. Calculate part of the cautionary component for period $k + 1$.
6. Repeat the calculation of the following components for periods $k + 1$ through $N - 1$:
   a. Deterministic
   b. Cautionary
   c. Probing
   d. Total cost-to-go
7. Choose a new control $\mathbf{u}_k^{\tau+1}$ in the search.
8. Repeat steps 1 through 7 until all the search points have been evaluated and then select the control which yields the minimum total cost-to-go.

In greater detail the eight steps are as follows.

Step 1 Use $\mathbf{u}_k^\tau$ in Eqs. (9-73) and (9-78) to project the future state $\hat{\mathbf{z}}_{k+1|k}$ and covariance $\Sigma_{k+1|k}$. These results are specialized in Appendix M to the components $\mathbf{x}$ and $\boldsymbol{\theta}$ of $\mathbf{z}$ for the linear problem and are given in Eqs. (M-8) and (M-9) as

$$\hat{\mathbf{x}}_{k+1|k} = \mathbf{A}_k \hat{\mathbf{x}}_{k|k} + \mathbf{B}_k \mathbf{u}_k^\tau + \mathbf{c}_k + \sum_{i \in X} \mathbf{e}^i \operatorname{tr}\left(\mathbf{a}_\theta^i \Sigma_{k|k}^{\theta x}\right) \quad (10\text{-}52)$$

and

$$\hat{\boldsymbol{\theta}}_{k+1|k} = \mathbf{D} \hat{\boldsymbol{\theta}}_{ok} \quad (10\text{-}53)$$

Also the covariance terms are given in Eqs. (M-16) to (M-19) as

$$\Sigma_{k+1|k} = \left[\begin{array}{c|c} \Sigma^{xx} & \Sigma^{\theta x} \\ \hline \Sigma^{\theta x} & \Sigma^{\theta\theta} \end{array}\right]_{k+1|k} \quad (10\text{-}54)$$

with the component matrices

$$\Sigma_{k+1|k}^{xx} = \mathbf{A}_k \Sigma_{k|k}^{xx} \mathbf{A}_k' + \mathbf{A}_k \Sigma_{k|k}^{x\theta}(\mathbf{f}_{\theta k}^x)'$$
$$+ \mathbf{f}_{\theta_k}^x \Sigma_{k|k}^{\theta x} \mathbf{A}_k' + \mathbf{f}_{\theta_k}^x \Sigma_{k|k}^{\theta\theta}(\mathbf{f}_{\theta_k}^x)' + \mathbf{Q}_k$$
$$+ \sum_{i \in X} \sum_{j \in X} \mathbf{e}^i \mathbf{e}^{j'} \operatorname{tr}\left[\mathbf{a}_\theta^i \Sigma_{k|k}^{\theta x} \mathbf{a}_\theta^j \Sigma_{k|k}^{\theta x} + \mathbf{a}_\theta^i \Sigma_{k|k}^{\theta\theta} \mathbf{a}_\theta^j \Sigma_{k|k}^{xx}\right] \quad (10\text{-}55)$$

$$\Sigma_{k+1|k}^{\theta x} = \mathbf{D}_k \Sigma_{k|k}^{\theta x} \mathbf{A}_k' + \mathbf{D}_k \Sigma_{k|k}^{\theta\theta}(\mathbf{f}_{\theta k}^x)' \quad (10\text{-}56)$$

$$\Sigma_{k+1|k}^{\theta\theta} = \mathbf{D}_k \Sigma_{k|k}^{\theta\theta} \mathbf{D}_k' + \mathbf{G}_k \quad (10\text{-}57)$$

Also recall that the $\mathbf{f}_{\theta k}^x$ term is given as

$$\mathbf{f}_{\theta k}^x = \sum_i \mathbf{e}_i \hat{\mathbf{x}}_{k|k}' \mathbf{a}_\theta^i + \sum_i \mathbf{e}_i (\mathbf{u}_k^\tau)' \mathbf{b}_\theta^i + \sum_i \mathbf{e}_i \mathbf{c}_\theta^i \quad (10\text{-}58)$$

The initial conditions for Eqs. (10-55) to (10-57) are normally set to be diffuse priors; i.e., the diagonal elements of $\Sigma_{0|0}^{\theta\theta}$ and $\Sigma_{0|0}^{xx}$ are set to large numbers and the other elements of these two matrices and the elements of $\Sigma_{0|0}^{\theta x}$ are set to zero.

Step 2 Obtain the nominal paths $(\mathbf{x}_{o,j})_{j=k+1}^{N}$ and $(\mathbf{u}_{o,j})_{j=k+1}^{N-1}$ by using $\hat{\mathbf{x}}_{k+1|k}$ as the initial state and solving the certainty-equivalence problem from period $k + 1$

to period N. This also provides the initial value of $\mathbf{u}_k^\tau$ for the search, i.e. for $\tau = 1$. Thus $\mathbf{u}_k^1 = \mathbf{u}_k^{CE}$.

Step 3 Compute the Riccati matrices $\mathbf{K}^{\theta x}$ and $\mathbf{K}^{\theta\theta}$ for periods $k + 1$ to period N. (Recall that $\mathbf{K}^{xx} = \tilde{\mathbf{K}}$ was computed during the initialization stage.) For these computations use the backward recursions (10-40) and (10-42). The matrix $\mathbf{K}_j$ can then be formed from the components by using Eq. (10-38).

Step 4 Calculate the deterministic component of the approximate cost-to-go for period k and for period N (but not for the periods in between) by using the first through third terms on the right-hand side of Eq. (10-49).

Step 5 Calculate the cautionary component for period $k + 1$ by using the first three terms in Eq. (10-50). This expression uses the terms $\Sigma_{k+1|k}$. They are available from step 1. It also uses the terms $\mathbf{K}_{k+1}$, which were calculated in step 3.

Step 6a: DETERMINISTIC COMPONENT For each period $j = k + 2, \ldots, N - 1$ evaluate the fourth through sixth terms in Eq. (10-49).

Step 6a: DETERMINISTIC COMPONENT For each period $j = k + 2, \ldots, N - 1$ evaluate the fourth through sixth terms in Eq. (10-49).

Step 6b: CAUTIONARY COMPONENT Use the fourth and fifth terms in Eq. (10-50).

Step 6c: PROBING COMPONENT Use the right-hand side of Eq. (10-51). The $\mathbf{K}_{j+1}$ matrices were calculated in step 3, but the $\Sigma_{j|j}$ matrices must be calculated. They are obtained by using Eqs. (10-55) to (10-57) to get $\Sigma_{j|j-1}$ from $\Sigma_{j-1|j-1}$. Then $\Sigma_{j|j}$ can be obtained from $\Sigma_{j|j-1}$ by using Eqs. (K-17) to (K-19).

$$\Sigma^{xx}_{k+1|k+1} = \left[\mathbf{I} - \Sigma^{xx}_{k+1|k}\mathbf{H}'_{k+1}\mathbf{S}^{-1}_{k+1}\mathbf{H}_{k+1}\right]\Sigma^{xx}_{k+1|k} \quad (10\text{-}59)$$

$$\Sigma^{\theta x}_{k+1|k+1} = \left(\Sigma^{x\theta}_{k+1|k+1}\right)' = \Sigma^{\theta x}_{k+1|k}\left[\mathbf{I} - \mathbf{H}'_{k+1}\mathbf{S}^{-1}_{k+1}\mathbf{H}_{k+1}\Sigma^{xx}_{k+1|k}\right] \quad (10\text{-}60)$$

$$\Sigma^{\theta\theta}_{k+1|k+1} = \Sigma^{\theta\theta}_{k+1|k} - \Sigma^{\theta x}_{k+1|k}\mathbf{H}'_{k+1}\mathbf{S}^{-1}_{k+1}\mathbf{H}_{k+1}\Sigma^{x\theta}_{k+1|k} \quad (10\text{-}61)$$

where, from Eq. (K-15),

$$\mathbf{S}_{k+1} = \mathbf{H}_{k+1}\Sigma^{xx}_{k+1|k}\mathbf{H}'_{k+1} + \mathbf{R}_{k+1} \quad (10\text{-}62)$$

Step 6d. TOTAL COST-TO-GO Sum the deterministic, cautionary, and probing terms over the periods $k + 1$ to N.

Step 7 Choose a new control $\mathbf{u}_k^{\tau+1}$ for the grid search. In practice the total cost-to-go in step 6 is evaluated at 20 to 30 points in the range where the optimal control is expected to lie. This is used when $\mathbf{u}_k$ consists of a single control and when there is concern that $J_d(\mathbf{u}_k)$ may have local optima. If local optima are not a concern, gradient methods can be employed at this step to get the new control $\mathbf{u}_k^{\tau+1}$.

Step 8 Repeat steps 1 through 7 until all the search points have been evaluated (for a grid-search technique) or until satisfactory convergence is obtained (for gradient methods).

This concludes the eight steps in the search for the optimal control $\mathbf{u}_k^*$ at time period k. The final part of the algorithm is the updating, outlined next.

10-5 UPDATING STATE AND PARAMETER ESTIMATES

Once the optimal control $\mathbf{u}_k^*$ has been determined, it is applied to the systems equations (10-13), (10-20), and (10-21) to obtain the two components of $\mathbf{z}_{k+1}$

$$\mathbf{z}_{k+1} = \begin{bmatrix} \mathbf{x}_{k+1} \\ \boldsymbol{\theta}_{k+1} \end{bmatrix} \tag{10-63}$$

where
$$\mathbf{x}_{k+1} = \mathbf{A}_k \hat{\mathbf{x}}_{k|k} + \mathbf{B}_k \mathbf{u}_k^* + \mathbf{c}_k + \mathbf{v}_k \tag{10-64}$$

and
$$\boldsymbol{\theta}_{k+1} = \mathbf{D}\hat{\boldsymbol{\theta}}_{k|k} + \boldsymbol{\eta}_k \tag{10-65}$$

A Monte Carlo procedure is used to generate the random variables $\mathbf{v}_k$ and $\boldsymbol{\eta}_k$ using the covariances $\mathbf{Q}_k$ and $\mathbf{G}_k$, respectively.

Next the values $\mathbf{x}_{k+1}$ and $\boldsymbol{\theta}_{k+1}$ are used in the measurement relationship (10-14) with (10-22) and (10-23) to obtain the measurement vector $\mathbf{y}_{k+1}$

$$\mathbf{y}_{k+1} = \begin{bmatrix} \mathbf{H}_{k+1} & \vdots & \mathbf{O} \end{bmatrix} \begin{bmatrix} \mathbf{x}_{k+1} \\ \hdashline \boldsymbol{\theta}_{k+1} \end{bmatrix} + \begin{bmatrix} \mathbf{w}_{k+1} \\ \hdashline \mathbf{O} \end{bmatrix}$$

or
$$\mathbf{y}_{k+1} = \mathbf{H}_{k+1}\mathbf{x}_{k+1} + \mathbf{w}_{k+1} \tag{10-66}$$

A Monte Carlo procedure is used to generate the random elements in $\mathbf{w}_{k+1}$ using the covariance $\mathbf{R}_{k+1}$.

Finally the measurement vector $\mathbf{y}_{k+1}$ is used in the augmented Kalman filter equations (N-7) and (N-8) to obtain updated estimates of the means of the initial states $\mathbf{x}$ and of the parameters $\boldsymbol{\theta}$

$$\hat{\mathbf{x}}_{k+1|k+1} = \hat{\mathbf{x}}_{k+1|k} + \Sigma_{k+1|k}^{xx} \mathbf{H}'_{k+1} \mathbf{S}_{k+1}^{-1} \left[\mathbf{y}_{k+1} - \mathbf{H}_{k+1}\hat{\mathbf{x}}_{k+1|k} \right] \tag{10-67}$$

$$\hat{\boldsymbol{\theta}}_{k+1|k+1} = \hat{\boldsymbol{\theta}}_{k+1|k} + \Sigma_{k+1|k}^{\theta x} \mathbf{H}'_{k+1} \mathbf{S}_{k+1}^{-1} \left[\mathbf{y}_{k+1} - \mathbf{H}_{k+1}\hat{\mathbf{x}}_{k+1|k} \right] \tag{10-68}$$

where
$$\mathbf{S}_{k+1} = \mathbf{H}_{k+1}\Sigma_{k+1|k}^{xx} \mathbf{H}'_{k+1} + \mathbf{R}_{k+1} \tag{10-69}$$

These estimates are then used as the starting values for the next time period. The algorithm is then repeated for each time period until the last period is reached.

If one wishes to make comparisons across Monte Carlo run, the entire multiperiod problem must be solved for each set of random elements obtained. This is the procedure used in Chap. 12.

CHAPTER ELEVEN

EXAMPLE: THE MACRAE PROBLEM

11-1 INTRODUCTION

Two examples are presented in this chapter and Chap. 12. The first is a problem drawn from MacRae (1972), with a single state variable and a single control variable. It was chosen both because it was simple enough to permit hand calculations and because a variant of it was used in Chap. 7 to illustrate the calculations used for passive-learning stochastic control. The calculations for this problem are shown in considerable detail, both to enhance understanding and to make them more useful for debugging computer programs. This same problem was used by Bar-Shalom and Tse (1976a) to compare the performance of a number of active-learning stochastic control algorithms.

The second problem is constructed from the small macroeconometric model used in the deterministic example in Chap. 4. Detailed calculations for the second problem are not given; instead the focus is on the final results and their economic implications.

11-2 PROBLEM STATEMENT: MACRAE PROBLEM

Find (u_0, u_1) to minimize

$$J = \tfrac{1}{2}qx_2^2 + \frac{1}{2}\sum_{k=0}^{1}(qx_k^2 + ru_k^2) \qquad (11\text{-}1)$$

subject to
$$x_{k+1} = ax_k + bu_k + c + \varepsilon_k \quad \text{for } k = 0, 1 \quad (11\text{-}2)$$
$$x_0 = 0$$

MacRae uses a set of different parameter values. For this example, let

$$a = .7 \quad b = -.5 \quad c = 3.5 \quad \sigma_\varepsilon = .2$$
$$q = 1 \quad r = 1 \quad \sigma_b = .5 \quad \sigma_a = \sigma_c = 0$$

Only the b parameter is treated in an adaptive manner. The parameters a and c are treated as though they were known perfectly.

In the notation used in the previous chapter the parameters of this problem are as follows:

$$\mathbf{A} = .7 \quad \mathbf{B} = -.5 \quad \mathbf{c} = 3.5 \quad \mathbf{x}_0 = 0$$
$$\tilde{\mathbf{x}}_2 = \tilde{\mathbf{x}}_1 = \tilde{\mathbf{x}}_0 = 0 \quad \tilde{\mathbf{u}}_1 = \tilde{\mathbf{u}}_0 = 0 \quad \hat{\boldsymbol{\theta}}_{0|0} = -.5 \quad \Sigma^{xx}_{0|0} = 0 \quad \Sigma^{\theta\theta}_{0|0} = .5$$
$$\Sigma^{\theta x}_{0|0} = 0 \quad \mathbf{Q} = .2 \quad \mathbf{W}_2 = \mathbf{W}_1 = \mathbf{W}_0 = 1 \quad \Lambda_1 = \Lambda_0 = 1$$

The only element in $\boldsymbol{\theta}$ is the single unknown parameter b. The desired paths are set to zero. Since the problem assumes perfect observation, the initial covariance of $\mathbf{x}$ is zero. Because $\mathbf{A}$ and $\mathbf{c}$ are not functions of $\boldsymbol{\theta}$ but b is, we have

$$\mathbf{x}_{k+1} = \mathbf{A}\mathbf{x}_k + \mathbf{B}(\boldsymbol{\theta})\mathbf{u}_k + \mathbf{c} + \boldsymbol{\varepsilon}_k \quad (11\text{-}3)$$

Also, since it is assumed the b is unknown but constant, the parameter equations (10-9) become

$$\boldsymbol{\theta}_{k+1} = \mathbf{D}\boldsymbol{\theta}_k + \boldsymbol{\gamma}_k \quad (11\text{-}4)$$

with $\mathbf{D} = 1$. It is assumed that

$$\hat{\gamma}_{0|0} = 0 \quad \text{and} \quad \sigma_\gamma = 0$$

So, in the notation of Chap. 10,

$$\gamma_k \sim N(0, \mathbf{G}_k) \quad \text{with } \mathbf{G}_k = 0$$

Since there is no measurement error, the measurement equation

$$\mathbf{y}_k = \mathbf{H}\mathbf{x}_k + \mathbf{w}_k \quad (11\text{-}5)$$

becomes

$$y_k = x_k + w_k \quad \text{with} \quad \begin{matrix} w_k \sim N(0, \mathbf{R}_k) \\ \mathbf{R}_k = 0 \end{matrix} \quad (11\text{-}6)$$

11-3 CALCULATION OF THE COST-TO-GO

The calculations performed here follow the description in Sec. 10-4.

Initialization

(a) Initialize with $k = 0$.
(b) Generate $\theta_{o,j}$ with Eq. (11-4). Since the parameter is assumed to be constant, one has

$$\theta_{o,j} = -.5 \qquad j = (0, 1)$$

(c) Compute $\tilde{K}_j$ and $\tilde{p}_j$ for $j = 1, 2$ from (10-33) and (10-34)

$$\tilde{K}_2 = W_2 = 1$$
$$\tilde{p}_2 = -W_2'\tilde{x}_2 = -(1)(0) = 0 \qquad (11\text{-}7)$$
$$\tilde{K}_1 = A'[I - \tilde{K}_2 B\mu_1 B']\tilde{K}_2 A + W_1$$

where, from Eq. (10-32),

$$\mu_1 = [\Lambda_1 + B'\tilde{K}_2 B]^{-1} = [1 + (-.5)(1)(-.5)]^{-1} = .8$$

Therefore,

$$\tilde{K}_1 = .7[1 - (1)(-.5)(.8)(-.5)](1)(.7) + 1 = 1.392$$

Also,

$$\tilde{p}_1 = -A\tilde{K}_2 B\mu_1 [B'(\tilde{K}_2 c + \tilde{p}_2) - \Lambda_1 \tilde{u}_1] + A'(\tilde{K}_2 c + \tilde{p}_2)$$
$$= -(.7)(1)(-.5)(.8)\{(-.5)[(1)(3.5) + 0] - (1)(0)\} + (.7)[(1)(3.5) + 0]$$
$$= 1.96 \qquad (11\text{-}8)$$

In summary,

k	$\tilde{K}_k$	$\tilde{p}_k$
2	1	0
1	1.392	1.96

(d) Set $u_k = u_k^{CE}$ as given by Eq. (10-30)

$$u_0 = -\mu_0 [B'(K_1 A x_0 + K_1 c + p_1) - \Lambda_0 \tilde{u}_1] \qquad (11\text{-}9)$$
$$\mu_0 = [\Lambda_0 + B'K_1 B]^{-1} = [1 + (-.5)(1.392)(-.5)]^{-1} = .742$$

Then, from Eq. (11-9),

$$u_0 = -(.742)\{(-.5)[(1.392)(.7)(0) + (1.392)(3.5) + 1.96] - (1)(0)\} = 2.534$$

Search for Optimal Control

Search for optimal control in period k as outlined in Sec. 10-4. Those steps are followed here.

Step 1 Apply $\mathbf{u}_k$ to get the predicted state $\hat{\mathbf{z}}_{k+1|k}$ and its covariance, $\Sigma_{k+1|k}$. Use

$$\hat{\mathbf{z}}_{k+1|k} = \begin{bmatrix} \hat{\mathbf{x}}_{k+1|k} \\ \hat{\boldsymbol{\theta}}_{k+1|k} \end{bmatrix}$$

and, from Eq. (10-52),

$$\hat{\mathbf{x}}_{1|0} = \mathbf{A}\hat{\mathbf{x}}_{0|0} + \mathbf{B}(\boldsymbol{\theta}_{0|0})\mathbf{u}_0^\tau + \mathbf{c} + \text{tr}\left[\mathbf{a}_{\boldsymbol{\theta}}\Sigma_{k|k}^{\boldsymbol{\theta} x}\right] \quad (11\text{-}10)$$

Since $\mathbf{A}$ is not a function of $\boldsymbol{\theta}$, $\mathbf{a}_{\boldsymbol{\theta}} = 0$. Also $\mathbf{u}_k^\tau = \mathbf{u}_0^{CE} = 2.534$ from the initialization above. Therefore,

$$\hat{\mathbf{x}}_{1|0} = (.7)(0) + (-.5)(2.534) + 3.5 + 0 = 2.233$$

Similarly, from Eq. (10-53),

$$\hat{\boldsymbol{\theta}}_{1|0} = \mathbf{D}\hat{\boldsymbol{\theta}}_{0|0} \quad (11\text{-}11)$$

and since $\mathbf{D} = 1$,

$$\hat{\boldsymbol{\theta}}_{1|0} = \hat{\boldsymbol{\theta}}_{0|0} = -.5$$

The covariance $\Sigma_{k+1|k}$ is obtained by using Eq. (10-54)

$$\Sigma_{k+1|k} = \begin{bmatrix} \Sigma^{xx} & \Sigma^{x\theta} \\ \hline \Sigma^{\theta x} & \Sigma^{\theta\theta} \end{bmatrix}_{k+1|k} \quad (11\text{-}12)$$

where, from Eq. (10-55),

$$\Sigma_{1|0}^{xx} = \mathbf{A}\Sigma_{0|0}^{xx}\mathbf{A}' + \mathbf{A}\Sigma_{0|0}^{x\theta}\mathbf{f}_{\boldsymbol{\theta}0}^{x'} + \mathbf{f}_{\boldsymbol{\theta}0}^{x}\Sigma_{0|0}^{\theta x}\mathbf{A}' + \mathbf{f}_{\boldsymbol{\theta}0}^{x}\Sigma_{0|0}^{\theta\theta}\mathbf{f}_{\boldsymbol{\theta}0}^{x'} + \mathbf{Q}_0$$
$$+ \text{tr}\left[\mathbf{a}_{\boldsymbol{\theta}}\Sigma_{0|0}^{\theta x}\mathbf{a}_{\boldsymbol{\theta}}\Sigma_{0|0}^{\theta x} + \mathbf{a}_{\boldsymbol{\theta}}\Sigma_{0|0}^{\theta\theta}\mathbf{a}_{\boldsymbol{\theta}}\Sigma_{0|0}^{xx}\right] \quad (11\text{-}13)$$

with, from Eq. (10-58),

$$\mathbf{f}_{\boldsymbol{\theta}0}^{x} = \hat{\mathbf{x}}_{0|0}\mathbf{a}_{\boldsymbol{\theta}} + \mathbf{u}_0^\tau \mathbf{b}_{\boldsymbol{\theta}} + \mathbf{c}_{\boldsymbol{\theta}} \quad (11\text{-}14)$$

Since $\mathbf{A}$ and $\mathbf{c}$ are not functions of $\boldsymbol{\theta}$, $\mathbf{a}_{\boldsymbol{\theta}}$ and $\mathbf{c}_{\boldsymbol{\theta}}$ equal zero. However, b is a function of θ and $\mathbf{b}_{\boldsymbol{\theta}} = 1$, so

$$\mathbf{f}_{\boldsymbol{\theta}0}^{x} = 0 + (2.534)(1) + 0 = 2.534$$

Therefore, Eq. (11-13) becomes

$$\Sigma_{1|0}^{xx} = (.7)(0)(.7) + (.7)(0)(2.534) + (2.534)(0)(.7)$$
$$+ (2.534)(.5)(2.534) + .2 + 0 = 3.410 \quad (11\text{-}15)$$

Next use Eq. (10-56) to obtain

$$\Sigma_{1|0}^{\theta x} = \mathbf{D}\Sigma_{0|0}^{\theta x}\mathbf{A}' + \mathbf{D}\Sigma_{0|0}^{\theta\theta}\mathbf{f}_{\boldsymbol{\theta}0}^{x'}$$
$$= (1)(0)(.7) + (1)(.5)(2.534) = 1.267 \quad (11\text{-}16)$$

Finally, use Eq. (10-57) to obtain
$$\Sigma^{\theta\theta}_{1|0} = D\Sigma^{\theta\theta}_{0|0}D' + G_0 = (1)(.5)(1) + 0 = .5 \tag{11-17}$$

In summary
$$\hat{x}_{1|0} = 2.233 \qquad \hat{\theta}_{1|0} = -.5$$
$$\Sigma^{xx}_{1|0} = 3.410 \qquad \Sigma^{\theta x}_{1|0} = 1.267 \qquad \Sigma^{\theta\theta}_{1|0} = .5$$

Step 2 Use $\hat{x}_{1|0}$ as the initial state and solve the certainty-equivalence problem from period 1 to 2 by computing $(x_{o,j})^2_{j=1}$ and $(u_{o,j})^1_{j=1}$ using Eqs. (10-30) and (10-28). From Eq. (10-30),
$$u_{o,1} = -\mu_1\left[B(\tilde{K}_2 A\hat{x}_{1|0} + \tilde{K}_2 c + \tilde{p}_2) - \Lambda_1\tilde{u}_1\right]$$
with $\mu_1 = [\Lambda_1 + B'K_2B]^{-1} = [1 + (-.5)(1.0)(-.5)]^{-1} = .8 \tag{11-18}$
$$u_{o,1} = -(.8)\{(-.5)[(1)(.7)(2.233) + (1)(3.5) + 0] - (1)(0)\} = 2.025$$
and, from Eq. (10-28),
$$x_{o,2} = A\hat{x}_{1|0} + B(\theta_{o,1})u_{o1} + c$$
$$= (.7)(2.233) + (-.5)(2.025) + 3.5 = 4.050 \tag{11-19}$$

Therefore, the nominal path is

k	$x_{o,k}$	$u_{o,k}$
1	2.233	2.025
2	4.050	

Step 3 Compute $K^{\theta x}_j$ and $K^{\theta\theta}_j$ for $j = 1, 2$ by using the backward recursions (10-40) and (10-42). Recall that $K^{xx}_j = \tilde{K}_j$ from Eq. (10-39); therefore it is not necessary to evaluate it since $\tilde{K}_j$ was computed above.

First compute $K^{\theta x}_j$ using Eq. (10-40)
$$K^{\theta x}_2 = 0 \tag{11-20}$$
$$K^{\theta x}_1 = \left[f^{x\prime}_{\theta 1}K^{xx}_2 + D'K^{\theta x}_2\right]A$$
$$- \left[(f^{x\prime}_{\theta 1}K^{xx}_2 + D'K^{\theta x}_2)B + (p^x_2 b_\theta)'\right]\mu_1[BK^{xx}_2 A]$$
$$+ p^x_1 a_\theta \tag{11-21}$$
where, from Eq. (10-43),
$$p^x_2 = \tilde{K}_2 x_{o2} + \tilde{p}_2 = (1)(4.050) + 0 = 4.050 \tag{11-22}$$
and, from Eq. (10-41),
$$f^x_{\theta 1} = \hat{x}_{o1} a_\theta + u_{o1} b_\theta + c_\theta$$
$$= (2.233)(0) + (2.025)(1) + 0 = 2.025 \tag{11-23}$$

and, from Eq. (10-32),

$$\mu_1 = [\Lambda_1 + B'K_2B]^{-1} = [1 + (-.5)(1.0)(-.5)] = (1.25)^{-1} = .8$$

Then Eq. (11-21) can be solved as

$$K_1^{\theta x} = [(2.025)(1) + (1)(0)](.7)$$
$$- \{[(2.025)(1) + (1)(0)](-.5) + (4.050)(1)\}.8(-.5)(1)(.7)$$
$$+ (4.050)(0) = 2.268 \qquad (11\text{-}24)$$

Next calculate $K_1^{\theta\theta}$ from Eq. (10-42) as

$$K_2^{\theta\theta} = 0 \qquad (11\text{-}25)$$

$$K_1^{\theta\theta} = f_{\theta 1}^{x'}[K_2^{xx}f_{\theta 1}^x + K_2^{x\theta}D] + D'[K_2^{\theta x}f_{\theta 1}^x + K_2^{\theta\theta}D]$$
$$- [(f_{\theta 1}^{x'}K_2^{xx} + D'K_2^{\theta x})B + p_2^x b_\theta]\mu_1$$
$$\times [B'(K_2^{xx}f_{\theta 1}^x + K_2^{x\theta}D) + p_2^x b_\theta]$$
$$= (2.025)[(1)(2.025) + (0)(1)] + (1)[(0)(2.025) + (0)(1)]$$
$$- \{[(2.025)(1) + (1)(0)](-.5) + (4.050)(1)\}(.8)$$
$$\times \{(-.5)[(1)(2.025) + (0)(1)] + (4.050)(1)\} = -3.282$$

In summary, the Riccati matrices for the augmented problem are

k	K_k^{xx}	$K_k^{\theta x}$	$K_k^{\theta\theta}$	p_k^x
1	1.392	2.268	-3.282	
2	1.000	0	0	4.050

In order to show the breakdown for the cost-to-go into deterministic, cautionary, and probing components, steps 4 through 6 from Sec. 10-4 will be used.

Step 4 Calculate the deterministic cost for period k and period N by using the first through third terms on the right-hand side of Eq. (10-49). Calling the sum of these terms $J_{D,N-k}^{Nk}$, one obtains

$$J_{D,N-k}^{Nk} = [x_k - \tilde{x}_k]'F_k[u_k - \tilde{u}_k] + \tfrac{1}{2}[u_k - \tilde{u}_k]'\Lambda_k[u_k - \tilde{u}_k]$$
$$+ \tfrac{1}{2}[x_{oN} - \tilde{x}_N]'W_N[x_{oN} - \tilde{x}_N]$$
$$J_{DN}^{Nk} = \tfrac{1}{2}(2.534 - 0)(1)(2.534 - 0)$$
$$+ \tfrac{1}{2}(4.050 - 0)(1)(4.050 - 0) = 11.412 \qquad (11\text{-}26)$$

Step 5 Calculate the cautionary cost for period $k + 1$ by using the first three terms in Eq. (10-50)

$$J_{C,N-k}^{k+1} = \tfrac{1}{2}\text{tr}(\mathbf{K}_{k+1}^{xx}\boldsymbol{\Sigma}_{k+1|k}^{xx}) + \text{tr}(\mathbf{K}_{k+1}^{\theta x}\boldsymbol{\Sigma}_{k+1|k}^{x\theta}) + \tfrac{1}{2}\text{tr}(\mathbf{K}_{k+1}^{\theta\theta}\boldsymbol{\Sigma}_{k+1|k}^{\theta\theta})$$

$$J_{C,N}^{k+1} = \tfrac{1}{2}\text{tr}(\mathbf{K}_1^{xx}\boldsymbol{\Sigma}_{1|0}^{xx}) + \text{tr}(\mathbf{K}_1^{\theta x}\boldsymbol{\Sigma}_{1|0}^{x\theta}) + \tfrac{1}{2}\text{tr}(\mathbf{K}_1^{\theta\theta}\boldsymbol{\Sigma}_{1|0}^{\theta\theta}) \qquad (11\text{-}27)$$

$$J_{CN}^{k+1} = \tfrac{1}{2}[(1.392)(3.410)] + (2.268)(1.267) + \tfrac{1}{2}[(-3.282)(.5)] = 4.426$$

Step 6 Repeat steps 6a through 6d for time periods $j = k + 1$ through $j = N - 1$, that is, from $j = 1$ through $j = 1$.

STEP 6a Calculate the future deterministic cost for period j by evaluating the fourth through sixth terms in Eq. (10-49) (using $\mathbf{F} = 0$)

$$J_{D,N-k}^F = \frac{1}{2}\sum_{j=1}^{1}\left([\mathbf{x}_{oj} - \tilde{\mathbf{x}}_j]'\mathbf{W}_j[\mathbf{x}_{oj} - \tilde{\mathbf{x}}_j] + [\mathbf{u}_{oj} - \tilde{\mathbf{u}}_j]'\Lambda_j[\mathbf{u}_{oj} - \tilde{\mathbf{u}}_j]\right)$$

$$J_{DN}^F = \tfrac{1}{2}[(2.233)(1)(2.233) + (2.025)(1)(2.025)] = 4.543 \qquad (11\text{-}28)$$

STEP 6b Calculate the future cautionary cost for period j by evaluating the fourth and fifth terms in Eq. (10-50)

$$J_{C,N-k}^F = \frac{1}{2}\sum_{j=1}^{1}\left(\text{tr}[\mathbf{K}_2^{xx}\mathbf{Q}_1] + \text{tr}[\mathbf{K}_2^{\theta\theta}\mathbf{G}_1]\right)$$

$$J_{CN}^F = \tfrac{1}{2}[\text{tr}(1.0)(.2) + \text{tr}(0)(0)] = \tfrac{1}{2}[(.2) + 0] = .100 \qquad (11\text{-}29)$$

STEP 6c Calculate the future probing cost for period j by evaluating the right-hand side of Eq. (10-51). The $\mathbf{K}_{j+1}$ matrices are available from step 3, but the $\boldsymbol{\Sigma}_{j|j}$ matrices must be computed. From Eq. (10-51)

$$J_{P,k} = \tfrac{1}{2}\text{tr}([\mathbf{A}'\mathbf{K}_2^{xx}\mathbf{B}]\mu_1[\mathbf{B}'\mathbf{K}_2^{xx}\mathbf{A}]\boldsymbol{\Sigma}_{1|1}^{xx})$$
$$+ \text{tr}([\mathbf{B}'\mathbf{K}_2^{xx}\mathbf{A}]'\mu_1(\mathbf{B}'[\mathbf{K}_2^{xx}\mathbf{f}_{\theta_1}^x + \mathbf{K}_2^{x\theta}\mathbf{D}] + \mathbf{p}^x\mathbf{b}_\theta)\boldsymbol{\Sigma}_{1|1}^{\theta x})$$
$$+ \tfrac{1}{2}\text{tr}([[\mathbf{D}'\mathbf{K}_2^{\theta x} + \mathbf{f}_{\theta_1}^{x'}\mathbf{K}_2^{xx}]\mathbf{B} + \mathbf{p}^x\mathbf{b}_\theta]$$
$$\times \mu_1[\mathbf{B}'[\mathbf{K}_2^{xx}\mathbf{f}_{\theta_1}^x + \mathbf{K}_2^{x\theta}\mathbf{D}] + \mathbf{p}^x\mathbf{b}_\theta]\boldsymbol{\Sigma}_{1|1}^{\theta\theta}) \qquad (11\text{-}30)$$

All the matrices in Eq. (11-30) except the $\boldsymbol{\Sigma}_{j|j}$ terms have been computed before. To obtain the $\boldsymbol{\Sigma}_{j|j}$'s use Eqs. (10-55) to (10-57) to get $\boldsymbol{\Sigma}_{j|j-1}$ from $\boldsymbol{\Sigma}_{j-1|j-1}$ and Eqs. (K-17) to (K-19) to get $\boldsymbol{\Sigma}_{j|j}$ from $\boldsymbol{\Sigma}_{j|j-1}$.

We need $\boldsymbol{\Sigma}_{1|1}$ in order to evaluate Eq. (11-30). This can be obtained by using Eqs. (10-55) to (10-57) to obtain $\boldsymbol{\Sigma}_{1|0}$ from $\boldsymbol{\Sigma}_{0|0}$, but this has already been accomplished in step 1, with the result

$$\boldsymbol{\Sigma}_{1|0}^{xx} = 3.410 \qquad \boldsymbol{\Sigma}_{1|0}^{\theta x} = 1.267 \qquad \boldsymbol{\Sigma}_{1|0}^{\theta\theta} = .5$$

Then, to obtain $\Sigma^{xx}_{1|1}$ use Eq. (10-59)

$$\Sigma^{xx}_{1|1} = \left[I - \Sigma^{xx}_{1|0}H'_1 S_1^{-1}H_1\right]\Sigma^{xx}_{1|0} \qquad (11\text{-}31)$$

where, from Eq. (10-62),

$$S_1 = H_1\Sigma^{xx}_{1|0}H'_1 + R_1$$
$$= (1)(3.410)(1) + 0 = 3.410$$

Therefore,

$$S_1^{-1} = .293$$

and thus

$$\Sigma^{xx}_{1|1} = [1 - (3.410)(1)(.293)(1)](3.410) = 0$$

In this situation with no measurement error and $H = 1$, the covariance of the state variables reduces to zero after the new measurement is taken.

Next, use Eq. (10-60) to obtain

$$\Sigma^{\theta x}_{1|1} = \Sigma^{\theta x}_{1|0}\left[I - H'_1 S_1^{-1}H_1\Sigma^{xx}_{1|0}\right]$$
$$= 1.267[1 - (1)(.293)(1)(3.410)] = 0 \qquad (11\text{-}32)$$

with the result that $\Sigma^{\theta x}_{1|1}$ also is zero after the measurement.

Finally, use Eq. (10-61) to obtain

$$\Sigma^{\theta\theta}_{1|1} = \Sigma^{\theta\theta}_{1|0} - \Sigma^{\theta x}_{1|0}H'_1 S_1^{-1}H_1\Sigma^{x\theta}_{1|0}$$
$$= .5 - (1.267)(1)(.293)(1)(1.267) = .03 \qquad (11\text{-}33)$$

Also, with perfect measurement and a single unknown parameter there is a substantial reduction in the uncertainty associated with the parameter θ. In this case the variance of b (the only element in θ) is reduced from .5 to .03 by a single measurement. In summary, from the initial data, from the initialization, and this step:

$j\|k$	$\Sigma^{xx}_{j\|k}$	$\Sigma^{\theta x}_{j\|k}$	$\Sigma^{\theta\theta}_{j\|k}$
0|0	0	0	.500
1|0	3.410	1.267	.500
1|1	0	0	.030

Now Eq. (11-30) can be evaluated. Since both $\Sigma^{xx}_{1|1}$ and $\Sigma^{\theta x}_{1|1}$ are equal to zero, it can be simplified substantially to

$$J_{P,N} = \tfrac{1}{2}\text{tr}\Big(\big[[D'K^{\theta x}_2 + \mathbf{fx}'_{\theta 1}K^{xx}_2]B + \mathbf{p}^x_2\mathbf{b}_\theta\big] \\ \times \mu_1\big[B'[K^{xx}_2\mathbf{f}^x_{\theta 1} + K^{x\theta}_2 D] + \mathbf{p}^x_2\mathbf{b}_\theta\big]\Sigma^{\theta\theta}_{1|1}\Big) \qquad (11\text{-}34)$$

Also, $f_{\theta1}^x$, μ_1, and p_2^x can be obtained from Eqs. (11-23) and (11-22), respectively, giving

$$J_{P,N} = \tfrac{1}{2}\text{tr}([[(1)(0) + (2.025)(1)](-.5) + (4.050)(1)](.8)$$
$$\{(-.5)[(1)(2.025) + (0)(1)] + (4.050)(1)\}(.03)) = .110$$

In summary, the deterministic component can be obtained from steps 4 and 6a as

$$J_{D,N} = J_{D,N}^{Nk} + J_{D,N}^{F} = 11.412 + 4.543 = 15.955 \tag{11-35}$$

The cautionary component is obtained from steps 5 and 6b as

$$J_{C,N} = J_{C,N}^{k+1} + J_{C,N}^{F} = 4.426 + .1 = 4.526 \tag{11-36}$$

Finally, the probing component is obtained from Eq. (11-34) in step 6c as

$$J_{P,N} = .110 \tag{11-37}$$

STEP 6d The total cost-to-go conditional on $\mathbf{u}_k$ is then obtained by summing the three components, as in Eq. (10-45)

$$J_{d,N-k}(\mathbf{u}_k) = J_{D,N-k} + J_{C,N-k} + J_{P,N-k} \tag{11-38}$$

or, for $\mathbf{u} = 2.534$ at time $k = 0$,

$$J_{d,N}(2.534) = J_{D,N} + J_{C,N} + J_{P,N}$$
$$= 15.955 + 4.526 + .110$$
$$= 20.591$$

This completes the evaluation of the approximate cost-to-go for a single value of the control, namely $\mathbf{u}_0 = 2.534$. As the search proceeds, the cost-to-go function is evaluated at other values of the control.

11-4 THE SEARCH

The search is then carried out to find that value of the control $\mathbf{u}_0^*$ which minimizes $J_{d,k}$.[1] Table 11-1 and Fig. 11-1 give the results of the evaluation of the deterministic, cautionary, and probing cost as well as the total cost for a number of values of the control $\mathbf{u}_0$.[2]

In Fig. 11-1 the deterministic cost component is relatively large and has the expected quadratic shape. The cautionary cost component rises with increases in the control value; i.e., caution results in a smaller control value than the deterministic component alone would imply. Finally, the probing cost component falls with increases in the control value. Thus, caution and probing work in

---

[1] For a discussion of this, see Kendrick (1978).
[2] See also Bar-Shalom and Tse (1976a, p. 331).

Table 11-1 Evaluation of cost-to-go and its components for the MacRae problem

Control u_0	Deterministic $J_{D,N}$	Cautionary $J_{C,N}$	Probing $J_{P,N}$	Total $J_{d,N}$
1.17	17.201	1.197	.496	18.894
1.28	17.005	1.434	.423	18.863
1.32	16.935	1.525	.400	18.860
1.37	16.869	1.616	.378	18.863
1.56	16.588	2.056	.294	18.938
2.53	15.957	4.527	.108	20.593

opposite directions; however, the probing term is smaller and has a smaller slope.

By way of contrast and in order to emphasize that the function $J_d(u_k)$ may have local minima, Fig. 11-2 provides a plot similar to Fig. 11-1 but for a slightly different problem. This problem is the same as the previous MacRae problem with two exceptions: (1) all three of the parameters a, b, and c are treated as unknown rather than only b (the initial variances of all three parameters are set

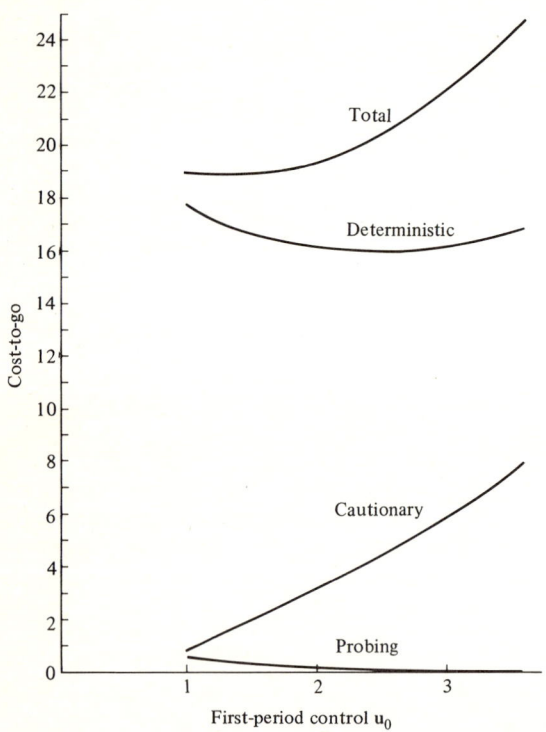

Figure 11-1 Total cost-to-go and components of two-period MacRae problem.

EXAMPLE: THE MACRAE PROBLEM

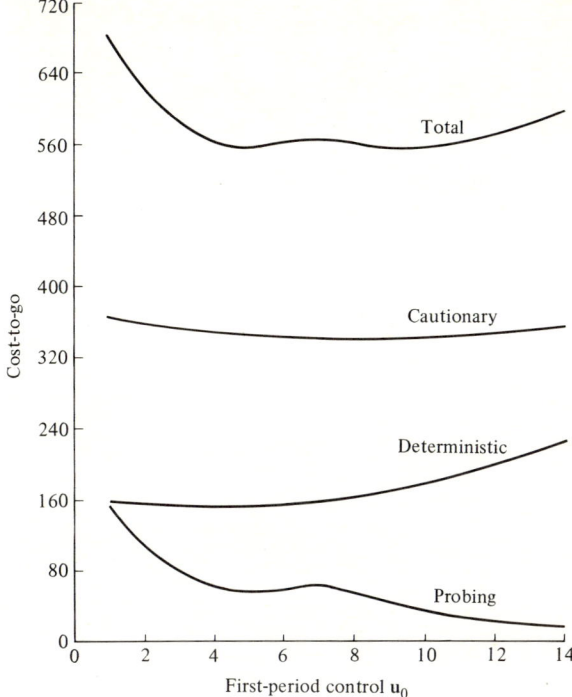

Figure 11-2 Total cost-to-go and components for 10-period MacRae problem.

at .5), and (2) the model is solved for 10 time periods instead of 2 (the penalty ratio of q to r is kept at 1 : 1 for all time periods).

As Fig. 11-2 shows, the probing cost component is nonconvex, and this produces two local optima in the total cost-to-go. This situation was discovered by accident. The author and Fred Norman were using this problem to debug their separately programmed codes. Both obtained the local optimum around 5 and concluded that the codes were debugged.

The author subsequently modified his code, solved the problem again, and found the local optimum near 10. At first it seemed that there was an error in the modified code, but subsequent analysis revealed the nonconvex shape of the cost-to-go function.

CHAPTER
TWELVE

EXAMPLE: A MACROECONOMIC MODEL WITH MEASUREMENT ERROR

12-1 INTRODUCTION

In Chap. 4 a small quarterly macroeconomic model of the United States economy was used as an example of deterministic control. Here that model is converted into a stochastic control model with measurement error and solved with the active-learning algorithm of Chap. 10.

Four sources of uncertainty are added to the model of Chap. 4:

1. An additive error (or noise) term in the system equations
2. An error term in the measurement equations
3. Uncertainty about initial conditions
4. Uncertainty about parameter values in the system equations

Of these four sources of uncertainty, the first is the most widely considered in economic models. It was discussed as additive uncertainty in Chap. 5. The fourth type of uncertainty, i.e., the parameter values, was discussed under multiplicative uncertainty in Chap. 6; however, the control was not chosen in an active-learning manner. Uncertainty of types 2 and 3 are much less widely used in economic models. There is a substantial literature in econometrics on measurement errors [see Geraci (1976)], but this has not previously been systematically incorporated into macroeconometric models to show the effect of measurement error on policy choice. A new start in this direction was made by Conrad

(1977) and the model of this chapter continues by including measurement error in a model with active learning.

Since different economic time series are of greatly varying accuracy, the use of measurement-error information provides a systematic way to take account of this fact while choosing policy levels. For example, the uncertainty associated with inventory investment data is much greater than that associated with aggregate consumption data; so one would like to discount somewhat inventory investment data relative to consumption data when making decisions about fiscal and monetary policy. The procedures outlined in Chaps. 9 and 10 provide a way to do this.

Also, once one introduces measurement error, it becomes apparent that the initial conditions of the model can no longer be treated as though they were known with certainty. Instead one must take account of the fact that policy makers do not know the present state of the economy exactly. However, economists frequently have information about the degree of uncertainty attached to each element in a state vector describing the economy. It is this information which is exhibited in the application discussed in this chapter.

12-2 THE MODEL AND DATA

Recall from Eq. (4-25) that the model can be written as

$$\mathbf{x}_{k+1} = \mathbf{A}\mathbf{x}_k + \mathbf{B}\mathbf{u}_k + \mathbf{c} \tag{12-1}$$

where

$$\mathbf{x}_k = \begin{bmatrix} C_k \\ I_k \end{bmatrix} = \begin{bmatrix} \text{consumption} \\ \text{investment} \end{bmatrix} \qquad \mathbf{u}_k = O_k = [\text{obligation}] \tag{12-2}$$

with

$$\mathbf{A} = \begin{bmatrix} 1.014 & .002 \\ .093 & .753 \end{bmatrix} \qquad \mathbf{B} = \begin{bmatrix} -.004 \\ -.100 \end{bmatrix} \qquad \mathbf{c} = \begin{bmatrix} -1.312 \\ .448 \end{bmatrix} \tag{12-3}$$

and

$$\mathbf{x}_0 = \begin{bmatrix} 460.1 \\ 113.1 \end{bmatrix} \tag{12-4}$$

Also from Eq. (4-26) the criterion function is

$$J = \tfrac{1}{2}[\mathbf{x}_N - \tilde{\mathbf{x}}_N]'\mathbf{W}_N[\mathbf{x}_N - \tilde{\mathbf{x}}_N]$$

$$+ \frac{1}{2}\sum_{k=0}^{N-1}([\mathbf{x}_k - \tilde{\mathbf{x}}_k]'\mathbf{W}_k[\mathbf{x}_k - \tilde{\mathbf{x}}_k] + [\mathbf{u}_k - \tilde{\mathbf{u}}_k]'\Lambda_k[\mathbf{u}_k - \tilde{\mathbf{u}}_k]) \tag{12-5}$$

where $\tilde{\mathbf{x}}$ = desired state vector
$\tilde{\mathbf{u}}$ = desired control vector
$\mathbf{W}$ = weights on state deviations
Λ = weights on control deviations

The paths $\tilde{x}$ and $\tilde{u}$ were chosen by assuming desired growth rates of .75 percent per quarter. The base for these desired paths are the actual data for 1969-I

$$\tilde{x}_0 = \begin{bmatrix} 460.1 \\ 113.1 \end{bmatrix} \qquad \tilde{u}_0 = [153.644] \qquad (12\text{-}6)$$

The weighting matrices were chosen to give greater weights to state deviations in the terminal year than in other years in order to model the fact that political leaders care much more about the state of the economy in quarters just before elections than in other quarters. Therefore, these matrices were set as

$$\mathbf{W}_N = \text{diag}[100, 100] \qquad \mathbf{W}_k = \text{diag}[1, 1] \qquad \Lambda_k = [1]$$
$$k = 0, 1, \ldots, N-1 \qquad (12\text{-}7)$$

The stochastic version of the model is obtained by minimizing the expected value of Eq. (12-5) subject to system equations

$$\mathbf{x}_{k+1} = \mathbf{A}\mathbf{x}_k + \mathbf{B}\mathbf{u}_k + \mathbf{c} + \mathbf{v}_k \qquad \begin{matrix} \mathbf{x}_0 \sim N[\hat{\mathbf{x}}_{0|0}, \Sigma^{xx}_{0|0}] \\ \mathbf{v}_k \sim N[\mathbf{0}, \mathbf{Q}] \end{matrix} \qquad (12\text{-}8)$$

and measurement relations

$$\mathbf{y}_k = \mathbf{H}\mathbf{x}_k + \mathbf{w}_k \qquad \mathbf{w}_k \sim N[\mathbf{0}, \mathbf{R}] \qquad (12\text{-}9)$$

where $\mathbf{v}$ = system-equation noises
$\mathbf{w}$ = measurement errors
$\mathbf{H}$ = measurement matrix
$\mathbf{y}$ = measurement vector

It is assumed here that the initial $\mathbf{x}$ is known imperfectly and that its estimate is normally distributed with mean $\hat{\mathbf{x}}_{0|0}$ and covariance $\Sigma^{xx}_{0|0}$. The system-equation noise $\mathbf{v}_k$ and the measurement noise are both assumed to be normally distributed and serially uncorrelated with means zero and covariances $\mathbf{Q}$ and $\mathbf{R}$, respectively. Although it is not true that the error terms are uncorrelated, that assumption has been used here for the sake of simplicity.

The diagonal elements of the covariance of the system-noise terms $\mathbf{Q}$ are the square of the standard errors of the reduced-form equation errors. The diagonal elements of this matrix are

$$\mathbf{Q} = \text{diag}[9.61, 18.92] \qquad (12\text{-}10)$$

The measurement-error covariance $\mathbf{R}$ was estimated from the revisions data by the procedure outlined in Appendix R. The resulting matrix is

$$\mathbf{R} = \begin{bmatrix} 2.71 & 1.12 \\ 1.12 & 2.78 \end{bmatrix} \qquad (12\text{-}11)$$

Note that the variance of the measurement error for consumption is low relative to its value of x_0 (2.71 on 460.1 billion) while that of investment is relatively high (2.78 on 113.1 billion). The algorithm described here takes account of this fact and relies less heavily on the observed value of investment y_2 than the observed value of consumption y_1 in updating estimates of both states and parameters and therefore in determining the control to be used in subsequent periods.

In the results reported here a single case of parameter uncertainty has been considered. In this case all eight of the coefficients in **A**, **B**, and **c** were learned.[1] As in Chap. 10, a parameter vector $\boldsymbol{\theta}$ consisting of the uncertain parameters is created and added to the initial state vector **x** to create a new state vector **z**. The state equations for the augmented model are

$$\mathbf{x}_{k+1} = \mathbf{A}(\boldsymbol{\theta}_k)\mathbf{x}_k + \mathbf{B}(\boldsymbol{\theta}_k)\mathbf{u}_k + \mathbf{c}(\boldsymbol{\theta}_k) + \mathbf{v}_k \qquad (12\text{-}12)$$

$$\boldsymbol{\theta}_{k+1} = \mathbf{D}\boldsymbol{\theta}_k + \boldsymbol{\eta}_k \qquad (12\text{-}13)$$

where **D** is assumed to be an identity matrix and $\boldsymbol{\eta}$ is assumed to have both mean and covariance equal to zero (to model the case of constant but unknown parameters).

Part of the system equations, namely Eq. (12-12), is now nonlinear in the new state vector

$$\mathbf{z}_k = \begin{bmatrix} \mathbf{x}_k \\ \boldsymbol{\theta}_k \end{bmatrix} \qquad (12\text{-}14)$$

Also, the covariance of the state vector at time k as estimated with data obtained through period k is now defined as

$$\Sigma_{k|k}^{zz} = \begin{bmatrix} \Sigma_{k|k}^{xx} & \Sigma_{k|k}^{x\theta} \\ \Sigma_{k|k}^{\theta x} & \Sigma_{k|k}^{\theta\theta} \end{bmatrix} \qquad (12\text{-}15)$$

With this notation the initial conditions for the augmented state equations (12-12) and (12-13) are

$$\hat{\mathbf{x}}_{0|0} = \begin{bmatrix} 460.1 \\ 113.1 \end{bmatrix} \qquad \hat{\boldsymbol{\theta}}_{0|0} = \begin{bmatrix} 1.014 \\ .002 \\ -.004 \\ -1.312 \\ .093 \\ .753 \\ -.100 \\ .448 \end{bmatrix} \qquad (12\text{-}16)$$

$$\Sigma_{0|0}^{xx} = \begin{bmatrix} 2.71 & 1.12 \\ 1.12 & 2.78 \end{bmatrix} \qquad (12\text{-}17)$$

---

[1] In contrast, in Kendrick (1979) only 5 of the 15 parameters were learned. The other 10 were assumed to be known perfectly.

$$\Sigma_{0|0}^{\theta x} = \left(\Sigma_{0|0}^{x\theta}\right)' = \begin{bmatrix} 0 & 0 \\ 0 & 0 \\ 0 & 0 \\ 0 & 0 \\ 0 & 0 \\ 0 & 0 \\ 0 & 0 \\ 0 & 0 \end{bmatrix} \quad (12\text{-}18)$$

$$\Sigma_{0|0}^{\theta\theta} = \begin{bmatrix} \begin{array}{cccc} .2690\text{E}{-}03 & -.5469\text{E}{-}03 & -.3743\text{E}{-}03 & -.5619\text{E}-02 \\ -.5469\text{E}{-}03 & .2297\text{E}{-}02 & .1590\text{E}{-}03 & -.1992\text{E}-01 \\ -.3743\text{E}{-}03 & .1590\text{E}{-}03 & .9675\text{E}{-}03 & .1039\text{E}-01 \\ -.5619\text{E}{-}02 & -.1992\text{E}{-}01 & .1039\text{E}{-}01 & .2316\text{E}+01 \end{array} & & \\ & 0 & \\ & & 0 \\ & \begin{array}{cccc} .5440\text{E}{-}03 & -.1106\text{E}{-}02 & -.7568\text{E}{-}03 & -.1136\text{E}-01 \\ -.1106\text{E}{-}02 & .4644\text{E}{-}02 & .3215\text{E}{-}03 & -.4028\text{E}-01 \\ -.7568\text{E}{-}03 & .3215\text{E}{-}03 & .1956\text{E}{-}02 & .2102\text{E}-01 \\ -.1136\text{E}{-}01 & -.4028\text{E}{-}01 & .2102\text{E}{-}01 & .4684\text{E}+01 \end{array} \end{bmatrix} \quad (12\text{-}19)$$

The prior mean of x is set to x_0, and the prior mean for θ is set to the estimated reduced-form parameter estimates. The state covariance (12-17) is set equal to the measurement-error covariance. The covariance (12-18) was set to zero.[1] The covariance (12-19) was estimated with the Time Series Processor (TSP) econometric package.

12-3 ADAPTIVE VERSUS CERTAINTY-EQUIVALENCE POLICIES

When measurement errors are considered, will adaptive-control methods yield substantially better results than certainty-equivalence and open-loop-feedback methods? Posed another way, the question is whether or not it is worthwhile to carry out the elaborate calculations which are required to consider the possibility of learning parameters and the gains which accrue from this learning. Results presented later in this section provide some evidence that it is not worthwhile; however, these results are based on assumptions that many economists—including the author—find unrealistic. Before presenting the results a word of

---

[1] This covariance could be estimated by applying a Kalman filter to the same data that were used for estimating the reduced form of the model. Some sensitivity tests on an earlier model indicated that the results were affected substantially by the choice of $\Sigma_{0|0}^{\theta x}$.

caution about numerical results obtained from complicated calculations is in order.

As is apparent from Chap. 10, the computer codes from which these results have been obtained are rather complex since they include both estimation and optimization procedures embedded in a Monte Carlo routine. Independently coded programs have therefore been used to check results. Fred Norman, Yaakov Bar-Shalom, and the author have independently coded various versions

Table 12-1 Comparison of criterion values (thousands)[†]

Monte Carlo run	Order	Certainty equivalence C	Open-loop feedback O	Dual D
1	O, D, C	22.450	22.240	22.320
2	O, C, D	28.710	28.610	28.730
3	C, D, O	31.850	32.000	31.870
4	O, D, C	23.941	23.695	23.717
5	D, O, C	23.020	22.917	22.909
6	O, D, C	29.229	28.787	28.867
7	C, D, O	21.597	21.759	21.637
8	O, D, C	19.219	19.139	19.213
9	D, O, C	25.392	25.324	25.278
10	O, D, C	27.907	27.418	27.504
11	D, O, C	25.975	22.242	22.115
12	O, D, C	26.402	25.818	25.975
13	D, O, C	21.615	21.438	21.298
14	O, C, D	27.810	27.705	27.853
15	D, O, C	15.893	15.701	15.563
16	D, O, C	23.078	22.862	22.811
17	O, D, C	23.545	23.084	23.107
18	C, O, D	26.899	26.934	27.013
19	O, D, C	22.366	21.820	22.092
20	O, D, C	18.360	18.283	18.349
21	D, O, C	22.069	21.745	21.512
22	D, O, C	20.177	19.914	19.904
23	O, C, D	17.938	17.879	17.976
24	O, D, C	36.133	35.678	36.057
25	O, C, D	24.143	24.128	24.182
26	C, D, O	27.871	27.943	27.911
27	O, D, C	21.019	20.678	20.905
28	O, D, C	26.181	26.080	26.082
29	O, D, C	27.344	27.123	27.276
30	D, C, O	18.488	18.498	18.458
31	D, C, O	29.107	29.156	28.977
32	D, O, C	26.894	26.581	26.496
33	O, D, C	16.811	16.312	16.523
34	D, O, C	28.878	28.708	28.678

[†] In these runs, the number of times each method had the lowest cost was
OLF = 18   Dual = 12   CE = 4

and parts of the adaptive algorithms. The most complicated part of the code is in the evaluation of the cost-to-go. Norman (using his program), Kent Wall (using Bar-Shalom's program), and the author have been able to duplicate each other's results on a number of other problems but have not fully checked the present problem. Therefore, the results presented here must be checked against one's intuition until complete numerical checking can be accomplished. It is in this spirit that the results are presented.

Table 12-1 shows the results from the 34 Monte Carlo runs completed. For each run random values of the systems noise v_k, the measurement noises w_k, the initial state estimate $\hat{x}_{0|0}$, and the initial parameter estimate $\hat{\theta}_{0|0}$ are generated using the means and covariances described above. The evidence suggests that the sequential certainty-equivalence procedure of Appendix O is inferior to both the open-loop-feedback method (OLF) of Chap. 6 and the adaptive-control (dual) method of Chap. 10. Of the two stochastic methods the OLF was superior in 18 and the dual method in 12 of the 34 runs. As more data are obtained, it will be useful to see whether there is a statistically significant difference between the three methods.

If the OLF results continue to appear to be better than the dual results, it would be possible to use the computationally simple OLF results rather than the computationally complex dual procedures in performing stochastic control on macroeconomic models. Of course this tendency may not continue as larger models are used for experimentation. Also, these results are for a model in which the parameters are assumed to be constant over time. If, alternatively, it had been assumed that some or all of the parameters were time-varying (a realistic assumption for some parameters), the ranking of the three methods might be different. Under the assumption of time-varying parameters the initial covariance matrix for the parameters $\Sigma^{\theta\theta}_{0|0}$ would probably have larger elements, representing the fact that the parameters would be known with less certainty. Then there would be more to learn, and the dual method might be superior to the OLF method. However, though more could be learned, the information obtained would be less valuable since its worth would decay over time with the time-varying paths of the parameters.

12-4 RESULTS FROM A SINGLE MONTE CARLO RUN

In order to provide more insight into the types of results obtained from stochastic control models the results of one of the Monte Carlo runs (run 4) are presented in detail in the following pages. This run is representative in the sense that the OLF solution was the least costly (23.695), the dual was next (23.717), and the certainty-equivalence solution was the worst (23.914). Also the results make clear that the model used has some characteristics which detract from its usefulness for testing the relative performance of different control-theory methods on economic models.

EXAMPLE: A MACROECONOMIC MODEL WITH MEASUREMENT ERROR 123

The input data which are specific to Monte Carlo run 4 and the numerical results for that particular run are included in Appendix T. The primary results are displayed graphically in the remainder of this section.

Time Paths of Variables and of Parameter Estimates

Figures 12-1 and 12-2 show the time paths of the two state variables, consumption and investment, under each of the three control schemes, and the desired path for each state variable. Figure 12-1 tells very little about the results but illustrates one of the undesirable properties of this model, the fact that the consumption path is explosive and that differences in controls have very little impact on the consumption path. These results come from the fact that the coefficient a_{11} is 1.014 and the coefficient b_1 is $-.004$. Thus consumption grows almost independently of changes in government expenditures.

Figure 12-2 displays the investment paths under the alternative control schemes and is considerably more interesting. It illustrates the difficulty of maintaining an economy on a steady path in the face of the various kinds of uncertainty which face economic policy makers. (1) There is the additive

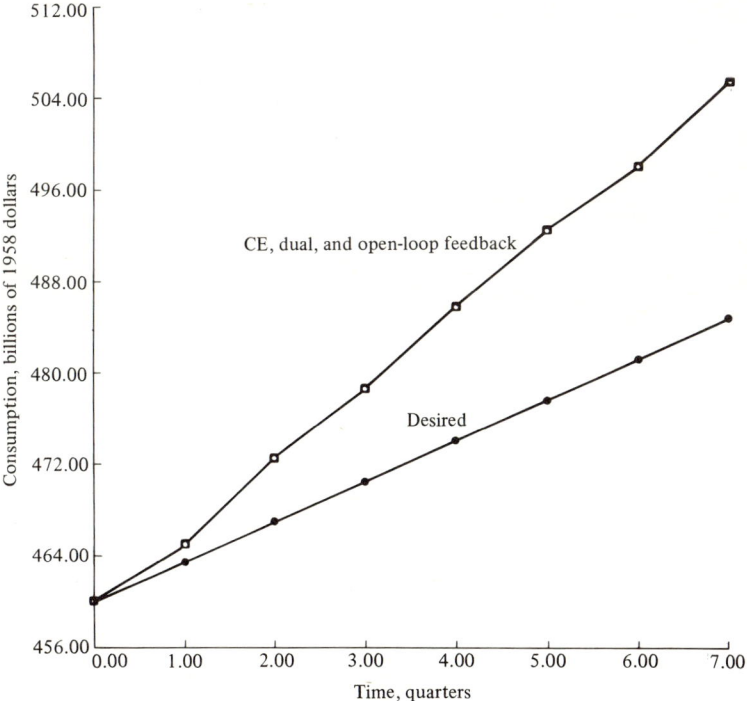

Figure 12-1 Consumption.

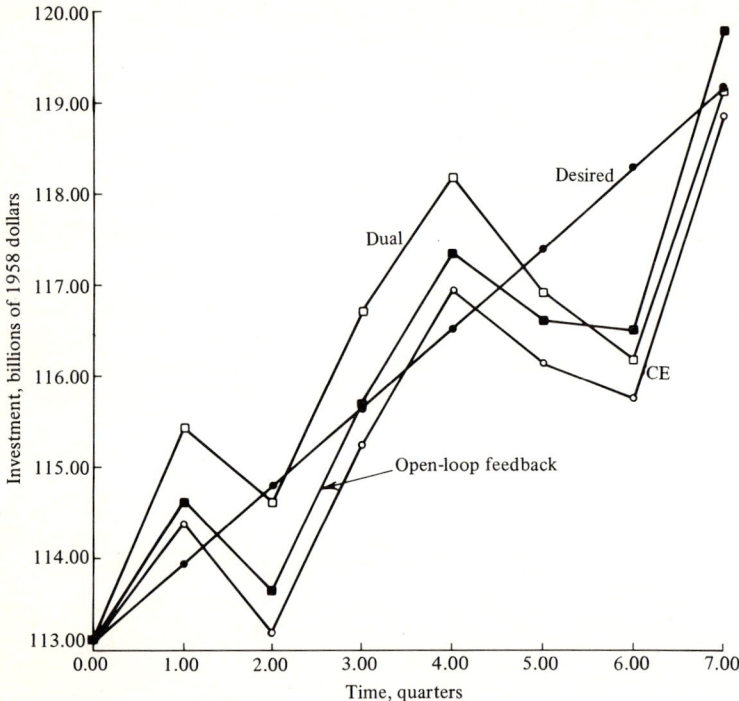

Figure 12-2 Investment.

uncertainty in the equation, representing the impact of unpredictable changes in investment which affect the level of investment additively. (2) The policy maker has an estimate of how the economy will respond to a policy measure but does not know what the actual response will be. (3) The policy maker does not know what the true state of the economy is at the moment because the statistics which report that state are affected by measurement errors.

Next compare the sequential certainty-equivalence path (CE) and the dual-control path (dual) in Fig. 12-2. Qualitatively, one would expect the dual-control path to deviate farther from the desired path than the certainty-equivalence path in the early time periods but be closer to the desired path in the terminal period (just before the election). This occurs in this particular Monte Carlo run. In the first time period desired investment is roughly 114.0 billion, the CE investment-path level is about 114.3, and the dual-path investment level is roughly 115.4. So the CE path deviates from the desired path by .3 billion while the dual path deviates by 1.4 billion. In contrast, in the last time period (period 7), supposedly the quarter just before the next presidential elections, the CE time path deviates from the desired by roughly .5 billion while the dual time path deviates by less than .1 billion. It should be emphasized that this kind of pattern is not observed

EXAMPLE: A MACROECONOMIC MODEL WITH MEASUREMENT ERROR 125

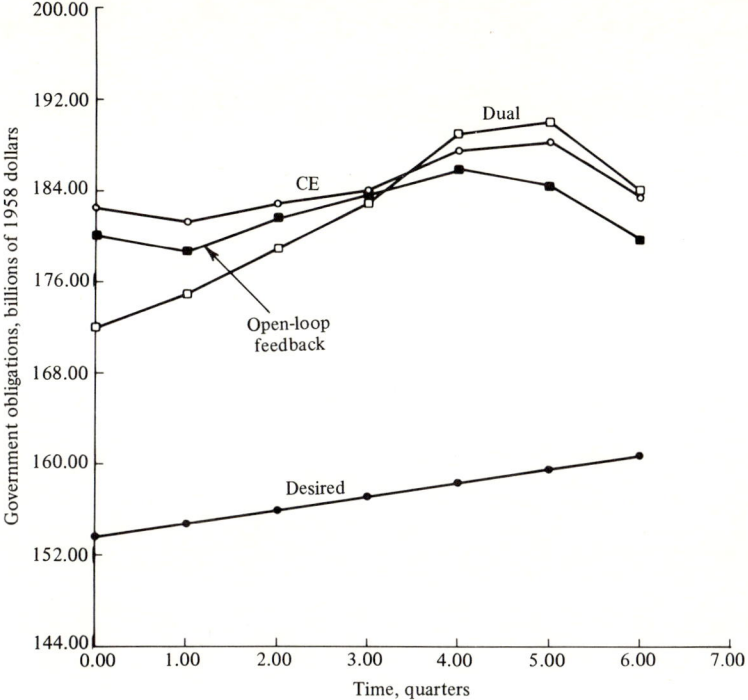

Figure 12-3 Government obligations.

in all the Monte Carlo runs but is illustrative of the kind of result that one expects when comparing certainty-equivalence results with dual-control results.

Next compare the OLF path with the adaptive-control (dual) path. This path is neither as far off the desired path in the first period nor as close to the desired path in the last period as the adaptive-control path. However, on average when all the costs are considered, including both the state and control cost, the OLF path has a slightly lower cost than the dual path.

If Fig. 12-2 seems to confirm one's preconceptions about adaptive-control results, Fig. 12-3 shows that matters are not so simple. This figure shows the desired, CE, OLF, and dual paths for the control variable, government obligations. The simplest preconceptions about the control path in the first time periods in stochastic control problems are (1) that solutions like OLF which consider uncertainty will be more "cautious," i.e., have smaller control values, than those like CE which do not consider uncertainty and (2) that solutions like dual which consider learning as well as uncertainty will do more "probing," i.e., have control values farther from the desired path, than solutions like OLF which consider the uncertainty but do not consider learning. One of these propositions is borne out by this particular Monte Carlo run, but the other is not. The OLF

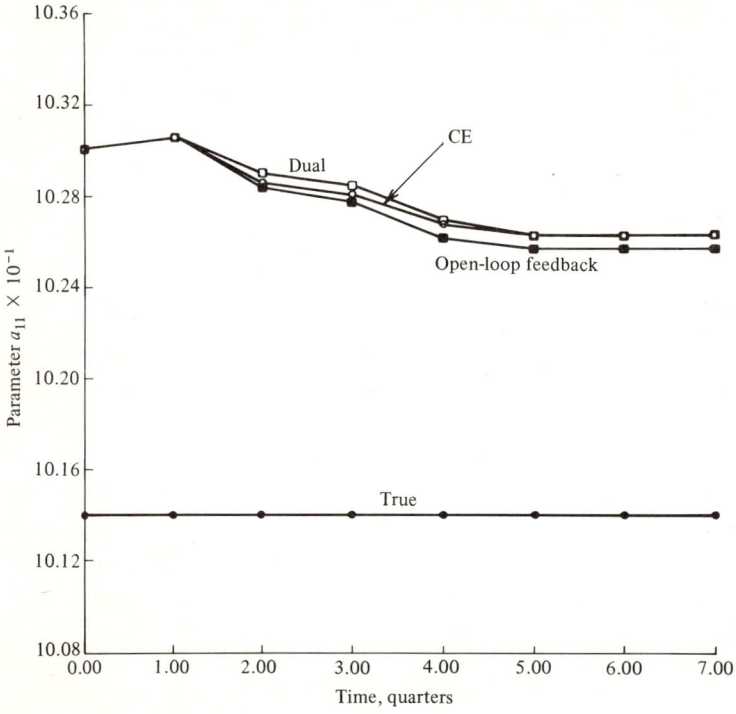

Figure 12-4 Parameter a_{11}.

path is indeed more cautious than the CE path in the first time period, but the dual path does not exhibit more probing than the OLF solution in the first few time periods. As work progresses in this field, it will be interesting to observe what classes of models will on average over many Monte Carlo runs exhibit both the caution and probing characteristics.[1]

Figures 12-4 to 12-11 show the paths of the eight parameter estimates in the vector $\hat{\boldsymbol{\theta}}$ for the eight time periods under each of the control methods. Figure 12-4 gives this information for the parameter a_{11}. The true value of the parameter is 1.014. The initial estimate of the parameter is 1.030, the same for all three methods. This initial estimate is generated by a Monte Carlo routine which uses the covariance of the parameter estimates.

---

[1]Preliminary results from dual control experiments on the Abel(1975) model with 2 state variables, 2 control variables, and 10 unknown parameters exhibit both the probing and the caution characteristics [Kendrick(1980a)].

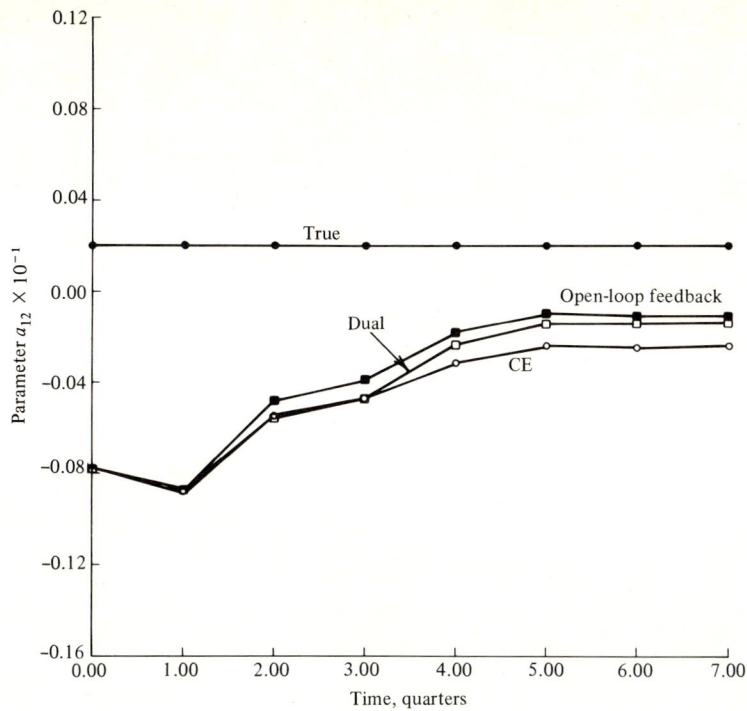

Figure 12-5 Parameter a_{12}.

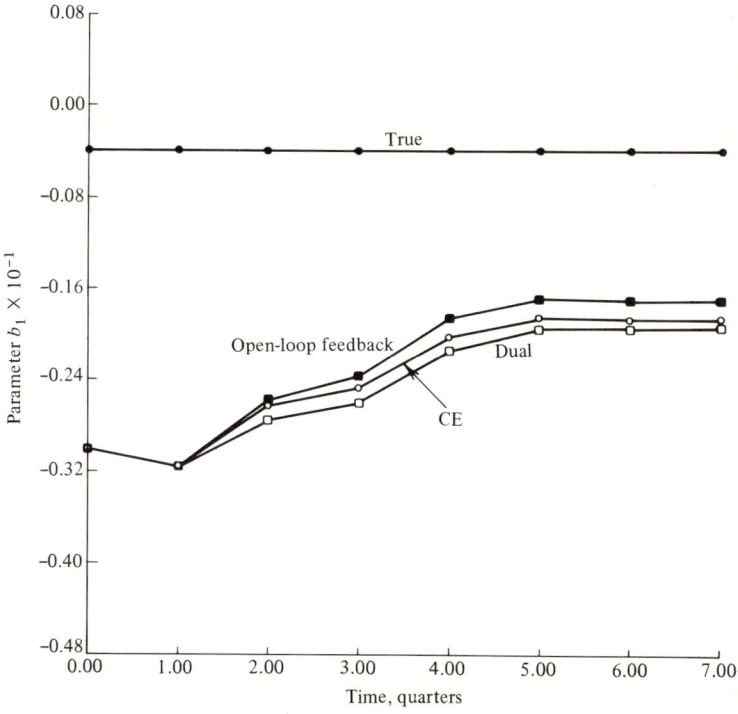

Figure 12-6 Parameter b_1.

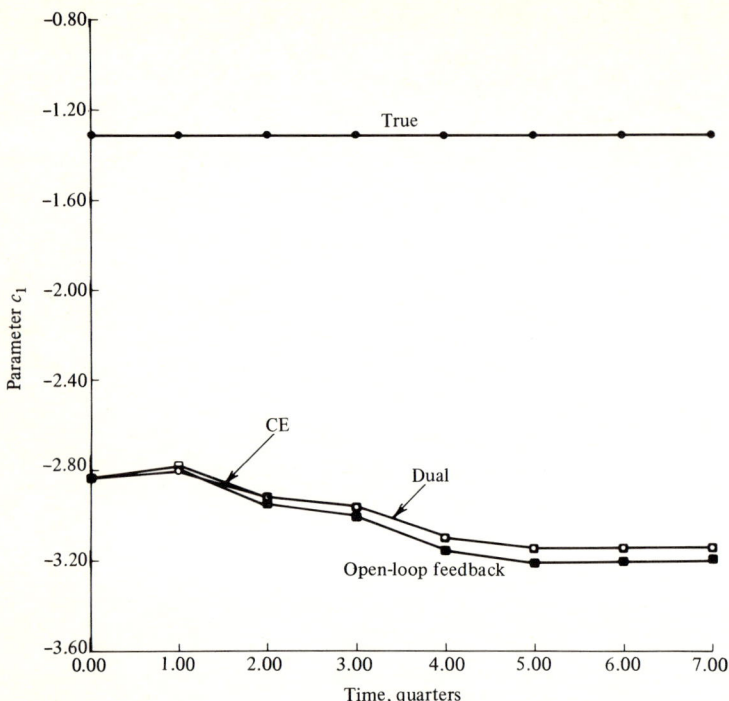

Figure 12-7 Parameter c_1.

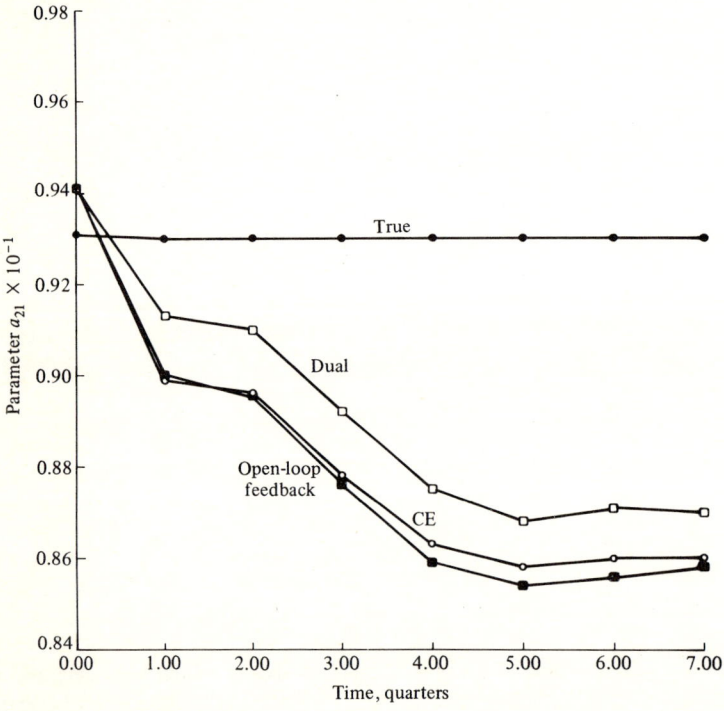

Figure 12-8 Parameter a_{21}.

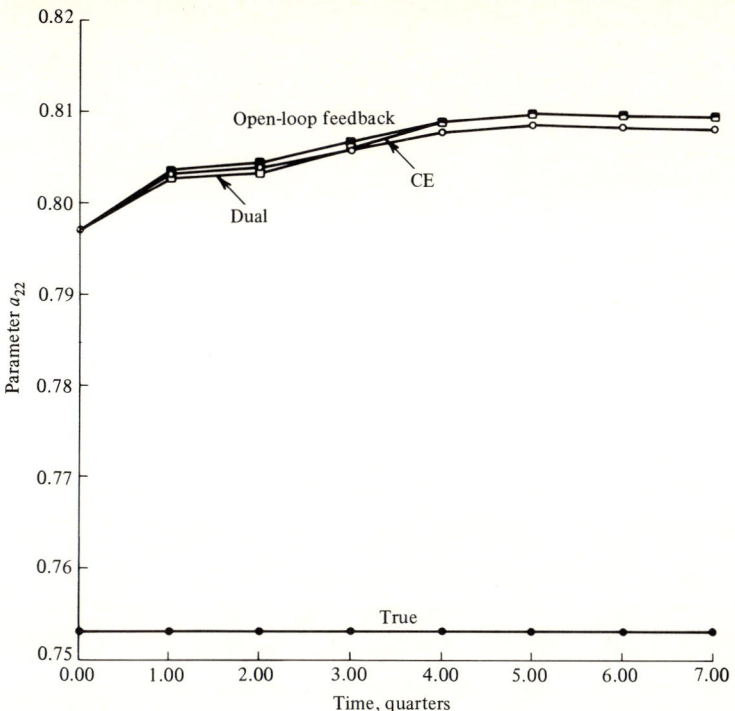

Figure 12-9 Parameter a_{22}.

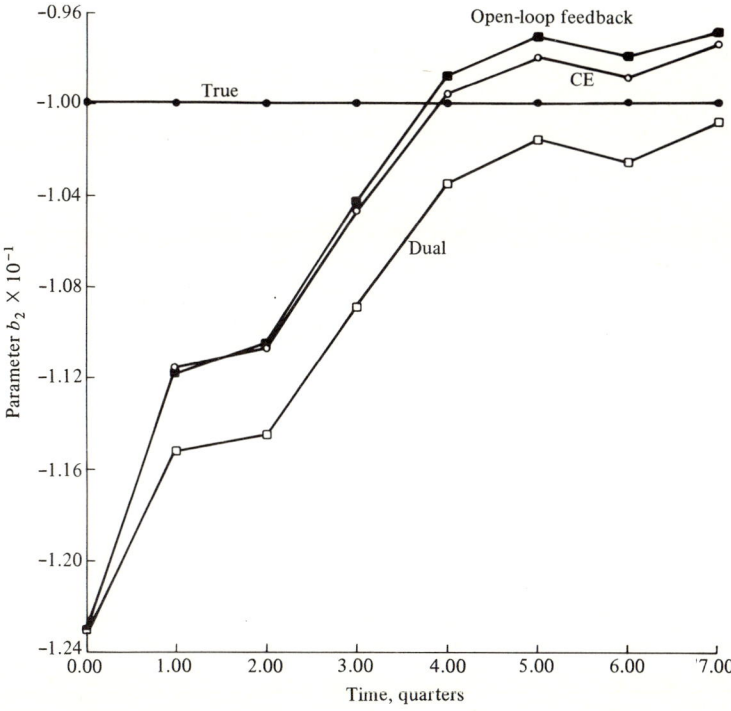

Figure 12-10 Parameter b_2.

130 ACTIVE-LEARNING STOCHASTIC CONTROL

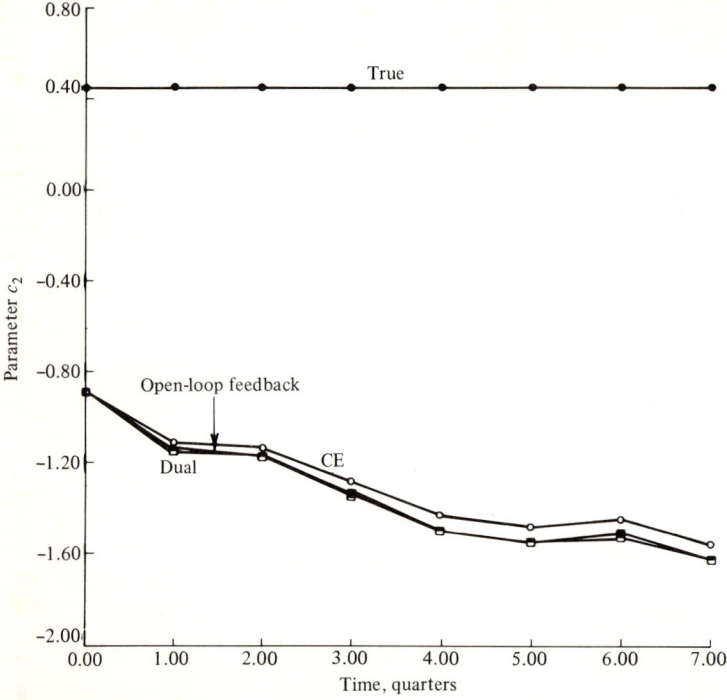

Figure 12-11 Parameter c_2.

In glancing at all eight of the parameter-estimate figures (12-4 to 12-11) one observes that for all three methods the estimates change substantially in the early periods and much less in the later periods. This is due to the fact that as more data are collected, the state and parameter-estimate covariance become smaller and the extended Kalman filter tends to assign lower weights to new observations in updating the parameter estimates. One can also observe that some of the parameter estimates actually diverge from, rather than converge to, the true values. While this is somewhat disturbing, it is worth remembering that the estimation done in the context of an optimal control algorithm does not treat all parameters equally. Some parameters are obviously more important than others when one considers the impact of uncertainty on the choice of control. For example, one of the most important parameters in this problem is b_2, the parameter for the government-obligations control variable in the investment equation. This parameter is shown in Fig. 12-10. The estimates for this parameter converge toward the true value. The estimate made in the adaptive-control (dual) solution is closer to the true value at the terminal time than either the CE or OLF estimates. However, in the problem at hand there is a heavy weight on deviations of the states from the desired path at the terminal time (period 7), so it may be more important to have a good estimate of b_2 in period 6 than in period 7. At period 6 the CE estimate is the closest, while the OLF and dual estimates are about equidistant from the true value.

This completes the discussion of the time paths of variables and of parameter estimates for the single Monte Carlo run. In order to understand these results better it is useful to separate the cost-to-go into several components.

Decomposition of the Cost-to-Go

As discussed in Sec. 10-3, it is possible to divide the approximate cost-to-go into three components, which were given the names deterministic, cautionary, and probing by Bar-Shalom and Tse (1976a). While there is debate about the efficacy of this particular separation and labeling of terms,[1] the separation into components has proved to be valuable in comparing results and debugging computer codes and in beginning to understand the character of the results.

In general functional form the three components are:

Deterministic: $\quad J_{D,N-k} = f\left(\mathbf{x}_k, \mathbf{u}_k, \mathbf{x}_{oN}, (\mathbf{x}_{oj}, \mathbf{u}_{oj})_{j=k+1}^{N-1}\right)$ (12-20)

Cautionary: $\quad J_{C,N-k} = f\left(\Sigma_{k+1|k}^{xx}, \Sigma_{k+1|k}^{\theta x}, \Sigma_{k+1|k}^{\theta\theta}, (\mathbf{Q}_j, \mathbf{G}_j)_{j=k+1}^{N-1}\right)$ (12-21)

Probing: $\quad J_{P,N-k} = f\left(\left(\Sigma_{j|j}^{xx}, \Sigma_{j|j}^{\theta x}, \Sigma_{j|j}^{\theta\theta}\right)_{j=k+1}^{N-1}\right)$ (12-22)

The detailed expressions are in Eqs. (10-49) to (10-51), and their derivation is given in Appendix Q.

The reader may recall from the earlier discussion that the deterministic component contains only nonrandom terms. All stochastic terms are in either the cautionary or the probing components. Of these stochastic terms the cautionary component includes terms in $\Sigma_{k+1|k}$, which represent the uncertainty in the system between the time a control is chosen at time k and the time the next control is chosen at time $k + 1$. In contrast, the probing component includes terms in $(\Sigma_{j|j})_{j=k+1}^{N-1}$, which is the uncertainty remaining in the system after measurements have been taken in each time period after the current time period k. In particular, this component includes the parameter covariance $\Sigma_{j|j}^{\theta\theta}$ for all future time periods. Since probing will serve to reduce the elements of this covariance, the component which includes the covariance is called the *probing component*.

Figures 12-12 to 12-18 show for each period the total cost-to-go and its breakdown into deterministic, cautionary, and probing terms as a function of the control $\mathbf{u}_k$ (government obligations).[2] Consider first Fig. 12-12 for period 0.

---

[1] See, for example, Dersin, Athans, and Kendrick (1979).

[2] A grid-search method was used to obtain the points shown in these figures. First the functions were evaluated at 20 points between $\mathbf{u}_k = 100$ and $\mathbf{u}_k = 195$. Then the function was evaluated at 10 points around the minimum found in the first grid search.

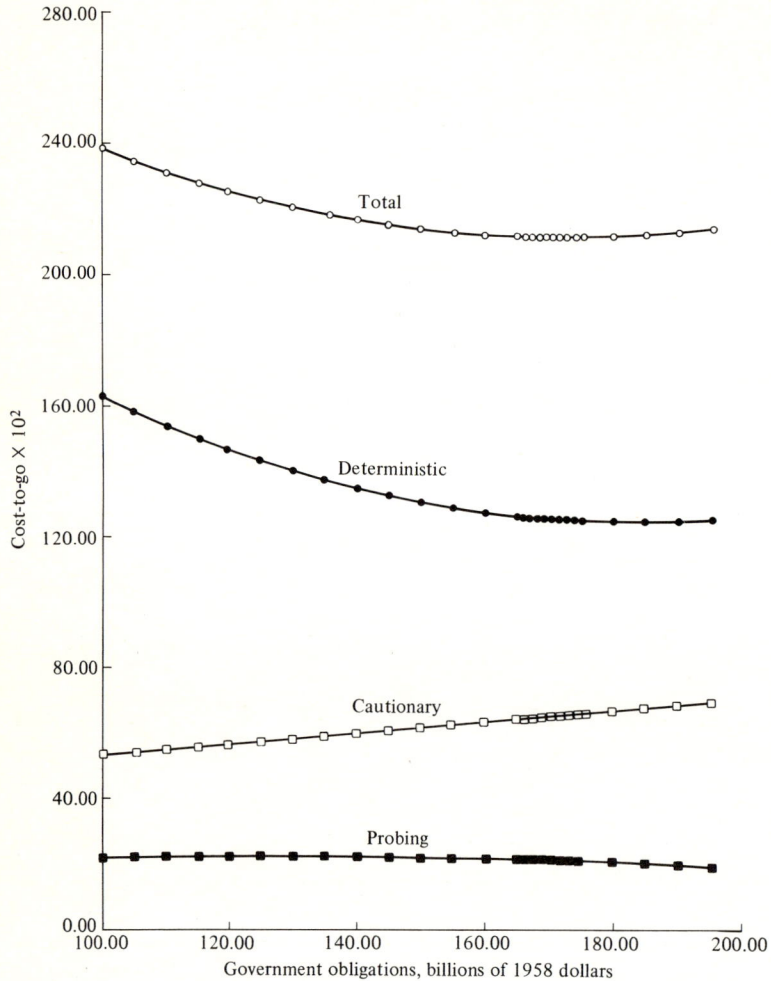

Figure 12-12 Period 0.

The deterministic component is the largest of the three, followed by the cautionary and the probing components. Also the deterministic component is a convex function, the cautionary component is roughly a linear function, and the probing component is concave. Since the cost-to-go is the sum of these three functions, it is not necessarily concave or convex and the problem of local optima is a real possibility. Recall that local optima did indeed occur in one variant of the MacRae problem discussed in Chap. 11 (see, for example, Fig. 11-2). For this reason a grid-search method was used in finding the minimum

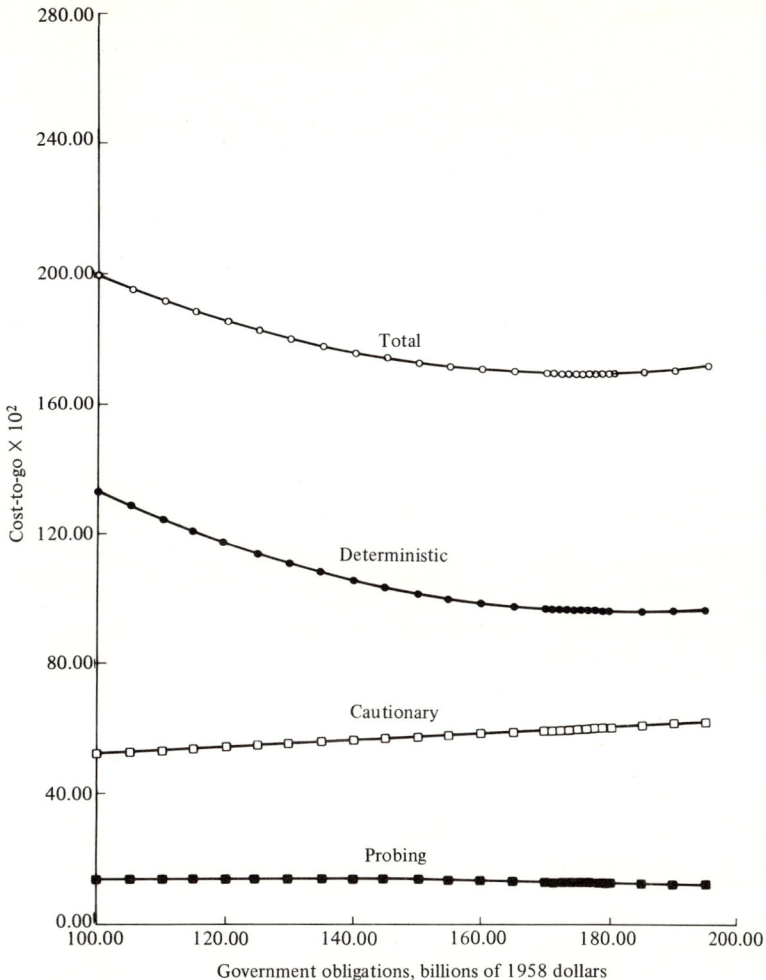

Figure 12-13 Period 1.

cost-to-go. The widely spaced points on each component represent the 20 values of government obligations at which the functions were evaluated. The closely spaced points in turn represent a finer grid evaluation at nine points centered on the minimum from the coarse-grid search.

A quick glance at Figs. 12-12 through 12-18 reveals that there is not a serious problem with local optima. Thus gradient methods probably could have been used. In fact this might have improved the relative standing on the dual method in the Monte Carlo runs. However, at this stage of the research, caution

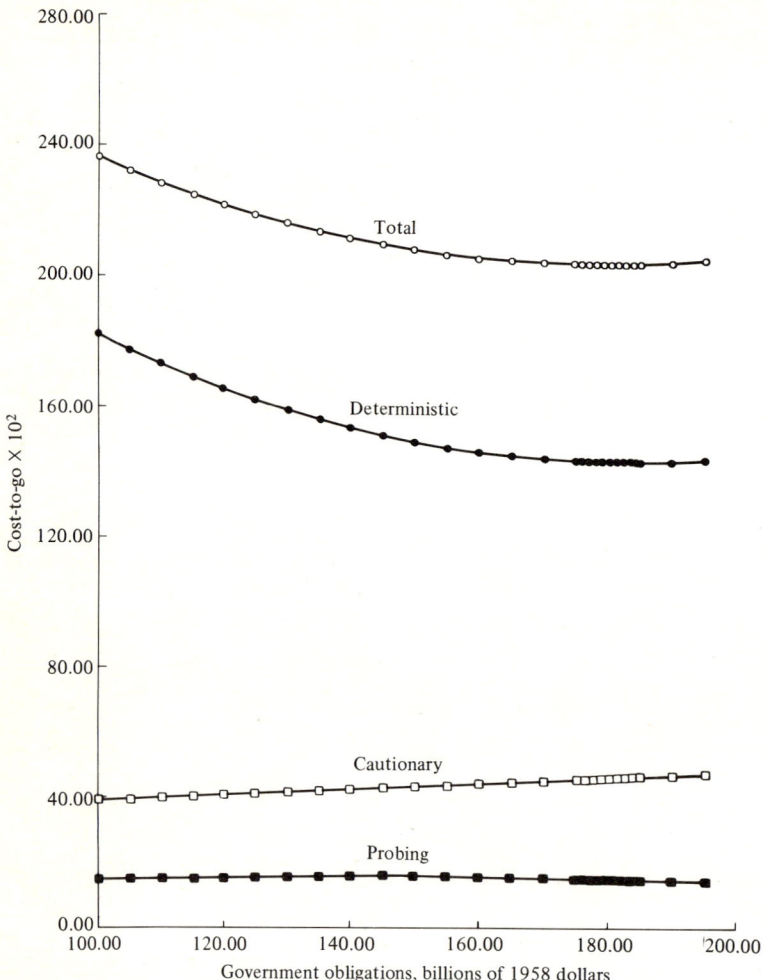

Figure 12-14 Period 2.

is advised. If it should result after a variety of macroeconomic models have been solved with grid-search methods that local optima are not a serious problem, gradient methods can be employed. This would be an important development because it would substantially reduce the cost of each Monte Carlo run, permitting wider experimentation.

Now consider the effect of each of the three components on the location of the minimum. The minimum of the *deterministic* cost component in Fig. 12-12 occurs at a government-obligation level of about 185 billion dollars. (The

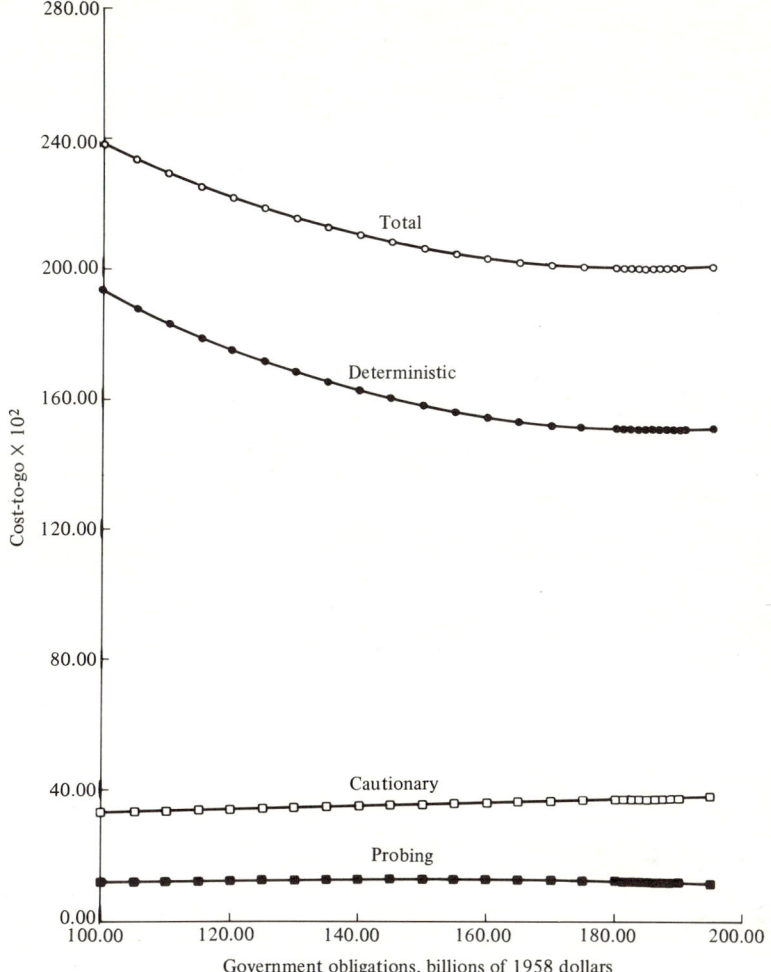

Figure 12-15 Period 3.

interested reader can find the numerical results in Appendix T, for period 0 in Table T-4.) In contrast, the minimum of the *total* cost occurs at roughly 170 billion dollars. Since the probing component is relatively flat, it is apparent that the positive slope of the cautionary term results in a decrease in the optimum level of the control from 185 to 170. Thus in this particular problem the cautionary term does indeed result in a more cautious policy. In contrast, the slope of the probing term near the optimum of 170 is small but negative; so the probing term has the effect of increasing the optimum level from the deterministic optimum.

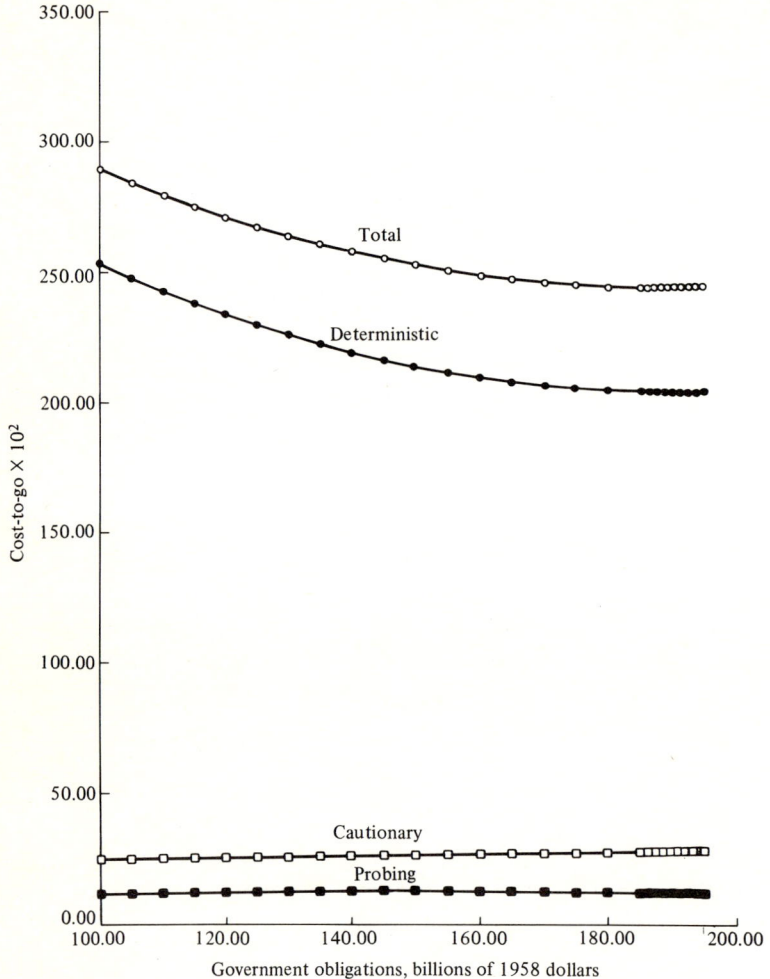

Figure 12-16 Period 4.

Thus in this problem for this time period the effect of the cautionary term is to result in a lower level of government expenditures, and the effect of the probing term is to cause a tendency toward higher levels of government expenditures. However, the cautionary term has a fairly large positive slope, and the probing form has a small negative slope. This suggests that, relative to the $\Sigma_{k+1|k}$ terms, the $(\Sigma_{j|j})_{j=k+1}^{N-1}$ terms are not changed much by changes in the government obligations. Another way to say this is that increases in government obligations have two effects. One is to increase the uncertainty about the levels of consumption and investment which will be obtained in the next period

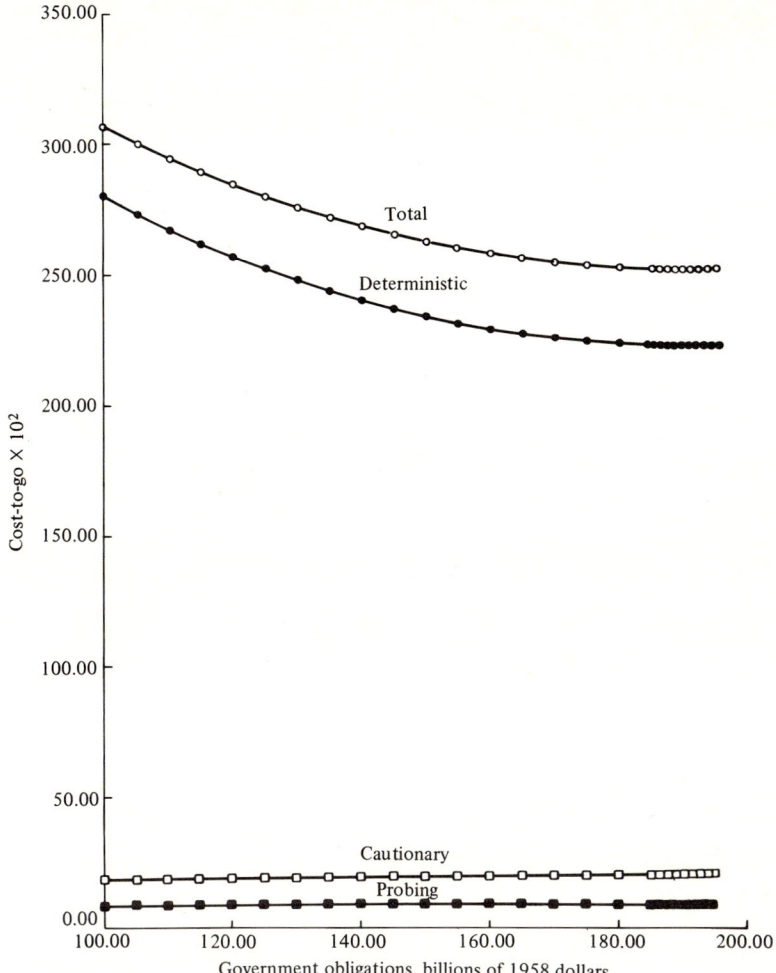

Figure 12-17 Period 5.

(period $k + 1$). The other is to decrease the uncertainty about postmeasurement values of the states and parameters in all future time periods. For this problem in this (and all other) time periods the two effects work in opposite directions, but the uncertainty in period $k + 1$ is the overriding effect.

It seems reasonable to conjecture that larger values of $\Sigma_{0|0}^{\theta\theta}$, that is, of the initial covariance matrix of the parameters, will result in relatively greater effects from the probing terms; i.e., if there was greater initial uncertainty about the parameters, probing would be more worthwhile. With the assumption used in this model that parameters are constant but unknown, the initial covariance of

138 ACTIVE-LEARNING STOCHASTIC CONTROL

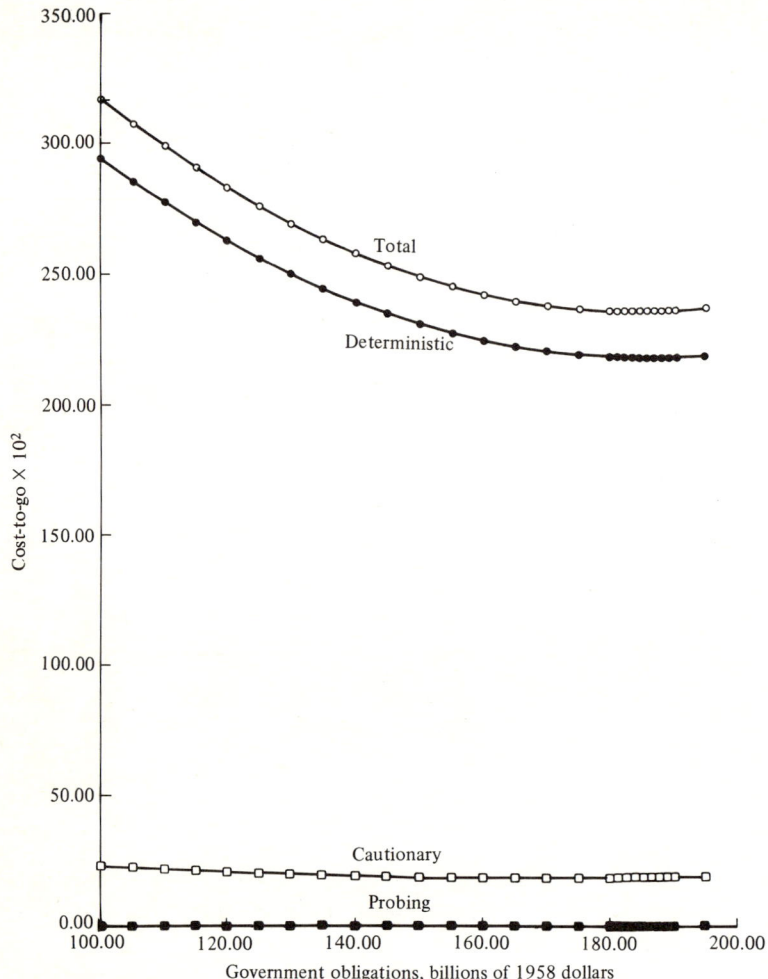

Figure 12-18 Period 6.

the parameters is sufficiently small for further learning from probing not to be a high priority. If, on the other hand, it was assumed that the parameters were time-varying, the initial parameter-covariance matrix elements would be larger and there would probably be more gain from active learning. However, the value of knowing the parameters better at any time is less when parameters are time-varying since the parameters will change. Therefore under the assumption of time-varying parameters it seems likely but not certain that there will be more active probing.

Against this one can ask whether or not economists really know the parameters of United States macroeconomic models as well as is represented by the covariance of coefficients when estimated on 20 to 30 years of quarterly data with the assumption that parameters are constant over that entire period. An assumption that at least some of the parameters are time-varying seems much more realistic.

This completes the discussion of the results for period 0. A comparison of the results across all of the time periods follows.

In looking at Figs. 12-13 to 12-18, the first thing one observes is that the deterministic cost term increases relative to the other two components. This is an artifact of the particular problem at hand and probably not a general result. The reason for this can be seen in Fig. 12-1, which shows the divergence of the dual path from the desired path for consumption. This divergence is a result of the explosive path of consumption in this particular model and thus is not a result that is likely to recur when more suitable models are used.

Next one can observe that the cautionary component becomes smaller and has a smaller positive slope as one moves from period 0 to period 6. This results from the fact that uncertainty about both states and parameters is reduced as time passes.

Also, the probing component becomes smaller with the passage of time and becomes zero in period 6 (Fig. 12-18) when only one period remains and there is therefore nothing to be gained from active learning.

Thus with a relatively high ratio of terminal-period penalties W_N to other period penalties W_k of 100 : 1 there is not much gain from active learning in this small model with constant but unknown parameters. It remains to be seen whether this result will hold with larger models, different assumptions about parameters, and different ratios of terminal to other period weights.

In summary the results show that (1) in the relevant range the slope of the cautionary term is positive and the slope of the probing term is negative; (2) the probing term is smaller in magnitude and has a smaller absolute value of the slope than the cautionary term; and (3) both the cautionary and the probing terms decrease with the passage of time.

12-5 SUMMARY

The methodology of control theory embodies a variety of notions which make it a particularly attractive means of analyzing many economic problems: (1) the focus on dynamics and thus on the evolution of an economic system over time, (2) the orientation toward reaching certain targets or goals and/or of improving the performance of an economic system, and (3) the treatment of uncertainty not only in additive-equation error terms but also in uncertain initial states, uncertain parameter estimates, and measurement errors.

APPENDICES

APPENDIX A

SECOND-ORDER EXPANSION OF THE SYSTEM EQUATIONS

For simplicity consider first an n vector $\mathbf{x}$, an m vector $\mathbf{u}$, and a set of n functions f^i of the form

$$\mathbf{x} = \mathbf{f}(\mathbf{u}) \tag{A-1}$$

where

$$\mathbf{x} = \begin{bmatrix} x_1 \\ \vdots \\ x_n \end{bmatrix} \quad \mathbf{u} = \begin{bmatrix} u_1 \\ \vdots \\ u_m \end{bmatrix} \quad \mathbf{f}(\mathbf{u}) = \begin{bmatrix} f^1(\mathbf{u}) \\ \vdots \\ f^n(\mathbf{u}) \end{bmatrix} \tag{A-2}$$

Then the derivative of a single function f^i with respect to the vector $\mathbf{u}$ is the column vector[1]

$$\mathbf{f}_\mathbf{u}^i = \begin{bmatrix} \dfrac{\partial f^i}{\partial u_1} \\ \vdots \\ \dfrac{\partial f^i}{\partial u_m} \end{bmatrix} \tag{A-3}$$

---

[1] This differs from the usual procedure of treating the gradient vector $\nabla \mathbf{f}$ of a function as a row vector. This means that all vectors are treated as column vectors unless they are explicitly transposed.

Also, the derivative of the column of functions **f** with respect to the vector **u** is defined to be the matrix

$$\mathbf{f_u} = \begin{bmatrix} (\mathbf{f_u^1})' \\ \vdots \\ (\mathbf{f_u^n})' \end{bmatrix} = \begin{bmatrix} \dfrac{\partial f^1}{\partial u_1} & \cdots & \dfrac{\partial f^1}{\partial u_m} \\ \cdots & \cdots & \cdots \\ \dfrac{\partial f^n}{\partial u_1} & \cdots & \dfrac{\partial f^n}{\partial u_m} \end{bmatrix} \quad (A\text{-}4)$$

The second derivative of a single function f^i with respect to the vector **u** is defined to be

$$\mathbf{f_{uu}^i} = \begin{bmatrix} \dfrac{\partial^2 f^i}{\partial u_1 \partial u_1} & \cdots & \dfrac{\partial^2 f^i}{\partial u_1 \partial u_m} \\ \cdots & \cdots & \cdots \\ \dfrac{\partial^2 f^i}{\partial u_m \partial u_1} & \cdots & \dfrac{\partial^2 f^i}{\partial u_m \partial u_m} \end{bmatrix} \quad (A\text{-}5)$$

Using the above notation, one can write the second-order Taylor expansion of the ith equation in (A-1) around $\mathbf{u}^\dagger$ as

$$x_i = f^i(\mathbf{u}^\dagger) + (\mathbf{f_u^i})'[\mathbf{u} - \mathbf{u}^\dagger] + \tfrac{1}{2}[\mathbf{u} - \mathbf{u}^\dagger]' \mathbf{f_{uu}^i}[\mathbf{u} - \mathbf{u}^\dagger] \quad (A\text{-}6)$$

Similarly the vector case of Eq. (A-6) can be written

$$\mathbf{x} = \mathbf{f}(\mathbf{u}^\dagger) + \mathbf{f_u}[\mathbf{u} - \mathbf{u}^\dagger] + \frac{1}{2} \sum_i \mathbf{e}^i [\mathbf{u} - \mathbf{u}^\dagger]' \mathbf{f_{uu}^i}[\mathbf{u} - \mathbf{u}^\dagger] \quad (A\text{-}7)$$

where

$$\mathbf{e}^i = \begin{bmatrix} 0 \\ 0 \\ \vdots \\ 0 \\ 1 \\ 0 \\ \vdots \\ 0 \end{bmatrix} \leftarrow i\text{th position}$$

The effect of the multiplication by $\mathbf{e}^i$ is to place the scalar quantity

$$[\mathbf{u} - \mathbf{u}^\dagger]' \mathbf{f_{uu}^i}[\mathbf{u} - \mathbf{u}^\dagger]$$

in the ith row of Eq. (A-7).

By analogy with Eq. (A-7) the second-order Taylor expansion of the system equations

$$\mathbf{x}_{k+1} = \mathbf{f}_k(\mathbf{x}_k, \mathbf{u}_k) + \boldsymbol{\xi}_k \quad (A\text{-}8)$$

SECOND-ORDER EXPANSION OF THE SYSTEM EQUATIONS 145

about $(\hat{\mathbf{x}}_{k|k}, \mathbf{u}_k^\dagger)$ is

$$\mathbf{x}_{k+1} = \mathbf{f}_k(\hat{\mathbf{x}}_{k|k}, \mathbf{u}_k^\dagger) + [\mathbf{f}_\mathbf{x}][\mathbf{x}_k - \hat{\mathbf{x}}_{k|k}] + [\mathbf{f}_\mathbf{u}][\mathbf{u}_k - \mathbf{u}_k^\dagger]$$
$$+ \frac{1}{2} \sum_i \mathbf{e}^i [\mathbf{x}_k - \hat{\mathbf{x}}_{k|k}]' \mathbf{f}_{\mathbf{xx}}^i [\mathbf{x}_k - \hat{\mathbf{x}}_{k|k}] + \frac{1}{2} \sum_i \mathbf{e}^i [\mathbf{u}_k - \mathbf{u}_k^\dagger]' \mathbf{f}_{\mathbf{uu}}^i [\mathbf{u}_k - \mathbf{u}_k^\dagger]$$
$$+ \sum_i \mathbf{e}^i [\mathbf{x}_k - \hat{\mathbf{x}}_{k|k}]' \mathbf{f}_{\mathbf{xu}}^i [\mathbf{u}_k - \mathbf{u}_k^\dagger] + \xi_k \tag{A-9}$$

where $\mathbf{f}_\mathbf{x}$ and $\mathbf{f}_\mathbf{u}$ denote the jacobians of $\mathbf{f}$ evaluated at $(\hat{\mathbf{x}}_{k|k}, \mathbf{u}_k^\dagger)$ and $\mathbf{f}_{\mathbf{xx}}, \mathbf{f}_{\mathbf{xu}}$, and $\mathbf{f}_{\mathbf{uu}}$ denote the hessians evaluated at $(\hat{\mathbf{x}}_{k|k}, \mathbf{u}_k^\dagger)$.

APPENDIX B

EXPECTED VALUE OF VECTOR AND MATRIX PRODUCTS

B-1 THE EXPECTED VALUE OF A QUADRATIC FORM

The purpose of this appendix is to show that the expected value of the quadratic form is

$$E\{\mathbf{x'Ax}\} = \hat{\mathbf{x}}'\mathbf{A}\hat{\mathbf{x}} + \text{tr}(\mathbf{A\Sigma}) \qquad \text{(B-1)}$$

where
- $\mathbf{x}$ = random vector of dimension n
- $\mathbf{A} = n \times n$ matrix
- $\hat{\mathbf{x}} = E\{\mathbf{x}\}$
- tr = trace operator
- $\mathbf{\Sigma}$ = covariance of $\mathbf{x} = E\{[\mathbf{x}-\hat{\mathbf{x}}][\mathbf{x}-\hat{\mathbf{x}}]'\}$

Following the line of argument in Goldberger (1964, p. 166), we obtain

$$\begin{aligned}
E\{\mathbf{x'Ax}\} &= E\{\text{tr}(\mathbf{x'Ax})\} &&\mathbf{x'Ax} = \text{scalar} \\
&= E\{\text{tr}[\mathbf{Axx'}]\} &&\text{since tr}[\mathbf{AB}] = \text{tr}[\mathbf{BA}] \\
&= \text{tr}\, E\{\mathbf{Axx'}\} &&\text{trace is a linear function} &&\text{(B-2)} \\
E\{\mathbf{x'Ax}\} &= \text{tr}[\mathbf{A}(E\{\mathbf{xx'}\})] &&\mathbf{A} \text{ is a constant matrix} &&\text{(B-3)}
\end{aligned}$$

Now consider the definition of the covariance matrix [see Goldberger (1964, p. 106) for related discussion]

$$\Sigma = E\{[\mathbf{x} - \hat{\mathbf{x}}][\mathbf{x} - \hat{\mathbf{x}}]'\}$$

$$= E\{\mathbf{xx}' - \mathbf{x}\hat{\mathbf{x}}' - \hat{\mathbf{x}}\mathbf{x}' + \hat{\mathbf{x}}\hat{\mathbf{x}}'\} \tag{B-4}$$

$$\Sigma = E\{\mathbf{xx}'\} - \hat{\mathbf{x}}\hat{\mathbf{x}}' \tag{B-5}$$

Therefore, from Eq. (B-5)

$$E\{\mathbf{xx}'\} = \hat{\mathbf{x}}\hat{\mathbf{x}}' + \Sigma \tag{B-6}$$

Substitution of Eq. (B-6) into Eq. (B-3) yields

$$E\{\mathbf{x}'\mathbf{Ax}\} = \mathrm{tr}\left[\mathbf{A}(\hat{\mathbf{x}}\hat{\mathbf{x}}' + \Sigma)\right]$$

$$= \mathrm{tr}\left[\hat{\mathbf{x}}'\mathbf{A}\hat{\mathbf{x}} + \mathbf{A}\Sigma\right] \quad \mathrm{tr}[\mathbf{AB}] = \mathrm{tr}[\mathbf{BA}] \tag{B-7}$$

$$E\{\mathbf{x}'\mathbf{Ax}\} = \hat{\mathbf{x}}'\mathbf{A}\hat{\mathbf{x}} + \mathrm{tr}\left[\mathbf{A}\Sigma\right] \quad \hat{\mathbf{x}}'\mathbf{A}\hat{\mathbf{x}} \text{ is a scalar} \tag{B-8}$$

and Eq. (B-8) is the same as Eq. (B-1).

B-2 THE EXPECTED VALUE OF A MATRIX TRIPLE PRODUCT

This section extends the result above to show that when d_{ij} is the (i,j)th element of $\mathbf{D}$ and

$$\mathbf{D} = E\{\mathbf{AKB}\} \tag{B-9}$$

where $\mathbf{A}$, $\mathbf{K}$, and $\mathbf{B}$ are conformable matrices with $\mathbf{A}$ and $\mathbf{B}$ random and $\mathbf{K}$ fixed, we have

$$d_{ij} = E\{\mathbf{a}_i\mathbf{K}\mathbf{b}_j\} = \hat{\mathbf{a}}_i\mathbf{K}\hat{\mathbf{b}}_j + \mathrm{tr}\left[\mathbf{K}\Sigma_{\mathbf{b}_j\mathbf{a}_i}\right] \tag{B-10}$$

First let

$$\mathbf{H} = \mathbf{AKB} \tag{B-11}$$

then

$$h_{ij} = \mathbf{a}_i' \begin{bmatrix} \sum_l k_{1l}b_{lj} \\ \sum_l k_{2l}b_{lj} \\ \vdots \\ \sum_l k_{nl}b_{lj} \end{bmatrix} \tag{B-12}$$

where $\mathbf{a}'_i$ is the ith row of $\mathbf{A}$.[1] Now

$$h_{ij} = a_{i1} \sum_l k'_{1l} b_{lj} + a_{i2} \sum_l k_{2l} b_{lj} + \cdots + a_{in} \sum_l k_{nl} b_{lj}$$

$$= \sum_\theta a_{i\theta} \left(\sum_l k_{\theta l} b_{lj} \right) = \sum_\theta \sum_l (a_{i\theta} k_{\theta l} b_{lj})$$

$$= \mathbf{a}'_i \mathbf{K} \mathbf{b}_j \tag{B-13}$$

where $\mathbf{b}_j$ is the jth column of $\mathbf{B}$.

Thus,

$$d_{ij} = E\{h_{ij}\} = E\{\mathbf{a}_i \mathbf{K} \mathbf{b}_j\} \tag{B-14}$$

Then, following the steps used in Sec. B-1, we have

$$E\{\mathbf{a}_i \mathbf{K} \mathbf{b}_j\} = E\{\operatorname{tr}[\mathbf{a}'_i \mathbf{K} \mathbf{b}_j]\} \quad \text{since } \mathbf{a}_i \mathbf{K} \mathbf{b}_j = \text{scalar} \tag{B-15}$$

$$= E\{\operatorname{tr}[\mathbf{K} \mathbf{b}_j \mathbf{a}'_i]\} \quad \text{since tr}[\mathbf{AB}] = \operatorname{tr}[\mathbf{BA}] \tag{B-16}$$

$$= \operatorname{tr}(E\{\mathbf{K} \mathbf{b}_j \mathbf{a}'_i\}) \quad \text{trace is a linear function} \tag{B-17}$$

$$= \operatorname{tr}(\mathbf{K} E\{\mathbf{b}_j \mathbf{a}'_i\}) \quad \mathbf{K} \text{ is a constant matrix} \tag{B-18}$$

Also,

$$\Sigma_{\mathbf{b}_j \mathbf{a}_i} = E\{[\mathbf{b}_j - \hat{\mathbf{b}}_j][\mathbf{a}_i - \hat{\mathbf{a}}_i]'\}$$

$$= E\{\mathbf{b}_j \mathbf{a}'_i - \hat{\mathbf{b}}_j \mathbf{a}'_i - \mathbf{b}_j \hat{\mathbf{a}}'_i + \hat{\mathbf{b}}_j \hat{\mathbf{a}}'_i\}$$

$$= E\{\mathbf{b}_j \mathbf{a}'_i\} - \hat{\mathbf{b}}_j \hat{\mathbf{a}}'_i \tag{B-19}$$

Therefore,

$$E\{\mathbf{b}_j \mathbf{a}'_i\} = \hat{\mathbf{b}}_j \hat{\mathbf{a}}'_i + \Sigma_{\mathbf{b}_j \mathbf{a}_i} \tag{B-20}$$

Substitution of Eq. (B-20) into Eq. (B-18) yields

$$E\{\mathbf{a}'_i \mathbf{K} \mathbf{b}_j\} = \operatorname{tr}\left[\mathbf{K}(\hat{\mathbf{b}}_j \hat{\mathbf{a}}'_i) + \mathbf{K} \Sigma_{\mathbf{b}_j \mathbf{a}_i}\right]$$

$$= \operatorname{tr}\left[\hat{\mathbf{a}}'_i \mathbf{K} \hat{\mathbf{b}}_j + \mathbf{K} \Sigma_{\mathbf{b}_j \mathbf{a}_i}\right] \tag{B-21}$$

or

$$E\{\mathbf{a}'_i \mathbf{K} \mathbf{b}_j\} = \hat{\mathbf{a}}'_i \mathbf{K} \hat{\mathbf{b}}_j + \operatorname{tr}\left[\mathbf{K} \Sigma_{\mathbf{b}_j \mathbf{a}_i}\right]$$

---

[1] To be consistent in the treatment of vectors, $\mathbf{a}_i$ contains the elements of the ith row of $\mathbf{A}$, but these elements are arranged as a column. Thus $\mathbf{a}'_i$ is a row vector.

APPENDIX
C

EQUIVALENCE OF SOME MATRIX RICCATI RECURSIONS

This appendix shows the equivalence of the g, $\mathbf{p}$, and $\mathbf{K}$ recursions in Bar-Shalom, Tse, and Larson (1974) (BTL) and in Tse, Bar-Shalom, and Meier (1973) (TBM). The recursions are given in the papers in the following forms: BTL (A.14) to (A.16):

$$g_j = g_{j+1} - \tfrac{1}{2}\mathbf{H}'_\mathbf{u}\mathcal{H}_\mathbf{uu}^{-1}\mathbf{H}_\mathbf{u} + \tfrac{1}{2}\operatorname{tr}\left[\mathbf{K}_{j+1}\mathbf{Q}_j + \mathcal{Q}_\mathbf{xx}\boldsymbol{\Sigma}_{j|j}\right] \qquad g_N = 0 \quad \text{(C-1)}$$

$$\mathbf{p}_j = \mathbf{H}_\mathbf{x} - \mathcal{H}'_\mathbf{ux}\mathcal{H}_\mathbf{uu}^{-1}\mathbf{H}_\mathbf{u} \qquad \mathbf{p}_N = L_{N\mathbf{x}} \quad \text{(C-2)}$$

$$\mathbf{K}_j = \mathcal{H}_\mathbf{xx} - \mathcal{Q}_\mathbf{xx} \qquad \mathbf{K}_N = L_{N,\mathbf{xx}} \quad \text{(C-3)}$$

TBM (A.7) to (A.9):

$$\hat{g}_j = \hat{g}_{j+1} - \tfrac{1}{2}\mathbf{H}'_\mathbf{u}\mathcal{H}_\mathbf{uu}^{-1}\mathbf{H}_\mathbf{u} + \tfrac{1}{2}\operatorname{tr}\left[\mathbf{H}_\mathbf{xx}\boldsymbol{\Sigma}_{j|j} + (\boldsymbol{\Sigma}_{j+1|j} - \boldsymbol{\Sigma}_{j+1|j+1})\mathbf{K}_{j+1}\right]$$

$$\text{(C-4)}$$

$$\hat{g}_N = \tfrac{1}{2}\operatorname{tr}\left[L_{N,\mathbf{xx}}\boldsymbol{\Sigma}_{N|N}\right]$$

$$\mathbf{p}_j = \mathbf{H}_\mathbf{x} - \mathcal{H}'_\mathbf{ux}\mathcal{H}_\mathbf{uu}^{-1}\mathbf{H}_\mathbf{u} \qquad \mathbf{p}_N = L_{N\mathbf{x}} \quad \text{(C-5)}$$

$$\mathbf{K}_j = \mathcal{H}_\mathbf{xx} - \mathcal{Q}_\mathbf{xx} \qquad \mathbf{K}_N = L_{N,\mathbf{xx}} \quad \text{(C-6)}$$

Since Eqs. (C-2) and (C-3) are the same as Eqs. (C-5) and (C-6), it is necessary only to show the equivalence for Eqs. (C-1) and (C-4). The method of doing this is to begin with Eq. (C-1) and derive Eq. (C-4).

First one needs a relationship between the g of Eq. (C-1) and the $\hat{g}$ of Eq. (C-4). This lies in the expected cost-to-go formulas of the two papers which are, respectively,

BTL (3.19): $\quad \Delta J^*_{N-j} = g_j + E\{\mathbf{p}'_j \delta \mathbf{x}_j + \tfrac{1}{2} \delta \mathbf{x}'_j \mathbf{K}_j \delta \mathbf{x}_j | \mathcal{P}^j\}$ (C-7)

and

TBM (A.3): $\quad \Delta J^*_j = \hat{g}_j + \mathbf{p}'_j \delta \mathbf{x}_{j|j} + \tfrac{1}{2} \delta \hat{\mathbf{x}}'_{j|j} \mathbf{K}_j \delta \hat{\mathbf{x}}_{j|j}$ (C-8)

First consider the terms ΔJ^*_{N-j} and ΔJ^*_j, which are equivalent even though the j's are not. In fact the subscripts on these terms could be written as $N - j_B = j_T$, where j_B is the j used in (C-7) and j_T is the j used in (C-8). Then

$$j_T + j_B = N \qquad \text{(C-9)}$$

makes it clear that j_T is an index for counting backward. Thus $\Delta J^*_{N-j_B}$ is the cost-to-go j_B periods from the end and $\Delta J^*_{j_T}$ is the cost-to-go at period j_T. So we can set Eq. (C-7) equal to Eq. (C-8) with the understanding of the indexing as stated above. Doing this and taking the expectation in Eq. (C-7) yields

$$g_j + \mathbf{p}'_j \delta \hat{\mathbf{x}}_{j|j} + \tfrac{1}{2} \delta \hat{\mathbf{x}}'_{j|j} \mathbf{K}_j \delta \hat{\mathbf{x}}_{j|j} + \tfrac{1}{2} \operatorname{tr}[\mathbf{K}_j \Sigma_{j|j}] = \hat{g}_j + \mathbf{p}'_j \delta \hat{\mathbf{x}}_{j|j} + \tfrac{1}{2} \delta \hat{\mathbf{x}}'_{j|j} \mathbf{K}_j \delta \hat{\mathbf{x}}_{j|j}$$

(C-10)

or $\quad g_j = \hat{g}_j - \tfrac{1}{2} \operatorname{tr}[\mathbf{K}_j \Sigma_{j|j}]$ (C-11)

Equation (C-11) can be substituted into Eq. (C-1) as the first step in the transformation of the BTL equation (C-1) into the TBM equation (C-4). This yields

$$\hat{g}_j - \tfrac{1}{2} \operatorname{tr}[\mathbf{K}_j \Sigma_{j|j}] = \hat{g}_{j+1} - \tfrac{1}{2} \operatorname{tr}[\mathbf{K}_{j+1} \Sigma_{j+1|j+1}]$$
$$- \tfrac{1}{2} \mathbf{H}'_\mathbf{u} \mathcal{H}_{\mathbf{uu}} \mathbf{H}_\mathbf{u} + \tfrac{1}{2} \operatorname{tr}[\mathbf{K}_{j+1} \mathbf{Q}_j + \mathcal{Q}_{\mathbf{xx}} \Sigma_{j|j}] \quad \text{(C-12)}$$

or

$$\hat{g}_j = \hat{g}_{j+1} - \tfrac{1}{2} \mathbf{H}'_\mathbf{u} \mathcal{H}_{\mathbf{uu}}^{-1} \mathbf{H}_\mathbf{u}$$
$$+ \tfrac{1}{2} \operatorname{tr}[\mathbf{K}_{j+1} \mathbf{Q}_j + \mathcal{Q}_{\mathbf{xx}} \Sigma_{j|j} + \mathbf{K}_j \Sigma_{j|j} - \mathbf{K}_{j+1} \Sigma_{j+1|j+1}] \quad \text{(C-13)}$$

A comparison of Eqs. (C-13) and (C-4) shows that all terms are the same except the trace term. Therefore consider only the trace term. Solve Eq. (C-3) for $\mathcal{Q}_{\mathbf{xx}}$ and substitute the result into the trace term to obtain

$$\operatorname{tr}[\mathbf{K}_{j+1} \mathbf{Q}_j + \mathcal{Q}_{\mathbf{xx}} \Sigma_{j|j} + \mathbf{K}_j \Sigma_{j|j} - \mathbf{K}_{j+1} \Sigma_{j+1|j+1}]$$
$$= \operatorname{tr}[\mathbf{K}_{j+1} \mathbf{Q}_j + \mathcal{H}_{\mathbf{xx}} \Sigma_{j|j} - \mathbf{K}_{j+1} \Sigma_{j+1|j+1}]$$
$$= \operatorname{tr}[\mathbf{K}_{j+1} \mathbf{Q}_j + \mathbf{H}_{\mathbf{xx}} \Sigma_{j|j} + \mathbf{f}'_\mathbf{x} \mathbf{K}_{j+1} \mathbf{f}_\mathbf{x} \Sigma_{j|j} - \mathbf{K}_{j+1} \Sigma_{j+1|j+1}] \quad \text{(C-14)}$$

by definition of $\mathcal{H}_{\mathbf{xx}}$

$$= \operatorname{tr}(\mathbf{H}_{\mathbf{xx}} \Sigma_{j|j} + \mathbf{K}_{j+1}[\mathbf{f}'_\mathbf{x} \Sigma_{j|j} \mathbf{f}_\mathbf{x} + \mathbf{Q}_j] - \mathbf{K}_{j+1} \Sigma_{j+1|j+1}) \quad \text{(C-15)}$$

$$\operatorname{tr}(\mathbf{AB}) = \operatorname{tr}(\mathbf{BA})$$

Now consider the middle term of Eq. (C-15). It can be shown that

$$\Sigma_{j+1|j} = \mathbf{f}'_\mathbf{x} \Sigma_{j|j} \mathbf{f}_\mathbf{x} + \mathbf{Q}_j \tag{C-16}$$

through the following steps. By definition

$$\Sigma_{j+1|j} = E\{[\mathbf{x}_{j+1} - \hat{\mathbf{x}}_{j+1|j}][\mathbf{x}_{j+1} - \hat{\mathbf{x}}_{j+1|j}]' | \mathcal{P}^j\} \tag{C-17}$$

The term $\hat{\mathbf{x}}_{j+1|j}$ was shown in Eq. (9-13) to be

$$\hat{\mathbf{x}}_{j+1|j} = \mathbf{f}_j(\hat{\mathbf{x}}_{j|j}, \mathbf{u}_k^\tau) + \frac{1}{2} \sum_i \mathbf{e}^i \operatorname{tr}(\mathbf{f}^i_{\mathbf{xx}} \Sigma_{j|j}) \tag{C-18}$$

Also a second-order expansion of the system equation (9-4) (setting $\mathbf{u}_k^\dagger = \mathbf{u}_k$) yields, from Eq. (9-10),

$$\mathbf{x}_{j+1} = \mathbf{f}_j(\hat{\mathbf{x}}_{j|j}, \mathbf{u}_k^\tau) + \mathbf{f}'_\mathbf{x}[\mathbf{x}_j - \hat{\mathbf{x}}_{j|j}] + \frac{1}{2} \sum_i \mathbf{e}^i [\mathbf{x}_j - \hat{\mathbf{x}}_{j|j}]' \mathbf{f}^i_{\mathbf{xx}}[\mathbf{x}_j - \hat{\mathbf{x}}_{j|j}] + \xi_j \tag{C-19}$$

Dropping the second-order terms from Eqs. (C-18) and (C-19) and subtracting one from the other results in

$$\mathbf{x}_{j+1} - \hat{\mathbf{x}}_{j+1|j} = \mathbf{f}'_\mathbf{x}[\mathbf{x}_j - \hat{\mathbf{x}}_{j|j}] + \xi_j \tag{C-20}$$

Substitution of Eq. (C-20) into Eq. (C-17) yields

$$\Sigma_{j+1|j} = E\{\mathbf{f}'_\mathbf{x}[\mathbf{x}_j - \hat{\mathbf{x}}_{j|j}][\mathbf{x}_j - \hat{\mathbf{x}}_{j|j}]' \mathbf{f}_\mathbf{x} + 2\mathbf{f}'_\mathbf{x}[\mathbf{x}_j - \hat{\mathbf{x}}_{j|j}]\xi'_j + \xi_j \xi'_j | \mathcal{P}^j\} \tag{C-21}$$

or

$$\Sigma_{j+1|j} = \mathbf{f}'_\mathbf{x} \Sigma_{j|j} \mathbf{f}_\mathbf{x} + \mathbf{Q}_j \tag{C-22}$$

by the definitions of $\Sigma_{j|j}$ and $\mathbf{Q}_j$ and the assumption of the independence of $\mathbf{x}_j$ and ξ_j. Expression (C-22) is then the same as Eq. (C-16) and can be substituted into Eq. (C-15) to obtain

$$\text{trace term} = \operatorname{tr}\left[\mathbf{H}_{\mathbf{xx}} \Sigma_{j|j} + \mathbf{K}_{j+1} \Sigma_{j+1|j} - \mathbf{K}_{j+1} \Sigma_{j+1|j+1}\right] \tag{C-23}$$

Substitution of Eq. (C-23) into the $\hat{g}$ expression (C-13) and use once again of $\operatorname{tr}(\mathbf{AB}) = \operatorname{tr}(\mathbf{BA})$ provides

$$\hat{g}_j = \hat{g}_{j+1} - \frac{1}{2} \mathbf{H}'_\mathbf{u} \mathcal{H}^{-1}_{\mathbf{uu}} \mathbf{H}_\mathbf{u} + \frac{1}{2} \operatorname{tr}\left(\mathbf{H}_{\mathbf{xx}} \Sigma_{j|j} + [\Sigma_{j+1|j} - \Sigma_{j+1|j+1}]\mathbf{K}_{j+1}\right) \tag{C-24}$$

which is the same as Eq. (C-4).

The initial condition for Eq. (C-4) can be obtained by using the relationship between $\hat{g}$ and g in Eq. (C-11)

$$\hat{g}_N = g_N + \frac{1}{2} \operatorname{tr}\left[\mathbf{K}_N \Sigma_{N|N}\right] \tag{C-25}$$

From Eqs. (C-1) and (C-3) $g_N = 0$ and $\mathbf{K}_N = \mathbf{L}_{N,\mathbf{xx}}$; therefore, Eq. (C-25) becomes

$$\hat{g}_N = \frac{1}{2} \operatorname{tr}(\mathbf{L}_{N,\mathbf{xx}} \Sigma_{N|N}) \tag{C-26}$$

as in Eq. (C-4).

Thus the equivalence between Eqs. (C-1) and (C-4), (C-2) and (C-5), and (C-3) and (C-6) has been shown.

APPENDIX D

SECOND-ORDER KALMAN FILTER

This appendix is about the use of bayesian methods to obtain estimates of $\hat{\mathbf{x}}_{k+1|k+1}$ and $\Sigma_{k+1|k+1}$ from $\hat{\mathbf{x}}_{k+1|k}$ and $\Sigma_{k+1|k}$ using the measurement $\mathbf{y}_{k+1}$. This is done with the method outlined in Bryson and Ho (1969, pp. 377–381, and probs. 12.2.2 to 12.2.5, pp. 357–358). Their method b(i) (p. 378) is employed here.

The problem is to use the measurement relationship

$$\mathbf{y}_k = \mathbf{h}_k(\mathbf{x}_k, \boldsymbol{\zeta}_k) \tag{D-1}$$

to improve the estimates of the mean and covariance of $\mathbf{x}$. Since neither $\mathbf{x}$ nor $\boldsymbol{\zeta}$ is directly observable, it is necessary to use the information in $\mathbf{y}$ to improve the estimate. In order to show how this is done, a general derivation will be accomplished by using the sections in Bryson and Ho mentioned above, and then these will be extended slightly through the use of a second-order expansion of the measurement relationship.

Bryson and Ho's (BH) notation for the measurement relationship (D-1) is {Bryson and Ho [1969, eq. (12.7.1)]}

$$\mathbf{z} = \mathbf{h}(\mathbf{x}, \mathbf{v}) \tag{D-2}$$

where $\mathbf{z} = m \times 1$ measurement vector
           $\mathbf{x} = n \times 1$ state vector
           $\mathbf{v} = q \times 1$ measurement-noise vector

It is desirable to obtain $p(\mathbf{x}|\mathbf{z})$, that is, the conditional distribution of the state given the measurement $\mathbf{z}$ actually obtained. Now by the definition of a conditional distribution

$$p(\mathbf{x}|\mathbf{z})p(\mathbf{z}) = p(\mathbf{x}, \mathbf{z}) \tag{D-3}$$

or

$$p(\mathbf{x}|\mathbf{z}) = \frac{p(\mathbf{x}, \mathbf{z})}{p(\mathbf{z})} \tag{D-4}$$

Therefore $p(\mathbf{x}|\mathbf{z})$ can be obtained from the joint distribution of $\mathbf{x}$ and $\mathbf{z}$ and the distribution of $\mathbf{z}$. Assume for the moment that $p(\mathbf{x}, \mathbf{z})$ is a joint normal distribution and $p(\mathbf{z})$ is a normal distribution. Then it is possible to derive a conditional distribution $p(\mathbf{x}|\mathbf{z})$ in terms of the parameters of the distributions $p(\mathbf{x}, \mathbf{z})$ and $p(\mathbf{z})$.[1]

Since it has been assumed that $p(\mathbf{x}, \mathbf{z})$ is normal, it can be written as

$$p(\mathbf{z}, \mathbf{x}) = \frac{1}{(2\pi)^{(m+n)/2}|\mathbf{P}|^{\frac{1}{2}}} \exp\left\{-\frac{1}{2}\left([\mathbf{z}-\bar{\mathbf{z}}]', [\mathbf{x}-\bar{\mathbf{x}}]'\right)\mathbf{P}^{-1}\begin{bmatrix}\mathbf{z}-\bar{\mathbf{z}}\\\mathbf{x}-\bar{\mathbf{x}}\end{bmatrix}\right\} \tag{D-5}$$

where $\quad \mathbf{P} = \begin{bmatrix}\mathbf{P}_{zz} & \mathbf{P}_{zx}\\\mathbf{P}_{xz} & \mathbf{P}_{xx}\end{bmatrix} = $ covariance matrix of $(\mathbf{z}, \mathbf{x})$ $\tag{D-6}$

Also since $p(\mathbf{z})$ is assumed to be normally distributed, it can be written as

$$p(\mathbf{z}) = \frac{1}{(2\pi)^{m/2}|\mathbf{P}_{zz}|^{\frac{1}{2}}} \exp\left\{-\frac{1}{2}([\mathbf{z}-\bar{\mathbf{z}}]'\mathbf{P}_{zz}^{-1}[\mathbf{z}-\bar{\mathbf{z}}])\right\} \tag{D-7}$$

Then substitution of Eqs. (D-5) and (D-7) into Eq. (D-4) yields

$$p(\mathbf{x}|\mathbf{z}) = \left\{\frac{(2\pi)^{m/2}|\mathbf{P}_{zz}|^{\frac{1}{2}}}{(2\pi)^{(m+n)/2}|\mathbf{P}|^{\frac{1}{2}}} \frac{\exp\left\{-\frac{1}{2}\left([\mathbf{z}-\bar{\mathbf{z}}]', [\mathbf{x}-\bar{\mathbf{x}}]'\right)\mathbf{P}^{-1}\begin{bmatrix}\mathbf{z}-\bar{\mathbf{z}}\\\mathbf{x}-\bar{\mathbf{x}}\end{bmatrix}\right\}}{\exp\left\{-\frac{1}{2}([\mathbf{z}-\bar{\mathbf{z}}]'\mathbf{P}_{zz}^{-1}[\mathbf{z}-\bar{\mathbf{z}}])\right\}}\right\} \tag{D-8}$$

In order to simplify this expression further it is necessary to obtain the inverse of the partitioned matrix $\mathbf{P}$. This can be done using, for example, the method outlined in Ayres (1962, p. 58)

$$\mathbf{P}^{-1} = \begin{bmatrix}\mathbf{P}_{zz}^{-1} + [\mathbf{P}_{zz}^{-1}\mathbf{P}_{zx}]\mathbf{\varsigma}^{-1}[\mathbf{P}_{zz}^{-1}\mathbf{P}_{zx}]' & -\mathbf{\varsigma}^{-1}[\mathbf{P}_{zx}\mathbf{P}_{zz}^{-1}]\\-[\mathbf{P}_{zz}^{-1}\mathbf{P}_{zx}]\mathbf{\varsigma}^{-1} & \mathbf{\varsigma}^{-1}\end{bmatrix} \tag{D-9}$$

where $\quad \mathbf{\varsigma} = \mathbf{P}_{xx} - \mathbf{P}_{xz}\mathbf{P}_{zz}^{-1}\mathbf{P}_{zx}$ $\tag{D-10}$

The first term on the right-hand side of Eq. (D-8) can also be simplified. For this

---

[1] The procedure followed here is the same as that used in solving prob. 12.2.4 in Bryson and Ho (1969).

it is necessary to obtain the determinant of the partitioned matrix [see Gantmacher (1960, vol. I, pp. 45–46)]

$$|P| = |P_{zz}||P_{xx} - P_{xz}P_{zz}^{-1}P_{zx}| = |P_{zz}||\varsigma| \qquad \text{(D-11)}$$

Substitution of Eqs. (D-9) and (D-11) into Eq. (D-8) then yields

$$p(x|z) = \frac{1}{(2\pi)^{n/2}|\varsigma|^{\frac{1}{2}}} \exp\left\{-\frac{1}{2}\left[[z-\bar{z}]',[x-\bar{x}]'\right]\right.$$

$$\left. \times \begin{bmatrix} (P_{zz}^{-1}P_{zx})\varsigma^{-1}(P_{zz}^{-1}P_{zx})' & -\varsigma^{-1}P_{zx}P_{zz}^{-1} \\ -P_{zz}^{-1}P_{zx}\varsigma^{-1} & \varsigma^{-1} \end{bmatrix} \begin{bmatrix} z-\bar{z} \\ x-\bar{x} \end{bmatrix}\right\} \qquad \text{(D-12)}$$

Note in particular that the P_{zz}^{-1} terms cancel. Also from Eq. (D-12)

$$p(x|z) = \frac{1}{(2\pi)^{n/2}|\varsigma|^{\frac{1}{2}}}$$

$$\times \exp\left\{-\frac{1}{2}\left(\left[[-P_{xz}P_{zz}^{-1}[z-\bar{z}]]', [x-\bar{x}]'\right]\begin{bmatrix}\varsigma^{-1} & \varsigma^{-1} \\ \varsigma^{-1} & \varsigma^{-1}\end{bmatrix}\right.\right.$$

$$\left.\left.\times \begin{bmatrix} -P_{xz}P_{zz}^{-1}[z-\bar{z}] \\ x-\bar{x} \end{bmatrix}\right)\right\} \qquad \text{(D-13)}$$

$$p(x|z) = \frac{1}{(2\pi)^{n/2}|\varsigma|^{\frac{1}{2}}}$$

$$\times \exp\left\{-\frac{1}{2}\left([x-\bar{x} - P_{xz}P_{zz}^{-1}[z-\bar{z}]]\varsigma^{-1}[x-\bar{x} - P_{xz}P_{zz}^{-1}[z-\bar{z}]]\right)\right\} \qquad \text{(D-14)}$$

and Eq. (D-14) is a normal distribution with mean

$$E\{x|z\} = \bar{x} + P_{xz}P_{zz}^{-1}[z-\bar{z}] \qquad \text{(D-15)}$$

and covariance

$$E\{[x-\bar{x}][x-\bar{x}]'|z\} = \varsigma = P_{xx} - P_{xz}P_{zz}^{-1}P_{xz}' \qquad \text{(D-16)}$$

Therefore it has been shown that if $p(x, z)$ and $p(z)$ are each normal densities, the conditional distribution $p(x|z)$ will also be normal and will have the mean and covariance given by Eqs. (D-15) and (D-16). Therefore the next step is to show that $p(z)$ and $p(x, z)$ are normal densities.

Consider first $p(z)$ and specialize the measurement relationship Eq. (D-2) to the linear (or linearized case)

$$z = Hx + v \qquad \text{(D-17)}$$

where **H** is an $n \times n$ matrix, and let

$$E\{\mathbf{x}\} = \bar{\mathbf{x}} \qquad E\{[\mathbf{x} - \bar{\mathbf{x}}][\mathbf{x} - \bar{\mathbf{x}}]'\} = \mathbf{M}$$
$$E\{\mathbf{v}\} = \mathbf{O} \qquad E\{\mathbf{vv}'\} = \mathbf{R}$$

In this case **z** is a linear combination of the two normally distributed random variables **x** and **v**; therefore, **z** is also normally distributed [see Bryson and Ho (1969, p. 312)]. Also the mean and covariance of **z** can be calculated as follows:

$$\bar{\mathbf{z}} = E\{\mathbf{z}\} = E\{\mathbf{Hx} + \mathbf{v}\} = \mathbf{H}\bar{\mathbf{x}} + \mathbf{O} = \mathbf{H}\bar{\mathbf{x}} \tag{D-18}$$

$$\mathbf{P}_{zz} = E\{[\mathbf{z} - \bar{\mathbf{z}}][\mathbf{z} - \bar{\mathbf{z}}]'\}$$

$$= E\{[\mathbf{Hx} + \mathbf{v} - \mathbf{H}\bar{\mathbf{x}}][\mathbf{Hx} + \mathbf{v} - \mathbf{H}\bar{\mathbf{x}}]'\}$$

$$= E\{[\mathbf{H}[\mathbf{x} - \bar{\mathbf{x}}] + \mathbf{v}][\mathbf{H}[\mathbf{x} - \bar{\mathbf{x}}] + \mathbf{v}]'\}$$

$$= E\{\mathbf{H}[\mathbf{x} - \bar{\mathbf{x}}][\mathbf{x} - \bar{\mathbf{x}}]'\mathbf{H}' + 2\mathbf{H}[\mathbf{x} - \bar{\mathbf{x}}]\mathbf{v} + \mathbf{vv}'\} \tag{D-19}$$

$$\mathbf{P}_{zz} = \mathbf{HMH}' + \mathbf{R} \tag{D-20}$$

Therefore **z** is normally distributed as

$$p(\mathbf{z}) = N(\mathbf{H}\bar{\mathbf{x}}, \mathbf{HMH}' + \mathbf{R}) \tag{D-21}$$

Next consider $p(\mathbf{x}, \mathbf{z})$. To show that $p(\mathbf{x}, \mathbf{z})$ is a normal density one can write

$$p(\mathbf{z}, \mathbf{x}) = p(\mathbf{z}|\mathbf{x})p(\mathbf{x}) \tag{D-22}$$

It will first be shown that $p(\mathbf{x})$ and $p(\mathbf{z}|\mathbf{x})$ are normal densities. Then $p(\mathbf{z}, \mathbf{x})$ will be derived, and it will be demonstrated that it is a normal density.

The density $p(\mathbf{x})$ is normal by assumption, i.e.,

$$p(\mathbf{x}) = N[\bar{\mathbf{x}}, \mathbf{M}] \tag{D-23}$$

Then the density $p(\mathbf{z}|\mathbf{x})$ is normal because

$$\mathbf{z} = \mathbf{Hx} + \mathbf{v}$$

and with **x** fixed, **z** is a linear function of **v**. Also **v** is normally distributed; therefore **z** is normally distributed. The mean and covariance of $p(\mathbf{z}|\mathbf{x})$ are

$$E\{\mathbf{z}|\mathbf{x}\} = E\{\mathbf{Hx} + \mathbf{v}|\mathbf{x}\} = \mathbf{Hx} + E\{\mathbf{v}|\mathbf{x}\} = \mathbf{Hx}$$

and $\qquad \text{cov}(\mathbf{z}|\mathbf{x}) = E\{[\mathbf{z} - \mathbf{Hx}][\mathbf{z} - \mathbf{Hx}]'|\mathbf{x}\} = E\{E\{\mathbf{vv}'|\mathbf{x}\}\} = \mathbf{R}$

Therefore,

$$p(\mathbf{z}|\mathbf{x}) = N[\mathbf{Hx}, \mathbf{R}] \tag{D-24}$$

Then using Eqs. (D-23) and (D-24) in Eq. (D-22) yields

$$p(\mathbf{z}, \mathbf{x}) = N[\mathbf{Hx}, \mathbf{R}] N[\bar{\mathbf{x}}, \mathbf{M}]$$

$$= \tfrac{1}{c} \exp\{-\tfrac{1}{2}([\mathbf{z} - \mathbf{Hx}]'\mathbf{R}^{-1}[\mathbf{z} - \mathbf{Hx}] + [\mathbf{x} - \bar{\mathbf{x}}]'\mathbf{M}^{-1}[\mathbf{x} - \bar{\mathbf{x}}])\}$$

where $\quad c = (2\pi)^{(m+n)/2}|\mathbf{R}|^{\frac{1}{2}}|\mathbf{M}|^{\frac{1}{2}}$

Next, complete the squares of the term in brackets in the exponent, i.e.,

$$G \equiv [z - Hx]'R^{-1}[z - Hx] + [x - \bar{x}]'M^{-1}[x - \bar{x}]$$
$$= z'R^{-1}z - 2zR^{-1}Hx + x'H'R^{-1}Hx + x'M^{-1}x - 2\bar{x}'M^{-1}x + \bar{x}'M^{-1}\bar{x}$$

Then, in order to complete the square add the zero term

$$\bar{x}'H'R^{-1}H\bar{x} - 2\bar{x}'H'R^{-1}H\bar{x} + \bar{x}'H'R^{-1}H\bar{x}$$
$$- 2z'R^{-1}H\bar{x} + 2z'R^{-1}H\bar{x} + 2\bar{x}'H'R^{-1}Hx - 2\bar{x}'H'R^{-1}Hx = 0$$

to the right-hand side of the G equation to obtain

$$G = z'R^{-1}z - 2z'R^{-1}H\bar{x} + \bar{x}'H'R^{-1}H\bar{x}$$
$$- 2\left[z'R^{-1}Hx - z'R^{-1}H\bar{x} - \bar{x}'H'R^{-1}Hx + \bar{x}'H'R^{-1}H\bar{x}\right]$$
$$+ x'\left[M^{-1} + H'R^{-1}H\right]x - 2\bar{x}'\left[M^{-1} + H'R^{-1}H\right]x$$
$$+ \bar{x}'\left[M^{-1} + H'R^{-1}H\right]\bar{x}$$
$$= \left[z - H\bar{x}\right]'R^{-1}\left[z - H\bar{x}\right] - \left[z - H\bar{x}\right]'R^{-1}H\left[x - \bar{x}\right]$$
$$- \left[x - \bar{x}\right]'H'R^{-1}\left[z - H\bar{x}\right] + \left[x - \bar{x}\right]'\left[M^{-1} + H'R^{-1}H\right]\left[x - \bar{x}\right]$$
$$= \left[\left[z - H\bar{x}\right]', \left[x - \bar{x}\right]'\right]\begin{bmatrix} R^{-1} & -R^{-1}H \\ -H'R^{-1} & M^{-1} + H'R^{-1}H \end{bmatrix}\begin{bmatrix} z - H\bar{x} \\ x - \bar{x} \end{bmatrix}$$

Also it can be shown that

$$\begin{bmatrix} R^{-1} & -R^{-1}H \\ -H'R^{-1} & M^{-1} + H'R^{-1}H \end{bmatrix}^{-1} = \begin{bmatrix} HMH' + R & HM \\ MH' & M \end{bmatrix}$$

Therefore $p(z, x)$ is a normal density[1]

$$p(z, x) = N\left[\ (H\bar{x}, \bar{x}),\ P\right] \qquad (D\text{-}25)$$

where
$$P = \begin{bmatrix} P_{zz} & P_{zx} \\ P_{xz} & P_{xx} \end{bmatrix} = \begin{bmatrix} HMH' + R & HM \\ MH' & M \end{bmatrix} \qquad (D\text{-}26)$$

Expressions (D-21), (D-25), and (D-26) provide the mean and covariance of $p(z)$ and $p(z, x)$ for the special case of a linear (or linearized) measurement relationship. These relationships can now be used in Eqs. (D-15) and (D-16) to yield the

---

[1] A simple derivation of this is to recall that $P_{zz} = HMH' + R$ from (D-21) and $P_{xx} = M$ by definition. So it remains only to obtain P_{xz} since P is symmetric and $P_{xz} = P'_{zx}$.

$$P_{xz} = E\{[x - \bar{x}][z - \bar{z}]'\}$$
$$= E\{[x - \bar{x}][H[x - \bar{x}] + v]'\}$$
$$= E\{[x - \bar{x}][x - \bar{x}]'H' + [x - \bar{x}][v]'\}$$
$$P_{xz} = MH'$$

conditional mean and variance of x given z, that is,

$$E\{x|z\} = \bar{x} + P_{xz}P_{zz}^{-1}[z - \bar{z}] \tag{D-27}$$

$$E\{x|z\} = \bar{x} + MH'[HMH' + R]^{-1}[z - H\bar{x}] \tag{D-28}$$

and[1]

$$\Sigma = E\{[x - \bar{x}][x - \bar{x}]'|z\} = P_{xx} - P_{xz}P_{zz}^{-1}P'_{xz} \tag{D-29}$$

$$\Sigma = M - MH'[HMH' + R]^{-1}HM \tag{D-30}$$

To derive the Kalman filter for a second-order expansion of the measurement equation with additive noise, consider first such a form to replace the linear equation (D-17)

$$z = h(x) + v \tag{D-31}$$

The second-order expansion of this expression is

$$z \approx h(\hat{x}) + h_x \delta x + \frac{1}{2}\sum_i e^i \delta x' h^i_{xx} \delta x + v \tag{D-32}$$

Then the expected value is

$$\bar{z} = E\{z\} = h(\hat{x}) + \frac{1}{2}\sum_i e^i \operatorname{tr}\left[h^i_{xx} M\right] \tag{D-33}$$

because $E\{\delta x\} = 0$, where

$$M = E\{(\delta x)(\delta x)'\}$$

Then

$$z - E(z) = h'_x \delta x + \frac{1}{2}\sum_i e^i \delta x' h^i_{xx} \delta x + v - \frac{1}{2}\sum_i e^i \operatorname{tr}\left[h^i_{xx} M\right] \tag{D-34}$$

The covariance for $p(z)$ is obtained as

$$P_{zz} = E\{[z - E\{z\}][z - E\{z\}]'\}$$

$$= E\left\{h'_x \delta x \delta x' h_x + vv' + \frac{1}{4}\sum_i\sum_j e^i e^{j\prime}\left[\delta x' h^i_{xx} \delta_x\right]\left[\delta x' h^j_{xx} \delta x\right]\right.$$

$$+ \frac{1}{4}\sum_i\sum_j e^i e^{j\prime} \operatorname{tr}\left[h^i_{xx} M\right] \operatorname{tr}\left[h^j_{xx} M\right]$$

$$\left. - \frac{2}{4}\sum_i\sum_j (e^i \operatorname{tr}\left[h^i_{xx} M\right])(e^{j\prime} \delta x' h^j_{xx} \delta x)\right\} \tag{D-35}$$

---

[1] Bryson and Ho use the notation P rather than Σ for the covariance matrix of x conditional on z. Thus Eqs. (D-28) and (D-30) provide the mean and covariance of $p(x|z)$ for a first-order expansion of the measurement relationship. However, TBM use a second-order expansion.

or
$$P_{zz} = h'_x M h_x + R + \frac{1}{4} \sum_i \sum_j e^i e^{j\prime} E\{(\delta x' h^i_{xx} \delta x)(\delta x' h^j_{xx} \delta x)\}$$

$$+ \frac{1}{4} \sum_i \sum_j e^i e^{j\prime} \operatorname{tr}[h^i_{xx} M] \operatorname{tr}[h^j_{xx} M]$$

$$- \frac{2}{4} \sum_i \sum_j e^i e^{j\prime} \operatorname{tr}[h^i_{xx} M] \operatorname{tr}[h^j_{xx} M] \qquad (D\text{-}36)$$

Now consider only the third term on the right-hand side of Eq. (D-36). This is a fourth moment, and under gaussian assumptions one has [see Appendix F or Athans, Wishner, and Bertolini (1968, eq. (48), p. 508)]

$$\frac{1}{4} \sum_i \sum_j e^i e^{j\prime} E\{(\delta x' h^i_{xx} \delta x)(\delta x' h^j_{xx} \delta x)\} = \frac{2}{4} \sum_i \sum_j e^i (e^j)' \operatorname{tr}[h^i_{xx} M h^j_{xx} M]$$

$$+ \frac{1}{4} \sum_i \sum_j e^i (e^j)' \operatorname{tr}[h^i_{xx} M] \operatorname{tr}[h^j_{xx} M]$$

$$(D\text{-}37)$$

Then, using Eq. (D-37) in Eq. (D-36) and collecting terms yields

$$P_{zz} = h'_x M h_x + R + \frac{1}{2} \sum_i \sum_j e^i e^{j\prime} \operatorname{tr}[h^i_{xx} M h^j_{xx} M] \qquad (D\text{-}38)$$

Using Eq. (D-27) and (D-29) again, one obtains

$$E\{x|z\} = \bar{x} + P_{xz} P_{zz}^{-1}[z - \bar{z}]$$

$$= \bar{x} + [M h_x] \left[h'_x M h_x + R + \frac{1}{2} \sum_i \sum_j e^i e^{j\prime} \operatorname{tr}[h^i_{xx} M h^j_{zz} M] \right]^{-1} [z - \bar{z}]$$

$$(D\text{-}39)$$

and $\quad \Sigma = P_{xx} - P_{xz} P_{zz}^{-1} P'_{xz} \qquad (D\text{-}40)$

$$\Sigma = M - [M h_x] \left[h_x M h'_x + R + \frac{1}{2} \sum_i \sum_j e^i e^{j\prime} \operatorname{tr}[h^i_{xx} M h^j_{xx} M] \right]^{-1} [h'_x M]$$

$$(D\text{-}41)$$

APPENDIX E

ALTERNATE FORMS OF THE COST-TO-GO EXPRESSION

This appendix shows the equivalence of Eq. (9-69), the Tse, Bar-Shalom, and Meier (1973) (TBM) result, and Eq. (9-68), the Bar-Shalom, Tse, and Larson (1974) (BTL) result.

Since $C_{o,N-k-1}$ and γ_{k+1} in BTL are equivalent to $J_{o,N-k-1}$ and $g_{o,k+1}$, respectively, in TBM, Eq. (9-68) is the same as Eq. (9-69) except for the term

$$\frac{1}{2} \sum_{j=k+1}^{N-1} \operatorname{tr} \left[\mathbf{K}_{j+1} \mathbf{Q}_j + \mathcal{Q}_{\mathbf{xx}} \boldsymbol{\Sigma}_{j|j} \right]$$

This term is derived here and then substituted into Eq. (9-68).

Start with a result from Appendix C, namely Eq. (C-11)

$$g_j = \hat{g}_j - \tfrac{1}{2} \operatorname{tr} \left[\mathbf{K}_j \boldsymbol{\Sigma}_{j|j} \right] \tag{C-11}$$

where $\quad g_j = g_{j+1} - \tfrac{1}{2} \mathbf{H}'_{\mathbf{u}} \mathcal{H}_{\mathbf{uu}}^{-1} \mathbf{H}_{\mathbf{u}} + \tfrac{1}{2} \operatorname{tr} \left[\mathbf{K}_{j+1} \mathbf{Q}_j + \mathcal{Q}_{\mathbf{xx}} \boldsymbol{\Sigma}_{j|j} \right] \quad g_N = 0 \quad$ (C-1)

$$\hat{g}_j = \hat{g}_{j+1} - \tfrac{1}{2} \mathbf{H}'_{\mathbf{u}} \mathcal{H}_{\mathbf{uu}}^{-1} \mathbf{H}_{\mathbf{u}} + \tfrac{1}{2} \operatorname{tr} \left[\mathbf{H}_{\mathbf{xx}} \boldsymbol{\Sigma}_{j|j} + (\boldsymbol{\Sigma}_{j+1|j} - \boldsymbol{\Sigma}_{j+1|j+1}) \mathbf{K}_{j+1} \right]$$
$$\tag{C-4}$$

$$\hat{g}_N = \tfrac{1}{2} \operatorname{tr} \left[L_{N,\mathbf{xx}} \boldsymbol{\Sigma}_{N|N} \right]$$

From Eq. (C-1) one can get

$$g_{k+1} = g_{k+2} - \tfrac{1}{2}\mathbf{H}'_\mathbf{u}\mathcal{H}_\mathbf{uu}^{-1}\mathbf{H}_\mathbf{u} + \tfrac{1}{2}\operatorname{tr}[\mathbf{K}_{k+2}\mathbf{Q}_{k+1} + \mathcal{Q}_{\mathbf{xx}}\Sigma_{k+1|k+1}]$$

$$g_{k+2} = g_{k+3} - \tfrac{1}{2}\mathbf{H}'_\mathbf{u}\mathcal{H}_\mathbf{uu}^{-1}\mathbf{H}_\mathbf{u} + \tfrac{1}{2}\operatorname{tr}[\mathbf{K}_{k+3}\mathbf{Q}_{k+2} + \mathcal{Q}_{\mathbf{xx}}\Sigma_{k+2|k+2}] \quad \text{(E-1)}$$

$$g_{N-1} = g_N - \tfrac{1}{2}\mathbf{H}'_\mathbf{u}\mathcal{H}_\mathbf{uu}^{-1}\mathbf{H}_\mathbf{u} + \tfrac{1}{2}\operatorname{tr}[\mathbf{K}_N\mathbf{Q}_{N-1} + \mathcal{Q}_{\mathbf{xx}}\Sigma_{N-1|N-1}]$$

Successive substitution of all expressions into the first expression in Eq. (E-1) leads to

$$g_{k+1} = g_N - \frac{1}{2}\sum_{j=k+1}^{N-1}\mathbf{H}'_\mathbf{u}\mathcal{H}_\mathbf{uu}^{-1}\mathbf{H}_\mathbf{u} + \frac{1}{2}\sum_{j=k+1}^{N-1}\operatorname{tr}[\mathbf{K}_{j+1}\mathbf{Q}_j + \mathcal{Q}_{\mathbf{xx}}\Sigma_{j|j}] \quad \text{(E-2)}$$

In exactly the same way, one gets from Eq. (C-4)

$$\hat{g}_{k+1} = \hat{g}_N - \frac{1}{2}\sum_{j=k+1}^{N-1}\mathbf{H}'_\mathbf{u}\mathcal{H}_\mathbf{uu}^{-1}\mathbf{H}_\mathbf{u}$$

$$+ \frac{1}{2}\sum_{j=k+1}^{N-1}\operatorname{tr}[\mathbf{H}_{\mathbf{xx}}\Sigma_{j|j} + (\Sigma_{j+1|j} - \Sigma_{j+1|j+1})\mathbf{K}_{j+1}] \quad \text{(E-3)}$$

On the other hand, by Eq. (C-11),

$$g_{k+1} = \hat{g}_{k+1} - \tfrac{1}{2}\operatorname{tr}[\mathbf{K}_{k+1}\Sigma_{k+1|k+1}] \quad \text{(E-4)}$$

Substituting Eqs. (E-2) and (E-3) into Eq. (E-4) and simplifying the result leads to

$$\frac{1}{2}\sum_{j=k+1}^{N-1}\operatorname{tr}[\mathbf{K}_{j+1}\mathbf{Q}_j + \mathcal{Q}_{\mathbf{xx}}\Sigma_{j|j}] + g_N = \frac{1}{2}\sum_{j=k+1}^{N-1}\{\operatorname{tr}[\mathbf{H}_{\mathbf{xx}}\Sigma_{j|j}$$

$$+ (\Sigma_{j+1|j} - \Sigma_{j+1|j+1})\mathbf{K}_{j+1}]\} + \hat{g}_N - \tfrac{1}{2}\operatorname{tr}[\mathbf{K}_{k+1}\Sigma_{k+1|k+1}] \quad \text{(E-5)}$$

Substituting $g_N = 0$ from Eq. (C-1) and $\hat{g}_N = \tfrac{1}{2}\operatorname{tr}[\psi_{\mathbf{xx}}\Sigma_{N|N}]$ from Eq. (C-4) into Eq. (E-5) yields

$$\frac{1}{2}\sum_{j=k+1}^{N-1}\operatorname{tr}[\mathbf{K}_{j+1}\mathbf{Q}_j + \mathcal{Q}_{\mathbf{xx}}\Sigma_{j|j}]$$

$$= \frac{1}{2}\sum_{j=k+1}^{N-1}\{\operatorname{tr}[\mathbf{H}_{\mathbf{xx}}\Sigma_{j|j} + (\Sigma_{j+1|j} - \Sigma_{j+1|j+1})\mathbf{K}_{j+1}]\}$$

$$+ \tfrac{1}{2}\operatorname{tr}[L_{N,\mathbf{xx}}\Sigma_{N|N}] - \tfrac{1}{2}\operatorname{tr}[\mathbf{K}_{k+1}\Sigma_{k+1|k+1}] \quad \text{(E-6)}$$

ALTERNATE FORMS OF THE COST-TO-GO EXPRESSION

Substituting Eq. (E-6) into Eq. (9-68) leads to

$$J_{d,N-k}^* = \min_{u_k} \Big\{ \mathcal{L}_k(\mathbf{x}_k, \mathbf{u}_k) + \phi_k(\mathbf{u}_k) + C_{o,N-k-1} + \gamma_{k+1}$$

$$+ \tfrac{1}{2} \operatorname{tr}\big[\Sigma_{k+1|k} - \Sigma_{k+1|k+1} \big] \mathbf{K}_{k+1} + \tfrac{1}{2} \operatorname{tr}\big[L_{N,\mathbf{xx}} \Sigma_{N|N} \big]$$

$$+ \frac{1}{2} \sum_{j=k+1}^{N-1} \operatorname{tr}\big[\mathbf{H}_{\mathbf{xx}} \Sigma_{j|j} + \big((\Sigma_{j+1|j} - \Sigma_{j+1|j+1}) \mathbf{K}_{j+1} \big) \big] \Big\} \quad \text{(E-7)}$$

Equation (E-7) is exactly the same as Eq. (9-69) since the notational difference between TBM and BTL is

TBM	BTL
$J_{o,N-k-1}$	$C_{o,N-k-1}$
$g_{o,k+1}$	γ_{k+1}

APPENDIX
F

EXPECTED VALUE OF THE PRODUCT OF TWO QUADRATIC FORMS

by
Jorge Rizo Patron

In Athans, Wishner, and Bertolini [1968, app. A, especially Eq. (48), p. 508], a formal derivation of $E\{(\mathbf{x}'\mathbf{A}\mathbf{x})(\mathbf{x}'\mathbf{B}\mathbf{x})\} = 2\,\mathrm{tr}[\mathbf{A}\boldsymbol{\Sigma}\mathbf{B}\boldsymbol{\Sigma}] + \mathrm{tr}[\mathbf{A}\boldsymbol{\Sigma}]\,\mathrm{tr}[\mathbf{B}\boldsymbol{\Sigma}]$ is given. However, Athans et al. take as given that for a vector of gaussian random variables with zero means one has

$$E\{x_i x_j x_k x_l\} = \sigma_{ij}\sigma_{kl} + \sigma_{ik}\sigma_{jl} + \sigma_{il}\sigma_{jk} \qquad \text{(F-1)}$$

where σ_{ij} is the covariance between x_i and x_j. In these notes, the derivation of Eq. (F-1) is developed. Thereafter, following closely the approach of the above article, a formal proof of equality

$$E\{[\mathbf{x}'\mathbf{A}\mathbf{x}][\mathbf{x}'\mathbf{B}\mathbf{x}]\} = 2\,\mathrm{tr}[\mathbf{A}\boldsymbol{\Sigma}\mathbf{B}\boldsymbol{\Sigma}] + \mathrm{tr}[\mathbf{A}\boldsymbol{\Sigma}]\,\mathrm{tr}[\mathbf{B}\boldsymbol{\Sigma}]$$

where $\boldsymbol{\Sigma}$ is the covariance matrix of the x's, is given.

As $E\{x_i x_j x_k x_l\}$ is a fourth moment, the point of departure of the derivation is the moment-generating function.[1] To make exposition easier, this appendix is

---

[1] The author has been helped in certain aspects of the derivation by notes of Yaakov Bar-Shalom.

divided into three sections. The first section provides a derivation of the fourth moment in the scalar case. The second section generalizes this to the vector case, and the third section applies the result to obtain the desired derivation.

F-1 FOURTH MOMENT OF A NORMAL DISTRIBUTION WITH ZERO MEAN: SCALAR CASE

$$x \sim N(0, \sigma^2)$$

where x is the normal variable and σ^2 is its variance. Therefore, $E\{x - \mu\}^2 = E\{x^2\} = \sigma^2$, as the mean (μ) is 0.

The moment-generating function would be [Thiel (1971, p. 75)]

$$Mx(t) = e^{(1/2)\sigma^2 t^2}$$

$$Mx'(t) = \frac{d}{dt} Mx(t) = \tfrac{1}{2}\sigma^2 2t e^{(1/2)\sigma^2 t^2} = \sigma^2 t e^{(1/2)\sigma^2 t^2} = \sigma^2 t Mx(t)$$

$$\frac{d^2}{dt^2} Mx(t) = \sigma^2 t Mx'(t) + Mx(t)\sigma^2 = \sigma^2 t (\sigma^2 t Mx(t)) + Mx(t)\sigma^2$$

$$= (\sigma^4 t^2 + \sigma^2) Mx(t)$$

$$\frac{d^3}{dt^3} Mx(t) = (\sigma^4 t^2 + \sigma^2) Mx'(t) + Mx(t) 2\sigma^4 t = (\sigma^4 t^2 + \sigma^2)(\sigma^2 t Mx(t))$$

$$+ Mx(t) 2\sigma^4 t$$

$$= (\sigma^6 t^3 + \sigma^4 t + 2\sigma^4 t) Mx(t) = (\sigma^6 t^3 + 3\sigma^4 t) Mx(t)$$

$$\frac{d^4}{dt^4} Mx(t) = (\sigma^6 t^3 + 3\sigma^4 t) Mx'(t) + (3\sigma^6 t^2 + 3\sigma^4) Mx(t)$$

$$= (\sigma^6 t^3 + 3\sigma^4 t)\sigma^2 t Mx(t) + (3\sigma^6 t^2 + 3\sigma^4) Mx(t)$$

$$= (\sigma^8 t^4 + 6\sigma^6 t^2 + 3\sigma^4) Mx(t)$$

From the definition of moment-generating function

$$E\{x^4\} = \frac{d^4}{dt^4} Mx(0)$$

Substituting 0 for t in the fourth derivative gives

$$E\{x^4\} = 3\sigma^4 (Mx(0))$$

As $Mx(0) = e^{(1/2)\sigma^2(0)} = 1$,

$$E\{x^4\} = 3\sigma^4$$

F-2 FOURTH MOMENT OF A NORMAL DISTRIBUTION WITH ZERO MEAN: VECTOR CASE

In this case

$$\mathbf{x} \sim N(\mathbf{0}, \Sigma)$$

where Σ is the variance-covariance matrix.

The moment-generating function when the mean is zero is given by {Thiel [1971, p. 77, eq. (5.7)]}

$$M_x(\mathbf{t}) = e^{(1/2)\mathbf{t}'\Sigma\mathbf{t}}$$

At this point it is useful to develop some derivations of matrix derivatives which will be used later.

Recall that if

$$\mathbf{f}(\mathbf{t}) = \begin{bmatrix} f_1(\mathbf{t}) \\ \vdots \\ f_i(\mathbf{t}) \\ \vdots \\ f_M(\mathbf{t}) \end{bmatrix} = M \times 1 \text{ vector} \quad \text{and} \quad \mathbf{t} = \begin{bmatrix} t_1 \\ \vdots \\ t_j \\ \vdots \\ t_N \end{bmatrix} = N \times 1 \text{ vector}$$

then according to the notation used in Appendix A,[1]

$$\frac{d}{d\mathbf{t}} f_i(\mathbf{t}) = \begin{bmatrix} \frac{d}{dt_1} f_i(\mathbf{t}) \\ \vdots \\ \frac{d}{dt_j} f_i(\mathbf{t}) \\ \vdots \\ \frac{d}{dt_N} f_i(\mathbf{t}) \end{bmatrix} = N \times 1 \text{ vector}$$

$$\frac{d}{d\mathbf{t}} \mathbf{f}(\mathbf{t}) = \begin{bmatrix} \frac{d}{dt_1} f_1(\mathbf{t}) & \cdots & \frac{d}{dt_j} f_1(\mathbf{t}) & \cdots & \frac{d}{dt_N} f_1(\mathbf{t}) \\ \frac{d}{dt_1} f_i(\mathbf{t}) & \cdots & \frac{d}{dt_j} f_i(\mathbf{t}) & \cdots & \frac{d}{dt_N} f_i(\mathbf{t}) \\ \frac{d}{dt_1} f_M(\mathbf{t}) & \cdots & \frac{d}{dt_j} f_M(\mathbf{t}) & \cdots & \frac{d}{dt_N} f_M(\mathbf{t}) \end{bmatrix}$$

which is an $M \times N$ matrix.

[1] In this appendix d is used to indicate partial derivatives.

The following rules apply.
Rule 1
$$\frac{d}{d\mathbf{t}}\mathbf{t}'\mathbf{A}\mathbf{t} = 2\mathbf{A}\mathbf{t}$$
where $\mathbf{A}$ is an $N \times N$ symmetric matrix and $\mathbf{t}$ is an $N \times 1$ vector. The prime stands for transpose.

Rule 2
$$\frac{d}{d\mathbf{t}}\mathbf{A}\mathbf{t} = \mathbf{A}$$
where $\mathbf{A}$ is an $M \times N$ matrix.

Rule 3
$$\frac{d}{d\mathbf{t}}\mathbf{a}'\mathbf{t} = \frac{d}{d\mathbf{t}}\mathbf{t}'\mathbf{a} = \mathbf{a}$$
where $\mathbf{a}$ is an $N \times 1$ vector.

Rule 4
$$\frac{d}{d\mathbf{t}}\mathbf{f}(\mathbf{t})g(\mathbf{t}) = \mathbf{f}(\mathbf{t})\left[\frac{d}{d\mathbf{t}}g(\mathbf{t})\right]' + \left[\frac{d}{d\mathbf{t}}\mathbf{f}(\mathbf{t})\right]g(\mathbf{t})$$
where $\mathbf{f}(\mathbf{t})$ is an $M \times 1$ vector and $g(\mathbf{t})$ is a scalar.

PROOF $\mathbf{f}(\mathbf{t})g(\mathbf{t})$ is a vector of the form

$$\begin{bmatrix} f_1(\mathbf{t}) & g(\mathbf{t}) \\ \cdots & \cdots \\ f_i(\mathbf{t}) & g(\mathbf{t}) \\ \cdots & \cdots \\ f_M(\mathbf{t}) & g(\mathbf{t}) \end{bmatrix}$$

$$\frac{d}{d\mathbf{t}}\mathbf{f}(\mathbf{t})g(\mathbf{t}) = \begin{bmatrix} \frac{d}{dt_1}f_1(\mathbf{t})g(\mathbf{t}) & \cdots & \frac{d}{dt_j}f_1(\mathbf{t})g(\mathbf{t}) & \cdots & \frac{d}{dt_N}f_1(\mathbf{t})g(\mathbf{t}) \\ \cdots & & \cdots & & \cdots \\ \frac{d}{dt_1}f_i(\mathbf{t})g(\mathbf{t}) & \cdots & \frac{d}{dt_j}f_i(\mathbf{t})g(\mathbf{t}) & \cdots & \frac{d}{dt_N}f_i(\mathbf{t})g(\mathbf{t}) \\ \cdots & & \cdots & & \cdots \\ \frac{d}{dt_1}f_M(\mathbf{t})g(\mathbf{t}) & \cdots & \frac{d}{dt_j}f_M(\mathbf{t})g(\mathbf{t}) & \cdots & \frac{d}{dt_N}f_M(\mathbf{t})g(\mathbf{t}) \end{bmatrix}$$

Therefore, calling $f_i(\mathbf{t})$ simply f_i and $g(\mathbf{t})$ simply g, we have

$$\frac{d}{d\mathbf{t}}\mathbf{f}(\mathbf{t})g(\mathbf{t}) = \begin{bmatrix} f_1\frac{dg}{dt_1} + g\frac{df_1}{dt_1} & \cdots & f_1\frac{dg}{dt_j} + g\frac{df_1}{dt_j} & \cdots & f_1\frac{dg}{dt_N} + g\frac{df_1}{dt_N} \\ \cdots & & \cdots & & \cdots \\ f_i\frac{dg}{dt_1} + g\frac{df_i}{dt_1} & \cdots & f_i\frac{dg}{dt_j} + g\frac{df_i}{dt_j} & \cdots & f_i\frac{dg}{dt_N} + g\frac{df_i}{dt_N} \\ \cdots & & \cdots & & \cdots \\ f_M\frac{dg}{dt_1} + g\frac{df_M}{dt_1} & \cdots & f_M\frac{dg}{dt_j} + g\frac{df_M}{dt_j} & \cdots & f_M\frac{dg}{dt_N} + g\frac{df_M}{dt_N} \end{bmatrix}$$

Therefore

$$\frac{d}{d\mathbf{t}}\mathbf{f}(t)g(t) = \begin{bmatrix} f_1\frac{dg}{dt_1} & \cdots & f_1\frac{dg}{dt_j} & \cdots & f_1\frac{dg}{dt_N} \\ \vdots & & \vdots & & \vdots \\ f_i\frac{dg}{dt_1} & \cdots & f_i\frac{dg}{dt_j} & \cdots & f_i\frac{dg}{dt_N} \\ \vdots & & \vdots & & \vdots \\ f_M\frac{dg}{dt_1} & \cdots & f_M\frac{dg}{dt_j} & \cdots & f_M\frac{dg}{dt_N} \end{bmatrix}$$

$$+ g\begin{bmatrix} \frac{df_1}{dt_1} & \cdots & \frac{df_1}{dt_j} & \cdots & \frac{df_1}{dt_N} \\ \vdots & & \vdots & & \vdots \\ \frac{df_i}{dt_1} & \cdots & \frac{df_i}{dt_j} & \cdots & \frac{df_i}{dt_N} \\ \vdots & & \vdots & & \vdots \\ \frac{df_M}{dt_1} & \cdots & \frac{df_M}{dt_j} & \cdots & \frac{df_M}{dt_N} \end{bmatrix}$$

$$= \begin{bmatrix} f_1 \\ \vdots \\ f_i \\ \vdots \\ f_M \end{bmatrix} \begin{bmatrix} \frac{dg}{dt_1} & \cdots & \frac{dg}{dt_j} & \cdots & \frac{dg}{dt_N} \end{bmatrix} + g\frac{d\mathbf{f}}{d\mathbf{t}}$$

Finally,

$$\frac{d}{d\mathbf{t}}\mathbf{f}(t)g(t) = \mathbf{f}(t)\left[\frac{d}{d\mathbf{t}}g(t)\right]' + \left[\frac{d}{d\mathbf{t}}\mathbf{f}(t)\right]g(t)$$

Rule 5

$$\frac{d}{dt}\mathbf{a}g(t) = \mathbf{a}\left[\frac{d}{d\mathbf{t}}g(t)\right]'$$

where $\mathbf{a}$ is an $M \times 1$ vector and $g(t)$ is a scalar.

PROOF

$$\mathbf{a}g(t) = \begin{bmatrix} a_1 g(t) \\ \vdots \\ a_i g(t) \\ \vdots \\ a_M g(t) \end{bmatrix}$$

EXPECTED VALUE OF THE PRODUCT OF TWO QUADRATIC FORMS 167

Then

$$\frac{d}{dt}\mathbf{a}g(t) = \begin{bmatrix} a_1\frac{d}{dt_1}g(t) & \cdots & a_1\frac{d}{dt_j}g(t) & \cdots & a_1\frac{d}{dt_N}g(g) \\ \cdots & & \cdots & & \cdots \\ a_i\frac{d}{dt_1}g(t) & \cdots & a_i\frac{d}{dt_j}g(t) & \cdots & a_i\frac{d}{dt_N}g(t) \\ \cdots & & \cdots & & \cdots \\ a_M\frac{d}{dt_1}g(t) & \cdots & a_M\frac{d}{dt_j}g(t) & \cdots & a_M\frac{d}{dt_N}g(t) \end{bmatrix}$$

$$= \begin{bmatrix} a_1 \\ \vdots \\ a_i \\ \vdots \\ a_m \end{bmatrix} \begin{bmatrix} \frac{d}{dt_1}g(t) & \cdots & \frac{d}{dt_i}g(t) & \cdots & \frac{d}{dt_N}g(t) \end{bmatrix} = \mathbf{a}\left[\frac{d}{dt}g(t)\right]'$$

Rule 6

$$\frac{d}{dt}\mathbf{A}\mathbf{f}(t) = \mathbf{A}\frac{d}{dt}\mathbf{f}(t)$$

where $\mathbf{A}$ is a $K \times M$ matrix and $\mathbf{f}(t)$ is an $M \times 1$ vector.

PROOF

$$\mathbf{A}\mathbf{f}(t) = \begin{bmatrix} \sum_h a_{1h}f_h(t) \\ \vdots \\ \sum_h a_{ki}f_h(t) \\ \vdots \\ \sum_h a_{Kh}f_h(t) \end{bmatrix}$$

Calling $f_h(t)$ simply f_h, we have

$$\frac{d}{dt}\mathbf{A}\mathbf{f}(t) = \begin{bmatrix} a_{11}\frac{df_1}{dt_1}+\cdots+a_{1M}\frac{df_M}{dt_1} & \cdots & a_{11}\frac{df_1}{dt_N}+\cdots+a_{1M}\frac{df_M}{dt_N} \\ \cdots & & \cdots \\ a_{k1}\frac{df_1}{dt_1}+\cdots+a_{kM}\frac{df_M}{dt_1} & \cdots & a_{k1}\frac{df_1}{dt_N}+\cdots+a_{kM}\frac{df_M}{dt_N} \\ \cdots & & \cdots \\ a_{K1}\frac{df_1}{dt_1}+\cdots+a_{KM}\frac{df_M}{dt_1} & \cdots & a_{K1}\frac{df_1}{dt_N}+\cdots+a_{KM}\frac{df_M}{dt_N} \end{bmatrix}$$

Therefore

$$\frac{d}{d(t)}\mathbf{Af(t)} = \begin{bmatrix} a_{11} & \cdots & a_{1i} & \cdots & a_{1M} \\ a_{k1} & \cdots & a_{ki} & \cdots & a_{kM} \\ a_{K1} & \cdots & a_{Ki} & \cdots & a_{KM} \end{bmatrix}$$

$$\times \begin{bmatrix} \dfrac{df_1}{dt_1} & \cdots & \dfrac{df_1}{dt_j} & \cdots & \dfrac{df_1}{dt_N} \\ \dfrac{df_i}{dt_1} & \cdots & \dfrac{df_i}{dt_j} & & \dfrac{df_i}{dt_N} \\ \dfrac{df_M}{dt_1} & \cdots & \dfrac{df_M}{dt_j} & & \dfrac{df_M}{dt_N} \end{bmatrix}$$

$$\frac{d}{d(t)}\mathbf{Af(t)} = \mathbf{A}\frac{d}{d\mathbf{t}}\mathbf{f(t)}$$

Rule 7

$$\frac{d\mathbf{t}}{d\mathbf{t}} = \mathbf{I}$$

PROOF

$$\frac{d\mathbf{t}}{d\mathbf{t}} = \begin{bmatrix} \dfrac{dt_1}{dt_1} & \dfrac{dt_1}{dt_2} & \cdots & \dfrac{dt_1}{dt_N} \\ \dfrac{dt_N}{dt_1} & \dfrac{dt_N}{dt_2} & \cdots & \dfrac{dt_N}{dt_N} \end{bmatrix} = \begin{bmatrix} 1 & & & 0 \\ & 1 & & \\ & & \ddots & \\ 0 & & & 1 \end{bmatrix}$$

With these rules in mind one can find the fourth derivative of the moment-generating function.

Recall that $Mx(\mathbf{t}) = e^{(1/2)\mathbf{t}'\Sigma\mathbf{t}}$, where x is normally distributed with zero mean.

First derivative Therefore[1]

$$\frac{d}{d\mathbf{t}}Mx(\mathbf{t}) = \left[\frac{d}{d\mathbf{t}}\tfrac{1}{2}\mathbf{t}'\Sigma\mathbf{t}\right]Mx(\mathbf{t})$$

By rule 1 above,

$$\frac{d}{d\mathbf{t}}Mx(\mathbf{t}) = \Sigma\mathbf{t}\,Mx(\mathbf{t})$$

---

[1] $Mx(\mathbf{t})$ is a scalar, the first derivative is a vector, the second derivative is a matrix, and the third derivative is a row vector of matrices.

Second derivative

$$\frac{d^2}{dt^2}Mx(t) = \frac{d}{dt}\Sigma t\, Mx(t)$$

$$= \Sigma \frac{d}{dt} t\, Mx(t) \qquad \text{by rule 6}$$

$$= \Sigma\left[t\left(\frac{d}{dt}Mx(t)\right)' + I Mx(t)\right] \qquad \text{by rules 4 and 7}$$

$$= \Sigma[t(\Sigma t\, Mx(t))' + I Mx(t)] \qquad \text{by substituting for } \frac{d}{dt}Mx(t)$$

$$= \Sigma[tt'\Sigma Mx(t) + I Mx(t)]$$

since Σ is symmetric and $Mx(t)$ is a scalar

Third derivative Recall that

$$\frac{d^2}{dt^2}Mx(t)$$

$$= \begin{bmatrix} \frac{d}{dt_1}\left(\frac{d}{dt_1}Mx(t)\right) & \cdots & \frac{d}{dt_j}\left(\frac{d}{dt_1}Mx(t)\right) & \cdots & \frac{d}{dt_N}\left(\frac{d}{dt_1}Mx(t)\right) \\ \vdots & & \vdots & & \vdots \\ \frac{d}{dt_1}\left(\frac{d}{dt_I}Mx(t)\right) & \cdots & \frac{d}{dt_j}\left(\frac{d}{dt_I}Mx(t)\right) & \cdots & \frac{d}{dt_N}\left(\frac{d}{dt_I}Mx(t)\right) \\ \vdots & & \vdots & & \vdots \\ \frac{d}{dt_1}\left(\frac{d}{dt_N}Mx(t)\right) & \cdots & \frac{d}{dt_j}\left(\frac{d}{dt_N}Mx(t)\right) & \cdots & \frac{d}{dt_N}\left(\frac{d}{dt_N}Mx(t)\right) \end{bmatrix}$$

Then

$$\frac{d^2}{dt^2}Mx(t) = \left[\frac{d}{dt_1}\left(\frac{d}{dt}Mx(t)\right) \; \vdots \; \frac{d}{dt_2}\left(\frac{d}{dt}Mx(t)\right) \; \vdots \; \cdots \; \vdots \; \frac{d}{dt_N}\left(\frac{d}{dt}Mx(t)\right) \right]$$

and

$$\frac{d^3}{dt^3}Mx(t) = \left[\frac{d}{dt}\left\{\frac{d}{dt_1}\left(\frac{d}{dt}Mx(t)\right)\right\} \; \vdots \; \cdots \; \vdots \; \frac{d}{dt}\left\{\frac{d}{dt_N}\left(\frac{d}{dt}Mx(t)\right)\right\} \right]$$

where all $\left\{\frac{d}{dt}\frac{d}{dt_i}\left(\frac{d}{dt}Mx(t)\right)\right\}$ are matrices

The problem then is to find the matrix

$$\frac{d^3(Mx(t))}{dt\, dt_i\, dt} = \frac{d}{dt}\left\{\frac{d}{dt_i}\left(\frac{d}{dt}Mx(t)\right)\right\} \qquad \text{for each } i$$

as

$$\frac{d}{dt_i}\left(\frac{d}{dt}Mx(t)\right) = \left(\frac{d^2}{dt^2}Mx(t)\right)e^i$$

where e^i is a vector of zero element except for the ith position, where the element is 1. Then replacing the value of $d^2(Mx(t))/dt^2$ gives

$$\frac{d}{dt_i}\left(\frac{d}{dt}Mx(t)\right) = \Sigma[tt'\Sigma Mx(t) + IMx(t)]e^i$$

and
$$\frac{d^3(Mx(t))}{dt\,dt_i\,dt} = \frac{d}{dt}\{\Sigma[tt'\Sigma Mx(t) + IMx(t)]e^i\}$$

$$= \Sigma\frac{d}{dt}\{[tt'\Sigma Mx(t) + IMx(t)]e^i\} \quad \text{by rule 6}$$

$$\frac{d^3(Mx(t))}{dt\,dt_i\,dt} = \Sigma\frac{d}{dt}[(tt'\Sigma e^i)(Mx(t))] + \Sigma\frac{d}{dt}e^iMx(t) \quad \text{(F-2)}$$

By rule 4 the first term in Eq. (F-2) equals

$$\Sigma\left[tt\Sigma e^i\left[\frac{d}{dt}Mx(t)\right]' + \left(\frac{d}{dt}tt'\Sigma e^i\right)Mx(t)\right]$$

By rule 5 the second term in Eq. (F-2) equals

$$\Sigma\frac{d}{dt}e^iMx(t) = \Sigma e^i\left(\frac{d}{dt}Mx(t)\right)'$$

Substituting these two last equalities in Eq. (F-2), one gets

$$\frac{d^3(Mx(t))}{dt\,dt_i\,dt} = \Sigma\left[tt'\Sigma e^i\left(\frac{d}{dt}Mx(t)\right)' + \left(\frac{d}{dt}tt'\Sigma e^i\right)Mx(t) + e^i\left(\frac{d}{dt}Mx(t)\right)'\right]$$

Substituting for $(d(Mx(t))/dt)'$, we get

$$\frac{d^3(Mx(t))}{dt\,dt_i\,dt} = \Sigma\left[tt'\Sigma e^it'\Sigma Mx(t) + e^it'\Sigma Mx(t) + \frac{d}{dt}(tt'\Sigma e^i)Mx(t)\right] \quad \text{(F-3)}$$

By rules 4 and 7, recalling $t'\Sigma e^i$ is a scalar, one has

$$\frac{d}{dt}tt'\Sigma e^i = \frac{d}{dt}t(t'\Sigma e^i) = t\left(\frac{d}{dt}t'\Sigma e^i\right) + I(t'\Sigma e^i)$$

$$= t(\Sigma e^i)' + I(t'\Sigma e^i) \quad \text{by rule 3}$$

Therefore, substituting this value into Eq. (F-3) gives

$$\frac{d^3(Mx(t))}{dt\,dt_i\,dt} = \Sigma[tt'\Sigma e^it'\Sigma + e^it'\Sigma + t(e^i)'\Sigma + I(t'\Sigma e^i)]Mx(t)$$

Fourth derivative Similarly to the third derivative, the value of the matrix $d^4(Mx(t))/(dt\,dt_i\,dt_j\,dt)$ is computed. Recall that

$$\frac{d^4(Mx(t))}{dt\,dt_i\,dt_j\,dt} = \frac{d}{dt}\frac{d^3(Mx(t))}{dt\,dt_i\,dt_j} = \frac{d}{dt}\left[\frac{d^3(Mx(t))}{dt\,dt_i\,dt}e^j\right]$$

where e^j is a vector of zero elements except in position j, where the element is 1.

Therefore,

$$\frac{d^4(Mx(t))}{dt\,dt_i\,dt_j\,dt} = \frac{d}{dt}\left\{Mx(t)\Sigma\left[tt'\Sigma e^i t'\Sigma + e^i t'\Sigma + t(e^i)'\Sigma + I(t'\Sigma e^i)\right]e^j\right\}$$

$$\frac{d^4(Mx(t))}{dt\,dt_i\,dt_j\,dt} = \Sigma\left[tt'\Sigma e^i t'\Sigma + e^i t'\Sigma + t(e^i)'\Sigma + I(t'\Sigma e^i)\right]e^j\left[\frac{d}{dt}Mx(t)\right]'$$

$$+ Mx(t)\frac{d}{dt}\left\{\Sigma\left[tt'\Sigma e^i t'\Sigma + e^i t'\Sigma + t(e^i)'\Sigma + I(t'\Sigma e^i)\right]e^j\right\}$$

by rule 4   (F-4)

The second term in Eq. (F-4) consists of a sum of four terms, each equal to $Mx(t)$ multiplied by a derivative. These derivatives will be found first.

$$\frac{d}{dt}\Sigma tt'\Sigma e^i t'\Sigma e^j = \frac{d}{dt}\left\{(\Sigma tt'\Sigma e^i)(t'\Sigma e^j)\right\}$$

As $t'\Sigma e^j$ is a scalar, rule 4 applies. Then

$$\frac{d}{dt}\Sigma tt'\Sigma e^i t'\Sigma e^j = \Sigma tt'\Sigma e^i\left(\frac{d}{dt}t'\Sigma e^j\right)' + (t'\Sigma e^j)\left(\frac{d}{dt}\Sigma tt'\Sigma e^i\right)$$

$$= \Sigma tt'\Sigma e'e^{j'}\Sigma + t'\Sigma e^j\left\{\frac{d}{dt}\left[(\Sigma t)(t'\Sigma e^i)\right]\right\} \qquad \text{by rule 3}$$

$$= \Sigma tt'\Sigma e'e^{j'}\Sigma + t'\Sigma e^j\left[\Sigma t\left(\frac{d}{dt}t'\Sigma e^i\right)' + \left(\frac{d}{dt}\Sigma t\right)(t'\Sigma e^i)\right] \qquad \text{by rule 4}$$

$$= \Sigma tt'\Sigma e^i(e^j)'\Sigma + t'\Sigma e^j\left[\Sigma t(e^i)'\Sigma + \Sigma(t'\Sigma e^i)\right] \qquad \text{by rules 2 and 3}$$

$$= \Sigma tt'\Sigma e^i(e^j)'\Sigma + t'\Sigma e^j \Sigma t(e^i)'\Sigma + (t'\Sigma e^j)\Sigma t'\Sigma e^i$$

On the other hand,

$$\frac{d}{dt}\Sigma(e^i)t'\Sigma e^j = \frac{d}{dt}\left\{(\Sigma e^i)(t'\Sigma e^j)\right\}$$

$$= \Sigma e^i\left(\frac{d}{dt}t'\Sigma e^j\right)' \qquad \text{by rule 5}$$

$$= \Sigma e^i(e^j)'\Sigma \qquad \text{by rule 3}$$

Also $\quad \dfrac{d}{dt}\Sigma te^{i'}\Sigma e^j = \dfrac{d}{dt}\Sigma t((e^i)'\Sigma e^j) = \dfrac{d}{dt}((e^i)'\Sigma e^j)\Sigma t$

as $(e^i)'\Sigma e^j$ is a scalar. Therefore

$$\frac{d}{dt}\Sigma t(e^i)'\Sigma e^j = ((e^i)'\Sigma e^j)\Sigma \qquad \text{by rule 2}$$

Finally,

$$\frac{d}{dt}\Sigma(t'\Sigma e^i)e^j = \frac{d}{dt}(t'\Sigma e^i)\Sigma e^j$$

$$= \Sigma e^j\left(\frac{d}{dt}t'\Sigma e^i\right)' \quad \text{by rule 5}$$

$$= \Sigma e^j(e^i)'\Sigma \quad \text{by rule 3}$$

Substituting these values into Eq. (F-4) leads to

$$\frac{d^4(Mx(t))}{dt\,dt_i\,dt_j\,dt} = \Sigma\big[tt'\Sigma e^i t'\Sigma + e^i t'\Sigma + t(e^i)'\Sigma + I(t'\Sigma e^i)\big]e^j\left(\frac{dMx(t)}{dt}\right)'$$

$$+ Mx(t)\big\{\Sigma tt'\Sigma e^i(e^j)'\Sigma + (t'\Sigma e^j)\Sigma t(e^i)'\Sigma + (t'\Sigma e^j)\Sigma t'\Sigma e^i$$

$$+ \Sigma e^i(e^j)'\Sigma + \big[(e^i)'\Sigma e^j\big]\Sigma + \Sigma e^j(e^i)'\Sigma\big\}$$

To find the fourth moment, one needs to substitute zero for t in this expression. Then all terms with t' or t on them vanish, and what remains is

$$\left[\frac{d^4(Mx(t))}{dt\,dt_i\,dt_j\,dt}\right]_{t=0} = Mx(0)\big[\Sigma e^i(e^j)'\Sigma + ((e^i)'\Sigma e^j)\Sigma + \Sigma e^j(e^i)'\Sigma\big]$$

As $Mx(0) = e^{-(1/2)(0)} = 1$,

$$\left[\frac{d^4(Mx(t))}{dt\,dt_i\,dt_j\,dt}\right]_{t=0} = \big\{\Sigma e^i(e^j)'\Sigma + \big[(e^i)'\Sigma e^j\big]\Sigma + \Sigma e^j(e^i)'\Sigma\big\}$$

$$= \Sigma\big\{e^i(e^j)'\Sigma + \big[(e^i)'\Sigma e^j\big]I + e^j(e^i)'\Sigma\big\}$$

Our goal is to obtain the $E\{x_i x_i x_j x_k\}$. It is most direct to show this by taking $E\{\mathbf{x} x_i x_j \mathbf{x}\}$ as follows for the case in which $E\{\mathbf{x}\} = 0$:

$$E\{\mathbf{x} x_i x_j \mathbf{x}'\} = \Sigma\left\{\begin{bmatrix} 0 & 0 & 0 & \cdots & 0 \\ 0 & 0 & 0 & \cdots & 0 \\ \cdots & \cdots & \cdots & 1 & \cdots \\ 0 & 0 & 0 & \cdots & 0 \end{bmatrix}\underset{(i,j)\text{th element}}{\Sigma + \sigma_{ij}I}\right.$$

$$+ \underset{\substack{(j,i)\text{th} \\ \text{element}}}{\begin{bmatrix} 0 & 0 & 0 & \cdots & 0 \\ 0 & 0 & 1 & \cdots & 0 \\ \cdots & \cdots & \cdots & \cdots & \cdots \\ 0 & 0 & 0 & \cdots & 0 \end{bmatrix}}\Sigma\bigg\}$$

Then

$$E\{\mathbf{x}x_i x_j \mathbf{x}'\} = \Sigma \left\{ \begin{bmatrix} 0 & 0 & 0 & \cdots & 0 \\ 0 & 0 & 0 & \cdots & 0 \\ \sigma_{j1} & \sigma_{j2} & \sigma_{j3} & \cdots & \sigma_{jN} \\ 0 & 0 & 0 & \cdots & 0 \\ 0 & 0 & 0 & \cdots & 0 \end{bmatrix} + \begin{bmatrix} \sigma_{ij} & & & & \\ & \sigma_{ij} & & & \\ & & \sigma_{ij} & & \\ & & & \ddots & \\ & & & & \sigma_{ij} \end{bmatrix} \right.$$

$$+ \left. \begin{bmatrix} 0 & 0 & 0 & \cdots & 0 \\ 0 & 0 & 0 & \cdots & 0 \\ \sigma_{i1} & \sigma_{i2} & \sigma_{i3} & \cdots & \sigma_{iN} \\ 0 & 0 & 0 & \cdots & 0 \\ 0 & 0 & 0 & \cdots & 0 \end{bmatrix} \right\}$$

$$= \begin{bmatrix} \sigma_{1i}\sigma_{j1} & \sigma_{1i}\sigma_{j2} & \cdots & \sigma_{1i}\sigma_{jN} \\ \sigma_{2i}\sigma_{j1} & \sigma_{2i}\sigma_{j2} & \cdots & \sigma_{2i}\sigma_{jN} \\ \sigma_{li}\sigma_{j1} & \sigma_{li}\sigma_{j2} & \cdots & \sigma_{li}\sigma_{jN} \end{bmatrix} + \begin{bmatrix} \sigma_{11}\sigma_{ij} & \sigma_{12}\sigma_{ij} & \cdots \\ \sigma_{l1}\sigma_{ij} & \sigma_{l2}\sigma_{ij} & \cdots \end{bmatrix}$$

$$+ \begin{bmatrix} \sigma_{1j}\sigma_{i1} & \sigma_{1j}\sigma_{i2} & \cdots \\ \sigma_{2j}\sigma_{i1} & \sigma_{2j}\sigma_{i2} & \cdots \\ \sigma_{lj}\sigma_{i1} & \sigma_{lj}\sigma_{i2} & \cdots \end{bmatrix}$$

Therefore, if $E\{\mathbf{x}\} = 0$,

$$E\{x_l x_i x_j x_k\} = \sigma_{li}\sigma_{jk} + \sigma_{lk}\sigma_{ij} + \sigma_{lj}\sigma_{ik}$$

F-3 PROOF OF $E\{[\mathbf{x}'\mathbf{A}\mathbf{x}][\mathbf{x}'\mathbf{B}\mathbf{x}]\} = 2\,\text{tr}[\mathbf{A}\Sigma\mathbf{B}\Sigma] + \text{tr}[\mathbf{A}\Sigma]\,\text{tr}[\mathbf{B}\Sigma]$

It is assumed that $\mathbf{A}$ and $\mathbf{B}$ are symmetric matrices. Because of the properties of the trace[1]

$$\mathbf{x}'\mathbf{A}\mathbf{x} = \text{tr}[\mathbf{x}'\mathbf{A}\mathbf{x}] = \text{tr}[\mathbf{A}\mathbf{x}\mathbf{x}'] \quad \text{and} \quad \mathbf{x}'\mathbf{B}\mathbf{x} = \text{tr}[\mathbf{B}\mathbf{x}\mathbf{x}']$$

As a result,

$$E\{[\mathbf{x}'\mathbf{A}\mathbf{x}][\mathbf{x}'\mathbf{B}\mathbf{x}]\} = E\{\text{tr}[\mathbf{A}\mathbf{x}\mathbf{x}']\,\text{tr}[\mathbf{B}\mathbf{x}\mathbf{x}']\}$$

Call

$$\mathbf{D} = \mathbf{A}\mathbf{x}\mathbf{x}' = \mathbf{A} \begin{bmatrix} x_1 x_1 & x_1 x_2 & \cdots & x_1 x_N \\ \vdots & \vdots & & \vdots \\ x_N x_1 & x_N x_2 & \cdots & x_N x_N \end{bmatrix}$$

---

[1] See Appendix B and/or Goldberger (1964, p. 166).

In this case

$$d_{11} = \sum_j a_{1j}x_jx_1 \qquad d_{22} = \sum_j a_{2j}x_jx_2 \qquad d_{ii} = \sum_j a_{ij}x_jx_i$$

$$\text{tr}(D) = \sum_i \sum_j a_{ij}x_jx_i$$

Call

$$\mathbf{F} = \mathbf{Bxx'} \qquad \text{tr}(F) = \sum_k \sum_l b_{kl}x_kx_l$$

and

$$\text{tr}(\mathbf{D})\,\text{tr}(\mathbf{F}) = \sum_i \sum_j \sum_k \sum_l a_{ij}b_{kl}x_ix_jx_kx_l$$

Then $E\{[\mathbf{x'Ax}][\mathbf{x'Bx}]\} = E\{\text{tr}[\mathbf{Axx'}]\,\text{tr}[\mathbf{B(xx')}]\} =$

$$E\{\text{tr}[\mathbf{D}]\,\text{tr}[\mathbf{F}]\} = \sum_i \sum_j \sum_k \sum_l a_{ij}b_{kl}E\{(x_ix_jx_kx_l)\}$$

From the development in Sec. F-2

$$E\{[\mathbf{x'Ax}][\mathbf{x'Bx}]\} = \sum_i \sum_j \sum_k \sum_l a_{ij}b_{kl}(\sigma_{ij}\sigma_{lk} + \sigma_{ik}\sigma_{jl} + \sigma_{il}\sigma_{jk})$$

$$= \sum_i \sum_j \sum_k \sum_l a_{ij}b_{kl}\sigma_{ij}\sigma_{lk} + \sum_i \sum_j \sum_k \sum_l a_{ij}b_{kl}\sigma_{ik}\sigma_{jl}$$

$$+ \sum_i \sum_j \sum_k \sum_l a_{ij}b_{kl}\sigma_{il}\sigma_{jk} \tag{F-5}$$

As subindices, k and l can be interchanged, the second term in the last expression can be written

$$\sum_i \sum_j \sum_k \sum_l a_{ij}b_{kl}\sigma_{ik}\sigma_{jl} = \sum_i \sum_j \sum_k \sum_l a_{ij}b_{lk}\sigma_{il}\sigma_{jk}$$

But as $b_{lk} = b_{kl}$ (**B** is symmetric), the term at the right of the last equation can be expressed differently, and

$$\sum_i \sum_j \sum_k \sum_l a_{ij}b_{kl}\sigma_{ik}\sigma_{jl} = \sum_i \sum_j \sum_k \sum_l a_{ij}b_{kl}\sigma_{il}\sigma_{jk}$$

Therefore in Eq. (F-5), the second and third terms are equal and

$$E\{[\mathbf{x'Ax}][\mathbf{x'Bx}]\} = \sum_i \sum_j \sum_k \sum_l a_{ij}b_{kl}\sigma_{ij}\sigma_{lk} + 2\sum_i \sum_j \sum_k \sum_l a_{ij}b_{kl}\sigma_{ik}\sigma_{jl}$$

$$\tag{F-6}$$

On the other hand,[1]

$$A\Sigma = \begin{bmatrix} \sum_j a_{1j}\sigma_{j1} & \sum_j a_{1j}\sigma_{j2} & \cdots \\ \sum_j a_{2j}\sigma_{j1} & \sum_j a_{2j}\sigma_{j2} & \cdots \\ \cdots & \cdots & \end{bmatrix} \qquad B\Sigma = \begin{bmatrix} \sum_k b_{1k}\sigma_{k1} & \sum_k b_{1k}\sigma_{k2} & \cdots \\ \sum_k b_{2k}\sigma_{k1} & \sum_k b_{2k}\sigma_{k2} & \cdots \\ \cdots & \cdots & \end{bmatrix}$$

Calling $P = A\Sigma B\Sigma$, we get

$$P_{11} = \left(\sum_j a_{1j}\sigma_{j1}\right)\left(\sum_k b_{1k}\sigma_{k1}\right) + \left(\sum_j a_{1j}\sigma_{j2}\right)\left(\sum_k b_{2k}\sigma_{k1}\right)\cdots$$

$$= \sum_j \sum_k a_{1j}\sigma_{j1}b_{1k}\sigma_{k1} + \sum_j \sum_k a_{1j}\sigma_{j2}b_{2k}\sigma_{k1}\cdots$$

$$= \sum_j \sum_k a_{1j}\sigma_{k1}\left(\sum_l \sigma_{jl}b_{lk}\right)$$

Similarly
$$P_{ii} = \sum_j \sum_k a_{ij}\sigma_{ki}\left(\sum_l \sigma_{jl}b_{lk}\right)$$

Therefore
$$\text{tr}[P] = \sum_i \sum_j \sum_k a_{ij}\sigma_{ki}\left(\sum_l \sigma_{jl}b_{lk}\right)$$

and
$$\text{tr}[A\Sigma B\Sigma] = \sum_i \sum_j \sum_k \sum_l a_{ij}\sigma_{ki}\sigma_{jl}b_{lk} \qquad \text{as } P = A\Sigma B\Sigma$$

As $\sigma_{ki} = \sigma_{ik}$ and $b_{lk} = b_{kl}$,

$$\text{tr}[A\Sigma B\Sigma] = \sum_i \sum_j \sum_k \sum_l a_{ij}\sigma_{ik}\sigma_{jl}b_{kl} \qquad (F\text{-}7)$$

Also, from the observation of matrices $A\Sigma$ and $B\Sigma$ shown above

$$\text{tr}[A\Sigma] = \sum_i \sum_j a_{ij}\sigma_{ji}$$

$$\text{tr}[B\Sigma] = \sum_l \sum_k b_{lk}\sigma_{kl} = \sum_l \sum_k b_{kl}\sigma_{kl} \qquad \text{as } b_{kl} = b_{lk}$$

Then

$$\text{tr}[A\Sigma]\,\text{tr}[B\Sigma] = \sum_i \sum_j \sum_k \sum_l a_{ij}b_{kl}\sigma_{ji}\sigma_{kl} = \sum_i \sum_j \sum_k \sum_l a_{ij}b_{kl}\sigma_{ij}\sigma_{lk} \qquad (F\text{-}8)$$

---

[1] The reader is cautioned to be aware of the difference between $\sum_j$ (summation over j) and Σ (variance-covariance matrix).

since $\sigma_{ij} = \sigma_{ji}$ and $\sigma_{lk} = \sigma_{kl}$. Therefore, from Eqs. (F-7) and (F-8)

$$2\,\text{tr}[\mathbf{A\Sigma B\Sigma}] + \text{tr}[\mathbf{A\Sigma}]\,\text{tr}[\mathbf{B\Sigma}] = 2\sum_i\sum_j\sum_k\sum_l a_{ij}\sigma_{lk}\sigma_{jl}b_{kl}$$
$$+ \sum_i\sum_j\sum_k\sum_l a_{ij}\sigma_{ij}b_{kl}\sigma_{lk} \quad \text{(F-9)}$$

As the right-hand sides in Eqs. (F-6) and (F-9) are identical, the left sides would also be equal and the equality

$$E\{[\mathbf{x'Ax}][\mathbf{x'Bx}]\} = 2\,\text{tr}[\mathbf{A\Sigma B\Sigma}] + \text{tr}[\mathbf{A\Sigma}]\,\text{tr}[\mathbf{B\Sigma}]$$

is proved.

APPENDIX
G

CERTAINTY-EQUIVALENCE OPTIMAL COST-TO-GO PROBLEM

The problem is to minimize

$$J_{o,N-k-1} = \tfrac{1}{2}[\mathbf{x}_{oN} - \tilde{\mathbf{x}}_N]'\mathbf{W}_N[\mathbf{x}_{oN} - \tilde{\mathbf{x}}_N]$$

$$+ \sum_{j=k+1}^{N-1} \left(\tfrac{1}{2}[\mathbf{x}_{oj} - \tilde{\mathbf{x}}_j]'\mathbf{W}_j[\mathbf{x}_{oj} - \tilde{\mathbf{x}}_j] + [\mathbf{x}_{oj} - \tilde{\mathbf{x}}_j]'\mathbf{F}_j[\mathbf{u}_{oj} - \tilde{\mathbf{u}}_j] \right.$$

$$\left. + \tfrac{1}{2}[\mathbf{u}_{oj} - \tilde{\mathbf{u}}_j]'\mathbf{\Lambda}_j[\mathbf{u}_{oj} - \tilde{\mathbf{u}}_j] \right) \qquad \text{(G-1)}$$

subject to

$$\mathbf{x}_{o,j+1} = \mathbf{A}_j(\boldsymbol{\theta}_{oj})\mathbf{x}_{oj} + \mathbf{B}_j(\boldsymbol{\theta}_{oj})\mathbf{u}_{oj} + \mathbf{c}_j(\boldsymbol{\theta}_{oj}) \qquad \mathbf{x}_{o,k+1} = \hat{\mathbf{x}}_{k+1|k} \qquad \text{(G-2)}$$

$$\boldsymbol{\theta}_{o,j+1} = \mathbf{D}_j \boldsymbol{\theta}_{oj} \qquad \boldsymbol{\theta}_{o,k+1} = \hat{\boldsymbol{\theta}}_{k+1|k} \qquad \text{(G-3)}$$

To simplify, substitute the results of the forward integration of Eq. (G-3) into Eq. (G-2) and then drop Eq. (G-3) from the problem. The resulting problem is similar to the problem (2-1) to (2-3) and can be converted into that form by completion of the square.

Therefore, rewrite Eq. (G-1) as

$$J_o(N - k - 1) = \tfrac{1}{2}\mathbf{x}'_{oN}\mathbf{W}_N\mathbf{x}_{oN} - \tilde{\mathbf{x}}'_N\mathbf{W}_N\mathbf{x}_{oN} + \tfrac{1}{2}\tilde{\mathbf{x}}'_N\mathbf{W}_N\tilde{\mathbf{x}}_N$$

$$+ \sum_{j=k+1}^{N-1} \left(\tfrac{1}{2}\mathbf{x}'_{oj}\mathbf{W}_j\mathbf{x}_{oj} - \tilde{\mathbf{x}}'_j\mathbf{W}_j\mathbf{x}_{oj} + \tfrac{1}{2}\tilde{\mathbf{x}}'_j\mathbf{W}_j\tilde{\mathbf{x}}_j \right.$$

$$+ \mathbf{x}'_{oj}\mathbf{F}_j\mathbf{u}_{oj} - \tilde{\mathbf{u}}'_j\mathbf{F}_j\mathbf{x}_{oj} - \tilde{\mathbf{x}}'_j\mathbf{F}_j\mathbf{u}_{oj} + \tilde{\mathbf{x}}'_j\mathbf{F}_j\tilde{\mathbf{u}}_{oj}$$

$$\left. + \tfrac{1}{2}\mathbf{u}'_{oj}\mathbf{\Lambda}_j\mathbf{u}_{oj} - \tilde{\mathbf{u}}'_j\mathbf{\Lambda}_j\mathbf{u}_{oj} + \tfrac{1}{2}\tilde{\mathbf{u}}'_j\mathbf{\Lambda}_j\tilde{\mathbf{u}}_j \right) \qquad \text{(G-4)}$$

Table G-1 Notational equivalence

Problem (2-1) and (2-3)	Problem (G-5) and (G-2)	Problem (2-1) and (2-3)	Problem (G-5) and (G-2)
$\mathbf{W}_N$	$\mathbf{W}_N$	Λ_k	Λ_j
$\mathbf{w}_N$	$-\mathbf{W}_N\tilde{\mathbf{x}}_N$	λ_k	$-(\mathbf{F}_j'\tilde{\mathbf{x}}_j + \Lambda_j\tilde{\mathbf{u}}_j)$
$\mathbf{W}_k$	$\mathbf{W}_j$	$\mathbf{A}_k$	$\mathbf{A}_j(\boldsymbol{\theta}_{oj})$
$\mathbf{w}_k$	$-(\mathbf{W}_j\tilde{\mathbf{x}}_j + \mathbf{F}_j\tilde{\mathbf{u}}_j)$	$\mathbf{B}_k$	$\mathbf{B}_j(\boldsymbol{\theta}_{oj})$
$\mathbf{F}_k$	$\mathbf{F}_j$	$\mathbf{c}_k$	$\mathbf{c}_j(\boldsymbol{\theta}_{oj})$

Dropping the constant terms and collecting terms yields

$$J_o(N - k - 1) = \tfrac{1}{2}\mathbf{x}'_{oN}\mathbf{W}_N\mathbf{x}_{oN} - \tilde{\mathbf{x}}'_N\mathbf{W}_N\mathbf{x}_{oN}$$

$$+ \sum_{j=k+1}^{N-1} \left(\tfrac{1}{2}\mathbf{x}'_{oj}\mathbf{W}_j\mathbf{x}_{oj} - \left[\tilde{\mathbf{x}}'_j\mathbf{W}_j + \tilde{\mathbf{u}}'_j\mathbf{F}'_j\right]\mathbf{x}_{oj}\right.$$

$$\left. + \mathbf{x}'_{oj}\mathbf{F}_j\mathbf{u}_{oj} + \tfrac{1}{2}\mathbf{u}'_{oj}\Lambda_j\mathbf{u}_{oj} - \left[\tilde{\mathbf{u}}'_j\Lambda_j + \tilde{\mathbf{x}}'_j\mathbf{F}_j\right]\mathbf{u}_{oj}\right) \quad \text{(G-5)}$$

The problem (G-5) and (G-2) is in the same form as the quadratic linear problem (2-1) to (2-3). The notational equivalence is shown in Table G-1.

The solution to problem (2-1) to (2-3) is given in Eqs. (2-51) and (2-52). Using these results and the notational equivalence in Table G-1 yields the feedback rule

$$\mathbf{u}_{oj} = \mathbf{G}_j\mathbf{x}_{oj} + \mathbf{g}_j \quad \text{(G-6)}$$

where

$$\mathbf{G}_j = -\left[\mathbf{B}_j(\boldsymbol{\theta}_{oj})'\mathbf{K}_{j+1}\mathbf{B}_j(\boldsymbol{\theta}_{oj}) + \Lambda_j\right]^{-1}\left[\mathbf{F}'_j + \mathbf{B}_j(\boldsymbol{\theta}_{oj})'\mathbf{K}_{j+1}\mathbf{A}_j(\boldsymbol{\theta}_{oj})\right] \quad \text{(G-7)}$$

$$\mathbf{g}_j = -\left[\mathbf{B}_j(\boldsymbol{\theta}_{oj})'\mathbf{K}_{j+1}\mathbf{B}_j(\boldsymbol{\theta}_{oj}) + \Lambda_j\right]^{-1}\left[\mathbf{B}_j(\boldsymbol{\theta}_{oj})'\left[\mathbf{K}_{j+1}\mathbf{c}_j(\boldsymbol{\theta}_{oj}) + \mathbf{p}_{j+1}\right]\right.$$
$$\left. - \mathbf{F}'_j\tilde{\mathbf{x}}_j - \Lambda_j\tilde{\mathbf{u}}_j\right] \quad \text{(G-8)}$$

with, from Eqs. (2-53) and (2-54),

$$\mathbf{K}_j = \mathbf{A}_j(\boldsymbol{\theta}_{oj})'\mathbf{K}_{j+1}\mathbf{A}_j(\boldsymbol{\theta}_{oj})$$
$$- \left[\mathbf{A}_j(\boldsymbol{\theta}_{oj})'\mathbf{K}_{j+1}\mathbf{B}_j(\boldsymbol{\theta}_{oj}) + \mathbf{F}_j\right]\left[\mathbf{B}_j(\boldsymbol{\theta}_{oj})'\mathbf{K}_{j+1}\mathbf{B}_j(\boldsymbol{\theta}_{oj}) + \Lambda_j\right]^{-1}$$
$$\times \left[\mathbf{F}'_j + \mathbf{B}_j(\boldsymbol{\theta}_{oj})'\mathbf{K}_{j+1}\mathbf{A}_j(\boldsymbol{\theta}_{oj})\right] + \mathbf{W}_j \quad \text{where } \mathbf{K}_N = \mathbf{W}_N \quad \text{(G-9)}$$

and with

$$\mathbf{p}_j = -\left[\mathbf{A}_j(\boldsymbol{\theta}_{oj})'\mathbf{K}_{j+1}\mathbf{B}_j(\boldsymbol{\theta}_{oj}) + \mathbf{F}_j\right]$$
$$\times \left[\mathbf{B}_j(\boldsymbol{\theta}_{oj})'\mathbf{K}_{j+1}\mathbf{B}_j(\boldsymbol{\theta}_{oj}) + \Lambda_j\right]^{-1}$$
$$\times \left[\mathbf{B}_j(\boldsymbol{\theta}_{oj})'\left[\mathbf{K}_{j+1}\mathbf{c}_j(\boldsymbol{\theta}_{oj}) + \mathbf{p}_{j+1}\right] - (\mathbf{F}'_j\tilde{\mathbf{x}}_j + \Lambda_j\tilde{\mathbf{u}}_j)\right]$$
$$+ \mathbf{A}_j(\boldsymbol{\theta}_{oj})'\left[\mathbf{K}_{j+1}\mathbf{c}_j(\boldsymbol{\theta}_{oj}) + \mathbf{p}_{j+1}\right] - \left[\mathbf{W}_j\tilde{\mathbf{x}}_j + \mathbf{F}_j\tilde{\mathbf{u}}_j\right]$$
$$\text{where } \mathbf{p}_N = -\mathbf{W}_N\tilde{\mathbf{x}}_N \quad \text{(G-10)}$$

APPENDIX
H

MATRIX RECURSIONS FOR THE AUGMENTED SYSTEM

The matrix **K** for the augmented system (10-38) can be partitioned as

$$\mathbf{K} = \begin{bmatrix} \mathbf{K}^{xx} & (\mathbf{K}^{\theta x})' \\ \mathbf{K}^{\theta x} & \mathbf{K}^{\theta\theta} \end{bmatrix} \tag{H-1}$$

where $\mathbf{K}^{xx} = \tilde{\mathbf{K}}$ and $\tilde{\mathbf{K}}$ is the recursion for the unaugmented system defined in Eq. (10-33). Similarly, **p** can be partitioned as

$$\mathbf{p} = \begin{bmatrix} \mathbf{p}^x \\ \mathbf{p}^\theta \end{bmatrix}$$

To begin the derivation of the recursions $\mathbf{K}^{\theta x}$ and $\mathbf{K}^{\theta\theta}$ recall the following definitions from Chap. 9 [see Eq. (9-45)]:

$$\mathbf{K}_j = \mathcal{H}_{xx} - \mathcal{Q}_{xx} \tag{H-2}$$

where, from Eq. (9-37),

$$\mathcal{Q}_{xx} = \mathcal{H}'_{ux} \mathcal{H}_{uu}^{-1} \mathcal{H}_{ux} \tag{H-3}$$

and, from Eq. (9-31),

$$\mathcal{H}_{xx} = \mathbf{H}_{xx} + \mathbf{f}'_x \mathbf{K}_{j+1} \mathbf{f}_x \quad \mathcal{H}_{ux} = \mathbf{H}_{ux} + \mathbf{f}'_u \mathbf{K}_{j+1} \mathbf{f}_x \quad \mathcal{H}_{uu} = \mathbf{H}_{uu} + \mathbf{f}'_u \mathbf{K}_{j+1} \mathbf{f}_u \tag{H-4}$$

where, from Eq. (9-28),

$$H_j = L_j(\mathbf{x}_j, \mathbf{u}_j) + \mathbf{p}'_{j+1}\mathbf{f}_j \tag{H-5}$$

and, from Eq. (9-29),[1]

$$\mathbf{H}_\mathbf{x} = \mathbf{L}_\mathbf{x} + \mathbf{f}'_\mathbf{x}\mathbf{p}_{j+1} \qquad \mathbf{H}_\mathbf{u} = \mathbf{L}_\mathbf{u} + \mathbf{f}'_\mathbf{u}\mathbf{p}_{j+1}$$

$$\mathbf{H}_{\mathbf{xx}} = \mathbf{L}_{\mathbf{xx}} + \sum_{i=1}^{N} \left[(\mathbf{e}^i)' \mathbf{p}_{j+1} \right] \mathbf{f}^i_{\mathbf{xx}}$$

$$\mathbf{H}_{\mathbf{uu}} = \mathbf{L}_{\mathbf{uu}} + \sum_{i=1}^{N} \left[(\mathbf{e}^i)' \mathbf{p}_{j+1} \right] \mathbf{f}^i_{\mathbf{uu}} \tag{H-6}$$

$$\mathbf{H}_{\mathbf{xu}} = \mathbf{L}_{\mathbf{xu}} + \sum_{i=1}^{N} \left[(\mathbf{e}^i)' \mathbf{p}_{j+1} \right] \mathbf{f}^i_{\mathbf{xu}}$$

The time subscript k is omitted from $\mathbf{H}$, $\mathcal{H}$, and $\mathcal{C}$ for simplicity. The subscript $\mathbf{x}$ now is changed to $\mathbf{z}$ where $\mathbf{z}$ is the augmented state vector. Hence, for example, Eq. (H-2) becomes

$$\mathbf{K}_j = \mathcal{H}_{\mathbf{zz}} - \mathcal{C}_{\mathbf{zz}} \tag{H-7}$$

The recursions $\mathbf{K}^{\theta\mathbf{x}}$ and $\mathbf{K}^{\theta\theta}$ can be obtained by expressing Eq. (H-7) in terms of $\mathbf{f}^\mathbf{x}$ and $\mathbf{f}^\theta$ from Eq. (10-20). This requires in turn expressing Eqs. (H-4) and (H-6) in terms of $\mathbf{f}^\mathbf{x}$ and $\mathbf{f}^\theta$ as the rest of this appendix will show.

From Eq. (10-20) it follows that

$$\mathbf{f}^\mathbf{z}_\mathbf{z} = \begin{bmatrix} \mathbf{f}^\mathbf{x}_\mathbf{x} & \mathbf{f}^\mathbf{x}_\theta \\ \mathbf{f}^\theta_\mathbf{x} & \mathbf{f}^\theta_\theta \end{bmatrix} \tag{H-8}$$

where the subscript denotes the gradient of each set of functions with respect to the state vector. Also

$$\mathbf{f}^\mathbf{z}_\mathbf{u} = \begin{bmatrix} \mathbf{f}^\mathbf{x}_\mathbf{u} \\ \mathbf{f}^\theta_\mathbf{u} \end{bmatrix} \tag{H-9}$$

and $H^\mathbf{z} = L^\mathbf{z} + \mathbf{p}'\mathbf{f}^\mathbf{z}$, from Eq. (H-5), where the time subscript is omitted for simplicity, or

$$H^\mathbf{z} = L^\mathbf{x} + L^\theta + \left[(\mathbf{p}^\mathbf{x})' \;\vdots\; (\mathbf{p}^\theta)' \right] \begin{bmatrix} \mathbf{f}^\mathbf{x} \\ \mathbf{f}^\theta \end{bmatrix} \tag{H-10}$$

Note that Eq. (H-10) is still a scalar.

---

[1] Since $(\mathbf{e}^i)'\mathbf{p}_{j+1}$ is a scalar quantity it is equal to the quantity $\mathbf{e}^i\mathbf{p}'_{j+1}$ which is used in Eq. (9-29).

Since $\boldsymbol{\theta}$ does not enter the cost function, $L^{\theta} = 0$, Eq. (H-10) becomes

$$H^z = L^x + \left[(\mathbf{p}^x)' \mid (\mathbf{p}^{\theta})'\right]\begin{bmatrix} \mathbf{f}^x \\ --- \\ \mathbf{f}^{\theta} \end{bmatrix} \tag{H-11}$$

and, from Eqs. (10-16) to (10-19),

$$L^x = \tfrac{1}{2}[\mathbf{x}_k - \tilde{\mathbf{x}}_k]'\mathbf{W}_k[\mathbf{x}_k - \tilde{\mathbf{x}}_k] + [\mathbf{x}_k - \tilde{\mathbf{x}}_k]'\mathbf{F}_k[\mathbf{u}_k - \tilde{\mathbf{u}}_k]$$
$$+ \tfrac{1}{2}[\mathbf{u}_k - \tilde{\mathbf{u}}_k]'\Lambda_k[\mathbf{u}_k - \tilde{\mathbf{u}}_k] \tag{H-12}$$

The gradient of H^z with respect to $\mathbf{z}$ is

$$H^z_\mathbf{z} = \begin{bmatrix} H^z_\mathbf{x} \\ --- \\ H^z_{\boldsymbol{\theta}} \end{bmatrix} \tag{H-13}$$

where

$$H^z_\mathbf{x} = L^x_\mathbf{x} + \left[(\mathbf{f}^x_\mathbf{x})' \mid (\mathbf{f}^{\theta}_\mathbf{x})'\right]\begin{bmatrix} \mathbf{p}^x \\ --- \\ \mathbf{p}^{\theta} \end{bmatrix} = L^x_\mathbf{x} + (\mathbf{f}^x_\mathbf{x})'\mathbf{p}^x \tag{H-14}$$

since $\mathbf{f}^{\theta}_\mathbf{x} = 0$ in view of the system equations and the criterion function

$$H^z_{\boldsymbol{\theta}} = L^x_{\boldsymbol{\theta}} + \left[(\mathbf{f}^x_{\boldsymbol{\theta}})' \mid (\mathbf{f}^{\theta}_{\boldsymbol{\theta}})'\right]\begin{bmatrix} \mathbf{p}^x \\ --- \\ \mathbf{p}^{\theta} \end{bmatrix} = (\mathbf{f}^x_{\boldsymbol{\theta}})'\mathbf{p}^x + (\mathbf{f}^{\theta}_{\boldsymbol{\theta}})'\mathbf{p}^{\theta} \tag{H-15}$$

since $L^x_{\boldsymbol{\theta}} = 0$ in view of the criterion function.
Hence,

$$H^z_\mathbf{z} = \begin{bmatrix} L^x_\mathbf{x} + (\mathbf{f}^x_\mathbf{x})'\mathbf{p}^x \\ ---------- \\ (\mathbf{f}^x_{\boldsymbol{\theta}})'\mathbf{p}^x + (\mathbf{f}^{\theta}_{\boldsymbol{\theta}})'\mathbf{p}^{\theta} \end{bmatrix} \tag{H-16}$$

Similarly, the gradient of H^z with respect to $\mathbf{u}$ is

$$H^z_\mathbf{u} = L^x_\mathbf{u} + \left[(\mathbf{f}^x_\mathbf{u})' \mid (\mathbf{f}^{\theta}_\mathbf{u})'\right]\begin{bmatrix} \mathbf{p}^x \\ --- \\ \mathbf{p}^{\theta} \end{bmatrix} \tag{H-17}$$

Since

$$L^x_\mathbf{u} = F'_k[\mathbf{x}_k - \tilde{\mathbf{x}}_k] + \Lambda_k[\mathbf{u}_k - \tilde{\mathbf{u}}_k] \qquad (\mathbf{f}^x_\mathbf{u})' = B' \qquad \mathbf{f}^{\theta}_\mathbf{u} = 0$$

Eq. (H-17) becomes

$$H^z_\mathbf{u} = L^x_\mathbf{u} + \left[(\mathbf{f}^x_\mathbf{u})' \mid 0\right]\begin{bmatrix} \mathbf{p}^x \\ --- \\ \mathbf{p}^{\theta} \end{bmatrix} = F'_k[\mathbf{x}_k - \tilde{\mathbf{x}}_k] + \Lambda\mathbf{u} - \Lambda\tilde{\mathbf{u}} + B'\mathbf{p}^x \tag{H-18}$$

The hessian of H^z with respect to $\mathbf{z}$ is given by

$$H^z_{\mathbf{zz}} = \begin{bmatrix} H^z_{\mathbf{xx}} & H^z_{\mathbf{x}\boldsymbol{\theta}} \\ H^z_{\boldsymbol{\theta}\mathbf{x}} & H^z_{\boldsymbol{\theta\theta}} \end{bmatrix} \tag{H-19}$$

Using Eqs. (H-14) and (H-15) and letting $i \in X$ and $i \in \Theta$ denote the indices of the original state equations and of the parameter equations, respectively, we get

$$\mathbf{H}_{xx}^z = \mathbf{L}_{xx} + \sum_{i \in X} (e_i' \mathbf{p}^x) \mathbf{f}_{xx}^i + \sum_{i \in \Theta} e_i' \mathbf{p}^\theta \mathbf{f}_{xx}^i = \mathbf{L}_{xx} \qquad (\text{H-20})$$

since $\mathbf{f}_{xx}^i = \mathbf{0}$ for all i, and

$$\mathbf{H}_{x\theta}^z = (\mathbf{H}_{\theta x}^z)' = \mathbf{L}_{x\theta} + \sum_{i \in X} e_i' \mathbf{p}^x \mathbf{f}_{x\theta}^i + \sum_{i \in \Theta} e_i' \mathbf{p}^x \mathbf{f}_{x\theta}^i = \sum_{i \in X} e_i' \mathbf{p}^x \mathbf{f}_{x\theta}^i \qquad (\text{H-21})$$

since $\mathbf{L}_{x\theta} = \mathbf{0}$ and $\mathbf{f}_{x\theta}^i = \mathbf{0}$ for $i \in \Theta$, and

$$\mathbf{H}_{\theta\theta} = \mathbf{L}_{\theta\theta} + \sum_{i \in X} e_i' \mathbf{p}^x \mathbf{f}_{\theta\theta}^i + \sum_{i \in \Theta} e_i' \mathbf{p}^\theta \mathbf{f}_{\theta\theta}^i = \mathbf{0} \qquad (\text{H-22})$$

since $\mathbf{L}_{\theta\theta} = \mathbf{0}$ and $\mathbf{f}_{\theta\theta}^i = \mathbf{0}$ for all i.

A 2×2 example will make the derivation of Eq. (H-20) from Eq. (H-14) clearer. Consider the following 2×2 case. Let

$$H = L(x_1, x_2) + [p_1 \mid p_2] \begin{bmatrix} f^1(x_1, x_2) \\ f^2(x_1, x_2) \end{bmatrix} \qquad (\text{H-23})$$

Note that p_1 and p_2 are scalars. Then

$$\mathbf{H}_x = \begin{bmatrix} H_{x_1} \\ H_{x_2} \end{bmatrix} \qquad (\text{H-24})$$

$$H_{x_1} = L_{x_1} + \begin{bmatrix} f_{x_1}^1 \\ f_{x_1}^2 \end{bmatrix}' \begin{bmatrix} p_1 \\ p_2 \end{bmatrix} \qquad H_{x_2} = L_{x_2} + \begin{bmatrix} f_{x_2}^1 \\ f_{x_2}^2 \end{bmatrix}' \begin{bmatrix} p_1 \\ p_2 \end{bmatrix}$$

or

$$\mathbf{H}_x = \begin{bmatrix} H_{x_1} \\ H_{x_2} \end{bmatrix} = \begin{bmatrix} L_{x_1} \\ L_{x_2} \end{bmatrix} + \begin{bmatrix} f_{x_1}^1 & f_{x_2}^1 \\ f_{x_1}^2 & f_{x_2}^2 \end{bmatrix}' \begin{bmatrix} p_1 \\ p_2 \end{bmatrix} \qquad (\text{H-25})$$

The hessian $\mathbf{H}_{xx}$ is obtained from Eq. (H-25)

$$\mathbf{H}_{xx} = \begin{bmatrix} H_{x_1 x_1} & H_{x_1 x_2} \\ \hline H_{x_2 x_1} & H_{x_2 x_2} \end{bmatrix} \qquad (\text{H-26})$$

Redefine $H_{11} = H_{x_1 x_1}$, $H_{12} = H_{x_1 x_2}$, $H_{22} = H_{x_2 x_2}$, $L_{11} = L_{x_1 x_1}$, and $f_{11} = f_{x_1 x_1}$, and so on. Then

$$\mathbf{H}_{xx} = \begin{bmatrix} H_{11} & H_{12} \\ H_{21} & H_{22} \end{bmatrix} \qquad (\text{H-27})$$

where

$$H_{11} = \frac{\partial}{\partial x_1} H_{x_1} = L_{11} + [p_1 \; p_2] \begin{bmatrix} f_{11}^1 \\ f_{11}^2 \end{bmatrix}$$

$$H_{12} = \frac{\partial}{\partial x_2} H_{x_1} = L_{12} + [p_1 \; p_2] \begin{bmatrix} f_{12}^1 \\ f_{12}^2 \end{bmatrix} = H_{21}' \qquad (\text{H-28})$$

$$H_{22} = \frac{\partial}{\partial x_2} H_{x_2} = L_{22} + \begin{bmatrix} p_1 & p_2 \end{bmatrix} \begin{bmatrix} f_{22}^1 \\ f_{22}^2 \end{bmatrix}$$

Substituting Eq. (H-28) into Eq. (H-27) leads, after simplification, to

$$\mathbf{H}_{xx} = \begin{bmatrix} L_{11} & L_{12} \\ \hline L_{21} & L_{22} \end{bmatrix} + \begin{bmatrix} p_1 f_{11}^1 + p_2 f_{11}^2 & p_1 f_{12}^1 + p_2 f_{12}^2 \\ \hline p_1 f_{21}^1 + p_2 f_{21}^2 & p_1 f_{22}^1 + p_2 f_{22}^2 \end{bmatrix}$$

$$= \begin{bmatrix} L_{11} & L_{12} \\ \hline L_{21} & L_{22} \end{bmatrix} + p_1 \begin{bmatrix} f_{11}^1 & f_{12}^1 \\ f_{21}^1 & f_{22}^1 \end{bmatrix} + p_2 \begin{bmatrix} f_{11}^2 & f_{12}^2 \\ f_{21}^2 & f_{22}^2 \end{bmatrix} \quad \text{(H-29)}$$

$$\mathbf{H}_{xx} = \mathbf{L}_{xx} + \sum_i e_i' \begin{bmatrix} p_1 \\ p_2 \end{bmatrix} \mathbf{f}_{xx}^i \quad \text{(H-30)}$$

where

$$\mathbf{L}_{xx} = \begin{bmatrix} L_{11} & L_{12} \\ \hline L_{21} & L_{22} \end{bmatrix} \quad \mathbf{f}_{xx}^i = \begin{bmatrix} f_{11}^i & f_{12}^i \\ f_{21}^i & f_{22}^i \end{bmatrix} \quad e_1 = \begin{bmatrix} 1 \\ 0 \end{bmatrix} \quad e_2 = \begin{bmatrix} 0 \\ 1 \end{bmatrix}$$

Notice that Eq. (H-20) is equivalent to Eq. (H-30).

Now, substituting Eqs. (H-20) to (H-22) into Eq. (H-19) leads to

$$\mathbf{H}_{zz}^z = \begin{bmatrix} \mathbf{L}_{xx} & 0 \\ \hline 0 & 0 \end{bmatrix} + \sum_{i \in X} e_i' \mathbf{p}^x \begin{bmatrix} 0 & \mathbf{f}_{x\theta}^i \\ \hline \mathbf{f}_{\theta x}^i & 0 \end{bmatrix} \quad \text{(H-31)}$$

From the criterion equation $\mathbf{L}_{xx} = \mathbf{W}$, and from the system equations $\mathbf{f}_{x\theta}^i = \mathbf{a}_\theta^i = (\mathbf{f}_{\theta x}^i)'$, where $\mathbf{a}_\theta^i$ denotes the gradient of the ith row of the coefficient matrix $\mathbf{A}_k(\theta_k)$ with respect to θ_k. Therefore,

$$\mathbf{H}_{zz}^z = \begin{bmatrix} \mathbf{W} & 0 \\ \hline 0 & 0 \end{bmatrix} + \sum_{i \in X} e_i' \mathbf{p}^x \begin{bmatrix} 0 & \mathbf{a}_\theta^i \\ \hline \mathbf{a}_\theta^{i\prime} & 0 \end{bmatrix} \quad \text{(H-32)}$$

which is the same as Eq. (10-37).

In exactly the same way, the hessian of $\mathbf{H}^z$ with respect to $\mathbf{u}$, that is, $\mathbf{H}_{uu}^z$ is obtained from Eq. (H-17)

$$\mathbf{H}_{uu}^z = \mathbf{L}_{uu}^x + \sum_{i \in X} e_i' \mathbf{p}^x \mathbf{f}_{uu}^i + \sum_{j \in \Theta} e_j' \mathbf{p}^\theta \mathbf{f}_{uu}^j \quad \text{(H-33)}$$

In view of the system equation and cost functional again,

$$\mathbf{L}_{uu}^x = \Lambda \quad \mathbf{f}_{uu}^i = 0 = \mathbf{f}_{uu}^j \quad \text{for } i \in X, j \in \Theta$$

Therefore

$$\mathbf{H}_{uu}^z = \Lambda \quad \text{(H-34)}$$

On the other hand, from Eq. (H-17),

$$\mathbf{H}_{zu}^z = \mathbf{L}_{zu}^x + \sum_{i \in X} e_i' \mathbf{p}^x \mathbf{f}_{zu}^i + \sum_{j \in \Theta} e_j' \mathbf{p}^\theta \mathbf{f}_{zu}^j \quad \text{(H-35)}$$

Recall that

$$\mathbf{f}_z = \begin{bmatrix} \mathbf{f}_x \\ \mathbf{f}_\theta \end{bmatrix} \quad \text{from which} \quad \mathbf{f}_{zu} = \begin{bmatrix} \mathbf{f}_{xu} \\ \mathbf{f}_{\theta u} \end{bmatrix}$$

is derived, hence, Eq. (H-35) can be rewritten as

$$\mathbf{H}_{zu}^z = \mathbf{L}_{zu}^x + \sum_{i \in X} e_i' \mathbf{p}^x \begin{bmatrix} \mathbf{f}_{xu}^i \\ \mathbf{f}_{\theta u}^i \end{bmatrix} + \sum_{j \in \Theta} e_j' \mathbf{p}^\theta \begin{bmatrix} \mathbf{f}_{xu}^j \\ \mathbf{f}_{\theta u}^j \end{bmatrix} \quad \text{(H-36)}$$

Again, from the system equation and cost function, the following facts are found:

$$\mathbf{L}_{zu}^x = \begin{bmatrix} \mathbf{F} \\ \hline 0 \end{bmatrix}$$

$$\mathbf{f}_{xu}^i = 0 \quad \text{for } i \in X$$

$$\mathbf{f}_{xu}^j = 0 \quad \text{for } j \in \Theta$$

$$\mathbf{f}_{\theta u}^i = \mathbf{b}_\theta^i \quad \text{for } i \in X$$

$$\mathbf{f}_{\theta u}^j = 0 \quad \text{for } j \in \Theta$$

where $\mathbf{b}_\theta^i$ denotes the gradient of the ith row of the coefficient matrix $\mathbf{B}_k(\boldsymbol{\theta}_k)$ with respect to $\boldsymbol{\theta}_k$.

Therefore Eq. (H-36) can be rewritten as

$$\mathbf{H}_{zu}^z = \begin{bmatrix} \mathbf{F} \\ \hline 0 \end{bmatrix} + \sum_{i \in X} e_i' \mathbf{p}^x \begin{bmatrix} 0 \\ \hline \mathbf{b}_\theta^{i\prime} \end{bmatrix} = \begin{bmatrix} \mathbf{F} \\ \hline \sum_{i \in X} e_i' \mathbf{p}^x (\mathbf{b}_\theta^i)' \end{bmatrix} \quad \text{(H-37)}$$

Now, using Eqs. (H-2) to (H-4), we can rewrite the recursion $\mathbf{K}$ for the augmented system as

$$\mathbf{K}_j = \mathcal{K}_{zz} - \mathcal{Q}_{zz}$$

$$\mathbf{K}_j = \mathbf{f}_z' \mathbf{K}_{j+1} \mathbf{f}_z + \mathbf{H}_{zz} - \mathcal{K}_{uz}' \mathcal{K}_{uu}^{-1} \mathcal{K}_{uz} \quad \text{(H-38)}$$

Then using Eqs. (H-38), (H-1), (H-8), (H-4), and (H-9), we can write the $\mathbf{K}$ recursion for the augmented system as

$$\mathbf{K}_j = \begin{bmatrix} \mathbf{K}^{xx} & (\mathbf{K}^{\theta x})' \\ \hline \mathbf{K}^{\theta x} & \mathbf{K}^{\theta\theta} \end{bmatrix}$$

$$= \begin{bmatrix} \mathbf{f}_x^x & \mathbf{f}_\theta^x \\ \hline \mathbf{f}_x^\theta & \mathbf{f}_\theta^\theta \end{bmatrix}' \begin{bmatrix} \mathbf{K}^{xx} & \mathbf{K}^{x\theta} \\ \hline \mathbf{K}^{\theta x} & \mathbf{K}^{\theta\theta} \end{bmatrix}_{j+1} \begin{bmatrix} \mathbf{f}_x^x & \mathbf{f}_\theta^x \\ \hline \mathbf{f}_x^\theta & \mathbf{f}_\theta^\theta \end{bmatrix} + \mathbf{H}_{zz}^z$$

$$- \left[\begin{bmatrix} \mathbf{f}_u^x \\ \hline \mathbf{f}_u^\theta \end{bmatrix}' \begin{bmatrix} \mathbf{K}^{xx} & \mathbf{K}^{x\theta} \\ \hline \mathbf{K}^{\theta x} & \mathbf{K}^{\theta\theta} \end{bmatrix}_{j+1} \begin{bmatrix} \mathbf{f}_x^x & \mathbf{f}_\theta^x \\ \hline \mathbf{f}_x^\theta & \mathbf{f}_\theta^\theta \end{bmatrix} + \mathbf{H}_{uz}^z \right]'$$

$$\left[\begin{bmatrix} f_u^x \\ \hline f_u^\theta \end{bmatrix}' \begin{bmatrix} K^{xx} & K^{x\theta} \\ \hline K^{\theta x} & K^{\theta\theta} \end{bmatrix}_{j+1} \begin{bmatrix} f_u^x \\ \hline f_u^\theta \end{bmatrix} + H_{uu}^z\right]^{-1}$$

$$\left[\begin{bmatrix} f_u^x \\ \hline f_u^\theta \end{bmatrix}' \begin{bmatrix} K^{xx} & K^{x\theta} \\ \hline K^{\theta x} & K^{\theta\theta} \end{bmatrix}_{j+1} \begin{bmatrix} f_x^x & f_\theta^x \\ \hline f_x^\theta & f_\theta^\theta \end{bmatrix} + H_{uz}^z\right] \quad \text{(H-39)}$$

Since, from (10-20), $f^x = Ax + Bu + c$ and $f^\theta = D\theta$,

$$f_x^x = A \quad f_u^x = B \quad f_\theta^\theta = D \quad f_x^\theta = f_u^\theta = 0 \quad \text{(H-40)}$$

Substituting Eqs. (H-32), (H-34), (H-37), and (H-40) into (H-39) yields

$$\begin{bmatrix} K^{xx} & (K^{\theta x})' \\ \hline K^{\theta x} & K^{\theta\theta} \end{bmatrix} = \begin{bmatrix} A & f_\theta^x \\ \hline 0 & D \end{bmatrix}' \begin{bmatrix} K^{xx} & K^{x\theta} \\ \hline K^{\theta x} & K^{\theta\theta} \end{bmatrix}_{j+1} \begin{bmatrix} A & f_\theta^x \\ \hline 0 & D \end{bmatrix}$$

$$+ \begin{bmatrix} W & 0 \\ \hline 0 & 0 \end{bmatrix} + \sum_{i \in X} e_i' p^x \begin{bmatrix} 0 & a_\theta^i \\ \hline (a_\theta^i)' & 0 \end{bmatrix}$$

$$- \left[\begin{bmatrix} B \\ \hline 0 \end{bmatrix}' \begin{bmatrix} K^{xx} & K^{x\theta} \\ \hline K^{\theta x} & K^{\theta\theta} \end{bmatrix} \begin{bmatrix} A & f_\theta^x \\ \hline 0 & D \end{bmatrix} + \begin{bmatrix} F' & \sum_{i \in X} e_i' p^x b_\theta^i \end{bmatrix}\right]'$$

$$\left[\begin{bmatrix} B \\ \hline 0 \end{bmatrix}' \begin{bmatrix} K^{xx} & K^{x\theta} \\ \hline K^{\theta x} & K^{\theta\theta} \end{bmatrix} \begin{bmatrix} B \\ \hline 0 \end{bmatrix} + \Lambda\right]^{-1}$$

$$\left[\begin{bmatrix} B \\ \hline 0 \end{bmatrix}' \begin{bmatrix} K^{xx} & K^{x\theta} \\ \hline K^{\theta x} & K^{\theta\theta} \end{bmatrix} \begin{bmatrix} A & f_\theta^x \\ \hline 0 & D \end{bmatrix} + \begin{bmatrix} F' & \sum_i e_i (p^x)' b_\theta^i \end{bmatrix}\right] \quad \text{(H-41)}$$

Consider the first term only:

$$\begin{bmatrix} A & f_\theta^x \\ \hline 0 & D \end{bmatrix}' \begin{bmatrix} K^{xx} & K^{x\theta} \\ \hline K^{\theta x} & K^{\theta\theta} \end{bmatrix}_{j+1} \begin{bmatrix} A & f_\theta^x \\ \hline 0 & D \end{bmatrix} = \begin{bmatrix} A' & 0 \\ \hline (f_\theta^x)' & D' \end{bmatrix} \begin{bmatrix} K^{xx}A & K^{xx}f_\theta^x + K^{x\theta}D \\ \hline K^{\theta x}A & K^{\theta x}f_\theta^x + K^{\theta\theta}D \end{bmatrix}$$

(H-42)

$$= \begin{bmatrix} A'K^{xx}A & A'(K^{xx}f_\theta^x + K^{x\theta}D) \\ \hline ((f_\theta^x)'K^{xx} + D'K^{\theta x})A & (f_\theta^x)'(K^{xx}f_\theta^x + K^{x\theta}D) + D'(K^{\theta x}f_\theta^x + K^{\theta\theta}D) \end{bmatrix}$$

(H-43)

Consider the term in the first brace after the minus sign:

$$\left[\begin{bmatrix} B \\ 0 \end{bmatrix}' \begin{bmatrix} K^{xx} & K^{x\theta} \\ \hline K^{\theta x} & K^{\theta\theta} \end{bmatrix} \begin{bmatrix} A & f_\theta^x \\ \hline 0 & D \end{bmatrix} + \begin{bmatrix} F' & \sum e_i' p^x b_\theta^j \end{bmatrix}\right]'$$

$$= \left[[B' \; 0] \begin{bmatrix} K^{xx}A & K^{xx}f_\theta^x + K^{x\theta}D \\ \hline K^{\theta x}A & K^{\theta x}f_\theta^x + K^{\theta\theta}D \end{bmatrix} + \begin{bmatrix} F' & \sum e_i' p^x b_\theta^j \end{bmatrix} \right]'$$

$$= \left[B'K^{xx}A + F' \;\middle|\; B'(K^{xx}f_\theta^x + K^{x\theta}D) + \sum e_i' p^x b_\theta^j \right]' \quad \text{(H-44)}$$

Next consider the inverse term:

$$\left[\begin{bmatrix} B \\ 0 \end{bmatrix}' \begin{bmatrix} K^{xx} & K^{x\theta} \\ \hline K^{\theta x} & K^{\theta\theta} \end{bmatrix} \begin{bmatrix} B \\ 0 \end{bmatrix} + \Lambda \right]^{-1} = \left[[B' \; 0] \begin{bmatrix} K^{xx}B \\ \hline K^{\theta x}B \end{bmatrix} + \Lambda \right]^{-1}$$

$$= [B'K^{xx}B + \Lambda]^{-1} \quad \text{(H-45)}$$

By using Eqs. (H-44) and (H-45) all terms after the minus sign in Eq. (H-41) can be rewritten as

$$[\;] = \left[B'K^{xx}A + F' \;\middle|\; B'(K^{xx}f_\theta^x + K^{x\theta}D) + \sum (e^i)' p^x b_\theta^j \right]' \mu \left[B'K^{xx}A + F' \right.$$
$$\left. \times B'(K^{xx}f_\theta^x + K^{x\theta}D) + \sum e_i' p^x b_\theta^j \right]$$

$$= \begin{bmatrix} A'K^{xx}B + F \\ ((f_\theta^x)'K^{xx} + D'K^{\theta x})B + (\sum e_i' p^x b_\theta^j)' \end{bmatrix}$$

$$\mu \left[B'K^{xx}A + F' \;\middle|\; B'(K^{xx}f_\theta^x + K^{x\theta}D) + \sum e_i' p^x b_\theta^j \right] \quad \text{(H-46)}$$

$$= \begin{bmatrix} \mathbb{A} & \mathbb{B} \\ \hline \mathbb{C} & \mathbb{D} \end{bmatrix} \quad \text{(H-47)}$$

where $\mathbb{A} = (A'K^{xx}B + F)\mu(B'K^{xx}A + F')$

$\mathbb{B} = (A'K^{xx}B + F)\mu\{B'(K^{xx}f_\theta^x + K^{x\theta}D) + \sum e_i' p^x b_\theta^j\}$

$\mathbb{C} = \{((f_\theta^x)'K^{xx} + D'K^{\theta x})B + (\sum e_i' p^x b_\theta^j)'\}\mu\{B'K^{xx}A + F'\}$

and

$\mathbb{D} = \{((f_\theta^x)'K^{xx} + D'K^{\theta x})B + (\sum e_i' p^x b_\theta^j)'\}\mu\{B'(K^{xx}f_\theta^x + K^{x\theta}D) + \sum e_i' p^x b_\theta^j\}$

and where $\mu = [\Lambda + B'K^{xx}B]^{-1}$.

Next, combine the second and third terms on the right-hand side of Eq. H-41 to obtain

$$\begin{bmatrix} W & 0 \\ \hline 0 & 0 \end{bmatrix} + \sum e_i' p^x \begin{bmatrix} 0 & a_\theta^i \\ \hline (a_\theta^i)' & 0 \end{bmatrix} = \begin{bmatrix} W & \sum e_i' p^x a_\theta^i \\ \hline \sum e_i' p^x (a_\theta^i)' & 0 \end{bmatrix} \quad \text{(H-48)}$$

Now Eq. (H-41) can be rewritten as a sum of partitioned matrices (H-43), (H-47), and (H-48). Without actually writing out this total expression, consider each of the component matrices of $\mathbf{K}_j$ in Eq. (H-41) one at a time. First consider $\mathbf{K}^{xx}$, which is

$$\mathbf{K}_j^{xx} = \mathbf{A}'\mathbf{K}_{j+1}^{xx}\mathbf{A} - [\mathbf{A}'\mathbf{K}^{xx}\mathbf{B} + \mathbf{F}]\mu[\mathbf{B}'\mathbf{K}^{xx}\mathbf{A} + \mathbf{F}'] + \mathbf{W}_j \quad (\text{H-49})$$

This is exactly the same as the certainty-equivalence Riccati matrix in Eq. (10-33). This proves Eq. (10-39). Then, consider $\mathbf{K}_j^{\theta x}$, which is

$$\mathbf{K}_j^{\theta x} = \left[(\mathbf{f}_\theta^x)'\mathbf{K}_{j+1}^{xx} + \mathbf{D}'\mathbf{K}_{j+1}^{\theta x}\right]\mathbf{A} - \left[((\mathbf{f}_\theta^x)'\mathbf{K}_{j+1}^{xx} + \mathbf{D}'\mathbf{K}_{j+1}^{\theta x})\mathbf{B} + \left(\sum e_i'\mathbf{p}^x(\mathbf{b}_\theta^i)'\right)\right]$$
$$\mu[\mathbf{B}'\mathbf{K}_{j+1}^{xx}\mathbf{A} + \mathbf{F}'] + \sum e_i'\mathbf{p}^x(\mathbf{a}_\theta^i)' \quad \text{with } \mathbf{K}_N^{\theta x} = \mathbf{0} \quad (\text{H-50})$$

This is the same as Eq. (10-40). Finally, consider $\mathbf{K}_j^{\theta\theta}$, which is

$$\mathbf{K}_j^{\theta\theta} = (\mathbf{f}_\theta^x)'(\mathbf{K}_{j+1}^{xx}\mathbf{f}_\theta^x + \mathbf{K}_{j+1}^{x\theta}\mathbf{D}) + \mathbf{D}'(\mathbf{K}_{j+1}^{\theta x}\mathbf{f}_\theta^x + \mathbf{K}_{j+1}^{\theta\theta}\mathbf{D})$$
$$- \left[\left[(\mathbf{f}_\theta^x)'\mathbf{K}_{j+1}^{xx} + \mathbf{D}'\mathbf{K}_{j+1}^{\theta x}\right]\mathbf{B} + \left[\sum e_i'\mathbf{p}^x\mathbf{b}_\theta^i\right]'\right]\mu\left[\mathbf{B}'\left[\mathbf{K}_{j+1}^{xx}\mathbf{f}_\theta^x + \mathbf{K}_{j+1}^{x\theta}\mathbf{D}\right]\right.$$
$$\left. + \sum e_i'\mathbf{p}^x\mathbf{b}_\theta^i\right] \quad \text{with } \mathbf{K}_N^{\theta\theta} = \mathbf{0} \quad (\text{H-51})$$

This is the same as Eq. (10-42). Thus, the Riccati matrix $\mathbf{K}_j$ is fully specified by Eqs. (H-49) to (H-51).

APPENDIX I

VECTOR RECURSIONS FOR THE AUGMENTED SYSTEM

Recall from Eq. (9-44) that

$$p_j = H_x - \mathcal{H}'_{ux}\mathcal{H}_{uu}^{-1}H_u$$

$$= H_x - [H_{ux} + f'_u K_{j+1} f_x]'[H_{uu} + f'_u K_{j+1} f_u]^{-1} H_u \quad \text{from Eq. (9-31)}$$

Writing this for the augmented system and using Eq. (9-31) again provides

$$p_j = \begin{bmatrix} p^x \\ p^\theta \end{bmatrix}_j = H_z^z - \mathcal{H}'_{uz}\mathcal{H}_{uu}^{-1}H_u$$

$$= H_z^z - \left[H_{uz}^z + [(f_u^x)' \vdots (f_u^\theta)'] \begin{bmatrix} K^{xx} & K^{x\theta} \\ K^{\theta x} & K^{\theta\theta} \end{bmatrix}_{j+1} \begin{bmatrix} f_x^x & f_\theta^x \\ f_x^\theta & f^\theta \end{bmatrix} \right],$$

$$\times \left[H_{uu}^z + [(f_u^x)' \vdots (f_u^\theta)'] \begin{bmatrix} K^{xx} & K^{x\theta} \\ K^{\theta x} & K^{\theta\theta} \end{bmatrix}_{j+1} \begin{bmatrix} f_u^x \\ f_u^\theta \end{bmatrix} \right]^{-1} H_u^z \quad \text{(I-1)}$$

but in this case

$$f_u^x = B \quad f_u^\theta = 0 \quad f_x^x = A \quad f_\theta^x = D \quad \text{and} \quad f_x^\theta = 0 \quad \text{(I-2)}$$

VECTOR RECURSIONS FOR THE AUGMENTED SYSTEM

Also,

$$\mathbf{H}_{uu}^z = \Lambda \qquad \text{from Eq. (H-34)}$$

$$\mathbf{H}_{uz}^z = (\mathbf{H}_{zu}^z)' = \left[\mathbf{F}' \; \vdots \; \sum_{i \in X} \mathbf{e}'_i \mathbf{p}^x \mathbf{b}^j_\theta \right] \qquad \text{from Eq. (H-37)}$$

$$\mathbf{H}_u^z = \mathbf{F}'_k(\mathbf{x}_k - \tilde{\mathbf{x}}_k) + \Lambda \mathbf{u} - \Lambda \tilde{\mathbf{u}} + \mathbf{B}' \mathbf{p}^x \qquad \text{from Eq. (H-18)}$$

$$\mathbf{H}_z^z = \begin{bmatrix} \mathbf{L}_x^x + \mathbf{A}' \mathbf{p}^x \\ (\mathbf{f}_\theta^x)' \mathbf{p}^x + (\mathbf{f}_\theta^\theta)' \mathbf{p}^\theta \end{bmatrix} \qquad \text{from Eq. (H-16)}$$

(I-3)

With the above, Eq. (I-1) becomes

$$\begin{bmatrix} \mathbf{p}^x \\ \mathbf{p}^\theta \end{bmatrix}_j = \begin{bmatrix} \mathbf{L}_x^x + \mathbf{A}' \mathbf{p}^x \\ (\mathbf{f}_\theta^x)' \mathbf{p}^x + (\mathbf{f}_\theta^\theta)' \mathbf{p}^\theta \end{bmatrix}$$

$$- \left[\left[\mathbf{F}' \; \vdots \; \sum \mathbf{e}'_i \mathbf{p}^x \mathbf{b}^j_\theta \right] + [\mathbf{B}' \; \vdots \; 0] \begin{bmatrix} \mathbf{K}^{xx} & \mathbf{K}^{x\theta} \\ \mathbf{K}^{\theta x} & \mathbf{K}^{\theta\theta} \end{bmatrix}_{j+1} \begin{bmatrix} \mathbf{A} & \mathbf{f}_\theta^x \\ 0 & \mathbf{D} \end{bmatrix} \right]'$$

$$\times \left[\Lambda + [\mathbf{B}' \; \vdots \; 0] \begin{bmatrix} \mathbf{K}^{xx} & \mathbf{K}^{x\theta} \\ \mathbf{K}^{\theta x} & \mathbf{K}^{\theta\theta} \end{bmatrix}_{j+1} \begin{bmatrix} \mathbf{B} \\ \overline{0} \end{bmatrix} \right]^{-1} \left[\mathbf{F}'_k[\mathbf{x}_k - \tilde{\mathbf{x}}_k] + \Lambda \mathbf{u} - \Lambda \tilde{\mathbf{u}} + \mathbf{B}' \mathbf{p}^x \right]$$

$$= \begin{bmatrix} \mathbf{L}_x^x + \mathbf{A}' \mathbf{p}^x \\ (\mathbf{f}_\theta^x)' \mathbf{p}^x + (\mathbf{f}_\theta^\theta)' \mathbf{p}^\theta \end{bmatrix} - \left[\left[\mathbf{F}' \; \vdots \; \sum \mathbf{e}'_i \mathbf{p}^x \mathbf{b}^j_\theta \right] \right.$$

$$\left. + [\mathbf{B}' \; \vdots \; 0] \begin{bmatrix} \mathbf{K}^{xx} \mathbf{A} & \mathbf{K}^{xx} \mathbf{f}_\theta^x + \mathbf{K}^{x\theta} \mathbf{D} \\ \mathbf{K}^{\theta x} \mathbf{A} & \mathbf{K}^{\theta x} \mathbf{f}_\theta^x + \mathbf{K}^{\theta\theta} \mathbf{D} \end{bmatrix} \right]'$$

$$\times \left[\Lambda + [\mathbf{B}' \; \vdots \; 0] \begin{bmatrix} \mathbf{K}^{xx} \mathbf{B} \\ \mathbf{K}^{\theta x} \mathbf{B} \end{bmatrix} \right]^{-1} \left[\mathbf{F}'[\mathbf{x} - \tilde{\mathbf{x}}] + \Lambda \mathbf{u} - \Lambda \tilde{\mathbf{u}} + \mathbf{B}' \mathbf{p}^x \right]$$

$$= \begin{bmatrix} \mathbf{L}_x^x + \mathbf{A}' \mathbf{p}^x \\ (\mathbf{f}_\theta^x)' \mathbf{p}^x + (\mathbf{f}_\theta^\theta)' \mathbf{p}^\theta \end{bmatrix} - \left[\mathbf{B}' \mathbf{K}^{xx} \mathbf{A} + \mathbf{F}' \; \vdots \; \sum \mathbf{e}'_i \mathbf{p}^x \mathbf{b}^j_\theta + \mathbf{B}' [\mathbf{K}^{xx} \mathbf{f}_\theta^x + \mathbf{K}^{x\theta} \mathbf{D}] \right]'$$

$$\times \mu \left[\mathbf{F}'(\mathbf{x} - \tilde{\mathbf{x}}) + \Lambda \mathbf{u} - \Lambda \tilde{\mathbf{u}} + \mathbf{B}' \mathbf{p}^x \right]$$

$$= \begin{bmatrix} \mathbf{L}_x^x + \mathbf{A}' \mathbf{p}^x \\ (\mathbf{f}_\theta^x)' \mathbf{p}^x + (\mathbf{f}_\theta^\theta)' \mathbf{p}^\theta \end{bmatrix}$$

$$- \begin{bmatrix} [\mathbf{A}' \mathbf{K}^{xx} \mathbf{B} + \mathbf{F}] \mu [\mathbf{F}'[\mathbf{x} - \tilde{\mathbf{x}}] + \Lambda \mathbf{u} - \Lambda \tilde{\mathbf{u}} + \mathbf{B}' \mathbf{p}^x] \\ \left[[(\mathbf{f}_\theta^x)' \mathbf{K}^{xx} + \mathbf{D}' \mathbf{K}^{\theta x}] \mathbf{B} + \left[\sum \mathbf{e}'_i \mathbf{p}^x \mathbf{b}^j_\theta \right]' \right] \mu [\mathbf{F}'[\mathbf{x} - \tilde{\mathbf{x}}] + \Lambda \mathbf{u} - \Lambda \tilde{\mathbf{u}} + \mathbf{B}' \mathbf{p}^x] \end{bmatrix}$$

(I-4)

where $\mu = [\Lambda + \mathbf{B} \mathbf{K}^{xx} \mathbf{B}]^{-1}$. Therefore

$$\mathbf{p}_j^x = \mathbf{L}_x^x + \mathbf{A}' \mathbf{p}_{j+1}^x - [\mathbf{A}' \mathbf{K}^{xx} \mathbf{B} + \mathbf{F}] \mu [\mathbf{F}'[\mathbf{x} - \tilde{\mathbf{x}}] + \Lambda [\mathbf{u} - \tilde{\mathbf{u}}] + \mathbf{B}' \mathbf{p}_{j+1}^x] \quad \text{(I-5)}$$

since
$$L_j^x = \tfrac{1}{2}[x_j - \tilde{x}_j]'W_j[x_j - \tilde{x}_j] + [x_j - \tilde{x}_j]'F_j[u_j - \tilde{u}_j] + \tfrac{1}{2}[u_j - \tilde{u}_j]'\Lambda_j[u_j - \tilde{u}_j] \quad \text{(I-6)}$$

we have
$$L_{jx}^x = L_x^x = W_j[x_j - \tilde{x}_j] + F_j[u_j - \tilde{u}_j]$$

Substitution of Eq. (I-6) into Eq. (I-5) yields
$$p_j^x = W_j[x_j - \tilde{x}_j] + F_j[u_j - \tilde{u}_j] + A'p_{j+1}^x$$
$$- [A'K_{j+1}^{xx}B + F_j]\mu_j[F_j'[x_j - \tilde{x}_j] + \Lambda_j[u_j - \tilde{u}_j] + B'p_{j+1}^x] \quad \text{(I-7)}$$

Now it is necessary to show that
$$p_j^x = \tilde{K}_j x_j + \tilde{p}_j \qquad \text{where } \tilde{K}_j = K_j^{xx} \quad \text{(I-8)}$$

and $\tilde{K}_j$ and $\tilde{p}_j$ are obtained from the certainty-equivalence (CE) solution in Appendix G.

It can be shown by induction that Eq. (I-7) and Eq. (I-8) are equivalent. First consider the last period, N. Then, from Eq. (I-7),
$$p_N^x = W_N[x_N - \tilde{x}_N] + F_N[u_N - \tilde{u}_N] + A'p_{N+1}^x$$
$$- [A'\tilde{K}_{N+1}B + F_N]\mu_N[F_N'[x_N - \tilde{x}_N] + \Lambda_N[u_N - \tilde{u}_N] + B'p_{N+1}^x]$$

but $F_N = \Lambda_N = p_{N+1}^x = 0$ from the CE solution. Therefore, the equation above becomes
$$p_N^x = W_N[x_N - \tilde{x}_N] \quad \text{(I-9)}$$

Also recall from the CE solution [Eqs. (10-33) and (10-34)] that $\tilde{K}_N = W_N$ and $\tilde{p}_N = -W_N\tilde{x}_N$. Therefore Eq. (I-9) can be written as
$$p_N^x = \tilde{K}_N x_N + \tilde{p}_N \quad \text{(I-10)}$$

Next consider the period $N - 1$. For this period Eq. (I-7) can be written as
$$p_{N-1}^x = W_{N-1}[x_{N-1} - \tilde{x}_{N-1}] + F_{N-1}[u_{N-1} - \tilde{u}_{N-1}] + A'p_N^x$$
$$- [A'\tilde{K}_N B + F_{N-1}]\mu_{N-1}[F_{N-1}'[x_{N-1} - \tilde{x}_{N-1}]$$
$$+ \Lambda_{N-1}[u_{N-1} - \tilde{u}_{N-1}] + B'p_N^x] \quad \text{(I-11)}$$

Let
$$\psi = \psi_{N-1} = A'\tilde{K}_N B + F_{N-1} = A'W_N B + F_{N-1}$$
$$\delta x = \delta x_{N-1} = x_{N-1} - \tilde{x}_{N-1} \quad \text{(I-12)}$$
$$\delta u = \delta u_{N-1} = u_{N-1} - \tilde{u}_{N-1}$$

Then Eq. (I-11) can be written as
$$p_{N-1}^x = W_{N-1}\delta x_{N-1} + F\delta u_{N-1} + A'p_N^x$$
$$- \psi_{N-1}\mu[F'\delta x_{N-1} + \Lambda \delta u_{N-1} + B'p_N^x]$$

$$
\begin{aligned}
&= \mathbf{W}_{N-1}\delta\mathbf{x}_{N-1} + \mathbf{F}\,\delta\mathbf{u}_{N-1} + \mathbf{A}'\mathbf{p}_N^x \\
&\quad - \psi\mu\mathbf{F}'\,\delta\mathbf{x}_{N-1} - \psi\mu\Lambda\,\delta\mathbf{u}_{N-1} - \psi\mu\mathbf{B}'\mathbf{p}_N^x \\
&= [\mathbf{W}_{N-1} - \psi\mu\mathbf{F}']\,\delta\mathbf{x}_{N-1} + [\mathbf{F} - \psi\mu\Lambda]\,\delta\mathbf{u}_{N-1} + [\mathbf{A} - \psi\mu\mathbf{B}']\mathbf{p}_N^x
\end{aligned}
\qquad (\text{I-13})
$$

From Eqs. (I-9) and (I-12)
$$
\mathbf{p}_N^x = \mathbf{W}_N[\mathbf{x}_N - \tilde{\mathbf{x}}_N] = \mathbf{W}_N\,\delta\mathbf{x}_N \qquad (\text{I-14})
$$
and from the system equations
$$
\delta\mathbf{x}_N = \mathbf{x}_N - \tilde{\mathbf{x}}_N = \mathbf{A}\mathbf{x}_{N-1} + \mathbf{B}\mathbf{u}_{N-1} + \mathbf{c} - \tilde{\mathbf{x}}_N \qquad (\text{I-15})
$$

For notational simplicity all variables without a time subscript are for period $N-1$. Using this convention and substituting Eqs. (I-14) and (I-15) into Eq. (I-13), we obtain

$$
\begin{aligned}
\mathbf{p}^x &= [\mathbf{W} - \psi\mu\mathbf{F}']\,\delta\mathbf{x} + [\mathbf{F} - \psi\mu\Lambda]\,\delta\mathbf{u} \\
&\quad + [\mathbf{A}' - \psi\mu\mathbf{B}'][\mathbf{W}_N\mathbf{A}\mathbf{x} + \mathbf{W}_N\mathbf{B}\mathbf{u} + \mathbf{W}_N\mathbf{c} - \mathbf{W}_N\tilde{\mathbf{x}}_N] \\
&= [\mathbf{W} - \psi\mu\mathbf{F}']\mathbf{x} - [\mathbf{W} - \psi\mu\mathbf{F}']\tilde{\mathbf{x}} + [\mathbf{F} - \psi\mu\Lambda]\mathbf{u} - [\mathbf{F} - \psi\mu\Lambda]\tilde{\mathbf{u}} \\
&\quad + \mathbf{A}'\mathbf{W}_N\mathbf{A}\mathbf{x} + \mathbf{A}'\mathbf{W}_N\mathbf{B}\mathbf{u} + \mathbf{A}'\mathbf{W}_N\mathbf{c} - \mathbf{A}'\mathbf{W}_N\tilde{\mathbf{x}}_N \\
&\quad - \psi\mu\mathbf{B}'\mathbf{W}_N\mathbf{A}\mathbf{x} - \psi\mu\mathbf{B}'\mathbf{W}_N\mathbf{B}\mathbf{u} - \psi\mu\mathbf{B}'\mathbf{W}_N\mathbf{c} + \psi\mu\mathbf{B}'\mathbf{W}_N\tilde{\mathbf{x}}_N
\end{aligned}
\qquad (\text{I-16})
$$

Collecting terms in $\mathbf{x}$, $\mathbf{u}$, and $\tilde{\mathbf{x}}$ yields
$$
\begin{aligned}
\mathbf{p}^x &= [\mathbf{W} - \psi\mu\mathbf{F}' + \mathbf{A}'\mathbf{W}_N\mathbf{A} - \psi\mu\mathbf{B}'\mathbf{W}_N\mathbf{A}]\mathbf{x} + \\
&\quad [\mathbf{F} - \psi\mu\Lambda + \mathbf{A}'\mathbf{W}_N\mathbf{B} - \psi\mu\mathbf{B}'\mathbf{W}_N\mathbf{B}]\mathbf{u} - [\mathbf{W} - \psi\mu\mathbf{F}']\tilde{\mathbf{x}} - [\mathbf{F} - \psi\mu\Lambda]\tilde{\mathbf{u}} \\
&\quad + [\psi\mu\mathbf{B}' - \mathbf{A}']\mathbf{W}_N\tilde{\mathbf{x}}_N + [\mathbf{A}' - \psi\mu\mathbf{B}']\mathbf{W}_N\mathbf{c}
\end{aligned}
\qquad (\text{I-17})
$$

Consider only the second term on the right-hand side of Eq. (I-17):
$$
\begin{aligned}
[\mathbf{F} - \psi\mu\Lambda + \mathbf{A}'\mathbf{W}_N\mathbf{B} - \psi\mu\mathbf{B}'\mathbf{W}_N\mathbf{B}]\mathbf{u} &= [\mathbf{F} + \mathbf{A}'\mathbf{W}_N\mathbf{B} - \psi\mu[\Lambda + \mathbf{B}'\mathbf{K}_N\mathbf{B}]]\mathbf{u} \\
&= [\psi - \psi\mu\mu^{-1}]\mathbf{u} = 0
\end{aligned}
\qquad (\text{I-18})
$$

Therefore Eq. (I-17) reduces to
$$
\begin{aligned}
\mathbf{p}^x &= [\mathbf{W} + \mathbf{A}'\mathbf{W}_N\mathbf{A} - \psi\mu\psi']\mathbf{x} - [\mathbf{W} - \psi\mu\mathbf{F}]\tilde{\mathbf{x}} - [\mathbf{F} - \psi\mu\Lambda]\tilde{\mathbf{u}} \\
&\quad + [\mathbf{A}' - \psi\mu\mathbf{B}']\mathbf{W}_N[\mathbf{c} - \tilde{\mathbf{x}}_N]
\end{aligned}
\qquad (\text{I-19})
$$

or
$$
\begin{aligned}
\mathbf{p}^x &= [\mathbf{A}'\mathbf{K}_N\mathbf{A} - \psi\mu\psi' + \mathbf{W}]\mathbf{x} + \psi\mu[\mathbf{F}\tilde{\mathbf{x}} + \Lambda\tilde{\mathbf{u}} - \mathbf{B}'\mathbf{W}_N[\mathbf{c} - \tilde{\mathbf{x}}_N]] \\
&\quad - \mathbf{W}\tilde{\mathbf{x}} - \mathbf{F}\tilde{\mathbf{u}} + \mathbf{A}\mathbf{W}_N[\mathbf{c} - \tilde{\mathbf{x}}_N]
\end{aligned}
\qquad (\text{I-20})
$$

or
$$
\begin{aligned}
\mathbf{p}^x &= [\mathbf{A}'\mathbf{K}_N\mathbf{A} - \psi\mu\psi' + \mathbf{W}]\mathbf{x} - \psi\mu[\mathbf{B}[\tilde{\mathbf{K}}_N\mathbf{c} + \tilde{\mathbf{p}}_N] - [\mathbf{F}\tilde{\mathbf{x}} + \Lambda\tilde{\mathbf{u}}]] \\
&\quad + \mathbf{A}[\tilde{\mathbf{K}}_N\mathbf{c} + \tilde{\mathbf{p}}_N] - [\mathbf{W}\tilde{\mathbf{x}} + \mathbf{F}\tilde{\mathbf{u}}]
\end{aligned}
\qquad (\text{I-21})
$$

Using Eqs. (10-33) and (I-12), we obtain

$$\tilde{\mathbf{K}}_{N-1} = \mathbf{A}'\tilde{\mathbf{K}}_N \mathbf{A} - \boldsymbol{\psi}_{N-1} \boldsymbol{\mu}_{N-1} \boldsymbol{\psi}'_{N-1} + \mathbf{W}_{N-1} \qquad \text{(I-22)}$$

and using Eqs. (10-34) and (I-12) provides

$$\tilde{\mathbf{p}}_{N-1} = -\boldsymbol{\psi}_{N-1} \boldsymbol{\mu}_{N-1} \big[\mathbf{B} [\tilde{\mathbf{K}}_N \mathbf{c} + \tilde{\mathbf{p}}_N] - [\mathbf{F}_{N-1} \tilde{\mathbf{x}}_{N-1} + \boldsymbol{\Lambda}_{N-1} \tilde{\mathbf{u}}_{N-1}] \big]$$
$$+ \mathbf{A}' [\tilde{\mathbf{K}}_N \mathbf{c} + \tilde{\mathbf{p}}_N] - [\mathbf{W}_{N-1} \tilde{\mathbf{x}}_{N-1} + \mathbf{F}_{N-1} \tilde{\mathbf{u}}_{N-1}] \qquad \text{(I-23)}$$

Then using Eqs. (I-22) and (I-23), we can write Eq. (I-21)

$$\mathbf{p}^x_{N-1} = \tilde{\mathbf{K}}_{N-1} \mathbf{x}_{N-1} + \tilde{\mathbf{p}}_{N-1} \qquad \text{(I-24)}$$

which establishes the second step of the induction. In the same manner it can be shown that for any period j, Eqs. (I-7) and (I-8) are equivalent. This proves the **p** recursion (10-43).

APPENDIX J

PROOF THAT A CONSTANT TERM IN THE COST-TO-GO IS ZERO

This appendix proves that γ_{k+1}^z in the approximate optimal cost-to-go [Eq. (10-24)] is zero. γ_k has been defined to be

$$\gamma_k = \gamma_{k+1} - \tfrac{1}{2}\mathbf{H}'_{\mathbf{u},k}\mathcal{H}_{\mathbf{uu},k}^{-1}\mathbf{H}_{\mathbf{u},k} \qquad \gamma_N = 0 \tag{J-1}$$

[See Eq. (9-60).] Similarly, γ_k^z is defined for the augmented system as

$$\gamma_k^z = \gamma_{k+1}^z - \tfrac{1}{2}[\mathbf{H}_{\mathbf{u},k}^z]'[\mathcal{H}_{\mathbf{uu},k}^z]^{-1}[\mathbf{H}_{\mathbf{u},k}^z] \qquad \text{with } \gamma_N^z = 0 \tag{J-2}$$

From Eq. (H-18)

$$(\mathbf{H}_{\mathbf{u},k}^z)' = [\mathbf{x}_k - \tilde{\mathbf{x}}_k]'\mathbf{F}_k + [\mathbf{u}_{ok} - \tilde{\mathbf{u}}_k]'\Lambda'_k + (\mathbf{p}_{k+1}^{\mathbf{x}})'\mathbf{B}_k \tag{J-3}$$

where $\mathbf{u}_{ok}$ is the nominal control obtained from the CE problem. From Eqs. (H-4), (H-34), (H-40), and (10-32)

$$[\mathcal{H}_{\mathbf{uu},k}^z]^{-1} = [\Lambda'_k + \mathbf{B}'\mathbf{K}_{k+1}^{\mathbf{xx}}\mathbf{B}]^{-1} = \mu_k \tag{J-4}$$

Hence Eq. (J-2) becomes

$$\gamma_k^z = \gamma_{k+1}^z - \tfrac{1}{2}([[\mathbf{x}_k - \tilde{\mathbf{x}}_k]'\mathbf{F}_k + [\mathbf{u}_{ok} - \tilde{\mathbf{u}}_k]'\Lambda'_k + (\mathbf{p}_{k+1}^{\mathbf{x}})'\mathbf{B}_k]$$
$$\times \mu[\mathbf{F}'_k[\mathbf{x}_k - \tilde{\mathbf{x}}_k] + \Lambda_k[\mathbf{u}_{ok} - \tilde{\mathbf{u}}_k] + \mathbf{B}'_k\mathbf{p}_{k+1}^{\mathbf{x}}]) \tag{J-5}$$

Now, by using Eq. (10-43) we obtain $\mathbf{p}_{k+1}^{x'}$ as
$$(\mathbf{p}_{k+1}^x)' = \mathbf{x}_{k+1}'\tilde{\mathbf{K}}_{k+1}' + \tilde{\mathbf{p}}_{k+1}' \tag{J-6}$$
Substituting the unaugmented system equation (10-7) into Eq. (J-6) gives
$$\begin{aligned}(\mathbf{p}_{k+1}^x)' &= [\mathbf{A}_k\mathbf{x}_{ok} + \mathbf{B}_k\mathbf{u}_{ok} + \mathbf{c}_k]'\tilde{\mathbf{K}}_{k+1}' + \tilde{\mathbf{p}}_{k+1}' \\ &= \mathbf{x}_{ok}'\mathbf{A}_k'\tilde{\mathbf{K}}_{k+1}' + \mathbf{u}_{ok}'\mathbf{B}_k'\tilde{\mathbf{K}}_{k+1}' + \mathbf{c}_k'\tilde{\mathbf{K}}_{k+1}' + \tilde{\mathbf{p}}_{k+1}'\end{aligned} \tag{J-7}$$
Now consider only the term
$$\begin{aligned}[\mathbf{x}_{ok} &- \tilde{\mathbf{x}}_k]'\mathbf{F}_k + [\mathbf{u}_{ok} - \tilde{\mathbf{u}}_k]'\Lambda_k' + (\mathbf{p}_{k+1}^x)'\mathbf{B}_k \\ &= [\mathbf{x}_{ok} - \tilde{\mathbf{x}}_k]'\mathbf{F}_k + [\mathbf{u}_{ok} - \tilde{\mathbf{u}}_k]'\Lambda_k + \mathbf{x}_{ok}'\mathbf{A}_k'\tilde{\mathbf{K}}_{k+1}'\mathbf{B}_k \\ &\quad + \mathbf{u}_{ok}'\mathbf{B}_k'\tilde{\mathbf{K}}_{k+1}'\mathbf{B}_k + \mathbf{c}_k'\tilde{\mathbf{K}}_{k+1}'\mathbf{B}_k + \tilde{\mathbf{p}}_{k+1}'\mathbf{B}_k \\ &= \mathbf{u}_{ok}'[\Lambda_k' + \mathbf{B}_k'\tilde{\mathbf{K}}_{k+1}'\mathbf{B}_k] + \mathbf{x}_{ok}'[\mathbf{F}_k + \mathbf{A}_k'\tilde{\mathbf{K}}_{k+1}'\mathbf{B}_k] \\ &\quad + \tilde{\mathbf{p}}_{k+1}'\mathbf{B}_k - \tilde{\mathbf{x}}_k'\mathbf{F}_k - \tilde{\mathbf{u}}_k'\Lambda_k' + \mathbf{c}_k'\mathbf{K}_{k+1}'\mathbf{B}_k\end{aligned} \tag{J-8}$$
Also let
$$\Psi_k = [\mathbf{F}_k + \mathbf{A}_k'\tilde{\mathbf{K}}_{k+1}'\mathbf{B}_k] \tag{J-9}$$
By using Eqs. (J-4) and (J-9) in Eq. (J-8) we get
$$\begin{aligned}[\mathbf{x}_{ok} &- \tilde{\mathbf{x}}_k]'\mathbf{F}_k + [\mathbf{u}_{ok} - \tilde{\mathbf{u}}_k]'\Lambda_k' + \mathbf{p}_{k+1}^{x'}\mathbf{B}_k \\ &= \mathbf{u}_{ok}'\mu_k^{-1} + \mathbf{x}_{ok}'\Psi_k + \tilde{\mathbf{p}}_{k+1}'\mathbf{B}_k - \tilde{\mathbf{x}}_k'\mathbf{F}_k - \tilde{\mathbf{u}}_k'\Lambda_k' + \mathbf{c}_k'\tilde{\mathbf{K}}_{k+1}\mathbf{B}_k\end{aligned} \tag{J-10}$$
The nominal control $\mathbf{u}_{ok}$ from Eq. (10-30) is
$$\mathbf{u}_{ok} = \mathbf{G}_k\mathbf{x}_{ok} + \mathbf{g}_k \tag{J-11}$$
where $\quad \mathbf{G}_k = -\mu_k\Psi_k'$

and $\quad \mathbf{g}_k = -\mu_k\bigl[\mathbf{B}'[\tilde{\mathbf{K}}_{k+1}\mathbf{c} + \tilde{\mathbf{p}}_{k+1}] - [\mathbf{F}_k'\tilde{\mathbf{x}}_k + \Lambda_k\tilde{\mathbf{u}}_k]\bigr]$

Substitution of Eq. (J-11) into Eq. (J-10) then yields
$$\begin{aligned}[\mathbf{x}_{ok} &- \tilde{\mathbf{x}}_k]'\mathbf{F}_k + [\mathbf{u}_{ok} - \tilde{\mathbf{u}}_k]'\Lambda_k' + (\mathbf{p}_{k+1}^x)'\mathbf{B}_k \\ &= -\bigl[[\mathbf{B}'[\tilde{\mathbf{K}}_{k+1}\mathbf{c} + \tilde{\mathbf{p}}_{k+1}] - [\mathbf{F}_k'\tilde{\mathbf{x}}_k + \Lambda_k\tilde{\mathbf{u}}_k]]'\mu_k' + \mathbf{x}_{ok}'\Psi\mu_k'\bigr]\mu_k^{-1} \\ &\quad + \mathbf{x}_{ok}'\Psi_k' + \tilde{\mathbf{p}}_{k+1}'\mathbf{B}_k - (\tilde{\mathbf{x}}_k'\mathbf{F}_k + \tilde{\mathbf{u}}_k'\Lambda_k') + \mathbf{c}'\tilde{\mathbf{K}}_{k+1}\mathbf{B}_k \\ &= 0\end{aligned} \tag{J-12}$$
Substituting Eq. (J-12) into Eq. (J-5) leads to
$$\gamma_k^z = \gamma_{k+1}^z \tag{J-13}$$
Since $\gamma_N^z = 0$, Eq. (J-13) implies
$$\gamma_{k+1}^z = 0 \tag{J-14}$$
which was sought for in Eq. (10-35).

… APPENDIX K

UPDATING THE AUGMENTED STATE COVARIANCE

Begin with Eqs. (9-84) and (9-85), that is,

$$\Sigma_{k+1|k+1} = [\mathbf{I} - \mathbf{V}_{k+1}\mathbf{h}_{z,k+1}]\Sigma_{k+1|k} \tag{K-1}$$

and

$$\mathbf{V}_{k+1} = \Sigma_{k+1|k}\mathbf{h}'_{z,k+1}\bigg[\mathbf{h}_{z,k+1}\Sigma_{k+1|k}\mathbf{h}'_{z,k+1} + \mathbf{R}_{k+1}$$

$$+ \tfrac{1}{2}\sum_i\sum_j \mathbf{e}^i(\mathbf{e}^j)' \,\mathrm{tr}\big[\mathbf{h}^i_{zz}\Sigma_{k+1|k}\mathbf{h}^j_{zz}\Sigma_{k+1|k}\big]\bigg]^{-1} \tag{K-2}$$

For the case at hand the observation relationship is Eq. (10-8), that is,

$$\mathbf{y}_k = \mathbf{H}_k(\boldsymbol{\theta}_k)\mathbf{x}_k + \mathbf{w}_k \tag{K-3}$$

Thus, in the notation of Eq. (9-5),

$$\mathbf{h}_k = \mathbf{H}_k(\boldsymbol{\theta}_k)\mathbf{x}_k \tag{K-4}$$

Therefore the observation relationship for the augmented system is

$$\mathbf{y}_k = \begin{bmatrix} \mathbf{H}_k(\boldsymbol{\theta}_k) & \vdots & \mathbf{0} \end{bmatrix}\begin{bmatrix} \mathbf{x}_k \\ \boldsymbol{\theta}_k \end{bmatrix} + \boldsymbol{\zeta}_k \tag{K-5}$$

and in the augmented system
$$\mathbf{h}_z = [\mathbf{h}_x \mid \mathbf{h}_\theta] \tag{K-6}$$

with
$$\mathbf{h}_x = \mathbf{H}_k(\theta_k) \quad \text{and} \quad \mathbf{h}_\theta = \sum_i e^i \hat{\mathbf{x}}'_{k+1|k} \mathbf{H}^i_\theta$$

by analogy with results in Appendix L. Also,

$$\mathbf{h}^i_{zz} = \begin{bmatrix} \mathbf{h}^i_{xx} & \mathbf{h}^i_{x\theta} \\ \mathbf{h}^i_{\theta x} & \mathbf{h}^i_{\theta\theta} \end{bmatrix} \tag{K-7}$$

and
$$\mathbf{h}^i_{xx} = 0 \qquad \mathbf{h}^i_{x\theta} = \mathbf{H}^i_\theta \qquad \mathbf{h}^i_{\theta\theta} = 0$$

Therefore

$$\mathbf{h}^i_{zz} \Sigma_{k+1|k} = \begin{bmatrix} 0 & \mathbf{H}^i_\theta \\ (\mathbf{H}^i_\theta)' & 0 \end{bmatrix} \begin{bmatrix} \Sigma^{xx} & \Sigma^{x\theta} \\ \Sigma^{\theta x} & \Sigma^{\theta\theta} \end{bmatrix}_{k+1|k}$$

$$= \begin{bmatrix} \mathbf{H}^i_\theta \Sigma^{\theta x} & \mathbf{H}^i_\theta \Sigma^{\theta\theta} \\ \mathbf{H}^{i\prime}_\theta \Sigma^{xx} & \mathbf{H}^{i\prime}_\theta \Sigma^{x\theta} \end{bmatrix} \tag{K-8}$$

and
$$\text{tr}\big[\mathbf{h}^i_{zz} \Sigma_{k+1|k} \mathbf{h}^j_{zz} \Sigma_{k+1|k}\big]$$

$$= \text{tr}\left(\begin{bmatrix} \mathbf{H}^i_\theta \Sigma^{\theta x} & \mathbf{H}^i_\theta \Sigma^{\theta\theta} \\ (\mathbf{H}^i_\theta)' \Sigma^{xx} & (\mathbf{H}^i_\theta)' \Sigma^{x\theta} \end{bmatrix} \begin{bmatrix} \mathbf{H}^j_\theta \Sigma^{\theta x} & \mathbf{H}^j_\theta \Sigma^{\theta\theta} \\ (\mathbf{H}^j_\theta)' \Sigma^{xx} & (\mathbf{H}^j_\theta)' \Sigma^{x\theta} \end{bmatrix} \right)$$

$$= \text{tr}\big[\mathbf{H}^i_\theta \Sigma^{\theta x} \mathbf{H}^j_\theta \Sigma^{\theta x} + \mathbf{H}^i_\theta \Sigma^{\theta\theta} (\mathbf{H}^j_\theta)' \Sigma^{xx}$$
$$+ (\mathbf{H}^i_\theta)' \Sigma^{xx} \mathbf{H}^j_\theta \Sigma^{\theta\theta} + (\mathbf{H}^i_\theta)' \Sigma^{x\theta} (\mathbf{H}^j_\theta)' \Sigma^{x\theta} \big]$$

$$= 2\,\text{tr}\big[\mathbf{H}^i_\theta \Sigma^{\theta x} \mathbf{H}^j_\theta \Sigma^{\theta x} + \mathbf{H}^i_\theta \Sigma^{\theta\theta} (\mathbf{H}^j_\theta)' \Sigma^{xx} \big] \tag{K-9}$$

Then substitution of Eq. (K-9) into Eq. (K-2) yields

$$\mathbf{V}_{k+1} = \Sigma_{k+1|k} \mathbf{h}'_{z,k+1} \bigg[\mathbf{h}_{z,k+1} \Sigma_{k+1|k} \mathbf{h}'_{z,k+1} + \mathbf{R}_{k+1}$$
$$+ \sum_i \sum_j e^i (e^j)' \text{tr}\big[\mathbf{H}^i_\theta \Sigma^{\theta x} \mathbf{H}^j_\theta \Sigma^{\theta x} + \mathbf{H}^i_\theta \Sigma^{\theta\theta} (\mathbf{H}^j_\theta)' \Sigma^{xx} \big] \bigg]^{-1} \tag{K-10}$$

For many problems $\mathbf{H}$ will not be a function of θ, so that

$$\mathbf{H}^i_\theta = 0 \qquad \text{for all } i$$

For this special case Eq. (K-6) becomes

$$\mathbf{h}_z = [\mathbf{H}_k \mid 0] \tag{K-11}$$

UPDATING THE AUGMENTED STATE COVARIANCE

and Eq. (K-7) becomes

$$h^i_{zz} = 0 \tag{K-12}$$

Thus Eq. (K-10) becomes

$$\mathbf{V}_{k+1} = \begin{bmatrix} \Sigma^{xx} & \Sigma^{x\theta} \\ \Sigma^{\theta x} & \Sigma^{xx} \end{bmatrix}_{k+1|k} \begin{bmatrix} \mathbf{H}'_{k+1} \\ 0 \end{bmatrix} \begin{bmatrix} \mathbf{H}_{k+1} & 0 \end{bmatrix}$$

$$\times \begin{bmatrix} \begin{bmatrix} \Sigma^{xx} & \Sigma^{x\theta} \\ \Sigma^{\theta x} & \Sigma^{\theta\theta} \end{bmatrix} \begin{bmatrix} \mathbf{H}'_{k+1} \\ 0 \end{bmatrix} + \mathbf{R}_{k+1} \end{bmatrix}^{-1} \tag{K-13}$$

or

$$\mathbf{V}_{k+1} = \begin{bmatrix} \Sigma^{xx}_{k+1|k} & \mathbf{H}'_{k+1} \\ \Sigma^{\theta x}_{k+1|k} & \mathbf{H}'_{k+1} \end{bmatrix} \begin{bmatrix} \mathbf{H}_{k+1}\Sigma^{xx}_{k+1|k} \mathbf{H}'_{k+1} + \mathbf{R}_{k+1} \end{bmatrix}^{-1}$$

$$= \begin{bmatrix} \Sigma^{xx}\mathbf{H}'_{k+1} & \mathbf{S}^{-1}_{k+1} \\ \Sigma^{\theta x}\mathbf{H}'_{k+1} & \mathbf{S}^{-1}_{k+1} \end{bmatrix} \tag{K-14}$$

where

$$\mathbf{S}_{k+1} = \mathbf{H}_{k+1}\Sigma^{xx}_{k+1|k}\mathbf{H}'_{k+1} + \mathbf{R}_{k+1} \tag{K-15}$$

Substitution of Eqs. (K-14) and (K-15) into Eq. (K-1) yields

$$\begin{bmatrix} \Sigma^{xx} & \Sigma^{x\theta} \\ \Sigma^{\theta x} & \Sigma^{\theta\theta} \end{bmatrix} = \begin{bmatrix} \begin{bmatrix} \mathbf{I} & 0 \\ 0 & \mathbf{I} \end{bmatrix} - \begin{bmatrix} \Sigma^{xx}\mathbf{H}'_{k+1}\mathbf{S}^{-1}_{k+1} \\ \Sigma^{\theta x}\mathbf{H}'_{k+1}\mathbf{S}^{-1}_{k+1} \end{bmatrix} \begin{bmatrix} \mathbf{H}_{k+1} & 0 \end{bmatrix} \end{bmatrix} \begin{bmatrix} \Sigma^{xx} & \Sigma^{x\theta} \\ \Sigma^{\theta x} & \Sigma^{\theta\theta} \end{bmatrix}_{k+1|k}$$

$$= \begin{bmatrix} \mathbf{I} - \Sigma^{xx}_{k+1|k}\mathbf{H}'_{k+1}\mathbf{S}^{-1}_{k+1}\mathbf{H}_{k+1} & 0 \\ -\Sigma^{\theta x}_{k+1|k}\mathbf{H}'_{k+1}\mathbf{S}^{-1}_{k+1}\mathbf{H}_{k+1} & \mathbf{I} \end{bmatrix} \begin{bmatrix} \Sigma^{xx} & \Sigma^{x\theta} \\ \Sigma^{\theta x} & \Sigma^{\theta\theta} \end{bmatrix}_{k+1|k} \tag{K-16}$$

Therefore

$$\Sigma^{xx}_{k+1|k+1} = \Sigma^{xx}_{k+1|k} - \Sigma^{xx}_{k+1|k}\mathbf{H}'_{k+1}\mathbf{S}^{-1}_{k+1}\mathbf{H}_{k+1}\Sigma^{xx}_{k+1|k} \tag{K-17}$$

$$\Sigma^{\theta x}_{k+1|k+1} = (\Sigma^{x\theta}_{k+1|k})' = \Sigma^{\theta x}_{k+1|k} - \Sigma^{\theta x}_{k+1|k}\mathbf{H}'_{k+1}\mathbf{S}^{-1}_{k+1}\mathbf{H}_{k+1}\Sigma^{xx}_{k+1|k} \tag{K-18}$$

$$\Sigma^{\theta\theta}_{k+1|k+1} = \Sigma^{\theta\theta}_{k+1|k} - \Sigma^{\theta x}_{k+1|k}\mathbf{H}'_{k+1}\mathbf{S}^{-1}_{k+1}\mathbf{H}_{k+1}\Sigma^{x\theta}_{k+1|k} \tag{K-19}$$

So for the case in which $\mathbf{H}$ is not a function of θ, the relationships (K-17)–(K-19) are used for obtaining $\Sigma_{k+1|k+1}$ from $\Sigma_{k+1|k}$. When $\mathbf{H}$ is a function of θ, Eqs. (K-1) and (K-10) should be used, along with Eq. (K-6).

APPENDIX L

DERIVATIVE OF THE SYSTEM EQUATIONS WITH RESPECT TO THE PARAMETERS

Recall (dropping the time subscript k) from Eq. (10-20) that

$$\mathbf{f}^x = \mathbf{A}(\boldsymbol{\theta})\mathbf{x} + \mathbf{B}(\boldsymbol{\theta})\mathbf{u} + \mathbf{c}(\boldsymbol{\theta}) \tag{L-1}$$

Rewrite Eq. (L-1) as

$$\mathbf{f}^x = \begin{bmatrix} \mathbf{a}^1(\boldsymbol{\theta})\mathbf{x} \\ \mathbf{a}^2(\boldsymbol{\theta})\mathbf{x} \\ \vdots \\ \mathbf{a}^n(\boldsymbol{\theta})\mathbf{x} \end{bmatrix} + \begin{bmatrix} \mathbf{b}^1(\boldsymbol{\theta})\mathbf{u} \\ \mathbf{b}^2(\boldsymbol{\theta})\mathbf{u} \\ \vdots \\ \mathbf{b}^n(\boldsymbol{\theta})\mathbf{u} \end{bmatrix} + \begin{bmatrix} c_2^1(\boldsymbol{\theta}) \\ c^2(\boldsymbol{\theta}) \\ \vdots \\ c^n(\boldsymbol{\theta}) \end{bmatrix} \tag{L-2}$$

where $\mathbf{a}^i(\boldsymbol{\theta}) = i$th row of $\mathbf{A}(\boldsymbol{\theta})$
$\mathbf{b}^i(\boldsymbol{\theta}) = i$th row of $\mathbf{B}(\boldsymbol{\theta})$
$c^i(\boldsymbol{\theta}) = i$th row of $\mathbf{c}(\boldsymbol{\theta})$

Then

$$\mathbf{f}^x_{\boldsymbol{\theta}} = \begin{bmatrix} \mathbf{x}'\dfrac{\partial}{\partial \theta_1}\mathbf{a}^1(\boldsymbol{\theta}) & \mathbf{x}'\dfrac{\partial}{\partial \theta_2}\mathbf{a}^1(\boldsymbol{\theta}) & \cdots & \mathbf{x}'\dfrac{\partial}{\partial \theta_r}\mathbf{a}^1(\boldsymbol{\theta}) \\ \mathbf{x}'\dfrac{\partial}{\partial \theta_1}\mathbf{a}^2(\boldsymbol{\theta}) & \mathbf{x}'\dfrac{\partial}{\partial \theta_2}\mathbf{a}^2(\boldsymbol{\theta}) & \cdots & \mathbf{x}'\dfrac{\partial}{\partial \theta_r}\mathbf{a}^2(\boldsymbol{\theta}) \\ \cdots & \cdots & \cdots & \cdots \\ \mathbf{x}'\dfrac{\partial}{\partial \theta_1}\mathbf{a}^n(\boldsymbol{\theta}) & \mathbf{x}'\dfrac{\partial}{\partial \theta_2}\mathbf{a}^n(\boldsymbol{\theta}) & \cdots & \mathbf{x}'\dfrac{\partial}{\partial \theta_r}\mathbf{a}^n(\boldsymbol{\theta}) \end{bmatrix}$$

$$+ \begin{bmatrix} \mathbf{u}'\frac{\partial}{\partial\theta_1}\mathbf{b}^1(\boldsymbol{\theta}) & \mathbf{u}'\frac{\partial}{\partial\theta_2}\mathbf{b}^1(\boldsymbol{\theta}) & \cdots & \mathbf{u}'\frac{\partial}{\partial\theta_r}\mathbf{b}^1(\boldsymbol{\theta}) \\ \mathbf{u}'\frac{\partial}{\partial\theta_1}\mathbf{b}^2(\boldsymbol{\theta}) & \mathbf{u}'\frac{\partial}{\partial\theta_2}\mathbf{b}^2(\boldsymbol{\theta}) & \cdots & \mathbf{u}'\frac{\partial}{\partial\theta_r}\mathbf{b}^2(\boldsymbol{\theta}) \\ \vdots & \vdots & & \vdots \\ \mathbf{u}'\frac{\partial}{\partial\theta_1}\mathbf{b}^n(\boldsymbol{\theta}) & \mathbf{u}'\frac{\partial}{\partial\theta_2}\mathbf{b}^n(\boldsymbol{\theta}) & \cdots & \mathbf{u}'\frac{\partial}{\partial\theta_r}\mathbf{b}^n(\boldsymbol{\theta}) \end{bmatrix}$$

$$+ \begin{bmatrix} \frac{\partial}{\partial\theta_1}c^1(\boldsymbol{\theta}) & \frac{\partial}{\partial\theta_2}c^1(\boldsymbol{\theta}) & \cdots & \frac{\partial}{\partial\theta_r}c^1(\boldsymbol{\theta}) \\ \frac{\partial}{\partial\theta_1}c^2(\boldsymbol{\theta}) & \frac{\partial}{\partial\theta_2}c^2(\boldsymbol{\theta}) & \cdots & \frac{\partial}{\partial\theta_r}c^2(\boldsymbol{\theta}) \\ \vdots & \vdots & & \vdots \\ \frac{\partial}{\partial\theta_1}c^n(\boldsymbol{\theta}) & \frac{\partial}{\partial\theta_2}c^n(\boldsymbol{\theta}) & \cdots & \frac{\partial}{\partial\theta_r}c^n(\boldsymbol{\theta}) \end{bmatrix} \quad \text{(L-3)}$$

Next define

$$\mathbf{a}^i_{\boldsymbol{\theta}} = \frac{\partial}{\partial\boldsymbol{\theta}}\mathbf{a}^i(\boldsymbol{\theta}) = \begin{bmatrix} \frac{\partial}{\partial\theta_1}a_{i1}(\boldsymbol{\theta}) & \frac{\partial}{\partial\theta_2}a_{i1}(\boldsymbol{\theta}) & \cdots & \frac{\partial}{\partial\theta_r}a_{i1}(\boldsymbol{\theta}) \\ \frac{\partial}{\partial\theta_1}a_{i2}(\boldsymbol{\theta}) & \frac{\partial}{\partial\theta_2}a_{i2}(\boldsymbol{\theta}) & \cdots & \frac{\partial}{\partial\theta_r}a_{i2}(\boldsymbol{\theta}) \\ \vdots & \vdots & & \vdots \\ \frac{\partial}{\partial\theta_1}a_{in}(\boldsymbol{\theta}) & \frac{\partial}{\partial\theta_2}a_{in}(\boldsymbol{\theta}) & \cdots & \frac{\partial}{\partial\theta_r}a_{in}(\boldsymbol{\theta}) \end{bmatrix} \quad \text{(L-4)}$$

Then

$$\mathbf{x}'\mathbf{a}^i_{\boldsymbol{\theta}} = \left[\sum_j x_j \frac{\partial}{\partial\theta_1}a_{ij}(\boldsymbol{\theta}) \quad \sum_j x_j \frac{\partial}{\partial\theta_2}a_{ij}(\boldsymbol{\theta}) \quad \cdots \quad \sum_j x_j \frac{\partial}{\partial\theta_r}a_{ij}(\boldsymbol{\theta}) \right] \quad \text{(L-5)}$$

and

$$\sum_i \mathbf{e}_i \mathbf{x}'\mathbf{a}^i_{\boldsymbol{\theta}} = \begin{bmatrix} \sum_j x_j \frac{\partial}{\partial\theta_1}a_{1j}(\boldsymbol{\theta}) & \sum_j x_j \frac{\partial}{\partial\theta_2}a_{1j}(\boldsymbol{\theta}) & \cdots & \sum_j x_j \frac{\partial}{\partial\theta_r}a_{1j}(\boldsymbol{\theta}) \\ \sum_j x_j \frac{\partial}{\partial\theta_1}a_{2j}(\boldsymbol{\theta}) & \sum_j x_j \frac{\partial}{\partial\theta_2}a_{2j}(\boldsymbol{\theta}) & \cdots & \sum_j x_j \frac{\partial}{\partial\theta_r}a_{2j}(\boldsymbol{\theta}) \\ \vdots & \vdots & & \vdots \\ \sum_j x_j \frac{\partial}{\partial\theta_1}a_{nj}(\boldsymbol{\theta}) & \sum_j x_j \frac{\partial}{\partial\theta_2}a_{nj}(\boldsymbol{\theta}) & \cdots & \sum_j x_j \frac{\partial}{\partial\theta_r}a_{nj}(\boldsymbol{\theta}) \end{bmatrix}$$

$$= \begin{bmatrix} \mathbf{x}'\dfrac{\partial}{\partial \theta_1}\mathbf{a}^1(\boldsymbol{\theta}) & \mathbf{x}'\dfrac{\partial}{\partial \theta_2}(\mathbf{a}^1(\boldsymbol{\theta})) & \cdots & \mathbf{x}'\dfrac{\partial}{\partial \theta_r}\mathbf{a}^1(\boldsymbol{\theta}) \\ \mathbf{x}'\dfrac{\partial}{\partial \theta_1}\mathbf{a}^2(\boldsymbol{\theta}) & \mathbf{x}'\dfrac{\partial}{\partial \theta_2}\mathbf{a}^2(\boldsymbol{\theta}) & \cdots & \mathbf{x}'\dfrac{\partial}{\partial \theta_r}\mathbf{a}^2(\boldsymbol{\theta}) \\ \cdots & \cdots & \cdots & \cdots \\ \mathbf{x}'\dfrac{\partial}{\partial \theta_1}\mathbf{a}^n(\boldsymbol{\theta}) & \mathbf{x}'\dfrac{\partial}{\partial \theta_2}\mathbf{a}^n(\boldsymbol{\theta}) & \cdots & \mathbf{x}'\dfrac{\partial}{\partial \theta_r}\mathbf{a}^n(\boldsymbol{\theta}) \end{bmatrix} \quad \text{(L-6)}$$

Similarly define

$$\mathbf{b}^i_{\boldsymbol{\theta}} = \frac{\partial}{\partial \boldsymbol{\theta}}\mathbf{b}^i(\boldsymbol{\theta}) = \begin{bmatrix} \dfrac{\partial}{\partial \theta_1}b_{i1}(\boldsymbol{\theta}) & \dfrac{\partial}{\partial \theta_2}b_{i1}(\boldsymbol{\theta}) & \cdots & \dfrac{\partial}{\partial \theta_r}b_{i1}(\boldsymbol{\theta}) \\ \dfrac{\partial}{\partial \theta_1}b_{i2}(\boldsymbol{\theta}) & \dfrac{\partial}{\partial \theta_2}b_{i2}(\boldsymbol{\theta}) & \cdots & \dfrac{\partial}{\partial \theta_r}b_{i2}(\boldsymbol{\theta}) \\ \cdots & \cdots & \cdots & \cdots \\ \dfrac{\partial}{\partial \theta_1}b_{im}(\boldsymbol{\theta}) & \dfrac{\partial}{\partial \theta_2}b_{im}(\boldsymbol{\theta}) & \cdots & \dfrac{\partial}{\partial \theta_r}b_{im}(\boldsymbol{\theta}) \end{bmatrix} \quad \text{(L-7)}$$

Then

$$\mathbf{u}'\mathbf{b}^i_{\boldsymbol{\theta}} = \left[\sum_j u_j \frac{\partial}{\partial \theta_1} b_{ij}(\boldsymbol{\theta}) \quad \sum_j u_j \frac{\partial}{\partial \theta_2} b_{ij}(\boldsymbol{\theta}) \quad \cdots \quad \sum_j u_j \frac{\partial}{\partial \theta_r} b_{ij}(\boldsymbol{\theta}) \right] \quad \text{(L-8)}$$

and $\displaystyle\sum_i \mathbf{e}_i \mathbf{u}'\mathbf{b}^i_{\boldsymbol{\theta}} = \begin{bmatrix} \sum_j u_j \dfrac{\partial}{\partial \theta_1} b_{1j}(\boldsymbol{\theta}) & \sum_j u_j \dfrac{\partial}{\partial \theta_2} b_{1j}(\boldsymbol{\theta}) & \cdots & \sum_j u_j \dfrac{\partial}{\partial \theta_r} b_{1j}(\boldsymbol{\theta}) \\ \sum_j u_j \dfrac{\partial}{\partial \theta_1} b_{2j}(\boldsymbol{\theta}) & \sum_j u_j \dfrac{\partial}{\partial \theta_2} b_{2j}(\boldsymbol{\theta}) & \cdots & \sum_j u_j \dfrac{\partial}{\partial \theta_r} b_{2j}(\boldsymbol{\theta}) \\ \cdots & \cdots & \cdots & \cdots \\ \sum_j u_j \dfrac{\partial}{\partial \theta_1} b_{nj}(\boldsymbol{\theta}) & \sum_j u_j \dfrac{\partial}{\partial \theta_2} b_{nj}(\boldsymbol{\theta}) & \cdots & \sum_j u_j \dfrac{\partial}{\partial \theta_r} b_{nj}(\boldsymbol{\theta}) \end{bmatrix}$

$$= \begin{bmatrix} \mathbf{u}'\dfrac{\partial}{\partial \theta_1}\mathbf{b}^1(\boldsymbol{\theta}) & \mathbf{u}'\dfrac{\partial}{\partial \theta_2}\mathbf{b}^1(\boldsymbol{\theta}) & \cdots & \mathbf{u}'\dfrac{\partial}{\partial \theta_r}\mathbf{b}^1(\boldsymbol{\theta}) \\ \mathbf{u}'\dfrac{\partial}{\partial \theta_1}\mathbf{b}^2(\boldsymbol{\theta}) & \mathbf{u}'\dfrac{\partial}{\partial \theta_2}\mathbf{b}^2(\boldsymbol{\theta}) & \cdots & \mathbf{u}'\dfrac{\partial}{\partial \theta_r}\mathbf{b}^2(\boldsymbol{\theta}) \\ \cdots & \cdots & \cdots & \cdots \\ \mathbf{u}'\dfrac{\partial}{\partial \theta_1}\mathbf{b}^n(\boldsymbol{\theta}) & \mathbf{u}'\dfrac{\partial}{\partial \theta_2}\mathbf{b}^n(\boldsymbol{\theta}) & \cdots & \mathbf{u}'\dfrac{\partial}{\partial \theta_r}\mathbf{b}^n(\boldsymbol{\theta}) \end{bmatrix} \quad \text{(L-9)}$$

Define

$$\mathbf{c}^i_{\boldsymbol{\theta}} = \frac{\partial}{\partial \boldsymbol{\theta}} c^i(\boldsymbol{\theta}) = \left[\frac{\partial}{\partial \theta_1} c_i(\boldsymbol{\theta}) \quad \frac{\partial}{\partial \theta_2} c_i(\boldsymbol{\theta}) \quad \cdots \quad \frac{\partial}{\partial \theta_r} c_i(\boldsymbol{\theta}) \right] \quad \text{(L-10)}$$

Then

$$\sum_i \mathbf{e}_i \mathbf{c}_\theta^i = \begin{bmatrix} \frac{\partial}{\partial \theta_1} c_1(\boldsymbol{\theta}) & \frac{\partial}{\partial \theta_2} c_1(\boldsymbol{\theta}) & \cdots & \frac{\partial}{\partial \theta_r} c_1(\boldsymbol{\theta}) \\ \frac{\partial}{\partial \theta_1} c_2(\boldsymbol{\theta}) & \frac{\partial}{\partial \theta_2} c_2(\boldsymbol{\theta}) & \cdots & \frac{\partial}{\partial \theta_r} c_2(\boldsymbol{\theta}) \\ \cdots \\ \frac{\partial}{\partial \theta_1} c_n(\boldsymbol{\theta}) & \frac{\partial}{\partial \theta_2} c_n(\boldsymbol{\theta}) & \cdots & \frac{\partial}{\partial \theta_r} c_n(\boldsymbol{\theta}) \end{bmatrix}$$

$$= \begin{bmatrix} \frac{\partial}{\partial \theta_1} c^1(\boldsymbol{\theta}) & \frac{\partial}{\partial \theta_2} c^1(\boldsymbol{\theta}) & \cdots & \frac{\partial}{\partial \theta_r} c^1(\boldsymbol{\theta}) \\ \frac{\partial}{\partial \theta_1} c^2(\boldsymbol{\theta}) & \frac{\partial}{\partial \theta_2} c^2(\boldsymbol{\theta}) & \cdots & \frac{\partial}{\partial \theta_r} c^2(\boldsymbol{\theta}) \\ \cdots \\ \frac{\partial}{\partial \theta_1} c^n(\boldsymbol{\theta}) & \frac{\partial}{\partial \theta_2} c^n(\boldsymbol{\theta}) & \cdots & \frac{\partial}{\partial \theta_r} c^n(\boldsymbol{\theta}) \end{bmatrix} \quad \text{(L-11)}$$

which c^i = the ith row in $\mathbf{c}(\boldsymbol{\theta}) = c_i$ = the ith element in $\mathbf{c}(\boldsymbol{\theta})$.

Then substitution of Eqs. (L-6), (L-9), and (L-11) into Eq. (L-3) yields

$$\mathbf{f}_\theta^x = \sum_i \mathbf{e}_i \mathbf{x}' \mathbf{a}_\theta^i + \sum \mathbf{e}_i \mathbf{u}' \mathbf{b}_\theta^j + \sum \mathbf{e}_i \mathbf{c}_\theta^i \quad \text{(L-12)}$$

In order to evaluate Eq. (L-12) at $(\hat{\mathbf{z}}_{k|k}, \mathbf{u}_k^\tau)$ one has

$$\mathbf{f}_\theta^x(k, \hat{\mathbf{z}}_{k|k}, \mathbf{u}_k^\tau) = \sum_{i \in X} \mathbf{e}_i \mathbf{x}'_{k|k} \mathbf{a}_\theta^i(k) + \sum_{i \in X} \mathbf{e}_i (\mathbf{u}_k^\tau)' \mathbf{b}_\theta^j(k) + \sum_{i \in X} \mathbf{e}_i \mathbf{c}_\theta^i(k) \quad \text{(L-13)}$$

which is the desired result.

APPENDIX M

PROJECTION OF THE AUGMENTED STATE VECTOR

This appendix details the one-period projection of the mean and covariance of the augmented state vector, i.e., the projection of $\hat{z}_{k+1|k}$ and $\Sigma_{k+1|k}$ from $\hat{z}_{k|k}$ and $\Sigma_{k|k}$.

Using Eq. (9-73), we have

$$\hat{z}_{k+1|k} \approx f(\hat{z}_{k|k}, u_k^\tau) + \frac{1}{2} \sum_{i \in I} e^i \, \text{tr}\left[f_{zz,k|k}^i\right] \tag{M-1}$$

where $I = X \cup \Theta$, X is the set of indices for the system equations for the original state variables, Θ is the set of indices for the parameter dynamics equations, and $X \cup \Theta$ means the union of the two sets.

For the linear case

$$f(\hat{z}_{k|k}, u_k^\dagger) = \left[\begin{array}{c} A_k(\theta_{o,k})\hat{x}_{k|k} + B_k(\theta_{o,k})u_k^\tau + c_k(\theta_{o,k}) \\ \hdashline D_k \theta_{ok} \end{array}\right] \tag{M-2}$$

Also

$$f_{zz}^i = \left[\begin{array}{c:c} f_{xx}^i & f_{x\theta}^i \\ \hdashline f_{\theta x}^i & f_{\theta\theta}^i \end{array}\right] = \left[\begin{array}{c:c} 0 & a_\theta^i \\ \hdashline a''_\theta & 0 \end{array}\right] \quad i \in X \tag{M-3}$$

$$f_{zz}^i = \left[\begin{array}{c:c} f_{xx}^i & f_{x\theta}^i \\ \hdashline f_{\theta x}^i & f_{\theta\theta}^i \end{array}\right] = \left[\begin{array}{c:c} 0 & 0 \\ \hdashline 0 & 0 \end{array}\right] \quad i \in \Theta \tag{M-4}$$

and
$$\Sigma_{k|k} = \begin{bmatrix} \Sigma^{xx} & \Sigma^{x\theta} \\ \hline \Sigma^{\theta x} & \Sigma^{\theta\theta} \end{bmatrix}$$

Therefore

$$\mathbf{f}_{zz}^i \Sigma_{k|k} = \begin{bmatrix} 0 & \mathbf{a}_\theta^i \\ \hline (\mathbf{a}_\theta^i)' & 0 \end{bmatrix} \begin{bmatrix} \Sigma^{xx} & \Sigma^{x\theta} \\ \hline \Sigma^{\theta x} & \Sigma^{\theta\theta} \end{bmatrix} = \begin{bmatrix} \mathbf{a}_\theta^i \Sigma^{\theta x} & \mathbf{a}_\theta^i \Sigma^{\theta\theta} \\ \hline (\mathbf{a}_\theta^i)' \Sigma^{xx} & (\mathbf{a}_\theta^i)' \Sigma^{x\theta} \end{bmatrix} \quad i \in X \tag{M-5}$$

and
$$\mathbf{f}_{zz}^i \Sigma_{k|k} = 0 \quad \text{for } i \in \Theta \tag{M-6}$$

Therefore

$$\frac{1}{2} \sum_{i \in I} \mathbf{e}^i \operatorname{tr}\left[\mathbf{f}_{zz}^i \Sigma_{k|k}\right] = \begin{bmatrix} \dfrac{1}{2} \sum_{i \in X} \mathbf{e}^i \operatorname{tr}\left[\mathbf{f}_{zz}^i \Sigma_{k|k}\right] \\ \hline \dfrac{1}{2} \sum_{i \in \Theta} \mathbf{e}^i \operatorname{tr}\left[\mathbf{f}_{zz}^i \Sigma_{k|k}\right] \end{bmatrix}$$

$$= \begin{bmatrix} \dfrac{1}{2} \sum_{i \in X} \mathbf{e}^i \operatorname{tr}\begin{bmatrix} \mathbf{a}_\theta^i \Sigma^{\theta x} & \mathbf{a}_\theta^i \Sigma^{\theta\theta} \\ \hline (\mathbf{a}_\theta^i)' \Sigma^{xx} & (\mathbf{a}_\theta^i)' \Sigma^{x\theta} \end{bmatrix} \\ \hline 0 \end{bmatrix}$$

$$= \begin{bmatrix} \dfrac{1}{2} \sum_{i \in X} \mathbf{e}^i \operatorname{tr}\left[\mathbf{a}_\theta^i \Sigma^{\theta x} + (\mathbf{a}_\theta^i)' \Sigma^{x\theta}\right] \\ \hline 0 \end{bmatrix}$$

$$= \begin{bmatrix} \sum_{i \in X} \mathbf{e}^i \operatorname{tr}\left[\mathbf{a}_\theta^i \Sigma^{\theta x}\right] \\ \hline 0 \end{bmatrix} \tag{M-7}$$

Hence, the use of Eqs. (M-2) and (M-7) in Eq. (M-1) yields

$$\hat{\mathbf{z}}_{k+1|k} = \begin{bmatrix} \hat{\mathbf{x}}_{k+1|k} \\ \hline \hat{\boldsymbol{\theta}}_{k+1|k} \end{bmatrix}$$

$$= \begin{bmatrix} \mathbf{A}_k(\boldsymbol{\theta}_{o,k})\hat{\mathbf{x}}_{k|k} + \mathbf{B}_k(\boldsymbol{\theta}_{o,k})\mathbf{u}_k^\tau + \mathbf{c}_k(\boldsymbol{\theta}_{o,k}) + \sum_{i \in X} \mathbf{e}^i \operatorname{tr}\left[\mathbf{a}_\theta^i \Sigma^{\theta x}\right] \\ \hline \mathbf{D}_k \hat{\boldsymbol{\theta}}_{o,k} \end{bmatrix} \tag{M-8}$$

and since $\hat{\boldsymbol{\theta}}$ does not differ from $\boldsymbol{\theta}_o$, we need to use only the top half of Eq. (M-8); i.e.,

$$\hat{\mathbf{x}}_{k+1|k} = \mathbf{A}_k(\boldsymbol{\theta}_{ok})\hat{\mathbf{x}}_{k|k} + \mathbf{B}_k(\boldsymbol{\theta}_{ok})\mathbf{u}_k^\tau + \mathbf{c}_k(\boldsymbol{\theta}_{ok}) + \sum_{i \in X} \mathbf{e}^i \operatorname{tr}\left[\mathbf{a}_\theta^i \Sigma^{\theta x}_{k|k}\right] \tag{M-9}$$

Next Eq. (9-78) can be used to project the variance one step ahead

$$\Sigma_{k+1|k} = \mathbf{f}_z \Sigma_{k|k} \mathbf{f}'_z + \mathbf{Q}^z_k + \frac{1}{2} \sum_i \sum_j \mathbf{e}^i (\mathbf{e}^j)' \operatorname{tr}\left[\mathbf{f}^i_{zz} \Sigma_{k|k} \mathbf{f}^j_{zz} \Sigma_{k|k}\right] \quad \text{(M-10)}$$

$$\Sigma_{k+1|k} = \begin{bmatrix} \mathbf{f}^x_x & \mathbf{f}^x_\theta \\ \hline \mathbf{f}^\theta_x & \mathbf{f}^\theta_\theta \end{bmatrix}_k \begin{bmatrix} \Sigma^{xx} & \Sigma^{x\theta} \\ \hline \Sigma^{\theta x} & \Sigma^{\theta\theta} \end{bmatrix}_{k|k} \begin{bmatrix} \mathbf{f}^x_x & \mathbf{f}^x_\theta \\ \hline \mathbf{f}^\theta_x & \mathbf{f}^\theta_\theta \end{bmatrix}'_k + \begin{bmatrix} \mathbf{Q}_k & 0 \\ \hline 0 & \mathbf{G}_k \end{bmatrix}$$

$$+ \frac{1}{2} \sum_{i \in I} \sum_{j \in I} \mathbf{e}^i (\mathbf{e}^j)' \operatorname{tr}\left(\begin{bmatrix} \mathbf{f}^i_{xx} & \mathbf{f}^i_{x\theta} \\ \hline \mathbf{f}^i_{\theta x} & \mathbf{f}^i_{\theta\theta} \end{bmatrix} \begin{bmatrix} \Sigma^{xx} & \Sigma^{x\theta} \\ \hline \Sigma^{\theta x} & \Sigma^{\theta\theta} \end{bmatrix}_{k|k}\right.$$

$$\left. \times \begin{bmatrix} \mathbf{f}^j_{xx} & \mathbf{f}^j_{x\theta} \\ \hline \mathbf{f}^j_{\theta x} & \mathbf{f}^j_{\theta\theta} \end{bmatrix} \begin{bmatrix} \Sigma^{xx} & \Sigma^{x\theta} \\ \hline \Sigma^{\theta x} & \Sigma^{\theta\theta} \end{bmatrix}_{k|k}\right) \quad \text{(M-11)}$$

And since

$$\mathbf{f}^x = \mathbf{A}_k(\boldsymbol{\theta}_k) \mathbf{x}_k + \mathbf{B}_k(\boldsymbol{\theta}_k) \mathbf{u}^\tau_k + \mathbf{c}_k(\boldsymbol{\theta}_k) \qquad \mathbf{f}^\theta = \mathbf{D}_k \boldsymbol{\theta}_k$$

so we have

$$\mathbf{f}^x_x = \mathbf{A}_k(\boldsymbol{\theta}_k)$$

and (see Appendix L)

$$\mathbf{f}^x_\theta = \sum_i \mathbf{e}_i \hat{\mathbf{x}}'_{k|k} \mathbf{a}^i_\theta + \sum_i \mathbf{e}_i (\mathbf{u}^\tau_k)' \mathbf{b}^i_\theta + \sum_i \mathbf{e}_i \mathbf{c}^i_\theta \qquad \mathbf{f}^\theta_x = 0 \qquad \mathbf{f}^\theta_\theta = \mathbf{D}_k \quad \text{(M-12)}$$

Substitution of Eqs. (M-3), (M-4), and (M-12) into Eq. (M-11) yields

$$\Sigma_{k+1|k} = \begin{bmatrix} \mathbf{A} & \mathbf{f}^x_\theta \\ \hline 0 & \mathbf{D} \end{bmatrix}_k \begin{bmatrix} \Sigma^{xx} & \Sigma^{x\theta} \\ \hline \Sigma^{\theta x} & \Sigma^{\theta\theta} \end{bmatrix}_{k|k} \begin{bmatrix} \mathbf{A}' & 0 \\ \hline \mathbf{f}^x_\theta & \mathbf{D}' \end{bmatrix}_k + \begin{bmatrix} \mathbf{Q} & 0 \\ \hline \mathbf{Q} & \mathbf{G} \end{bmatrix}_k + \begin{bmatrix} \mathbb{A} & 0 \\ \hline 0 & 0 \end{bmatrix} \quad \text{(M-13)}$$

where[1]

$$\mathbb{A} = \frac{1}{2} \sum_{i \in X} \sum_{j \in X} \mathbf{e}^i (\mathbf{e}^j)' \operatorname{tr}\left\{\begin{bmatrix} 0 & \mathbf{a}^i_\theta \\ \hline (\mathbf{a}^i_\theta)' & 0 \end{bmatrix} \begin{bmatrix} \Sigma^{xx} & \Sigma^{x\theta} \\ \hline \Sigma^{\theta x} & \Sigma^{\theta\theta} \end{bmatrix} \begin{bmatrix} 0 & \mathbf{a}^j_\theta \\ \hline (\mathbf{a}^j_\theta)' & 0 \end{bmatrix} \begin{bmatrix} \Sigma^{xx} & \Sigma^{x\theta} \\ \hline \Sigma^{\theta x} & \Sigma^{\theta\theta} \end{bmatrix}\right\}$$

Then

$$\Sigma_{k+1|k} = \begin{bmatrix} \mathbf{A} & \mathbf{f}^x_\theta \\ \hline 0 & \mathbf{D} \end{bmatrix}_k \begin{bmatrix} \Sigma^{xx} \mathbf{A}' + \Sigma^{x\theta}(\mathbf{f}^x_\theta)' & \Sigma^{x\theta} \mathbf{D}' \\ \hline \Sigma^{\theta x} \mathbf{A}' + \Sigma^{\theta\theta}(\mathbf{f}^x_\theta)' & \Sigma^{\theta\theta} \mathbf{D}' \end{bmatrix} + \begin{bmatrix} \mathbf{Q} & 0 \\ \hline 0 & \mathbf{G} \end{bmatrix}_k + \begin{bmatrix} \mathbb{B} & 0 \\ \hline 0 & 0 \end{bmatrix} \quad \text{(M-14)}$$

where $\mathbb{B} = \frac{1}{2} \sum_{i \in X} \sum_{j \in X} \mathbf{e}^i (\mathbf{e}^j)' \operatorname{tr}\begin{bmatrix} \mathbf{a}^i_\theta \Sigma^{\theta x} & \mathbf{a}^i_\theta \Sigma^{\theta\theta} \\ \hline (\mathbf{a}^i_\theta)' \Sigma^{xx} & (\mathbf{a}^i_\theta)' \Sigma^{x\theta} \end{bmatrix} \begin{bmatrix} \mathbf{a}^j_\theta \Sigma^{\theta x} & \mathbf{a}^j_\theta \Sigma^{\theta\theta} \\ \hline (\mathbf{a}^j_\theta)' \Sigma^{xx} & (\mathbf{a}^j_\theta)' \Sigma^{x\theta} \end{bmatrix}$

[1] Note that the summations below are over X while the summations in Eq. (M-11) are over I. This explains why $\mathbb{A}$ is in the upper left hand corner in Eq. (M-13).

Then

$$\Sigma_{k+1|k} = \begin{bmatrix} \Sigma^{xx} & \Sigma^{x\theta} \\ \hline \Sigma^{\theta x} & \Sigma^{\theta\theta} \end{bmatrix}_{k+1|k}$$

$$= \begin{bmatrix} A\Sigma^{xx}A' + A\Sigma^{x\theta}(f_\theta^x)' + f_\theta^x\Sigma^{\theta x}A' + f_\theta^x\Sigma^{\theta\theta}(f_\theta^x)' & A\Sigma^{x\theta}D' + f_\theta^x\Sigma^{\theta\theta}D' \\ \hline D\Sigma^{\theta x}A' + D\Sigma^{\theta\theta}(f_\theta^x)' & D\Sigma^{\theta\theta}D' \end{bmatrix}$$

$$+ \begin{bmatrix} Q & 0 \\ \hline 0 & G \end{bmatrix}_k + \begin{bmatrix} \mathbb{C} & 0 \\ \hline 0 & 0 \end{bmatrix}$$

where
$$\mathbb{C} = \frac{1}{2} \sum_{i \in X} \sum_{j \in X} e^i(e^j)' \mathrm{tr}\Big[a_\theta^i \Sigma^{\theta x} a_\theta^j \Sigma^{\theta x} + a_\theta^i \Sigma^{\theta\theta}(a_\theta^j)' \Sigma^{xx}$$
$$+ (a_\theta^i)' \Sigma^{xx} a_\theta^j \Sigma^{\theta\theta} + (a_\theta^i)' \Sigma^{x\theta}(a_\theta^j)' \Sigma^{x\theta} \Big] \tag{M-15}$$

Then the component matrices of Eq. (M-15) can be rewritten as

$$\Sigma^{xx}_{k+1|k} = A_k \Sigma^{xx}_{k|k} A'_k + A_k \Sigma^{x\theta}_{k|k}(f_{\theta k}^x)' + f_{\theta k}^x \Sigma^{\theta x}_{k|k} A'_k + f_{\theta k}^x \Sigma^{\theta\theta}_{k|k}(f_{\theta k}^x)' + Q_k$$
$$+ \sum_{i \in X} \sum_{j \in X} e^i(e^j)' \mathrm{tr}\big(a_\theta^i \Sigma^{\theta x}_{k|k} a_\theta^j \Sigma^{\theta x}_{k|k} + a_\theta^i \Sigma^{\theta\theta}_{k|k}(a_\theta^j)' \Sigma^{xx}_{k|k}\big) \tag{M-16}$$

$$\Sigma^{x\theta}_{k+1|k} = \big(\Sigma^{\theta x}_{k+1|k}\big)' = A_k \Sigma^{x\theta}_{k|k} D'_k + f_{\theta k}^x \Sigma^{\theta\theta}_{k|k} D'_k \tag{M-17}$$

or $\quad \Sigma^{\theta x}_{k+1|k} = D_k \Sigma^{\theta x}_{k|k} A'_k + D_k \Sigma^{\theta\theta}_{k|k}(f_{\theta k}^x)' \tag{M-18}$

$$\Sigma^{\theta\theta}_{k+1|k} = D_k \Sigma^{\theta\theta}_{k|k} D'_k + G_k \tag{M-19}$$

APPENDIX N

UPDATING THE AUGMENTED STATE VECTOR

Begin with the augmented equation like Eq. (9-86)

$$\hat{\mathbf{z}}_{k+1|k+1} = \hat{\mathbf{z}}_{k+1|k} + \mathbf{V}_{k+1}\left[\mathbf{y}_{k+1} - \mathbf{h}_{z,k+1}\hat{\mathbf{z}}_{k+1|k}\right] \tag{N-1}$$

and write it in augmented form as

$$\begin{bmatrix}\hat{\mathbf{x}}\\\hat{\boldsymbol{\theta}}\end{bmatrix}_{k+1|k+1} = \begin{bmatrix}\hat{\mathbf{x}}\\\hat{\boldsymbol{\theta}}\end{bmatrix}_{k+1|k} + \mathbf{V}_{k+1}\left[\mathbf{y}_{k+1} - [\mathbf{h}_{\mathbf{x},k+1}, \mathbf{h}_{\boldsymbol{\theta},k+1}]\begin{bmatrix}\hat{\mathbf{x}}\\\hat{\boldsymbol{\theta}}\end{bmatrix}_{k+1|k}\right] \tag{N-2}$$

where, from Eq. (K-6), for the case in which noisy measurements of $\mathbf{x}$ alone are available,

$$\mathbf{h}_{\mathbf{x},k+1} = \mathbf{H}_{k+1}\left(\hat{\boldsymbol{\theta}}_{k+1|k}\right) \qquad \mathbf{h}_{\boldsymbol{\theta},k+1} = \sum_{i} e^{i}\hat{\mathbf{x}}'_{k+1|k}\mathbf{H}^{i}_{\boldsymbol{\theta},k+1} \tag{N-3}$$

For the case in which $\mathbf{h}$ and $\mathbf{H}$ are not functions of $\boldsymbol{\theta}$, Eq. (N-3) can be rewritten as

$$\mathbf{h}_{\mathbf{x},k+1} = \mathbf{H}_{k+1} \qquad \mathbf{h}_{\boldsymbol{\theta},k+1} = 0 \tag{N-4}$$

Substitution of Eq. (N-3), (N-4), and (K-14) into Eq. (N-2) yields

$$\begin{bmatrix}\hat{\mathbf{x}}\\\hat{\boldsymbol{\theta}}\end{bmatrix}_{k+1|k+1} = \begin{bmatrix}\hat{\mathbf{x}}\\\hat{\boldsymbol{\theta}}\end{bmatrix}_{k+1|k} + \begin{bmatrix}\Sigma^{\mathbf{xx}}_{k+1|k}\mathbf{H}'_{k+1}\mathbf{S}^{-1}_{k+1}\\ \hline \Sigma^{\boldsymbol{\theta}\mathbf{x}}_{k+1|k}\mathbf{H}'_{k+1}\mathbf{S}^{-1}_{k+1}\end{bmatrix}\left[\mathbf{y}_{k+1} - \mathbf{H}_{k+1}\hat{\mathbf{x}}_{k+1|k}\right] \tag{N-5}$$

where, from Eq. (K-15),

$$S_{k+1} = H_{k+1}\Sigma^{xx}_{k+1|k}H'_{k+1} + R_{k+1} \qquad (N\text{-}6)$$

Then Eq. (N-5) can be rewritten

$$\hat{x}_{k+1|k+1} = \hat{x}_{k+1|k} + \Sigma^{xx}_{k+1|k}H'_{k+1}S^{-1}_{k+1}\left[y_{k+1} - H_{k+1}\hat{x}_{k+1|k}\right] \qquad (N\text{-}7)$$

and

$$\hat{\theta}_{k+1|k+1} = \hat{\theta}_{k+1|k} + \Sigma^{\theta x}_{k+1|k}H'_{k+1}S^{-1}_{k+1}\left[y_{k+1} - H_{k+1}\hat{x}_{k+1|k}\right] \qquad (N\text{-}8)$$

APPENDIX O

THE SEQUENTIAL CERTAINTY-EQUIVALENCE METHOD

Repeat the following calculations for each time period beginning with $k = 0$.

Step 1 Generate the random vectors for the system noise $\mathbf{v}_k$ and the measurement noise $\mathbf{w}_{k+1}$.

Step 2 Solve the certainty-equivalence problem from period k to period N and set $\mathbf{u}_k^\tau = \mathbf{u}_k^{CE}$, as given by Eq. (10-30).

Step 3 Obtain the actual value of the state vector with

$$\mathbf{x}_{k+1} = \mathbf{A}\mathbf{x}_k + \mathbf{B}\mathbf{u}_k^\tau + \mathbf{c}_k + \mathbf{v}_k \tag{O-1}$$

and the actual value of the measurement vector with

$$\mathbf{y}_{k+1} = \mathbf{H}_{k+1}\mathbf{x}_{k+1} + \mathbf{w}_{k+1} \tag{O-2}$$

Step 4 Get $\hat{\mathbf{x}}_{k+1|k}$ and $\hat{\boldsymbol{\theta}}_{k+1|k}$ by using Eqs. (M-8) and (M-9)

$$\hat{\mathbf{x}}_{k+1|k} = \mathbf{A}_k(\hat{\boldsymbol{\theta}}_{k|k})\hat{\mathbf{x}}_{k|k} + \mathbf{B}_k(\hat{\boldsymbol{\theta}}_{k|k})\mathbf{u}_k^\tau + \mathbf{c}_k(\hat{\boldsymbol{\theta}}_{k|k}) + \sum_{i \in X} \mathbf{e}^i \operatorname{tr}\left[\mathbf{a}_\theta^i \Sigma_{k|k}^{\theta x}\right] \tag{O-3}$$

and

$$\hat{\boldsymbol{\theta}}_{k+1|k} = \mathbf{D}_k \boldsymbol{\theta}_{k|k} \tag{O-4}$$

Step 5 Get $\Sigma_{k+1|k}$ by using Eqs. (M-16) to (M-19)

$$\Sigma^{xx}_{k+1|k} = A_k \Sigma^{xx}_{k|k} A'_k + A_k \Sigma^{x\theta}_{k|k} (f^x_{\theta k})' + f^x_{\theta k} \Sigma^{\theta x}_{k|k} A_k$$
$$+ f^x_{\theta k} \Sigma^{\theta\theta}_{k|k} (f^x_{\theta k})' + Q_k$$
$$+ \sum_{i \in X} \sum_{j \in X} e^i (e^j)' \operatorname{tr}\left(a^i_\theta \Sigma^{\theta x}_{k|k} a^j_\theta \Sigma^{\theta x}_{k|k} + a^i_\theta \Sigma^{\theta\theta}_{k|k} (a^j_\theta)' \Sigma^{xx}_{k|k}\right) \quad \text{(O-5)}$$

$$\Sigma^{\theta x}_{k+1|k} = D_k \Sigma^{\theta x}_{k|k} A'_k + D_k \Sigma^{\theta\theta}_{k|k} (f^x_{\theta k})' \tag{O-6}$$

$$\Sigma^{\theta\theta}_{k+1|k} = D_k \Sigma^{\theta\theta}_{k|k} D'_k + G_k \tag{O-7}$$

Step 6 For the case in which H is not a function of θ use Eqs. (K-17) to (K-19) to get $\Sigma_{k+1|k+1}$

$$\Sigma^{xx}_{k+1|k+1} = \Sigma^{xx}_{k+1|k} - \Sigma^{xx}_{k+1|k} H'_{k+1} S^{-1}_{k+1} H_{k+1} \Sigma^{xx}_{k+1|k} \tag{O-8}$$

$$\Sigma^{\theta x}_{k+1|k+1} = \left(\Sigma^{x\theta}_{k+1|k}\right)' = \Sigma^{\theta x}_{k+1|k} - \Sigma^{\theta x}_{k+1|k} H'_{k+1} S^{-1}_{k+1} H_{k+1} \Sigma^{xx}_{k+1|k} \tag{O-9}$$

$$\Sigma^{\theta\theta}_{k+1|k+1} = \Sigma^{\theta\theta}_{k+1|k} - \Sigma^{\theta x}_{k+1|k} H'_{k+1} S^{-1}_{k+1} H_{k+1} \Sigma^{x\theta}_{k+1|k} \tag{O-10}$$

Step 7 Update the means $\hat{x}_{k+1|k+1}$ and $\hat{\theta}_{k+1|k+1}$ by using Eqs. (N-7) and (N-8)

$$\hat{x}_{k+1|k+1} = \hat{x}_{k+1|k} + \Sigma^{xx}_{k+1|k} H'_{k+1} S^{-1}_{k+1} \left[y_{k+1} - H_{k+1} \hat{x}_{k+1|k}\right] \tag{O-11}$$

and
$$\hat{\theta}_{k+1|k+1} = \hat{\theta}_{k+1|k} + \Sigma^{\theta x}_{k+1|k} H'_{k+1} S^{-1}_{k+1} \left[y_{k+1} - H_{k+1} \hat{x}_{k+1|k}\right] \tag{O-12}$$

Step 8 Set $k = k + 1$ and get the new $\hat{x}_{k|k}$, $\hat{\theta}_{k|k}$, and $\Sigma_{k|k}$ from the old $\hat{x}_{k+1|k+1}$, $\hat{\theta}_{k+1|k+1}$, and $\Sigma_{k+1|k+1}$. Then repeat steps 1 through 8.

Store the control value u^r_k at each step since it is the optimal control for the sequential certainty-equivalence method.[1]

---

[1] The interested reader may wish to turn back to Sec. 7-3 to see how results from this appendix were used in that example.

APPENDIX
P

THE REESTIMATION METHOD

In this method the econometric model is reestimated each time period with the assumption of perfect measurement of the state vector. Then the certainty-equivalence path is calculated, and the control for the next period only is applied. After the period the model is reestimated and the process continues.

The steps are to repeat the following calculations for each time period beginning with $k = 0$:

1. Generate the random vectors for the system noise $\mathbf{v}_k$ and the measurement noise $\mathbf{w}_{k+1}$.
2. Solve the certainty-equivalence problem from period k to period N and set $\mathbf{u}_k^\tau = \mathbf{u}_k^{CE}$, as given by Eq. (10-30).
3. Obtain the actual value of the state vector with

$$\mathbf{x}_{k+1} = \mathbf{A}\mathbf{x}_k + \mathbf{B}\mathbf{u}_k^\tau + \mathbf{c} + \mathbf{v}_k \tag{P-1}$$

and the actual value of the measurement vector with

$$\mathbf{y}_{k+1} = \mathbf{x}_{k+1} + \mathbf{w}_{k+1} \tag{P-2}$$

(assuming that $\mathbf{H} = \mathbf{I}$).

4. Set

$$\hat{\mathbf{x}}_{k+1|k+1} = \mathbf{y}_{k+1}$$

and estimate $\hat{\boldsymbol{\theta}}_{k+1|k+1}$ by using ordinary least squares on the reduced form or two-stage least squares on the structural form as appropriate.

5. Set

$$\Sigma_{k+1|k+1}^{xx} = 0 \qquad \Sigma_{k+1|k+1}^{\theta x} = 0$$

and obtain $\Sigma_{k+1|k+1}^{\theta\theta}$ from the estimation method used in step 4.

6. Set $k = k + 1$ and get the new $\hat{\mathbf{x}}_{k|k}$, $\hat{\boldsymbol{\theta}}_{k|k}$, and $\Sigma_{k|k}$ from the old $\hat{\mathbf{x}}_{k+1|k+1}$, $\hat{\boldsymbol{\theta}}_{k+1|k+1}$, and $\Sigma_{k+1|k+1}$, respectively. Store $\mathbf{u}_k^\tau$ as $\mathbf{u}_k^{RE}$ since it is the reestimation-method control value. Then repeat steps 1 through 6.

APPENDIX
Q

DETERMINISTIC, CAUTIONARY, AND PROBING COMPONENTS OF THE COST-TO-GO

In this appendix the deterministic, cautionary, and probing components of the approximate cost-to-go are derived.

Begin with the deterministic component in Eq. (10-44), that is, Eq. (10-46)

$$J_{D,N-k} = \omega_k(\mathbf{z}_k, \mathbf{u}_k) + \phi_k(\mathbf{u}_k) + C_{o,k+1} + \gamma_{k+1} \qquad \text{(Q-1)}$$

Recalling that $C_{o,k+1}$ is the deterministic cost-to-go along the nominal path [Eq. (9-17)] and using the fact that $\gamma = 0$ (from Appendix J), we can write the general form of this component as

$$J_{D,N-k} = \omega_k(\mathbf{z}_k, \mathbf{u}_k) + \phi_k(\mathbf{u}_k) + L_N(\mathbf{x}_{o,N}) + \sum_{j=k+1}^{N-1} L_j(\mathbf{x}_{oj}, \mathbf{u}_{oj}) \qquad \text{(Q-2)}$$

For the linear problem at hand one can use Eqs. (10-2) to (10-6) in Eq. (Q-2) to obtain

$$\begin{aligned}J_{D,N-k} &= [\mathbf{x}_k - \tilde{\mathbf{x}}_k]'\mathbf{F}_k[\mathbf{u}_k - \tilde{\mathbf{u}}_k] + \tfrac{1}{2}[\mathbf{u}_k - \tilde{\mathbf{u}}_k]'\Lambda_k[\mathbf{u}_k - \tilde{\mathbf{u}}_k] \\ &+ \tfrac{1}{2}[\mathbf{x}_{o,N} - \tilde{\mathbf{x}}_N]'\mathbf{W}_N[\mathbf{x}_{o,N} - \tilde{\mathbf{x}}_N] + \sum_{j=k+1}^{N-1}\left(\tfrac{1}{2}[\mathbf{x}_{o,j} - \tilde{\mathbf{x}}_j]'\mathbf{W}_j[\mathbf{x}_{oj} - \tilde{\mathbf{x}}_j]\right. \\ &\left. + [\mathbf{x}_{oj} - \tilde{\mathbf{x}}_{oj}]'\mathbf{F}_j[\mathbf{u}_{oj} - \tilde{\mathbf{u}}_j] + \tfrac{1}{2}[\mathbf{u}_{oj} - \tilde{\mathbf{u}}_j]'\Lambda_j[\mathbf{u}_{oj} - \tilde{\mathbf{u}}_j]\right) \qquad \text{(Q-3)}\end{aligned}$$

This expression then provides the deterministic component of the cost-to-go.

Next consider the cautionary term from Eq. (10-47)

$$J_{C,N-k} = \tfrac{1}{2} \operatorname{tr}\left[\mathbf{K}_{k+1}\Sigma_{k+1|k}\right] + \frac{1}{2}\sum_{j=k+1}^{N-1} \operatorname{tr}\left[\mathbf{K}_{j+1}\mathbf{Q}_j^z\right] \qquad (Q\text{-}4)$$

Begin with only the first term in this expression,

$$\begin{aligned}
\operatorname{tr}\left[\mathbf{K}_{k+1}\Sigma_{k+1|k}\right] &= \operatorname{tr}\left(\begin{bmatrix} \mathbf{K}^{xx} & \mathbf{K}^{x\theta} \\ \mathbf{K}^{\theta x} & \mathbf{K}^{\theta\theta} \end{bmatrix}_{k+1} \begin{bmatrix} \Sigma^{xx} & \Sigma^{x\theta} \\ \Sigma^{\theta x} & \Sigma^{\theta\theta} \end{bmatrix}_{k+1|k}\right) \\
&= \operatorname{tr}(\mathbf{K}^{xx}\Sigma^{xx} + \mathbf{K}^{x\theta}\Sigma^{\theta x}) + \operatorname{tr}(\mathbf{K}^{\theta x}\Sigma^{x\theta} + \mathbf{K}^{\theta\theta}\Sigma^{\theta\theta}) \\
&= \operatorname{tr}(\mathbf{K}^{xx}_{k+1}\Sigma^{xx}_{k+1|k}) + 2\operatorname{tr}(\mathbf{K}^{\theta x}_{k+1}\Sigma^{x\theta}_{k+1|k}) + \operatorname{tr}(\mathbf{K}^{\theta\theta}_{k+1}\Sigma^{\theta\theta}_{k+1|k})
\end{aligned} \qquad (Q\text{-}5)$$

Similarly the second term in Eq. (Q-4) can be written as

$$\operatorname{tr}(\mathbf{K}_{j+1}\mathbf{Q}_j^z) = \operatorname{tr}\left(\begin{bmatrix} \mathbf{K}^{xx} & \mathbf{K}^{x\theta} \\ \mathbf{K}^{\theta x} & \mathbf{K}^{\theta\theta} \end{bmatrix}_{j+1} \begin{bmatrix} \mathbf{Q}_j & 0 \\ 0 & \mathbf{G}_j \end{bmatrix}\right) \qquad (Q\text{-}6)$$

This expression uses the assumptions in Eq. (10-10) about the covariance of the system-equation noise terms. From Eq. (Q-6) one obtains

$$\operatorname{tr}(\mathbf{K}_{j+1}\mathbf{Q}_j^z) = \operatorname{tr}(\mathbf{K}^{xx}_{j+1}\mathbf{Q}_j) + \operatorname{tr}(\mathbf{K}^{\theta\theta}_{j+1}\mathbf{G}_j) \qquad (Q\text{-}7)$$

Substitution of Eqs. (Q-5) and (Q-7) into (Q-4) yields

$$\begin{aligned}
J_{C,N-k} = & \tfrac{1}{2}\operatorname{tr}(\mathbf{K}^{xx}_{k+1}\Sigma^{xx}_{k+1|k}) + \operatorname{tr}(\mathbf{K}^{\theta x}_{k+1}\Sigma^{x\theta}_{k+1|k}) + \tfrac{1}{2}\operatorname{tr}(\mathbf{K}^{\theta\theta}_{k+1}\Sigma^{\theta\theta}_{k+1|k}) \\
& + \frac{1}{2}\sum_{j=k+1}^{N-1}\left[\operatorname{tr}(\mathbf{K}^{xx}_{j+1}\mathbf{Q}_j) + \operatorname{tr}(\mathbf{K}^{\theta\theta}_{j+1}\mathbf{G}_j)\right]
\end{aligned} \qquad (Q\text{-}8)$$

which is the cautionary component.

It remains only to evaluate the probing component Eq. (10-48)

$$J_{P,N-k} = \frac{1}{2}\sum_{j=k+1}^{N-1} \operatorname{tr}\left[\mathcal{Q}_{zz,j}\Sigma_{j|j}\right] \qquad (Q\text{-}9)$$

From Eq. (9-37)

$$\mathcal{Q}_{zz,j} = \mathcal{H}'_{uz,j}\mathcal{H}^{-1}_{uu,j}\mathcal{H}_{uz,j} \qquad (Q\text{-}10)$$

For the quadratic linear problem at hand, use Eqs. (H-44) and (H-45) to rewrite Eq. (Q-10) as

$$\mathcal{Q}_{zz} = \left[\mathbf{B}'\mathbf{K}^{xx}\mathbf{A} + \mathbf{F}' \;\Big|\; \mathbf{B}'\left[\mathbf{K}^{xx}\mathbf{f}^x_\theta + \mathbf{K}^{x\theta}\mathbf{D}\right] + \sum_i \mathbf{e}'_i \mathbf{p}^x \mathbf{b}^i_\theta \right]' [\mathbf{B}'\mathbf{K}^{xx}\mathbf{B} + \Lambda]^{-1}$$
$$\times \left[\mathbf{B}'\mathbf{K}^{xx}\mathbf{A} + \mathbf{F}' \;\Big|\; \mathbf{B}'\left[\mathbf{K}^{xx}\mathbf{f}^x_\theta + \mathbf{K}^{x\theta}\mathbf{D}\right] + \sum_i \mathbf{e}'_i \mathbf{p}^x \mathbf{b}^i_\theta \right] \qquad (Q\text{-}11)$$

and $\mathcal{Q}_{zz} = \begin{bmatrix} \mathbf{A} & \mathbf{B} \\ \mathbf{C} & \mathbf{D} \end{bmatrix}$ \qquad (Q-12) where

$$\mathbb{A} = [A'K^{xx}B + F]\mu[B'K^{xx}A + F']$$

$$\mathbb{B} = [B'K^{xx}A + F']'\mu\left[B'[K^{xx}f_\theta^x + K^{x\theta}D] + \sum_i e_i' p^x b_\theta^i\right]$$

$$\mathbb{C} = \left[[D'K^{\theta x} + f_\theta^{x'}K^{xx}]B + \left[\sum_i e_i' p^x b_\theta^i\right]'\right]\mu[B'K^{xx}A + F^x]$$

and

$$\mathbb{D} = \left[[D'K^{\theta x} + f_\theta^{x'}K^{xx}]B + \left[\sum_i e_i' p^x b_\theta^i\right]'\right]\mu\left[B'[K^{xx}f_\theta^x + K^{x\theta}D] + \sum_i e_i' p^x b_\theta^i\right]$$

From Eqs. (Q-9) and (Q-12) we can then determine the probing term

$$J_{P,N-k} = \frac{1}{2} \sum_{j=k+1}^{N-1} \Big\{ \text{tr}([A'K_{j+1}^{xx}B + F]\mu_j[B'K_{j+1}^{xx}A + F']\Sigma_{j|j}^{xx})$$

$$+ 2\,\text{tr}\Big([B'K_{j+1}^{xx}A + F']'\mu_j\Big[B'[K_{j+1}^{xx}f_\theta^x + K_{j+1}^{x\theta}D] + \sum e_i' p^x b_\theta^i\Big]\Sigma_{j|j}^{\theta x}\Big)$$

$$+ \text{tr}\Big(\Big[[D'K_{j+1}^{\theta x} + (f_\theta^x)'K_{j+1}^{xx}]B + \Big[\sum e_i' p^x b_\theta^i\Big]'\Big]\mu_j$$

$$\times \Big[B'[K_{j+1}^{xx}f_\theta^x + K_{j+1}^{x\theta}D] + \sum e_i' p^x b_\theta^i\Big]\Sigma_{j|j}^{\theta\theta}\Big) \quad \text{(Q-13)}$$

APPENDIX R

THE MEASUREMENT-ERROR COVARIANCE

Following the work of Conrad (1977), the revisions of the national-income accounts were used to obtain an estimate of the covariance matrix of the noise term of the measurement equations. This was done by assuming that the latest revision available is the true value and that the difference between this and the initial estimate is the size of the measurement error.

Table R-1 gives the first reported value of GC58, GPI58, and GNP58, and Table R-2 gives the latest revision used in this study (those published in the *Survey of Current Business* on or before the November 1968 issue).

Table R-1 First reported values, billions of 1958 dollars

Quarter	GC58	GPI58	GNP58
64-I	364.5	83.8	567.1
II	369.8	85.2	575.9
III	377.3	86.0	582.6
IV	376.8	90.2	584.7
65-I	385.9	94.7	597.5
II	390.2	93.0	601.4
III	396.7	92.9	609.7
IV	403.3	100.5	624.4
66-I	409.9	100.9	633.6
II	412.2	106.3	643.5
III	418.3	102.5	649.3
IV	418.5	106.4	657.2
67-I	422.0	95.7	656.7
II	430.6	91.3	664.7
III	431.5	96.4	672.0
IV	434.0	103.0	679.6

The difference between these two series, of course, understates the magnitude of the true measurement error. Worse still, they may provide misleading estimates of the true measurement error since those series which have the largest true measurement error may be the most difficult to revise and thus be the series that shows the least revision and therefore the smallest error. So, the measurement errors shown in the revisions in Table R-3 reflect lower bounds on the true measurement error. As this kind of work proceeds, it will be useful to attempt to obtain independent information on the magnitudes of the measurement errors by making detailed studies on some elements of the time series.

A glance at Table R-3 confirms that the revisions are serially correlated and have nonzero means. However, for purposes of this study, we have assumed that the measurement errors have zero means and are uncorrelated over time. For a study which exploits the information in the serial correlation and nonzero means of these statistics see Bar-Shalom and Wall (1978).

The covariance of these time series is given in Table R-4. This is the 3 × 3 matrix used for **R**, the covariance of the measurement noise. There is a slight inconsistency in the components for GNP58 since the model actually uses GNP58 − GNET58, that is, GNP net of net exports. However, the magnitude of this inconsistency is small.

Table R-2 Latest revision, billions of 1958 dollars

Quarter	GC58	GPI58	GNP58
64-I	366.3	85.3	571.1
II	370.7	87.3	578.6
III	378.6	87.6	585.8
IV	379.3	90.8	588.5
65-I	387.9	96.9	601.6
II	393.4	96.8	610.4
III	400.3	99.6	622.5
IV	409.2	103.4	636.6
66-I	415.7	106.1	648.6
II	414.8	109.5	653.3
III	420.0	107.4	659.5
IV	420.6	112.3	667.1
67-I	424.8	99.8	665.7
II	431.2	94.2	669.2
III	431.8	99.3	675.6
IV	434.1	104.7	681.8

Table R-3 Size of revisions, billions of 1958 dollars

Quarter	GC58	GPI58	GNP58
64-I	−1.8	−1.5	−4.0
II	−0.9	−2.1	−2.7
III	−1.3	−1.6	−3.2
IV	−2.5	−0.6	−3.8
65-I	−2.0	−2.2	−4.1
II	−3.2	−3.8	−9.0
III	−3.6	−6.7	−12.8
IV	−5.9	−2.9	−12.2
66-I	−5.8	−5.2	−15.0
II	−2.6	−3.2	−9.8
III	−1.7	−4.9	−10.2
IV	−2.1	−5.9	−9.9
67-I	−2.8	−4.1	−9.0
II	−0.6	−2.9	−4.5
III	−0.3	−2.9	−3.6
IV	−0.1	−1.7	−2.2

Table R-4 Covariance of revisions

	GC58	GPI58	GNP58
GC58	2.71	1.12	5.52
GPI58	1.12	2.78	5.42
GNP58	5.52	5.42	16.22

APPENDIX S

DATA FOR DETERMINISTIC PROBLEM

Quarter	GC58	GPI58	YN	GNET58	GGE58
47-I	203.4	51.3	293.3	13.1	38.6
II	207.0	48.9	295.7	13.3	39.8
III	207.4	48.6	296.6	13.0	40.7
IV	207.3	57.1	304.8	9.70	40.3
48-I	208.5	59.8	309.4	7.70	41.1
II	210.7	60.9	317.1	5.80	45.5
III	211.1	61.3	320.2	5.60	47.8
IV	212.8	59.7	323.2	5.50	50.7
49-I	213.2	52.3	316.7	7.80	51.3
II	216.3	45.0	315.0	7.50	53.8
III	216.8	48.6	319.6	6.50	54.2
V	219.7	46.0	319.5	3.80	53.8
50-I	223.5	59.1	336.0	3.60	53.4
II	227.6	66.3	345.1	3.40	51.3
III	238.8	70.8	361.3	1.50	51.7
IV	232.1	81.0	367.8	2.30	54.8
51-I	236.0	71.7	372.1	2.70	64.4
II	230.0	75.1	376.7	4.80	71.7
III	232.0	70.0	381.9	6.80	79.9
IV	233.3	63.0	381.9	6.80	85.6

Quarter	GC58	GPI58	YN	GNET58	GGE58
52-I	233.7	63.8	385.4	6.00	87.8
II	238.1	56.0	385.8	3.80	91.7
III	239.1	58.6	392.3	1.60	94.6
IV	246.8	63.6	404.7	.60	94.4
53-I	250.1	63.4	411.1	1.00	97.7
II	251.5	64.2	415.6	.80	99.9
III	251.1	61.5	412.6	1.10	100.0
IV	250.4	55.7	407.3	1.50	101.3
54-I	250.8	56.3	401.1	1.80	94.1
II	253.3	57.0	399.1	3.00	88.8
III	256.9	59.8	403.9	3.30	87.2
IV	261.9	64.3	411.7	4.00	85.4
55-I	267.6	70.8	423.9	4.10	85.5
II	273.0	75.5	432.7	2.70	84.2
III	276.3	76.9	439.0	3.10	85.8
IV	279.0	78.5	443.6	2.80	85.1
56-I	279.8	75.5	440.4	3.20	85.2
II	280.3	74.5	440.6	5.00	85.8
III	280.8	74.0	439.2	5.30	84.3
IV	284.7	73.3	443.6	6.70	85.7
57-I	286.6	70.5	446.1	7.30	89.0
II	287.0	69.9	446.2	7.00	89.4
III	289.3	70.9	449.2	6.00	89.1
IV	289.7	64.0	443.6	4.60	89.9
58-I	285.6	57.50	435.0	2.5	91.80
II	287.5	56.00	437.0	2.5	93.60
III	291.9	61.60	448.3	2.4	94.80
IV	295.2	68.50	460.3	1.3	96.50
59-I	302.3	70.90	468.7	− .10	95.50
II	307.0	78.50	480.6	− .70	95.10
III	310.0	70.20	474.4	.60	94.30
IV	310.1	75.00	479.2	1.2	94.20
60-I	313.9	79.90	487.6	2.6	93.90
II	317.8	73.50	485.9	3.9	94.70
III	316.5	71.00	482.9	4.5	95.40
IV	316.5	65.20	477.6	6.2	95.90
61-I	316.3	62.40	476.3	6.4	97.60
II	320.5	67.80	487.9	5.0	99.50
III	324.0	71.20	497.2	4.4	102.0
IV	329.6	74.70	507.2	4.7	102.9
62-I	333.5	77.20	516.2	3.5	105.5
II	335.9	79.00	522.7	5.2	107.8
III	340.3	80.60	528.7	4.9	107.8
IV	344.8	80.70	534.1	4.4	108.5
63-I	348.3	78.70	537.2	4.0	110.3
II	350.0	80.50	539.1	5.8	108.7
III	355.1	83.00	548.2	5.5	110.0
IV	356.4	86.90	552.9	7.1	109.6

Quarter	GC58	GPI58	YN	GNET58	GGE58
64-I	366.3	85.30	562.0	9.1	110.4
II	370.7	87.30	570.6	8.0	112.6
III	378.6	87.60	577.4	8.4	111.2
IV	379.3	90.80	580.6	7.9	110.5
65-I	387.9	96.90	596.2	5.4	111.4
II	393.4	96.80	603.4	7.0	113.1
III	400.3	99.60	615.8	6.7	115.9
IV	409.2	103.4	630.9	5.7	118.4
66-I	415.7	106.1	643.3	5.3	121.5
II	414.8	109.5	649.0	4.3	124.7
III	420.0	107.4	655.9	3.6	128.5
IV	420.6	112.3	664.2	2.9	131.3
67-I	424.8	99.80	662.7	3.0	138.1
II	431.2	94.20	666.4	2.8	141.0
III	431.8	99.30	672.5	3.1	141.4
IV	434.1	104.7	680.8	1.0	142.0
68-I	444.9	101.5	692.8	− .10	146.5
II	447.5	107.3	704.0	− .60	149.2
III	455.7	105.8	711.6	.70	150.1
IV	455.4	113.1	719.7	− 1.3	151.2
69-I	460.1	113.1	725.8	− 2.3	152.5

APPENDIX T

SOLUTION TO THE MACROECONOMIC MODEL WITH MEASUREMENT ERROR

This appendix presents the detailed results for one Monte Carlo run of the macroeconomic model with measurement error discussed in Chap. 12. In particular the results are for the fourth Monte Carlo run. Graphical results are displayed in the chapter. This appendix contains both the actual random elements used in the run and the numerical results, so that others can check these results and debug their own computer codes.

T-1 RANDOM ELEMENTS

Four sets of random elements are required for each Monte Carlo run:

1. The system noise terms $\mathbf{v}_k$ in Eq. (12-8) for each time period, $k = 0, 1, \ldots, N-1$
2. The measurement-noise terms $\mathbf{w}_k$ in Eq. (12-9) for each time period, $k = 1, 2, \ldots, N$
3. The initial state-variable measurement error $\boldsymbol{\xi}$, defined by

$$\hat{\mathbf{x}}_{0|0} = \mathbf{x}_0 + \boldsymbol{\xi} \tag{T-1}$$

where $\hat{\mathbf{x}}_{0|0}$ is the initial estimate of the state vector and $\boldsymbol{\xi}$ is the initial-state-variable measurement error

4. The initial-parameter-vector error η, defined by

$$\hat{\theta}_{0|0} = \theta_0 + \eta \tag{T-2}$$

where $\hat{\theta}_{0|0}$ = initial estimate of parameter vector
θ_0 = true value of parameter
η = initial-parameter-vector error

For all the Monte Carlo runs x_0 and θ_0 were set as

$$x_0 = \begin{bmatrix} 460.1 \\ 113.1 \end{bmatrix} \tag{T-3}$$

and

$$\theta_0 = \begin{bmatrix} 1.014 \\ .002 \\ -.004 \\ -1.312 \\ .093 \\ .753 \\ -.100 \\ .448 \end{bmatrix} \tag{T-4}$$

The covariance Q for the additive-error terms [see Eq. (12-10)] was used in the Monte Carlo routine to generate the system noise terms v_k. For Monte Carlo run 4 these values were

$$v_0 = \begin{bmatrix} .27538 \\ 4.2377 \end{bmatrix} \quad v_1 = \begin{bmatrix} 2.8660 \\ 1.4935 \end{bmatrix} \quad v_2 = \begin{bmatrix} 1.2624 \\ 3.9079 \end{bmatrix} \quad v_3 = \begin{bmatrix} 2.2937 \\ 3.6310 \end{bmatrix}$$

$$v_4 = \begin{bmatrix} 1.7421 \\ 1.1975 \end{bmatrix} \quad v_5 = \begin{bmatrix} .36733 \\ .88018 \end{bmatrix} \quad v_6 = \begin{bmatrix} 2.1751 \\ 3.2589 \end{bmatrix} \tag{T-5}$$

The covariance R for the measurement-error term [see Eq. (12-11)] was used to generate the measurement-noise terms w_k. For Monte Carlo run 4 these values were

$$w_1 = \begin{bmatrix} .49625 \\ .93212 \end{bmatrix} \quad w_2 = \begin{bmatrix} .40668 \\ .25947 \end{bmatrix} \quad w_3 = \begin{bmatrix} .12890 \\ .05578 \end{bmatrix} \quad w_4 = \begin{bmatrix} 1.22890 \\ .50955 \end{bmatrix}$$

$$w_5 = \begin{bmatrix} .89972 \\ 1.39700 \end{bmatrix} \quad w_6 = \begin{bmatrix} 1.17250 \\ .71312 \end{bmatrix} \quad w_7 = \begin{bmatrix} .26480 \\ .91895 \end{bmatrix} \tag{T-6}$$

The covariance $\Sigma_{0|0}^{xx}$ for the initial-state vector [see Eq. (12-17)] was used to generate the initial-state-vector measurement error ξ. For Monte Carlo run 4 these values were

$$\xi = \begin{bmatrix} 1.16820 \\ .53328 \end{bmatrix} \tag{T-7}$$

The covariance $\Sigma_{0|0}^{\theta\theta}$ for the initial-parameter vector [see Eq. (12-19)] was used to generate the initial-parameter vector error η. For Monte Carlo run 4 these values were

$$\eta = \begin{bmatrix} .01606 \\ -.00983 \\ -.02613 \\ -1.52010 \\ .00112 \\ .04410 \\ -.02295 \\ -1.33760 \end{bmatrix} \qquad (T\text{-}8)$$

One of the links between these numerical input values and the results which are displayed graphically in Chap. 12 can be seen by using (T-4) and (T-8) in (T-2) to construct

$$\theta_{0|0} = \begin{bmatrix} 1.0301 \\ -.0078 \\ -.0301 \\ -2.8321 \\ .0941 \\ .7971 \\ -.1230 \\ -.8896 \end{bmatrix}$$

The value for parameter a_{11} in this vector is the first element, 1.0301, and this is used for the initial value of the parameter a_{11} in Fig. 12-4 for all three control methods.

T-2 RESULTS

This section presents the results for Monte Carlo run 4. The cost (in thousands) for the three methods for this particular run were

$$\text{Dual} = 23.72 \qquad \text{OLF} = 23.69 \qquad \text{CE} = 23.94$$

The results for this particular run are consistent with the overall results which found the Dual and OLF cost to be close to each other and somewhat better (lower) than the CE solution cost.

The state-variable results are given in Table T-1, the control-variable results are in Table T-2, and the parameter-estimation results are in Table T-3. These results correspond to Figs. 12-1 and 12-2, 12-3, and 12-4 to 12-11, respectively.

Table T-1 State-variable results

Period	Desired	Dual	OLF	CE
		Consumption		
0	460.10	460.10	460.10	460.10
1	463.55	465.04	465.01	465.00
2	467.03	472.64	472.59	472.57
3	470.53	478.72	478.66	478.63
4	474.06	485.90	485.84	485.81
5	477.61	492.62	492.56	492.52
6	481.20	498.04	498.01	497.95
7	484.81	505.38	505.36	505.28
		Investment		
0	113.10	113.10	113.10	113.10
1	113.95	115.44	114.63	114.39
2	114.80	114.62	113.64	113.19
3	115.66	116.72	115.71	115.25
4	116.53	118.19	117.36	116.96
5	117.41	116.93	116.62	116.15
6	118.29	116.19	116.51	115.76
7	119.17	119.12	119.78	118.85

Table T-2 Control-variable results: Government obligations

Period	Desired	Dual	OLF	CE
0	153.64	172.00	180.06	182.50
1	154.80	175.00	178.65	181.30
2	155.96	179.00	181.64	182.91
3	157.13	183.00	183.68	184.08
4	158.31	189.00	185.82	187.54
5	159.49	190.00	184.41	188.28
6	160.69	184.00	179.71	183.39

Table T-3 Parameter-estimation results

Parameter	Period	True	Dual	OLF	CE
a_{11}	0	1.0140	1.0301	1.0301	1.0301
	1	1.0140	1.0306	1.0306	1.0306
	2	1.0140	1.0290	1.0284	1.0286
	3	1.0140	1.0285	1.0278	1.0281
	4	1.0140	1.0270	1.0262	1.0268
	5	1.0140	1.0263	1.0257	1.0263
	6	1.0140	1.0263	1.0257	1.0263
	7	1.0140	1.0263	1.0257	1.0263
a_{12}	0	.0020	− .0078	− .0078	− .0078
	1	.0020	− .0089	− .0087	− .0087
	2	.0020	− .0055	− .0048	− .0054
	3	.0020	− .0047	− .0039	− .0047
	4	.0020	− .0023	− .0018	− .0031
	5	.0020	− .0014	− .0010	− .0024
	6	.0020	− .0014	− .0011	− .0025
	7	.0020	− .0014	− .0011	− .0024
b_1	0	− .0040	− .0301	− .0301	− .0301
	1	− .0040	− .0316	− .0316	− .0317
	2	− .0040	− .0275	− .0258	− .0263
	3	− .0040	− .0260	− .0237	− .0247
	4	− .0040	− .0214	− .0185	− .0202
	5	− .0040	− .0195	− .0169	− .0186
	6	− .0040	− .0195	− .0171	− .0187
	7	− .0040	− .0194	− .0171	− .0187
c_1	0	− 1.3120	− 2.8321	− 2.8321	− 2.8321
	1	− 1.3120	− 2.7819	− 2.7989	− 2.8011
	2	− 1.3120	− 2.9199	− 2.9537	− 2.9270
	3	− 1.3120	− 2.9636	− 3.0079	− 2.9672
	4	− 1.3120	− 3.0985	− 3.1565	− 3.0921
	5	− 1.3120	− 3.1477	− 3.2125	− 3.1396
	6	− 1.3120	− 3.1473	− 3.2018	− 3.1366
	7	− 1.3120	− 3.1492	− 3.1948	− 3.1366
a_{21}	0	.0930	.0941	.0941	.0941
	1	.0930	.0913	.0900	.0899
	2	.0930	.0910	.0895	.0896
	3	.0930	.0892	.0876	.0878
	4	.0930	.0875	.0859	.0863
	5	.0930	.0868	.0854	.0858
	6	.0930	.0871	.0856	.0860
	7	.0930	.0870	.0858	.0860

Table T-3 Parameter-estimation results

Parameter	Period	True	Dual	OLF	CE
a_{22}	0	.7530	.7971	.7971	.7971
	1	.7530	.8027	.8036	.8033
	2	.7530	.8033	.8044	.8039
	3	.7530	.8062	.8068	.8059
	4	.7530	.8089	.8091	.8078
	5	.7530	.8098	.8098	.8085
	6	.7530	.8095	.8095	.8082
	7	.7530	.8093	.8094	.8080
b_2	0	−.1000	−.1230	−.1230	−.1230
	1	−.1000	−.1152	−.1118	−.1116
	2	−.1000	−.1145	−.1105	−.1107
	3	−.1000	−.1089	−.1043	−.1047
	4	−.1000	−.1035	−.0988	−.0996
	5	−.1000	−.1016	−.0971	−.0980
	6	−.1000	−.1026	−.0980	−.0989
	7	−.1000	−.1008	−.0969	−.0974
c_2	0	.4480	−.8896	−.8896	−.8896
	1	.4480	−1.1525	−1.1382	−1.1142
	2	.4480	−1.1751	−1.1690	−1.1355
	3	.4480	−1.3435	−1.3341	−1.2837
	4	.4480	−1.4988	−1.4949	−1.4294
	5	.4480	−1.5487	−1.5507	−1.4798
	6	.4480	−1.5185	−1.5060	−1.4450
	7	.4480	−1.6254	−1.6312	−1.5580

Table T-4 contains the approximate cost-to-go for periods 0, 1, and 6. These results correspond to Figs. 12-12, 12-13, and 12-18. A discussion of these results is given in Chap. 12 along with the figures.

Table T-4 Approximate cost-to-go and its components

Government obligations	Deterministic	Cautionary	Probing	Total
		Period 0		
100.00	16,219.92	5342.64	2187.56	23,750.12
105.00	15,778.62	5419.73	2198.98	23,397.32
110.00	15,364.90	5497.78	2208.72	23,071.40
115.00	14,978.76	5576.80	2216.46	22,772.02
120.00	14,620.20	5656.79	2221.86	22,498.86
125.00	14,289.22	5737.75	2224.63	22,251.61
130.00	13,985.82	5819.69	2224.47	22,029.98
135.00	13,710.01	5902.59	2221.13	21,833.73
140.00	13,461.77	5986.46	2214.41	21,662.64
145.00	13,241.11	6071.30	2204.15	21,516.57

Table T-4 Approximate cost-to-go and its components

Government obligations	Deterministic	Cautionary	Probing	Total
Period 0				
150.00	13,048.04	6157.11	2190.27	21,395.42
155.00	12,882.54	6243.89	2172.74	21,299.18
160.00	12,744.63	6331.65	2151.62	21,227.89
165.00	12,634.29	6420.37	2127.02	21,181.68
166.00	12,615.54	6438.23	2121.69	21,175.46
167.00	12,597.88	6456.13	2116.24	21,170.25
168.00	12,581.33	6474.07	2110.66	21,166.06
169.00	12,565.89	6492.04	2104.95	21,162.88
170.00	12,551.54	6510.06	2099.12	21,160.72
171.00	12,538.30	6528.11	2093.17	21,159.58
172.00	12,526.16	6546.21	2087.09	21,159.46
173.00	12,515.13	6564.34	2080.90	21,160.37
174.00	12,505.20	6582.51	2074.59	21,162.30
175.00	12,496.37	6600.72	2068.17	21,165.26
180.00	12,468.78	6692.35	2034.45	21,195.57
185.00	12,468.76	6784.95	1998.27	21,251.99
190.00	12,496.33	6878.52	1960.00	21,334.86
195.00	12,551.48	6973.07	1919.98	21,444.53
Period 1				
100.00	13,275.01	5252.92	1367.78	19,895.72
105.00	12,837.21	5297.48	1377.31	19,512.00
110.00	12,427.19	5342.93	1385.71	19,155.84
115.00	12,044.97	5389.27	1392.74	18,826.98
120.00	11,690.54	5436.50	1398.17	18,525.22
125.00	11,363.91	5484.62	1401.79	18,250.32
130.00	11,065.07	5533.63	1403.38	18,002.08
135.00	10,794.02	5583.52	1402.77	17,780.32
140.00	10,550.76	5634.31	1399.82	17,584.89
145.00	10,335.30	5685.99	1394.41	17,415.70
150.00	10,147.63	5738.56	1386.50	17,272.69
155.00	9,987.76	5792.01	1376.06	17,155.83
160.00	9,855.67	5846.36	1363.15	17,067.18
165.00	9,751.38	5901.59	1347.85	17,000.83
170.00	9,674.89	5957.72	1330.30	16,962.91
171.00	9,662.92	5969.05	1326.54	16,958.51
172.00	9,652.07	5980.42	1322.69	16,955.18
173.00	9,642.33	5991.82	1318.76	16,952.92
174.00	9,633.70	6003.26	1314.76	16,951.72
175.00	9,626.18	6014.74	1310.68	16,951.60
176.00	9,619.78	6026.25	1306.52	16,952.55
177.00	9,614.48	6037.79	1302.29	16,954.57
178.00	9,610.30	6049.37	1297.99	16,957.67
179.00	9,607.23	6060.99	1293.63	16,961.85
180.00	9,605.27	6072.64	1289.19	16,967.10

Table T-4 Approximate cost-to-go and its components

Government obligations	Deterministic	Cautionary	Probing	Total
\multicolumn{5}{c}{Period 1}				
185.00	9,612.16	6131.44	1266.07	17,009.66
190.00	9,646.83	6191.12	1241.57	17,079.52
195.00	9,709.30	6251.69	1215.94	17,176.93
\multicolumn{5}{c}{Period 6}				
100.00	29,380.71	2299.60	0.00	31,680.31
105.00	28,514.79	2224.35	0.00	30,739.13
110.00	27,701.15	2154.75	0.00	29,855.90
115.00	26,939.79	2090.82	0.00	29,030.61
120.00	26,230.72	2032.55	0.00	28,263.27
125.00	25,573.93	1979.95	0.00	27,553.88
130.00	24,969.42	1933.00	0.00	26,902.43
135.00	24,417.20	1891.72	0.00	26,308.92
140.00	23,917.26	1856.10	0.00	25,773.36
145.00	23,469.61	1826.14	0.00	25,295.74
150.00	23,074.24	1801.84	0.00	24,876.07
155.00	22,731.15	1783.20	0.00	24,514.35
160.00	22,440.34	1770.22	0.00	24,210.57
165.00	22,201.82	1762.91	0.00	23,964.73
170.00	22,015.59	1761.26	0.00	23,776.84
175.00	21,881.63	1765.27	0.00	23,646.90
180.00	21,799.96	1774.94	0.00	23,574.90
181.00	21,789.90	1777.55	0.00	23,567.45
182.00	21,781.93	1780.39	0.00	23,562.32
183.00	21,776.06	1783.46	0.00	23,559.51
184.00	21,772.27	1786.75	0.00	23,559.02
185.00	21,770.57	1790.27	0.00	23,560.84
186.00	21,770.97	1794.02	0.00	23,564.99
187.00	21,773.46	1797.99	0.00	23,571.45
188.00	21,778.04	1802.19	0.00	23,580.23
189.00	21,784.71	1806.61	0.00	23,591.32
190.00	21,793.47	1811.26	0.00	23,604.74
195.00	21,868.65	1837.92	0.00	23,706.57

REFERENCES

Abel, Andrew B. (1975): A Comparison of Three Control Algorithms to the Monetarist-Fiscalist Debate, *Ann. Econ. Soc. Meas.*, **4**(2):239–252, Spring.
Ando, Albert, Alfred Norman, and Carl Palash (1978): On the Application of Optimal Control to a Large Scale Econometric Model, in "Applied Optimal Control," vol. 9 in A. Bensoussan, T. Kleindorfer, and S. H. S. Tapiero (eds.), "Studies in the Management Sciences," North-Holland, Amsterdam.
Aoki, Masanao (1967): "Optimization of Stochastic Systems," Academic, NY.
―――(1973): Sufficient Conditions for Optimal Stabilization Policies, *Rev. Econ. Stud.*, **40**:131–138, January.
―――(1974): Noninteracting Control of Macroeconomic Variables: Implication on Policy Mix Considerations, *J. Econometr.*, **2**(4):261–281.
―――(1974b): Stochastic Control Theory in Economics: Applications and New Problems, *IFAC Symp. Stochastic Control, Budapest*.
―――(1976): "Dynamic Economic Theory and Control in Economics," American Elsevier, New York.
Arrow, Kenneth J. (1968): Applications of Control Theory to Economic Growth, *Lect. Appl. Math. Math. Decision Sci.*, pt. 2, vol. 12, American Mathematical Society, Providence, R.I.
Ashley, Richard Arthur (1976): Postponed Linear Approximation in Stochastic Multiperiod Problems, Ph.D. dissertation, University of California, Department of Economics, San Diego.

———— (1979): Postponed Linear Approximations and Adaptive Control with Non-quadratic Losses, *J. Econ. Dynam. Control*, **1**(4):347–360, November.

Athans, Michael (1972): The Discrete Time Linear-Quadratic-Gaussian Stochastic Control Problem, *Ann. Econ. Soc. Meas.*, **1**(4):449–492.

————, and Peter L. Falb (1966): "Optimal Control," McGraw-Hill, New York.

————, and D. Kendrick (1974): Control Theory and Economics: A Survey, Forecast, and Speculations, *IEEE Trans. Autom. Control*, **19**(5):518–523, October.

————, Richard Ku, and Stanley B. Gershwin (1977): The Uncertainty Threshold Principle, *IEEE Trans. Autom. Control*, June, **AC-22**:491–495.

————, Edwin Kuh, Lucas Papademos, Robert Pindyck, Richard Ku, Turgay Ozkan, and Kent Wall (1975): Sequential Open Loop Optimal Control of a Nonlinear Macroeconomic Model, *3d World Congr. Econometric Soc.*, Toronto.

————, R. P. Wishner, and A. Bertolini (1968): Suboptimal State Estimation for Continuous Time Nonlinear Systems with Discrete Noise Measurements, *IEEE Trans. Autom. Control*, **13**(5):504–514, October.

Ayres, Frank, Jr. (1962): "Theory and Problems of Matrices," Schaum, Waltham, Mass.

Bar-Shalom, Yaakov, and R. Sivan (1969): On the Optimal Control of Discrete-Time Linear Systems with Random Parameters, *IEEE Trans. Autom. Control*, **AC-14**:3–8, February.

————, and Edison Tse (1976*a*): Caution, Probing and the Value of Information in the Control of Uncertain Systems, *Ann. Econ. Soc. Meas.*, **5**(2):323–338, Spring.

————, and ———— (1976*b*): Concepts and Methods in Stochastic Control, *Control Dynam. Syst.: Adv. Theory Appl.*, **12**:99–172.

————, ————, and R. E. Larson (1974): Some Recent Advances in the Development of Closed-Loop Stochastic Control and Resource Allocation Algorithms, *Proc. IFAC Symp. Adaptive Control*, Budapest.

————, and Kent Wall (1978): Effect of Uncertainties on the Adaptive Control of Macroeconomic Systems, *International Federation of Automatic Control (IFAC) Conference*, Sweden, 1978.

Bellman, Richard (1957): "Dynamic Programming," Princeton University Press, Princeton, N.J.

————, and Stuart Dreyfus (1962): "Applied Dynamic Programming," Princeton University Press, Princeton, N.J.

Bogaard, P. J. M. van den, and H. Theil (1959): Macrodynamic Policy Making: An Application of Strategy and Certainty Equivalence Concepts to the Economy of the United States, 1933–36, *Metroeconomica*, **11**:149–167.

Bowman, H. Woods, and Anne Marie Laporte (1972): Stochastic Optimization in Recursive Equation Systems and Random Parameters, *Ann. Econ. Soc. Meas.*, **1**(4):419–436.

Bray, Jeremy (1974): Predictive Control of a Stochastic Model of the U.K. Economy Simulating Present Policy Making Practice by the U.K. Government, *Ann. Econ. Soc. Meas.*, **3**(1):239–256, January.

———— (1975): Optimal Control of a Noisy Economy with the U.K. as an Example, *J. Statist. Soc.*, **138A**:339–366.

Brito, D. L., and D. D. Hester (1974): Stability and Control of the Money Supply, *Q. J. Econ.*, **88**(2):278–303, May.

Bryson, Arthur E., Jr., and Yu-Chi Ho (1969): "Applied Optimal Control," Blaisdell, Waltham, Mass.

Burger, Albert E., Lionel Kalish III, and Christopher T. Babb (1971): Money Stock Control and Its Implications for Monetary Policy, *Fed. Reserv. Bank St. Louis Rev.*, **53**:6–22, October.

Cheng, David C., and San Wan (1972): Time Optimal Control of Inflation, Georgia Institute of Technology, College of Industrial Management (photocopy).

Chow, Gregory C. (1967): Multiplier, Accelerator, and Liquidity Preference in the Determination of National Income in the United States, *Rev. Econ. Statist.*, **49**(1):1–15, February.

———— (1970): Optimal Stochastic Control of Linear Economic Systems, *J. Money Credit Banking*, **1**:411–425.

———— (1972): How Much Could Be Gained by Optimal Stochastic Control Policies, *Ann. Econ. Soc. Meas.*, **1**(4):391–406.

———— (1973): Effect of Uncertainty on Optimal Control Policies, *Int. Econ. Rev.*, **14**:632–645.

———— (1975): "Analysis and Control of Dynamic Systems," Wiley, New York.

Conrad, William E. (1977): Imperfect Observation and Systematic Policy Error, *Ann. Econ. Soc. Meas.*, **6**:3.

Cooper, J. Phillip, and Stanley Fischer (1975): A Method for Stochastic Control of Nonlinear Econometric Models and an Application, *Econometrica*, **4**(1):147–162, January.

Craine, Roger, Arthur Havenner, and Peter Tinsley (1976): Optimal Macroeconomic Control Policies, *Ann. Econ. Soc. Meas.*, **5**(2):191–203, Spring.

Curry, R. E. (1969): A New Algorithm for Suboptimal Stochastic Control, *IEEE Trans. Autom. Control*, **AC-14**:533–536.

Davidon, W. C. (1959): Variable Metric Method for Minimization, *AEC Res. Dev. Rep. ANL-5990*.

Denham, W. (1964): Choosing the Nominal Path for a Dynamic System with Random Forcing Function to Optimize Statistical Performance, *Harvard Univ. Div. Eng. Appl. Phys.*, TR449.

Dersin, Pierre, Michael Athans, and David A. Kendrick (1979): Some Properties of the Dual Adaptive Stochastic Control Algorithm, *M.I.T. Lab. Inf. Decis. Sci.*, LIDS-P-936, August.

Deshpande, J. G., T. N. Upadhyay, and D. G. Lainoitis (1973): Adaptive Control of Linear Stochastic Systems, *Automatica*, **9**:107–115, January.

Dobell, A. R. (1969): Some Characteristic Features of Optimal Problems in Economic Theory, *IEEE Trans. Autom. Control*, **AC-14**(1):39–46, February.

———— and Y. C. Ho (1967): Optimal Investment Policy: An Example of a

Control Problem in Economic Theory, *IEEE Trans. Autom. Control*, AC-12(1):4–14, February.

Drud, Arne (1976): "Methods for Control of Complex Dynamic Systems," *Tech. Univ. Denmark, Inst. Math. Statist. Oper. Res.*, no. 27.

―――― (1977): An Optimization Code for Nonlinear Econometric Models Based on Sparse Matrix Techniques and Reduced Gradients, I: Theory, Technical University of Denmark, Department of Mathematical Statistics and Operations Research (photocopy).

Eijk, C. J. van, and J. Sandee (1959): Quantitative Determination of an Optimal Economic Policy, *Econometrica*, **27**:1–13.

Erickson, D. L. (1968): Sensitivity Constrained Optimal Control Policies for a Dynamic Model of the U.S. National Economy, Ph.D. dissertation, University of California, School of Engineering, Los Angeles.

――――, C. T. Leondes, and F. E. Norton (1970): Optimal Decision and Control Policies in the National Economy, *Proc. 9th IEEE Symp. Adaptive Process. Decis. Control, Univ. Texas, Austin, December*, pp. XII.2.1–XII.2.6.

――――, and F. E. Norton (1973): Application of Sensitivity Constrained Optimal Control to National Economic Policy, *Control Dynam. Syst.*, **9**:131–237.

Fair, Ray C. (1974): On the Solution of Optimal Control Problems as Maximization Problems, *Ann. Econ. Soc. Meas.*, 3(1):135–154, January.

―――― (1976): "A Model of Macroeconomic Activity," vol. II; "The Empirical Model," Ballinger, Cambridge, Mass.

―――― (1978a): The Effects of Economic Events on Votes for President, *Rev. Econ. Statist.*, **60**:159–173, May.

―――― (1978b): The Use of Optimal Control Techniques to Measure Economic Performance, *Int. Econ. Rev.*, **19**:289–309, June.

Farison, J. B., R. E. Graham, and R. C. Shelton (1967): Identification and Control of Linear Discrete Systems, *IEEE Trans. Autom. Control*, AC-12(4):438–442, August.

Fischer, Joachim, and Götz Uebe (1975): Stability and Optimal Control of a Large Linearized Econometric Model for Germany, Technische Universität München, Institut für Statistik und Unternehmensforschung (photocopy).

Fisher, W. D. (1962): Estimation in the Linear Decision Model, *Int. Econ. Rev.*, **3**:1–29.

Fitzgerald, V. W., H. N. Johnston, and A. J. Bayes (1973): An Interactive Computing Algorithm for Optimal Policy Selection with Nonlinear Econometric Models, Commonwealth Bureau of Census and Statistics, Canberra, Australia (photocopy).

Fletcher, R., and M. J. D. Powell (1963): A Rapidly Convergent Descent Method of Minimization, *Comp. J.*, **6**:163–168.

――――, and C. M. Reeves (1964): Function Minimization for Conjugate Gradients, *Br. Comput. J.*, **7**:149–154, July.

Friedman, Benjamin M. (1972): Optimal Economic Stabilization Policy: An Extended Framework, *J. Polit. Econ.*, **80**:1002–1022, September-October.

———, and E. Phillip Howrey (1973): Nonlinear Models and Linear Optimal Policies: An Evaluation, *Harvard Inst. Econ. Res., Discuss. Pap.* 316.

Gantmacher, F. R. (1960): "The Theory of Matrices," Chelsea, New York.

Garbade, Kenneth D. (1975*a*): "Discretionary Control of Aggregate Economic Activity," Lexington, Lexington, Mass.

——— (1975*b*): Discretion in the Choice of Macroeconomic Policies, *Ann. Econ. Soc. Meas.*, **4**(2):215–238, Spring.

——— (1976): On the Existence and Uniqueness of Solutions of Multiperiod Linear Quadratic Control Problems, *Int. Econ. Rev.*, **17**(3):719–732, October.

Geraci, Vincent J. (1976): Identification of Simultaneous Equation Models with Measurement Error, *J. Econometr.*, **4**(3):263–283, August.

Gill, P. E., W. Murray, S. M. Picken, H. M. Barber, and H. M. Wright (1976): Subroutine LNSRCH and NEWPTC, National Physical Laboratory, Teddington, NPL Algorithm Library, Ef/16/0 Fortran/02/76.

Goldberger, Arthur S. (1964): "Econometric Theory," Wiley, New York.

Gordon, Roger H. (1974): The Investment Tax Credit as a Supplementary Discretionary Stabilization Tool, Harvard University, Department of Economics, Cambridge, Mass. (photocopy).

Gupta, Surender K., Laurence H. Meyer, Fredric Q. Raines, and Tzyh-Jong Tarn (1975): Optimal Coordination of Aggregate Stabilization Policies: Some Simulation Results, *Ann. Econ. Soc. Meas.*, **4**:253–270, Spring.

Healey, A. J., and F. Medina (1975): Economic Stabilization from the Monetaristic Viewpoint Using the Dynamic Phillips Curve Concept, University of Texas, Department of Mechanical Engineering, Austin (photocopy).

———, and S. Summers (1974): A Suboptimal Method for Feedback Control of the St. Louis Econometric Model, *Trans. ASME, J. Dynam. Syst., Meas. Control*, **96**(4):446–454, December.

Henderson, D. W., and S. J. Turnovsky (1972): Optimal Macroeconomic Policy Adjustment under Conditions of Risk, *J. Econ. Theory*, **4**:58–71.

Holbrook, Robert S. (1973): An Approach to the Choice of Optimal Policy Using Large Econometric Models, *Bank Can. Staff Res. Stud.*, No. 8, Ottawa.

——— (1974): A Practical Method for Controlling a Large Nonlinear Stochastic System, *Ann. Econ. Soc. Meas.*, **3**(1):155–176, January.

——— (1975): Optimal Policy Choice under a Nonlinear Constraint: An Iterative Application of Linear Techniques, *J. Money, Credit Banking*, **7**(1):33–49, February.

Holly, Sean, Berc Rustem, and Martin B. Zarrop (eds.) (1979): "Optimal Control for Econometric Models: An Approach to Economic Policy Formulation," Macmillan, London.

Holt, C. C. (1962): Linear Decision Rules for Economic Stabilization and Growth, *Q. J. Econ.*, **76**:20–45.

IMSL Library 3 (1974): Edition 3 (Fortran 2.4), International Mathematical and Statistical Libraries, 6200 Hilcroft, Suite 510, Houston, Tex.

Intriligator, Michael D. (1971): "Mathematical Optimization and Economic Theory," Prentice-Hall, Englewood Cliffs, N.J.

───── (1975): Applications of Optimal Control Theory in Economics, *Synthese*, **31**:271–288.

Jacobson, D. H., and D. Q. Mayne (1970): "Differential Dynamic Programming." American Elsevier, New York.

Kareken, J. H., T. Muench, and N. Wallace (1973): Optimal Open Market Strategy: The Use of Information Variables, *Am. Econ. Rev.*, **63**:156–172.

Kaul, T. K., and D. S. Rao (1975): Digital Simulation and Optimal Control of International Short-Term Capital Movements, *3d World Congr. Econometric Soc.*, Toronto.

Kendrick, D. A. (1973): Stochastic Control in Macroeconomic Models, *Inst. Elec. Eng. IEEE Conf. publ.* 101, pp. 200–207.

───── (1976): Applications of Control Theory to Macroeconomics, *Ann. Econ. Soc. Meas.*, **5**(2):171–190.

───── (1978): Non-convexities from Probing an Adaptive Control Problem, *J. Econ. Lett.*, **1**:347–351.

───── (1979): Adaptive Control of Macroeconomic Models with Measurement Error, chap. 9 in Holly, Rustem, and Zarrop (1979).

───── (1980): Control Theory with Application to Economics, chap. 4 in Kenneth J. Arrow and Michael D. Intriligator (eds.), "Handbook of Mathematical Economics," North-Holland, Amsterdam.

───── (1980a): "Caution and Probing in Macroeconomic Model," Center for Economic Research, Univ. of Texas, Austin, Texas. Presented at the World Congress of the Econometric Society, Aix-en-Provence, France, August 1980.

─────, and J. Majors (1974): Stochastic Control with Uncertain Macroeconomic Parameters, *Automatica*, **10**(2):587–594.

─────, H. Rao, and C. Wells (1970): Optimal Operation of a System of Waste Water Treatment Facilities, *Proc. 9th IEEE Symp. Adaptive Process. Decis. Control, Univ. Texas, Austin.*

─────, and Lance Taylor (1970): Numerical Solutions of Nonlinear Planning Models, *Econometrica*, **38**(3):453–467.

─────, and ───── (1971): Numerical Methods and Nonlinear Optimizing Models for Economic Planning, chap. 1 in Holls B. Chenery (ed.), "Studies in Development Planning," Harvard University Press, Cambridge, Mass.

Kim, Han K., Louis M. Goreux, and David A. Kendrick (1975): Feedback Control Rule for Cocoa Market Stabilization, chap. 9 in Walter C. Labys (ed.), "Quantitative Models of Commodity Markets," Ballinger, Cambridge, Mass.

Klein, Lawrence R. (1979): Managing the Modern Economy: Econometric Specification, chap. 11 in Holly, Rustem, and Zarrop (1979).

Kmenta, Jan (1971): "Elements of Econometrics," Macmillan, New York.

Ku, R., and M. Athans (1973): On the Adaptive Control of Linear Systems Using the Open Loop Feedback Optimal Approach, *IEEE Trans. Autom. Control*, **AC-18**:489–493.

───── and ───── (1977): Further Results on the Uncertainty Threshold Principle, *IEEE Trans. Autom. Control*, **AC-22**(5):866–868.

Kydland, Finn (1973): Decentralized Macroeconomic Planning, Ph.D. dissertation, Carnegie-Mellon University, Pittsburgh.
_____ (1975): Decentralized Stabilization Policies: Optimization and the Assignment Problem, *Ann. Econ. Soc. Meas.*, **5**(2):249–262.
Lasdon, L. S., S. K. Mitter, and A. D. Warren (1967): The Conjugate Gradient Method for Optimal Control Problems, *IEEE Trans. Autom. Control*, **12**:132–138, April.
Livesey, D. A. (1971): Optimizing Short-Term Economic Policy, *Econ. J.*, **81**:525–546.
_____ (1976): A Minimal Realization of the Leontief Dynamic Input-Output Model, chap. 25 in K. Polenske and J. Skolka (eds.), "Advances in Input-Output Analysis," Ballinger, Cambridge, Mass.
_____ (1977): On the Specification of Unemployment and Inflation in the Objective Function: A Comment, *Ann. Econ. Soc. Meas.*, **6**(3):291–293, Summer.
_____ (1978): Feasible Directions in Economic Policy, *J. Optimization Theory Appl.*, **25**(3):383–406.
MacRae, Elizabeth Chase (1972): Linear Decision with Experimentation, *Ann. Econ. Soc. Meas.*, **1**:437–447.
_____ (1975): An Adaptive Learning Role for Multiperiod Decision Problems, *Econometrica*, **43**(5-6):893–906.
Mantell, J. B., and L. S. Lasdon (1977): Algorithms and Software for Large Econometric Control Problems, *NBER Conf. Econ. Control, New Haven, Conn.*, May.
Miller, Ronald E. (1979): "Dynamic Optimization and Economic Applications," McGraw-Hill, New York.
Murtagh, Bruce A., and Michael A. Saunders (1977): MINOS, A Large-Scale Nonlinear Programming System, *Stanford Univ. Syst. Optimization Lab. Tech. Rep.* SOL 77-9, February.
Norman, A. L. (1976): First Order Dual Control, *Ann. Econ. Soc. Meas.*, **5**(3):311–322, Spring.
_____ (1979): Dual Control of Perfect Observations, pp. 343–349 in J. N. L. Janssen, L. M. Pau, and A. Straszak (eds.), "Models and Decision Making in National Economies," North-Holland, Amsterdam.
_____, and M. R. Norman (1973): Behavioral Consistency Test of Econometric Models, *IEEE Trans. Autom. Control*, **AC-18**:465–472, October.
_____, and Woo Sik Jung (1977): Linear Quadratic Control Theory for Models with Long Lags, *Econometrica*, **45**(4):905–918.
Oudet, B. A. (1976): Use of the Linear Quadratic Approach as a Tool for Analyzing the Dynamic Behavior of a Model of the French Economy, *Ann. Econ. Soc. Meas.*, **5**(2):205–210, Spring.
Pagan, Adrien (1975): Optimal Control of Econometric Models with Autocorrelated Disturbance Terms, *Int. Econ. Rev.*, **16**(1):258–263, February.
Palash, Carl J. (1977): On the Specification of Unemployment and Inflation in the Objective Function, *Ann. Econ. Soc. Meas.*, **6**(3):275–300.
Paryani, K. (1972): Optimal Control of Linear Macroeconomic Systems, Ph.D.

thesis, Michigan State University, Department of Electrical Engineering, East Lansing.

Perry, A. (1976): An Improved Conjugate Gradient Algorithm, *Northwestern Univ. Dept. Decis. Sci. Tech. Note*, Evanston, Ill.

Phelps, Edmund S., and John B. Taylor (1977): Stabilizing Properties of Monetary Policy under Rational Price Expectations, *J. Polit. Econ.*, **85**:163–190, February.

Phillips, A. W. (1954): Stabilization Policy in a Closed Economy, *Econ. J.*, **64**:290–323, June.

―――― (1957): Stabilization Policy and the Time Form of the Lagged Responses, *Econ. J.*, **67**:265–277, June.

Pindyck, Robert S. (1972): An Application of the Linear Quadratic Tracking Problem to Economic Stabilization Policy, *IEEE Trans. Autom. Control*, **AC-17**(3):287–300, June.

―――― (1973a): "Optimal Planning for Economic Stabilization," North-Holland, Amsterdam.

―――― (1973b): Optimal Policies for Economic Stabilization, *Econometrica*, **41**(3):529–560, May.

――――, and Steven M. Roberts (1974): Optimal Policies for Monetary Control, *Ann. Econ. Soc. Meas.*, **3**(1):207–238, January.

Pitchford, John, and Steve Turnovsky (1977): "Application of Control Theory to Economic Analysis," North-Holland, Amsterdam.

Polack, E., and G. Ribière (1969): Note sur la convergence de méthodes de directions conjugées, *Rev. Fr. Inf. Rech. Oper.*, **16RI**:35–43.

Prescott, E. C. (1967): Adaptive Decision Rules for Macroeconomic Planning, doctoral dissertation, Carnegie-Mellon University, Graduate School of Industrial Administration.

―――― (1971): Adaptive Decision Rules for Macroeconomic Planning, *West. Econ. J.*, **9**:369–378.

―――― (1972): The Multi-period Control Problem under Uncertainty, *Econometrica*, **40**:1043–1058.

Preston, A. J., and K. D. Wall (1973): Some Aspects of the Use of State Space Models in Econometrics, *Univ. London, Programme Res. Econometr. Methods Discuss. Pap.* 5.

Rausser, Gordon (1978): Active Learning, Control Theory, and Agricultural Policy, *Amer. J. Agricultural Economics*, **60**(3):476–490, 1978.

――――, and J. Freebairn (1974): Approximate Adaptive Control Solution to the U.S. Beef Trade Policy, *Ann. Econ. Soc. Meas.*, **3**(1):177–204.

Rouzier, P. (1974): "The Evaluation of Optimal Monetary and Fiscal Policy with a Macroeconomic Model for Belgium," Catholic University of Louvain, Belgium, 1974.

Sandblom, C. L. (1970): On Control Theory and Economic Stabilization, Ph.D. dissertation, Lund University, Sweden, National Economy Institution.

―――― (1975): Stabilization of a Fluctuating Simple Macroeconomic Model, *Cybern. Syst. Res.*, **2**:251–262.

Sargent, T. J., and N. Wallace (1975): "Rational" Expectations, the Optimal

Monetary Instrument and the Optimal Money Supply Rule, *J. Polit. Econ.*, **83**:241–254, April.

Sarris, Alexander H., and Michael Athans (1973): Optimal Adaptive Control Methods for Structurally Varying Systems, *Natl. Bur. Econ. Res. Working Pap.* 24, Cambridge, Mass., December.

Shanno, D. F. (1977): Conjugate Gradient Methods with Inexact Searches, *Univ. Arizona Coll. Bus. Public Admin. Manage. Inf. Syst. Working Pap.* Tempe, Ariz.

Shupp, Franklin R. (1972): Uncertainty and Stabilization Policies for a Nonlinear Macroeconomic Model, *Q. J. Econ.*, **80**(1):94–110, February.

―――― (1976a): Optimal Policy Rules for a Temporary Incomes Policy, *Rev. Econ. Stud.*, **43**(2):249–259, June.

―――― (1976b): Uncertainty and Optimal Policy Intensity in Fiscal and Incomes Policies, *Ann. Econ. Soc. Meas.*, **5**(2):225–238, Spring.

―――― (1976c): Uncertainty and Optimal Stabilization Policies, *J. Public Financ.*, **6**(4):243–253, November.

―――― (1977): Social Performance Functions and the Dichotomy Argument: A Comment, *Ann. Econ. Soc. Meas.*, **6**(3):295–300, Summer.

Simon, H. A. (1956): Dynamic Programming under Uncertainty with a Quadratic Criterion Function, *Econometrica*, **24**:74–81, January 1956.

Taylor, J. B. (1973): A Criterion for Multiperiod Control in Economic Models with Unknown Parameters, *Columbia Univ. Dept. Econ. Discuss. Pap.* 73-7406.

―――― (1974): Asymptotic Properties of Multiperiod Control Rules in the Linear Regression Model, *Int. Econ. Rev.*, **15**(2):472–482, June.

Thalberg, Bjorn (1971a): Stabilization Policy and the Nonlinear Theory of the Trade Cycle, *Swed. J. Econ.*, **73**:294–310.

―――― (1971b): A Note on Phillips' Elementary Conclusions on the Problems of Stabilization Policy, *Swed. J. Econ.*, **73**:385–408.

Theil, H. (1957): A Note on Certainty Equivalence in Dynamic Planning, *Econometrica*, **25**:346–349, April.

―――― (1964): "Optimal Decision Rules for Government and Industry," North-Holland, Amsterdam.

―――― (1965): Linear Decision Rules for Macro-dynamic Policy Problems, in B. Hickman (ed.), "Quantitative Planning of Economic Policy," The Brookings Institute, Washington.

―――― (1971): "Principles of Econometrics," Wiley, New York.

Tinsley, P., R. Craine, and A. Havenner (1974): On NEREF Solutions of Macroeconomic Tracking Problems, *3d NBER Stochastic Control Conf.*, Washington.

Tse, Edison, and Michael Athans (1972): Adaptive Stochastic Control for a Class of Linear Systems, *IEEE Trans. Autom. Control*, **AC-17**:38–52, February.

――――, and Y. Bar-Shalom (1973): An Actively Adaptive Control for Linear Systems with Random Parameters, *IEEE Trans. Autom. Control*, **AC-18**:109–117, April.

———, ———, and L. Meier (1973): Wide Sense Adaptive Dual Control for Nonlinear Stochastic Systems, *IEEE Trans. Autom. Control*, **AC-18**:98–108, April.

Turnovsky, Stephen J. (1973): Optimal Stabilization Policies for Deterministic and Stochastic Linear Systems, *Rev. Econ. Stud.*, **40**(121):79–96, January.

——— (1974): Stability Properties of Optimal Economic Policies, *Am. Econ. Rev.*, **44**:136–147.

——— (1975): Optimal Choice of Monetary Instruments in a Linear Economic Model with Stochastic Coefficients, *J. Money Credit Banking*, **7**:51–80.

——— (1977): Optimal Control of Linear Systems with Stochastic Coefficients and Additive Disturbances, chap. 11, in Pitchford and Turnovsky (1977).

Tustin, A. (1953): "The Mechanism of Economic Systems," Harvard University Press, Cambridge, Mass.

Upadhyay, Treveni (1975): Application of Adaptive Control to Economic Stabilization Policy, *Int. J. Syst. Sci.*, **6**(10):641–650.

Wall, K. D., and J. H. Westcott (1974): Macroeconomic Modelling for Control, *IEEE Trans. Autom. Control*, **AC-19**:862–873, December.

———, and ——— (1975): Policy Optimization Studies with a Simple Control Model of the U.K. Economy, *Proc. IFAC/75 Congress, Boston and Cambridge, Mass.*

Walsh, Peter, and J. B. Cruz (1975): Neighboring Stochastic Control of an Econometric Model, *4th NBER Stochastic Control Conf., Cambridge, Mass.*

Woodside, M. (1973): Uncertainty in Policy Optimization: Experiments on a Large Econometric Model, *Inst. Elect. Eng. IEE Conf. Publ.* 101. pp. 418–429.

You, Jong Keun (1975): A Sensitivity Analysis of Optimal Stochastic Control Policies, *4th NBER Stochastic Control Conf., Cambridge, Mass.*

Zellner, Arnold (1966): On Controlling, and Learning about a Normal Regression Model, University of Chicago, School of Business, Chicago (photocopy).

——— (1971): "An Introduction to Bayesian Inference in Econometrics," Wiley, New York.

———, and M. V. Geisel (1968): Sensitivity of Control to Uncertainty and Form of the Criterion Function, pp. 269–283 in D. G. Watts (ed.), "The Future of Statistics," Academic, New York.

INDEX

Abel, Andrew B., 64, 126*n*., 228
Active-learning stochastic control (*see* Learning, active)
Adaptive control, 2, 63, 64, 68, 120, 122, 125
Additive error terms, 39–40
Additive uncertainty, 35–40
Agricultural problems, 41
Ando, Albert, 17*n*., 24*n*., 228
Aoki, Masanao, 1, 2, 43*n*., 50*n*., 52*n*., 69, 228
Arrow, Kenneth J., 1, 228
Ashley, Richard Arthur, 40, 228
Astrom, Karl, 37
Athans, Michael, xi, 1, 2, 17*n*., 36*n*., 40, 43*n*., 50*n*., 64, 87*n*., 131*n*., 158, 162, 229, 230, 233, 236
Augmented state vector, 9, 202–207
Augmented system, 93–94
  matrix recursions for, 179–187
  vector recursions for, 188–192
Ayres, Frank, Jr., 153, 229

Babb, Christopher T., 52*n*., 230
Backward integration, 48, 71–72
Bacon, Francis, 61
Barber, H. M., 232
Bar-Shalom, Yaakov, x, xi, 37, 38, 43*n*., 50*n*., 64, 70, 73–76, 79, 82, 85*n*., 90, 91, 96*n*., 97, 105, 113*n*., 121, 122, 131, 149, 159, 162*n*., 216, 229, 237
  (*See also* BTL; TBM)
Bayes, A. J., 17*n*., 231
Bellman, Richard, 11*n*., 229
Bensoussan, A., 228
Bertolini, A., 87*n*., 158, 162, 229
Bogaard, P. J. M. van der, 8*n*., 229
Bowman, H. Woods, 52*n*., 229
Bray, Jeremy, 40*n*., 229
Brito, D. L., 40*n*., 230
Bryson, Arthur E., Jr., 2, 5, 23*n*., 88, 152–157, 230
BTL (Bar-Shalom, Tse, and Larson), 43*n*., 74*n*., 79, 82, 85*n*., 149, 159, 161, 229
Buffer-stock level, ix, 11–12

Burger, Albert E., 52*n*., 230

Cautionary term (component), 70, 71, 97, 98, 102, 103, 111, 113, 114, 131–139, 211–212, 225
CE (*see* Certainty equivalence)
Certainty equivalence (CE), 35, 36, 40, 67, 68, 76, 95, 102, 109, 120–123, 208
  heuristic, 50
  optimal cost-to-go problem, 177–178
  sequential, 50, 56, 122, 124, 208–209, 222
  update, 50
Chenery, Hollis B., 233
Cheng, David C., 17*n*., 230
Chow, Gregory, 1, 7, 40*n*., 43*n*., 50*n*., 52*n*., 64, 72, 73, 230
Closed-loop policy, 39, 75
Commodity stabilization, ix, 11, 12
Conditional distribution, 153
Conjugate gradient, 24, 77
Conrad, William E., 116, 214, 230
Consumption, 6, 8, 10, 26, 27, 117–119, 123, 136, 139, 223
Continuous-time problems, 5, 17
Control variables, 6–10
Control vector, 11
Cooper, J. Phillip, 52*n*., 230
Cost-to-go, 43, 69, 71, 76, 96, 107, 131–138, 159–161, 193–194, 211–213, 225
  deterministic, 43, 211
  expected, 43
  optimal, 10–13, 44–46, 70, 77–79, 177–178
  random, 64
Costate equations, 18, 23
Costate variables, 23
Covariance matrices:
  projection of, 85–89
  updating, 90
Craine, Roger, 8*n*., 17*n*., 230, 236
Criterion function, 31–32
  quadratic, 31–32
Cruz, J. B., 52*n*., 237

238

Curry, R. E., 43n., 50n., 230

Davidon, W. C., 24n., 230
Denham, W., 40n., 230
Dersin, Pierre, 131n., 230
Deshpande, J. G., 64, 230
Deterministic control, 2, 5—32, 67
   examples of, 26—32
      criterion function, 31—32
      system equations, 26—31
   nonlinear problems (see **Nonlinear problems**)
   quadratic linear problems (see **Quadratic linear problems**)
Deterministic cost-to-go, 43, 211
Deterministic problem, data for, 217—219
Deterministic term (component), 70, 71, 97, 98, 101, 103, 110, 113, 114, 131—139, 211, 225
Difference equations:
   first-order, 8, 9
   nth-order, 6, 7, 9
   second-order, 8
Discrete-time problems, 5
Dobell, A. R., 1, 231
Dreyfus, Stuart, 11n., 229
Drud, Arne, 25, 231
Dual control, 2, 63, 121, 122, 124, 126n., 222
Dual-control algorithm, 98—104
Dynamic programming, 6, 10—13, 43, 76

Eijk, C. J. van, 8n., 231
Endogenous variables, 29
Erickson, D. L., 8n., 231
Error terms, additive, 39—40
Expected cost-to-go, 43
Expected values of matrix products, 49—50
Expenditure, government, 6, 10, 26, 27, 136
Explicit form, 19, 24

Fair, Ray C., 17n., 231
Falb, Peter L., 2, 229
Farison, J. B., 43n., 231
Feedback-gain matrices, 48
Feedback policy, 38, 75
Feedback rule, 6, 11, 12, 14
   for deterministic problems, 15, 16, 178
   for stochastic problems, 40, 47, 48
Fiscal policy, ix, 117
Fischer, Joachim, 8n., 231
Fischer, Stanley, 52n., 230
Fisher, W. D., 1, 52n., 231
Fitzgerald, V. W., 17n., 231
Fletcher, R., 24n., 231
Forward integration, 72
Freebairn, J., 50n., 64, 235
Friedman, Benjamin M., 8n., 17n., 32n., 231

Gantmacher, F. R., 154, 232
Garbade, Kenneth D., 19n., 40, 232
Geisel, M. V., 52n., 237
Generalized reduced gradient (GRG), 25
Geraci, Vincent J., 36n., 116, 232
Gershwin, Stanley B., 229
Gill, P. E., 24, 232
Goldberger, Arthur S., 146, 147, 173n., 232
Gordon, Roger H., 40n., 232
Goreux, Louis M., 12n., 40, 233
Government expenditure, 6, 10, 26, 27, 136
Government obligations, 10, 30, 117, 125, 132—138, 223, 225
Government taxation, 6
Gradient conjugate, 24, 77
Gradient methods, 71, 76
   for nonlinear problems, 22—24
Gradient vector, 143, 180, 181, 184
Graham, R. E., 43n., 231
Grid search (see Search, grid)
Gross national product, 6, 10, 26, 27
Gupta, Surender K., 17n., 232

Hamiltonian, 23
Havenner, Arthur, 8n., 17n., 230, 236
Healey, A. J., 17n., 232
Henderson, D. W., 52n., 232
Hessians, 145
Hester, D. D., 40n., 230
Heuristic certainty equivalence, 50
Hewett, Ed, xi
Ho, Yu-Chi, 1, 2, 5, 23n., 88, 152—157, 230
Holbrook, Robert S., 17n., 232
Holly, Sean, 232
Holt, Charles C., 1, 8n., 232
Howrey, E. Phillip, 17n., 232

Identifiability, 29
Identification, 29—30
Implicit form, 19, 24
IMSL (International Mathematical and Statistical Libraries), 76, 232
Inflation, ix, 6
Initial conditions, 23
Initialization, 101, 107
Integration:
   backward, 48, 71—72
   forward, 72
Interest rates, 8
International Mathematical and Statistical Libraries (IMSL), 76, 232
Intriligator, Michael D., xi, 1, 10n., 17n., 233
Inventory, ix, 117
Investment, ix, 6, 10, 26, 27, 117, 119, 123, 124, 136, 223
   inventory, 117

Investment (*Cont.*):
  nonresidential, 8
  residential, 8

Jacobians, 145
Jacobson, D. H., 40, 233
Johnston, H. N., 17*n.*, 231
Joint distribution, 153
Jung, Woo Sik, 9, 72, 234

Kalish, Lionel, III, 52*n.*, 230
Kalman filter, 87, 88, 101, 104, 120*n.*, 130
  second-order, 90, 152–158
Kang, Bo Hyun, vii, xi, 74, 91
Kareken, J. H., 40*n.*, 233
Kaul, T. K., 8*n.*, 233
Kendrick, David A., xi, 1, 12*n.*, 23*n.*, 24*n.*, 40, 52*n.*, 64, 76, 77, 113*n.*, 119*n.*, 126*n.*, 131*n.*, 229, 230, 233
Kim, Han K., 12*n.*, 40, 233
Kirkland, Connie, xi
Klein, Lawrence R., 17*n.*, 233
Kleindorfer, T., 228
Kmenta, Jan, 29*n.*, 30*n.*, 233
Ku, Richard, 43*n.*, 50*n.*, 229, 233
Kuh, Edwin, 229
Kydland, Finn, 234

Lagrangian variable, 23
Lags, second-order, 8
Lainoitis, D. G., 64, 230
Lane, Susan, xi
Laporte, Anne Marie, 52*n.*, 229
Larson, R. E., 43*n.*, 74*n.*, 79, 82, 85*n.*, 149, 159, 229
  (*See also* BTL)
Lasdon, Leon S., 24*n.*, 25, 234
Learning:
  active, 2, 37–39, 63, 67
    examples of: MacRae problem, 105–115
      macroeconomic model with measurement error, 116–139
    nonlinear, 74–90
      cost-to-go: computing the approximate, 76–83
      obtaining a deterministic approximation for, 84–85
    quadratic linear, 91–104
      approximate optimal cost-to-go, 94–98
      dual-control algorithm, 98–104
  passive, 2, 37–39, 50, 67
    example of, 51–59
  (*See also* Riccati equations, stochastic)
Leondes, C. T., 8*n.*, 231
Line-search methods, 24
Livesey, David, 1, 17*n.*, 31*n.*, 234
Local optima, 103, 114, 115, 132

MacRae, Elizabeth Chase, 1, 51, 52, 56, 64, 72, 73, 105, 234
MacRae problem, 105–115, 132
Majors, Joe, 233
Mantell, J. B., 24*n.*, 25, 234
Matrix products, expected value of, 146–148
Matrix recursions for augmented systems, 179–187
Maximum-principle method, 6
Mayne, D. Q., 40, 233
Measurement-equation noise terms, 68, 220–221
Measurement error, 36–38, 65, 116, 117, 216, 220–227
Measurement-error covariance, 118, 214–216
Measurement-noise terms, 68, 220–221
  (*See also* Measurement error)
Measurement relationships, 38, 65, 75, 92, 106, 118, 152
Measurement vector, 65, 75
Measurements, multiple, 65
Medina, F., 17*n.*, 232
Meeraus, Alex, 25
Meier, L., 43*n.*, 64, 73, 74, 82, 85*n.*, 90, 149, 159, 237
  (*See also* TBM)
Meyer, Laurence H., 232
Miller, Ronald E., 17*n.*, 234
Mills, Peggy, xi
Mitter, S. K., 24*n.*, 234
Moment-generating function, 163, 164
Monetary policy, ix, 64, 117
Money supply, 8, 65
Monte Carlo, 64, 66–68, 72, 100, 101, 104, 121–126, 133, 134, 220–222
Motamen, Homa, xi
Muench, T., 40*n.*, 233
Multiplicative uncertainty, 41–50
Multiplier-accelerator model, 10, 26
Murray, W., 232
Murtagh, Bruce A., 24*n.*, 25, 234

National Bureau of Economic Research, 27
Noise terms, 36, 38
  measurement-equation, 68, 220–221
  system-equation, 68, 220–221
Nominal path, 22, 40, 70, 76–77, 99, 109
Nonconvex shape, 115
Nonlinear active-learning stochastic control (*see* Learning, active, nonlinear)
Nonlinear problems, 17–25
  gradient methods, 22–24
  problem statement, 18–19
  quadratic linear approximation method, 19–22
  special problems: accuracy and roundoff errors, 24
    inequality constraints on state variables, 25
    large model size, 25
Norman, Alfred L., x, xi, 1, 9, 17*n.*, 24*n.*, 50, 64, 72, 77, 93*n.*, 115, 121, 122, 228, 234
Norman, M. R., 1, 17*n.*, 77, 234

Norton, F. E., 8*n*., 231
Notational equivalence, 28, 29, 88

Obligations (*see* Government obligations)
Observation vector (*see* Measurement vector)
OLF (*see* Open-loop feedback)
Open-loop feedback (OLF), 50, 52, 56, 59, 121, 122, 125, 222
Open-loop policy, 38
Open-market purchases, 6
Optima, local (*see* Local optima)
Optimal cost-to-go (*see* Cost-to-go, optimal)
Optimal feedback rule (*see* Feedback rule)
Optimality, principle of, 45
Optimality conditions, 23
Oudet, B. A., 8*n*., 234
Ozkan, Turgay, 229

Pagan, Adrien, 39*n*., 234
Palash, Carl J., 17*n*., 24*n*., 31*n*., 228, 235
Papademos, Lucas, 229
Parameter uncertainty, 36
Paryani, K., 8*n*., 235
Passive-learning stochastic control (*see* Learning, passive)
Penalties, 139
   (*See also* Weighting matrices)
Perry, A., 24*n*., 235
Perturbations, 37, 39, 63, 71
Phelps, Edmund S., 40*n*., 235
Phillips, A. W., 1, 235
Picken, S. M., 232
Pindyck, Robert S., 1, 7–9, 30*n*., 32*n*., 40*n*., 229, 235
Pitchford, John, 1, 17*n*., 235
Polack, E., 24*n*., 235
Postponed-linear-approximation method, 40
Powell, M. J. D., 24*n*., 231
Predetermined variables, 29
Prescott, E. C., 1, 50*n*., 64, 235
Preston, A. J., 235
Price level, 8, 9
Prices, ix
Principle of optimality, 45
Probing, 71
Probing term (component), 70, 71, 97, 98, 102, 103, 111, 113, 114, 131–139, 211–213, 225
Production, ix
Profit, ix
Projections, 56, 70, 71, 85, 89, 202

QLP (*see* Quadratic linear problems)
Quadratic criterion function, 31–32
Quadratic forms, 162–176
  scalar case, 163–164
  vector case, 164–173

Quadratic linear active-learning stochastic control (*see* Learning, active, quadratic linear)
Quadratic linear problems (QLP), 5–16
  approximation, 19–22
  problem statement, 6–10
  solution method, 10–16
Quadratic linear tracking problems, 6–8

Raines, Fredric Q., 232
Random cost-to-go, 64
Random error term, 39
Rao, D. S., 8*n*., 233
Rao, H., 40*n*., 233
Rausser, Gordon, 37*n*., 50, 64, 235
Recursions, 47, 82–83, 96
  for augmented system: matrix, 179–187
    vector, 188–192
  (*See also* Riccati equations)
Reduced-form equation, 28
Reduced gradient, generalized, 25
Reestimation method, 210
Reeves, C. M., 24*n*., 231
Ribière, G., 24*n*., 235
Riccati equations:
  deterministic, 12, 15, 16
  stochastic: active-learning, 82, 96, 149
    passive-learning, 47–49
  terminal conditions, 45, 48
Riccati matrices, 12, 47, 71, 101, 103, 110, 149–151, 187
Rismanchian, Mohamad, xi
Rizo-Patron, Jorge, viii, xi, 162
Roberts, Steven M., 40*n*., 235
Roundoff errors, 24
Rouzier, P., 17*n*., 235
Rustem, Berc, 232

Sales, ix
Sandblom, C. L., 8*n*., 17*n*., 235
Sandee, J., 8*n*., 231
Sargent, T. J., 40*n*., 236
Sarris, Alexander H., 36*n*., 64, 236
Saunders, Michael A., 24*n*., 25, 234
Search, 67–69, 71, 72, 76, 89, 98, 100, 101, 108, 113–115
  grid, 67, 69, 71, 131, 132
Search-iteration counter, 68, 69, 71, 72
Sequential certainty equivalence (*see* Certainty equivalence, sequential)
Serial correlation, 39
Shanno, D. F., 24, 236
Shelton, R. C., 43*n*., 231
Shupp, Franklin R., 1, 8*n*., 17*n*., 31*n*., 52*n*., 236
Simon, H. A., 1, 40, 236
Sivan, R., 43*n*., 50*n*., 229
Sparsity, 18, 25

Stabilization:
  cocoa-market, 40
  commodity, ix, 11, 12
State equations, 18, 23
State variables, 6–10
  inequality constraints on, 25
State vector, 11
  augmented, 9, 202–207
Structural form, 28
Summers, S., 17n., 232
System-equation noise terms, 68, 220–221
System equations, 26–31, 198–201
  second-order expansion of, 143–145

Tapiero, S. H. S., 228
Tarn, Tzyh-Jong, 232
Taxation, 6
Taylor, John B., 40n., 64, 235, 236
Taylor, Lance, 1, 23n., 24n., 77, 233
TBM (Tse, Bar-Shalom, and Meier), 43n., 64, 73, 74, 82, 85n., 90, 149, 157n., 159, 161, 237
Terminal conditions, 23
Thalberg, Bjorn, 8n., 236
Theil, Henri, 1, 8n., 40, 163, 164, 229, 236
Time Series Processor (TSP), 120
Time-varying parameters, 122, 138
Tinsley, Peter, 8n., 17n., 230, 236
Tracking problems, quadratic linear, 6–8
TROLL system at M.I.T., 30
Tse, Edison, x, xi, 37, 38, 43n., 50n., 64, 70, 73–76, 79, 82, 85n., 90, 91, 96n., 97, 105, 113n., 131, 149, 159, 229, 236
  (*See also* BTL; TBM)
Turnovsky, Stephen J., xi, 1, 17n., 43n., 52n., 232, 235, 237
Tustin, A., 1, 8n., 237

Uebe, Götz, 8n., 231
Uncertainty, 116
  additive, 35–40
  multiplicative, 41–50
  parameter, 36
Unemployment, ix, 6, 8, 9
Upadhyay, Treveni, 64, 230, 237
Update, 67, 69, 72, 73, 89, 98, 100, 101, 206
  of augmented state covariance, 195–197
  of covariance matrix, 90
  of state and parameter estimates, 104
Update certainty equivalence, 50

Vector products, expected value of, 146–148
Vector recursions for augmented system, 188–192

Wall, Kent, 40n., 122, 216, 229, 235, 237
Wallace, N., 40n., 233, 236
Walsh, Peter, 52n., 237
Wan, San, 17n., 230
Warren, A. D., 24n., 234
Weighting matrices, 32, 118
Wells, C., 40n., 233
Westcott, J. H., 40n., 237
Wide-sense method, 75
Wishner, R. P., 87n., 158, 162, 229
Woodside, M., 17n., 237
Wright, H. M., 232

You, Jong Keun, 8n., 237

Zarrop, Martin B., 232
Zellner, Arnold, 1, 50n., 52n., 237